MATHS IN ACTION

Intermediate 1
MATHEMATICS

D. Brown
R. Howat
G. Marra
E. Mullan
R. Murray
K. Nisbet
J. Thomson

Nelson

Published in 1999 by:
Thomas Nelson and Sons Ltd

Reprinted in 2003 by:
Nelson Thornes Ltd
Delta Place
27 Bath Road
CHELTENHAM
GL53 7TH
United Kingdom

05 06 07 / 13 12 11 10 9 8 7 6

A catalogue record for this book is available from the British Library

ISBN 0 17 431497 3

Page make-up by Upstream, London

Printed and bound in China by L. Rex

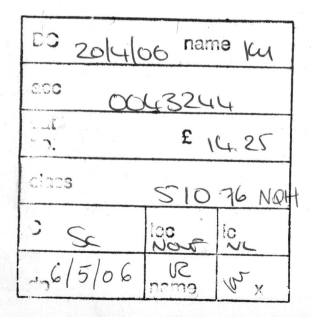

Contents

Preface

The purpose of this volume is to provide a comprehensive package of work, study and practice for the student attempting Intermediate 1 Mathematics.

It contains four units of work providing a course of study for Mathematics 1, Mathematics 2, Mathematics 3 and Applications of Mathematics.

All topics mentioned in the Arrangements documents are well covered.

It is assumed that the student has access to a scientific calculator, but as many students may only be familiar with the arithmetic calculator, Units 1 and 2 begin with short calculator primers. Within these short chapters the seeds of many a good habit are sown. Whenever you use a calculator, an idea of the result expected should already have formed in your mind. *Estimate, calculate* and *check* are the buzzwords. You should be aware, of course, that there are many makes of scientific calculator and that variations of procedures exist. Selecting one calculator and sticking to it throughout the course is recommended. If you are already familiar with the scientific calculator then you will not miss any of the unit syllabus by bypassing these introductions.

Although you are primarily following the Intermediate 1 course to pass exams and gain qualifications, remember that maths can be fun. There is a lot more to the subject than the bare syllabus content. Look for mathematics everywhere. Graphics calculators and computers open many doors; the Internet is simply bulging with ideas.

A companion Resource book has also been written to supplement this volume. It contains a bank of material to assist in revision, homework and extension.

Some questions and exercises are deliberately more difficult than the rest, and these have a tint behind them. Some explanations are also tinted, and you only need to do this material if you are aiming for one of the higher grades.

1 Using Your Calculator in Unit 1

Estimate, calculate and check

Calculators are easy to use but it is also easy to make mistakes.

Develop good habits when you are using a calculator.

Get to know your own machine.

Do some simple checks to make sure your calculator does what you expect it to.

a $4 + 3 \times 3$ ... Your calculator should give 13 and not 21.

b $1 \div 3 \times 3$ ... Your calculator should give 1 and not 0.999 999 99.

Not all calculators behave in the same way.
Check your manual.

Example 1 Find 19×6.1.

Estimate   Calculate a rough answer mentally.
$$19 \times 6.1 \approx 20 \times 6$$
$$\approx 120$$

Reminder
'$\approx$' means 'roughly equals'.

Calculate   Use your calculator. | 115.9 |

Check 1   Compare the calculator answer with your rough answer. $115.9 \approx 120$
Check 2   Reverse the process. $115.9 \div 6.1$ should give 19.

Example 2 Calculate $26.37 \div 4.5$.

Estimate $26.37 \div 4.5 \approx 24 \div 4 \approx 6$ (24 is picked because it is easily divided by 4)
Calculate $26.37 \div 4.5 = 5.86$
Check 1 $5.86 \approx 6$
Check 2 $5.86 \times 4.5 = 26.37$

EXERCISE 1

1 A choice of answers is given for each question.
Pick out the correct answer without the aid of a calculator.

a 12.2×1.7	**(i)** 2.074	**(ii)** 20.74	**(iii)** 207.4	**(iv)** 2074
b $29.7 + 126$	**(i)** 1.557	**(ii)** 15.57	**(iii)** 155.7	**(iv)** 1557
c $298 - 63.2$	**(i)** 23.48	**(ii)** 234.8	**(iii)** 2348	**(iv)** 23 480
d $578.2 \div 4.9$	**(i)** 0.118	**(ii)** 1.18	**(iii)** 11.8	**(iv)** 118

2 Do the following calculations. Write out your working as in Example 2.

    a $188 + 59$ (Hint for check: *answer* $- 59 = 188$)

    b 11×49 (Hint for check: *answer* $\div 49 = 11$)

    c $249 - 87$ (Hint for check: *answer* $+ 87 = 249$)

    d $150.4 \div 47$ (Hint for check: *answer* $\times 47 = 150.4$)

    e $26.7 + 39.8$ **f** 9.8×5.6 **g** $30.2 - 9.8$ **h** $422.96 \div 68$

Check the final digit

It is easy to check the last digit of your answer, except in the case of division.

Example 1 $25.\mathbf{4} \times 17.\mathbf{2}$ will end in $4 \times 2 = \mathbf{8}$.

Example 2 $25.\mathbf{4} + 17.\mathbf{2}$ will end in $4 + 2 = \mathbf{6}$.

Example 3 $25.\mathbf{4} - 17.\mathbf{2}$ will end in $4 - 2 = \mathbf{2}$.

Be careful when adding and subtracting.

Example 4 $7.4 + 8.21$

You must imagine the numbers as $7.\mathbf{40} + 8.\mathbf{21}$ to see it will end in $0 + 1 = \mathbf{1}$.

Example 5 $841 - 27$

Instead of $1 - 7$, think of $11 - 7$ to see it will end in **4**.

Remember to estimate, calculate and check.

Example 6 Calculate 26×5.2.

Estimate	$26 \times 5.2 \approx 30 \times 5 \approx 150$
Estimate	$6 \times 2 = \mathbf{12} \dots$ last digit is **2**
Calculate	$26 \times 5.2 = 135.2$
Check 1	$135.2 \approx 150$
Check 2	$135.2 \div 5.2 = 26$
Check 3	Answer ends in a 2.

EXERCISE 2

1 A selection of answers is given for each of the following questions. Pick the correct answer without using your calculator.

    a 17.4×18.3 **(i)** 318.42   **(ii)** 3184.2   **(iii)** 31 842

    b $243 + 54$ **(i)** 296   **(ii)** 297   **(iii)** 298

    c $8723 - 481$ **(i)** 8240   **(ii)** 8241   **(iii)** 8242

    d $561 + 843$ **(i)** 11 404   **(ii)** 1404   **(iii)** 144

    e 82×3.4 **(i)** 278.6   **(ii)** 278.7   **(iii)** 278.8

    f $19.9 - 4.74$ **(i)** 15.16   **(ii)** 151.6   **(iii)** 15.14

    g 8.9×72.8 **(i)** 647.94   **(ii)** 647.92   **(iii)** 647.90

2 Do these problems, following the steps in Example 6.

    a $23.7 + 4.5$ **b** 17×15.4 **c** $567 - 145$ **d** 45×63

    e $43 + 226$ **f** $67.4 - 54.8$ **g** 8×2.7 **h** $342 + 678$

    i $34.4 - 3.88$ **j** 26×9.7 **k** $753 + 11 + 39$ **l** 3.4×1.32

3 A customer bought 17 stamps at 27p each.

   a The shopkeeper asked for 468 pence.

      How did the customer know there had been a mistake?

   b How much *did* he pay? (Estimate, calculate and check.)

Miss Smith
2 Cold Street
London SE4 7PL

Fractions

Example 1 Simplify $\frac{15}{20}$.

15 20   `15 r 20`

   =   `3 r 4` $\frac{15}{20} = \frac{3}{4}$

Example 2 $\frac{1}{3} + \frac{2}{5}$

1 3   `1 r 3`

   +

2  5   `2 r 5`

   =   `11 r 15` $\frac{1}{3} + \frac{2}{5} = \frac{11}{15}$

Check: reverse the process.

 2  5 =    `1 r 3`

Example 3 Calculate $\frac{3}{4}$ of 36.

3 4   `3 r 4`

   × 36 =   `27` $\frac{3}{4}$ of 36 = 27

> *Reminder*
> 'of' means '×'.

Check: reverse the process.

 3  4 =   `36`

EXERCISE 3

1 Simplify the following.

  a $\frac{5}{10}$ **b** $\frac{4}{6}$ **c** $\frac{12}{20}$ **d** $\frac{6}{9}$ **e** $\frac{35}{35}$ **f** $\frac{81}{108}$

2 Work out the following. Check your answers by reversing the process.

  a $\frac{1}{3} + \frac{1}{4}$ **b** $\frac{2}{5} + \frac{1}{6}$ **c** $\frac{4}{5} - \frac{2}{3}$ **d** $\frac{7}{8} - \frac{1}{4}$

3 Calculate, then check your answers.

  a $\frac{2}{3}$ of 24   **b** $\frac{4}{5}$ of 60   **c** $\frac{2}{7}$ of 14   **d** $\frac{3}{8}$ of 16

Fix mode

On many calculators, **Mode 7** makes the machine work to a fixed number of decimal places.

Example 1   makes the machine work to 2 decimal places, which is handy for money problems.

While in this mode, enter 5 ÷ 2 = | £5 shared between two people.

The calculator returns 2.50 and not 2.5.

Example 2 Round 12.3456 to 2 decimal places.
With 12.3456 in the display, enter MODE 7 2.

The calculator display becomes | 12.35 |

Example 3 Round 12.3456, 3.4765 and 56.7123 to 2 decimal places.
Enter MODE 7 2
Enter 12.3456
Press =

The calculator display becomes | 12.35 |

When you enter a list of numbers, the machine automatically rounds them to 2 decimal places when 'equals' is pressed.

Example 4   makes the machine work to 3 decimal places, which is handy for weight problems.

While in this mode, enter 5 ÷ 4 = | 5 kg divided into four parts.

The calculator returns 1.250 and not 1.25.

  returns you to normal use.

Most scientific calculators have a **fix** mode.
You may have to check your manual to find out about your own machine.

EXERCISE 4

1 Use your calculator to round the following numbers to 2 decimal places.

    a 12.3875   **b** 0.4812   **c** 12.2   **d** 176.5487   **e** 0.009

2 While in fix mode for 2 decimal places, calculate:

    a £34 ÷ 3   **b** £77 ÷ 8   **c** £3.59 ÷ 4   **d** £5 ÷ 9   **e** £17 ÷ 2

3 Check each result in question **2** by multiplication.

4 Seven friends share the bill for a meal at a Chinese restaurant.

    a If the total bill is £62.70, how much should each pay? (Use **fix mode** for 2 decimal places.)

    b Without clearing your answer from the display, multiply by 7.
Check that this gives you 62.70.

> **Hint**
> The calculator remembers the original number even though it has been rounded.

5 Ken is saving for his holiday. He needs to save £250. He has 45 weeks to go. He saves the same amount each week.
What is the minimum saving he should make each week?

> **Reminder**
> Check your answer before clearing the display.

6 For each question choose a suitable fix mode.

    a Jenny, Jan and Bob share the bill for a day trip.
The bill comes to £74.
How much does each pay? (Answer to 2 d.p.)

> **Reminder**
> Remember to estimate, calculate and check.

    b Raj is making a model car one twelfth the size of the original.
If the real length is 555 cm, how long is his model? (Answer to 1 d.p.)

    c A coal merchant divides 34 kg of coal into six equal amounts.
What weight of coal is in each pile? (Answer to 3 d.p.)

    d Eleven people in a syndicate win a lottery prize of £24 000.
How much does each person get? (Answer to 2 d.p.)

    e Tracey works 11 hours and is paid £45.
How much is she paid per hour? (Answer to 2 d.p.)

    f A chef divides 3 litres of milk into eight equal parts.
How much is in each part? (Answer to 3 d.p.)

Using the constant facility

The constant facility allows you to do repetitive calculations.
Each calculator has its own way of doing it, so check your manual.

Example An architect has a scale model one sixth actual size.
She must multiply each length by 6 to get the actual sizes.
She sets up the constant facility to *multiply by 6*.
After that
4 = , 8 = , 2 = , ... will produce 24, 48, 12, ...

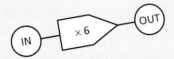

EXERCISE 5

1 Dr Cuthbertson has a set of marks out of 25.
To turn them into percentage marks he multiplies each by 4.
Set your calculator for a constant multiplier of 4.
Work out the percentage mark for each student.

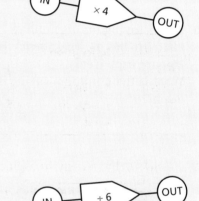

Akmal	23	Jill	10
Alison	20	Lisa	13
Betty	17	Claire	15
Karen	18	Sarah	25
Ashley	14.5	Derek	13.5
Faizel	12	May	18
Rizwan	24	Lee	16.5
Stephen	18	Ricky	11
Cari	19	Ross	5
Danny	7	Graeme	9

2 Six people are to share the cost of a holiday.
Use a constant divisor of 6.
Find the cost for one share for each of the holiday expenses.

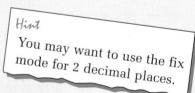

Travel	£425.00
Food	£137.00
Entertainment	£328.50
Insurance	£35.69

Hint
You may want to use the fix mode for 2 decimal places.

3 A computer catalogue lists the prices before tax is added.
Multiplying a price by 1.175 will let you know what the real cost is.
What does each of these systems cost?

a £2505 before tax **b** £1230 before tax **c** £899 before tax

2 *Basic Calculations*

STARTING POINTS

1 Complete these bills from a catalogue.

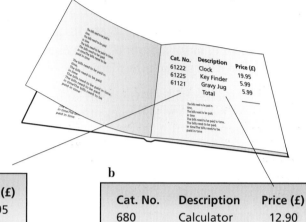

a

Cat. No.	Description	Price (£)
61222	Clock	19.95
61225	Key Finder	5.99
61121	Gravy Jug	5.99
	Total	

b

Cat. No.	Description	Price (£)
680	Calculator	12.90
214	Video Tapes	9.50
511	Audio Tapes	3.85
	Total	

2 Calculate the net pay in each case.

a

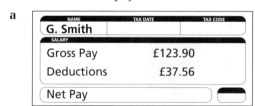

NAME	TAX DATE	TAX CODE
G. Smith		

SALARY

Gross Pay	£123.90
Deductions	£37.56
Net Pay	

b

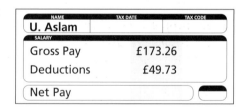

NAME	TAX DATE	TAX CODE
U. Aslam		

SALARY

Gross Pay	£173.26
Deductions	£49.73
Net Pay	

c

NAME	TAX DATE	TAX CODE
P. Grant		

SALARY

Gross Pay	£211.45
Deductions	£53.94
Net Pay	

3 Copy the table.
Enter the following numbers in your table.
The first one has been done for you.

a 23.47 **b** 2.504 **c** 10 **d** 8324
e 55.253 **f** 1001.01 **g** 0.22 **h** 83.24

Th	H	T	U	•	t	h	th
		2	3	•	4	7	

4 Ms Gordon needs 130 copies of her lecture notes.
Each copy costs 29p.
How much will it cost altogether?

5 Calculate the following.
  a 43 × 10   **b** 43 × 100   **c** 43 × 1000   **d** 4.3 × 10   **e** 4.3 × 100
  f 4.3 × 1000   **g** 26 ÷ 10   **h** 26 ÷ 100   **i** 324 ÷ 1000   **j** 118 ÷ 10
  k 3984 ÷ 100   **l** 4536 ÷ 1000

6 A shopkeeper purchases alarm clocks for £5 each.
She sells them to make a profit of £1.50 on each.
At what price does she sell the alarm clocks?

7 In a 100 m race the runners' times (in alphabetical order) are:
  C. Adams 10.8   F. Bothwick 10.08   H. Cairns 10.18   A. Duncan 10.79
  P. Everett 10.54
  Put the runners in order, fastest first.

Rounding

Many numbers do not need to be given *exactly*.
2626 people attend a golf tournament.
This might be reported in the paper as any of the following:

Attendance 3000 (rounded to the nearest thousand)

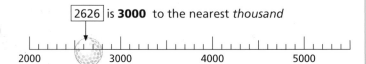

2626 is **3000** to the nearest *thousand*

or

Attendance 2600 (rounded to the nearest hundred)

2626 is **2600** to the nearest *hundred*

or

Attendance 2630 (rounded to the nearest ten)

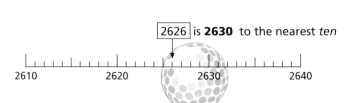

2626 is **2630** to the nearest *ten*

EXERCISE 1

1 Round these numbers to the nearest 10. A hint is given in brackets.

   a 23 (20 or 30)   **b** 46 (40 or 50)   **c** 129 (120 or 130)

   d 849 (840 or 850)   **e** 972 (970 or 980)   **f** 337 (330 or 340)

2 Round these numbers to the nearest 100. A hint is given in brackets for some questions.

   a 89 (0 or 100)   **b** 322 (300 or 400)   **c** 2189 (2100 or 2200)

   d 3107 (3100 or 3200)   **e** 4361 (4300 or 4400)   **f** 1999 (1900 or 2000)

   g 147   **h** 301   **i** 555

3 Round these numbers to the nearest 1000. A hint is given in brackets for some questions.

   a 4900 (4000 or 5000)   **b** 3012 (3000 or 4000)   **c** 53019 (53 000 or 54 000)

   d 72 345 (72 000 or 73 000) **e** 21 295   **f** 21 032

   g 3447   **h** 987   **i** 2500

4 Round these numbers to the nearest whole number. A hint is given in brackets for some questions.

   a 5.8 (5 or 6)   **b** 12.6 (12 or 13)   **c** 136.78 (136 or 137)

   d 530.26 (530 or 531)   **e** 95.5   **f** 0.5

   g 13.319   **h** 19.54   **i** 200.4

5 Round these football attendance figures to the nearest 100.

Venue	Attendance
Dens Park	8542
Ibrox Park	15 887
Tannadice	11 973
Celtic Park	16 739
Hampden Park	23 156
Bayview	1879
Starks Park	5421
Pittodrie	13 754

Hint

8500 or 8600 at Dens Park?

6 Round the number of exam candidates in each school to the nearest 10.

School	No. of candidates
Hillview H. S.	154
Blake H. S.	316
Norton Academy	271
Linfield H. S.	123
Freel College	511
Longside H. S.	68
Trest Academy	362
Forthill H. S.	206

Hint

150 or 160 at Hillview?

Decimal places

Some calculations produce numbers which need to be rounded.

Example 1

Calculate $19 \div 7$ to 2 decimal places.
      $19 \div 7 = 2.714\ 285\ 7$ (using a calculator)

Step 1   Score out the decimal places that you don't want.   **2.714 285 7**

Step 2   Note the first figure scored out. In this example it is a 4.

Step 3   If this figure is *4 or less*, you can ignore it.
          In this example your answer is 2.71.

Example 2

Calculate $20 \div 7$ to 2 decimal places.
      $20 \div 7 = 2.857\ 142\ 9$ (using a calculator)

Step 1   Score out the decimal places you don't want.   **2.857 142 9**

Step 2   Note the first figure scored out. In this example it is a 7.

Step 3   If this figure is *5 or more*, then add 1 to the last digit of
          your answer. In this example 2.85 becomes 2.86.

> *Reminder*
> 4 or less, then round down.
> 5 or more, then round up.

EXERCISE 2

1 Write down the number of decimal places in each of these numbers.
   a 234.512   **b** 7.423 312 5   **c** 0.7   **d** 34   **e** 17.42
   f 320.000 000 7 **g** 64.51   **h** 42 356   **i** 31.214 57   **j** 7

2 Work out the following.
   Write down the number of decimal places in each answer.
   a $25 \div 2$ **b** 36×1.8 **c** $6.4 + 5.63$ **d** $41 \div 4$ **e** 3×0.55
   f 5.7×8.8114 **g** $13.6 + 53$ **h** $23 - 11.548$ **i** 2.58×100 **j** $17 \div 5$

3 Calculate correct to 1 decimal place.
   a $2.7 + 3.56$ **b** $12 - 4.921$ **c** 5.3×6.81 **d** $17 \div 3$ **e** $57 \div 1.84$
   f 10.65×3.77 **g** $105 \div 17$ **h** $6 + 1.6623$ **i** $5.1 \div 0.8$

4 Calculate correct to 2 decimal places.
   a $13 - 7.392$ **b** $2.65 + 4.3813$ **c** 45.3×5.711 **d** $11 \div 7$ **e** $61 \div 17$
   f 7.84×2.99 **g** $25.66 \div 31$ **h** $2.13 + 5.888$ **i** $113 \div 37$

Rounding in context

Example 1   Six people share £1. How much does each get?

£1 ÷ 6 = 0.166 666 66
The answer could be £0.16 or £0.17.
But £0.17 each is more than £1 (£0.17 × 6 = £1.02).
So each person gets £0.16.

Example 2   Nine people need a taxi from the church to the reception.
A taxi will only take four passengers. How many taxis are needed?

9 ÷ 4 = 2.25
The answer could be two or three taxis.
Two taxis are not enough (2 × 4 = 8 passengers). So three taxis are needed.

Example 3   Find the cost of 8.23 m of material at £3.25 per metre.

8.23 × 3.25 = 26.7475
The answer could be £26.74 or £26.75.
If the shop rounded down, it would make a loss over many sales.
So the cost is £26.75.

Example 4   A 4 kg joint of beef is carved into three equal portions.
What does each portion weigh?

In examples like this we normally round to the nearest gram (3 decimal places).
4 kg ÷ 3 = 1.333 333 3. To the nearest gram this is 1.333 kg.

EXERCISE 3

1 Work out the following.
   a Share £3 equally amongst 7 people.
   b Share £9.40 equally amongst 6 people.
   c Share 144 eggs equally amongst 10 people.
   d A lift holds a maximum of 8 people. How many trips must it make to transport
       29 people from the ground to the fourth floor tea room?
   e James is saving for a stereo unit which costs £250. He saves just the right
       amount each week so that he can buy the unit after 12 weeks.
       How much does he save a week?

Reminder
When rounding, always consider the storyline.

2  A plank is 2.25 m long. A joiner
   wants to cut it into equal strips. How
   long is each strip (to the nearest
   centimetre) if he cuts it into:
   a 2 parts   **b** 3 parts   **c** 4 parts
   d 5 parts   **e** 6 parts   **f** 7 parts?

Reminder
Remember that the parts should not add up to more than the original.

3 A ham joint weighs 5.3 kg.
   How heavy is each part, to the nearest gram (3 d.p.), when it is cut into:
   a 2 parts   **b** 3 parts   **c** 4 parts   **d** 5 parts   **e** 6 parts   **f** 7 parts?

Scientific calculators can be set to give a **fixed** number of decimal places.
Fix your calculator to work with 2 decimal places.

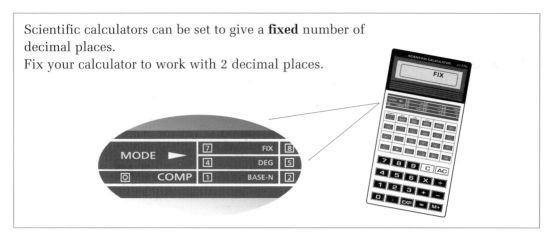

EXERCISE 4

1 Some office staff decide to have Christmas dinner in a local restaurant.
At each table they share the bill equally.
Calculate how much a person at each table should pay for his or her meal.

TABLE 1

No. of people   8

Total   £86.19

TABLE 2

No. of people 7

Total   £81.65

TABLE 3

No. of people 9

Total   £88.50

TABLE 4

No. of people   17

Total   £198.93

2 Jimal has been surfing the Internet three times every day.
Calculate the total telephone charge for each day to the nearest penny.

Monday Charges
£1.674
£0.443
£0.289

Wednesday Charges
£1.263
£0.73
£0.39

Tuesday Charges
£2.228
£1.507
£0.552

Thursday Charges
£1.658
£0.225
£1.249

3 Calculate the cost of each of these electricity bills to the nearest penny.

a   1305 units at £0.0743 per unit   **b**   896 units at £0.0743 per unit

Percentage

Example 1

Write 50% as a common fraction and as a decimal.

$$50\% = \frac{50}{100} = 50 \div 100 = 0.5$$

Percentage: 50%   Common fraction: $\frac{50}{100}$ Decimal fraction: 0.5

Example 2

Find 25% of 60.

$$25\% \text{ of } 60 = \frac{25}{100} \text{ of } 60$$
$$= 25 \div 100 \times 60$$
$$= 15$$

EXERCISE 5

1 Write these percentages as common fractions.

    a 25%   **b** 50%   **c** 75%   **d** 12%   **e** 10%

    f 1%   **g** 5%   **h** 20%   **i** 80%   **j** 100%

2 Write these percentages as decimal fractions.

    a 54%   **b** 17%   **c** 33%   **d** 6%   **e** 12.5%

    f 125%   **g** 17.5%   **h** 8%   **i** 250%   **j** 24%

3 Calculate.

    a 25% of 60   **b** 60% of 90   **c** 10% of 35   **d** 40% of £9   **e** 5% of £125

    f 20% of 450   **g** 12% of 500   **h** 75% of £37   **i** 12.5% of 86   **j** 2% of 444

4 You have to pay 8% tax on fuel bills.
Calculate 8% of the following amounts.

    a £250   **b** £360   **c** £190   **d** £550

5 15% is taken off each holiday.
    a Calculate the reduction on each holiday.
    b Calculate the cost of each holiday.

ROME	£317
CORFU	£290
PARIS	£189
ATHENS	£455
BRUSSELS	£266

15% REDUCTION ON ALL HOLIDAYS

6

The Regal Bank charges 6% per year when it lends money.
Calculate the charge for each of these loans, which have been taken out over one year.
Give your answer correct to the nearest penny.

a £345

b £1243

c £120.56

d £211

e £108.40

f £2320

g £578.60

h £75.74

7 Computer prices in a catalogue do not include value added tax (VAT).
VAT is 17.5% of the price.

Example

VAT = 17.5% of £1800
  = 17.5 ÷ 100 × 1800
  = £315

Actual cost = £1800 + £315
       = £2115

Calculate the actual cost of each item.

a

b

c

One quantity as a percentage of another

Example 1

Gerry scored 18 marks out of 25 in a maths test.
What is his mark expressed as a percentage?

18 out of 25 means $\frac{18}{25}$ of 100% = 18 ÷ 25 × 100%
$$= 72\%$$

Example 2

250 students voted in the election for Year Captain.
55 students voted for Tina.
What percentage of the votes did Tina get?

55 out of 250 voted for Tina, so
$$\frac{55}{250} \text{ of } 100\% = 55 \div 250 \times 100\%$$
$$= 22\%$$

EXERCISE 6

1 Work out these exam marks as percentages to the nearest per cent.

   a   **b**   **c**   **d**   **e**

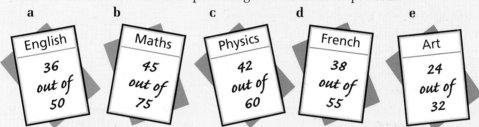

English	Maths	Physics	French	Art
36 out of 50	45 out of 75	42 out of 60	38 out of 55	24 out of 32

2 Find each profit as a percentage of the cost price.

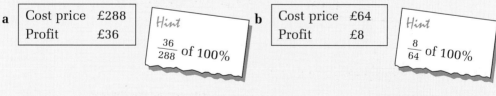

a
Cost price	£288
Profit	£36

Hint $\frac{36}{288}$ of 100%

b
Cost price	£64
Profit	£8

Hint $\frac{8}{64}$ of 100%

c
Cost price	£120
Profit	£12

d
Cost price	£864
Profit	£54

e
Cost price	£2345
Profit	£185

3 Asha bought a personal CD player for £120.
   She resold it for £132.
   a Calculate her profit.
   b Express this profit as a percentage of £120.

4 A crate holds 120 apples. 18 apples are damaged.
   a What percentage of the apples are damaged?
   b What percentage of the apples are undamaged?

5 A car salesman earns a basic wage of £120 per week plus commission from his sales.
   One week he earns £192.
   a How much commission did he make?
   b What percentage of his basic wage is the commission?

EXERCISE 7

1

   A couple buy a house for £35 500.
   They sell it a few years later for £42 000.
   a What profit did they make?
   b What percentage profit did they make?
      Give your answer to the nearest whole number.

2 A bicycle is bought for £120.
   It is sold for £95.
   a Calculate the loss.
   b Find the loss as a percentage of £120.

3 The cost price of an article is £146.
   The selling price is £159.52.
   a Calculate the profit.
   b Find the profit as a percentage of the cost price.

4 A car costing £10 930 was later sold for £9550.
   Find the loss as a percentage of the cost price.

Simple interest

Banks give **interest** to encourage people to save with them.

'p.a.' stands for 'per annum' which means 'for a year'.

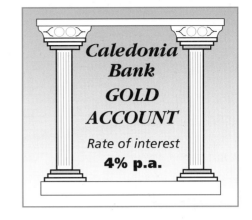

Caledonia
Bank
**GOLD
ACCOUNT**

Rate of interest
4% p.a.

Example   Colin put £200 in a bank account. The rate of interest was 4% p.a.
  a How much interest did Colin earn after a year?
  b How much money had he in the bank after a year?

a 4% of 200 = 4 ÷ 100 × 200 = 8
   So Colin had £8 in interest.

b £200 + £8 = £208.
   Colin had £208 in the bank.

EXERCISE 8

1 The Northern Building Society offers interest at 6% per annum.
  a Calculate a year's interest on the following amounts.
    (i) £60   **(ii)** £450   **(iii)** £1000   **(iv)** £550   **(v)** £3500   **(vi)** £110
  b How much money is in each account after a year?

2 Three people each put £300 in a different bank.
   Work out each person's interest after a year.

Northern Star	Berwick Bank	Caledonia Bank
6% p.a.	7% p.a.	8% p.a.

3

**Every penny counts
in our
GOLD ACCOUNT**

Up to £500	interest = 3.5%
£501–£1000	interest = 7%
£1001–£10 000	interest = 7.4%

Sam puts £780 into this account.
  a What rate of interest does Sam get?
  b How much interest does he get on his money?
  c How much is in his account after a year?

Interest for part of a year

Reminders

1 year = 12 months   1 month = $\frac{1}{12}$ of a year

1 year = 365 days   1 day = $\frac{1}{365}$ of a year

Example

Lucy puts £84 in a building society.

The rate of interest is 7% per annum.

How much interest is Lucy paid after:

a 1 month   **b** 8 months   **c** 100 days?

Interest for 1 year is 7% of £84.

$7 \div 100 \times 84 = £5.88$

a Interest for 1 month is $\frac{1}{12}$ of £5.88 = £0.49.

b Interest for 8 months is $8 \times 0.49 = £3.92$.

c Interest for 100 days is $\frac{100}{365}$ of £5.88 = $100 \div 365 \times 5.88 = £1.61$.

EXERCISE 9

1 Copy and complete this table.

	Amount	Rate	Time	Interest
a	£1000	6%	4 months	
b	£120	9%	5 months	
c	£4380	4%	130 days	

2

Bank of Scotia

Savers' Account

INTEREST PAID

TWICE YEARLY

Interest on this account is paid every 6 months.

Dave invests £280 at 6% p.a.

How much interest will Dave receive after 6 months?

3 A bank offers 8% interest.

Peter put £540 in the bank and withdrew it after 5 months.

Margaret put £600 in the bank and took it out after 4 months.

a How much interest did Peter get?

b Who was paid more in interest?

Direct proportion

Example 1   Four issues of a magazine cost a total of £2.80.
Find the cost of seven issues.

Find the cost for **1 item.** ⟶

4 cost	£2.80.
So	1 costs	£2.80 ÷ 4 = £0.70
and	7 cost	£0.70 × 7 = £4.90.

Example 2   Three panels of fence cover a distance of 18 m.
What distance do five panels cover?

Find out about **1.** ⟶

3 panels cover	18 m.
So	1 panel covers	18 ÷ 3 = 6 m
and	5 panels cover	6 × 5 = 30 m

EXERCISE 10

1 Cream cakes are 48p each.
Copy and complete the table.

Number of cream cakes	1	2	3	4	5
Cost		96p			

2 Each drawer in the filing cabinet contains 30 files.
Copy and complete the table.

Number of drawers	1	2	3	4	5
Number of files			90		

3 A baker can ice 3 cakes in 30 minutes.
How long does he take to ice:
  a 1 cake
  b 5 cakes
  c 9 cakes?

4 Amy inspects 5 new television sets each hour.
How many minutes does it take to inspect:
  a 1 set
  b 7 sets
  c 13 sets?

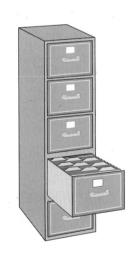

5 36 cm of ribbon cost 90p.
  a How much does 1 cm of ribbon cost?
  b How much does 70 cm cost?

6 Five of the same books cost £11.25.
  a How much does 1 book cost?
  b How much do 6 books cost?

7 A bus uses 2 gallons of petrol for a journey of 72 miles.
  a How far will it travel on 1 gallon?
  b How far will it travel on 5 gallons?

Sometimes finding out about one item does not make practical sense, but that doesn't matter.

Example

If 65 loaves of bread can be made from 100 kg of flour, how many can be made from a sack containing 280 kg?

    100 kg of flour can make 65 loaves.

So 1 kg of flour makes $65 \div 100 = 0.65$ loaf!

So 280 kg of flour can make $0.65 \times 280 = 182$ loaves.

EXERCISE 11

1 A company can clean 3 buses in 60 minutes.
  a How many buses can they clean in 1 minute?
  b How many can they clean in 100 minutes?

2 Four athletes can be trained for £500 a day.
  a How many athletes can be trained for £1?
  b How many can be trained for £750?

3

NOTICES

Collect your tokens!

Buy musical instruments for your school.

In a supermarket scheme, 2500 tokens will buy 5 violins.
  a How many violins can be bought for 1 token?
  b How many can be bought for 7000 tokens?

4 A kennel owner reckons she needs £702 a day to keep 12 dogs.
  a How many dogs can she keep for £1? (Don't clear your calculator.)
  b How many dogs can she keep for £819?

Now try these. Remember to find out about one item first.

EXERCISE 12

1 Graham pays £1000 to rent a house for 4 weeks.
   How much would it cost him for 7 weeks?

2 An excavator clears a trench 18 m long in 30 minutes.
   How much would it clear in 50 minutes?

3 A candle burns 14 mm in 16 minutes.
   How far does it burn in 40 minutes?

4

   At a vintage car rally, a car uses 5 gallons of petrol to cover 60 miles.
   a How far does it travel on 4 gallons?
   b How many gallons does it need to travel 72 miles?

5 In the High Street it costs £1 to park for 5 hours.
   a How long can you park for £3.60?
   b How much will it cost to park for 3 hours?

6 Trish types 300 words in 2 minutes.
   Working at this rate:
   a how many words can she type in 7 minutes?
   b how long will it take her to type 400 words?

CHAPTER 2 REVIEW

1 Round to the nearest whole number.

a 6.3   **b** 12.8   **c** 305.1

2 Copy and complete the table.

		To the nearest 10	To the nearest 100	To the nearest 1000
a	5672	5670	5700	6000
b	899			
c	1005			

3 Round these numbers to 1 decimal place: **a** 3.68   **b** 13.5328   **c** 0.7662

4 Calculate correct to 2 decimal places: **a** 25 ÷ 16   **b** 1.23 × 4.78   **c** 17 ÷ 7

5 Write these percentages as common fractions: **a** 23%   **b** 87%   **c** 9%

6 Write these percentages as decimal fractions:

a 25%   **b** 72%   **c** 19%

7 Calculate: **a** 25% of 128   **b** 50% of 48   **c** 10% of 125

8 a Calculate the discount on each item.
   b Calculate the sale price for each item.

10% OFF ALL GOODS!

Microwave £100
TV £330
Video £268

9 Work out Ken's test results as percentages.

$$\boxed{\text{English } \frac{24}{40}} \qquad \boxed{\text{Maths } \frac{36}{48}}$$

10 A storekeeper buys cameras for £130 and sells them for £145.60.
   a Calculate the profit.
   b Calculate the profit as a percentage of £130.

11 Twenty-four micro chips from a batch of 480 are faulty.
What is the percentage of micro chips which are faulty?

12 Wilf deposits £460 in the Scotia Bank Gold Deposit Account.
   a How much interest does he get at the end of a year?
   b How much money will be in his account after one year?

Scotia Bank
Gold Deposit Account
INTEREST RATE
5% p.a.

13 Jill puts £2000 in a bank. The rate of interest is 8% p.a. It is paid every 6 months.
   a What is 8% of £2000?
   b How much interest is Jill paid after 6 months?

14 An assembly line produces 180 microbuses per hour. How long does it take to make:
   a 1 microbus   **b** 6 microbuses   **c** 11 microbuses?

15 It costs £7.20 to feed a large cat for 3 days.
   a How much does it cost to feed it for 5 days?
   b For how many days can you feed the cat with £19.20?

3 Basic Geometry

 Each tiny square in the portcullis is about 1 square millimetre (1 mm^2).

100 mm^2 = 1 cm^2

Each face of a standard small dice is about 1 square centimetre (1 cm^2).

 A car door is about 1 square metre (1 m^2).

Very large areas are measured in square kilometres (km^2).

79 000 km^2

Measuring area means counting squares. The area of this rectangle is 6 cm^2.

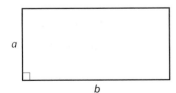

The area of the rectangle is equal to the length times the breadth.

$$A = a \times b$$

a

b

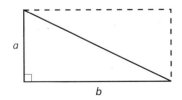

a

b

A right-angled triangle is half of a rectangle. The area of the right-angled triangle is equal to half the length times the breadth of the surrounding rectangle.

$$A = \frac{1}{2}a \times b$$

STARTING POINTS

1 Work out the area of shapes **a–c** by counting squares. Each square is 1 cm² .

a

b

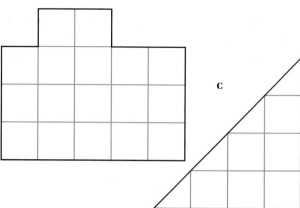

c

2 Which unit would you use to measure the area of:
  a a postage stamp   **b** the kitchen floor
  c a football pitch   **d** a country?

3 Calculate the area of this rectangle.

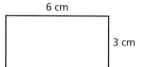

6 cm

3 cm

4

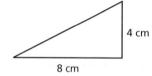

4 cm   What is the area of this triangle?

8 cm

5 Work out the area of:
  a the playing card   **b** the sail.

5.6 cm

8.2 cm

6.6 cm

3.2 cm

6

Measuring volume means counting cubes. represents a cubic centimetre (1 cm³).

How many cubic centimetres are needed to make the following solids?

A

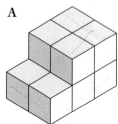

B

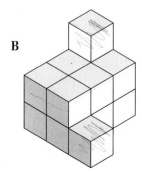

7 Which unit of volume would you use to measure:

   a a shoe box   **b** a room in a house

   c a cereal box   **d** a small button?

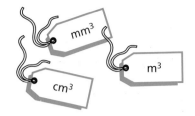

Area of composite shapes

To find the area of a composite shape:

- split the shape up into rectangles and right-angled triangles
- find the area of each piece
- add the areas.

Example

$A = l \times b$

   $= 10 \times 9$

$A = 90$ cm^2

$B = l \times b$

   $= 4 \times 4$

$B = 16$ cm^2

$A + B = 90 + 16$

       $= 106$ cm^2

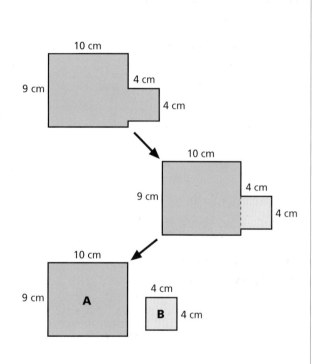

EXERCISE 1

Find the areas of these letters of the alphabet.

1

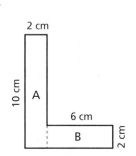

2

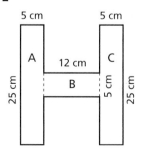

3

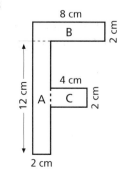

25

To calculate an area we sometimes have to work out the length of an unlabelled side.

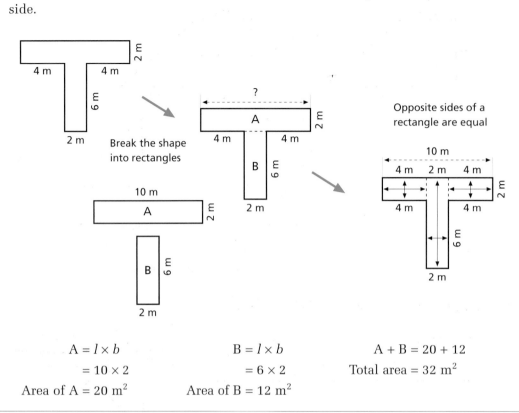

$A = l \times b$

$= 10 \times 2$

Area of A $= 20 \text{ m}^2$

$B = l \times b$

$= 6 \times 2$

Area of B $= 12 \text{ m}^2$

$A + B = 20 + 12$

Total area $= 32 \text{ m}^2$

EXERCISE 2

1 Use this method to find the area of each of these shapes.

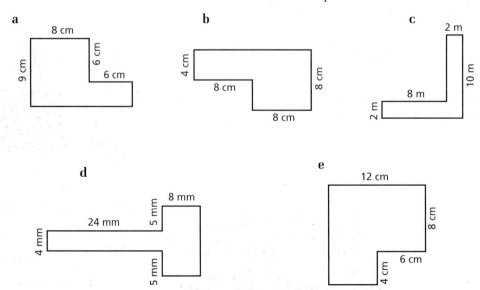

Example

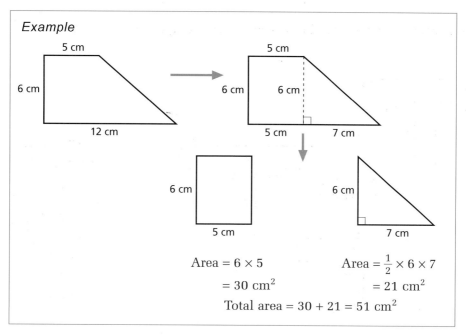

$$\text{Area} = 6 \times 5$$
$$= 30 \text{ cm}^2$$

$$\text{Area} = \frac{1}{2} \times 6 \times 7$$
$$= 21 \text{ cm}^2$$

$$\text{Total area} = 30 + 21 = 51 \text{ cm}^2$$

2 Calculate the area of each of the following shapes.

a

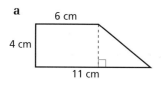

b

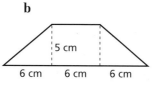

c

4 identical triangles and a square

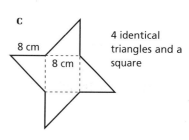

3

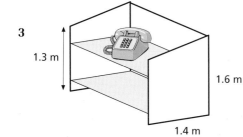

Calculate the area of the side of the telephone table.

4 The sign for a forestry firm is made out of wood as shown. Calculate the area of wood needed for the sign.

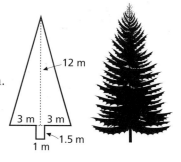

5 Calculate the area of the roof section shown.

EXERCISE 3

1 George and Frances move into a new house.
They want to buy a new carpet for the living room and dining area.
   a What area of carpet do they need to buy?
   b The carpet they like costs £8.50 per square metre. How much does it cost them?

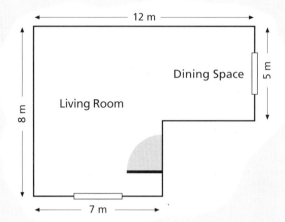

2 Windpower Industries use a child's toy as their logo.

Each part of the windmill is either a square or part of a square of side 9 cm.
The logo is cut from a larger square as shown.

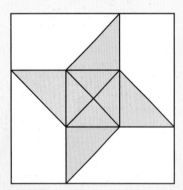

   a What is the shaded area?
   b What is the length of the side of the large square?
   c What is the area wasted?

3 A fireside rug measures 1 m by 75 cm. Calculate the area of the rug in square centimetres.

Reminder

Area = length × breadth but the length and breadth must be in the *same units*.

Sometimes it is easier to use subtraction to find an area.

Tom's garden is a patch of grass surrounded by a path.
Tom wants to find out the area of the path.

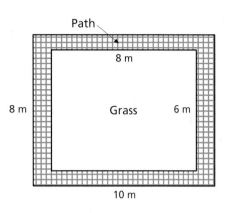
Path

8 m

8 m   Grass   6 m

10 m

Step 1 Garden: $A = l \times b$
$$= 8 \times 10 = 80$$

Area of whole garden = 80 m^2

Step 2 Grass: $A = l \times b$
$$= 6 \times 8 = 48$$

Area of the grass = 48 m^2

Step 3 Path: $80 - 48 = 32$

Area of path = area of garden – area of grass = 32 m^2

EXERCISE 4

Use subtraction to calculate each area mentioned below.

1 The path

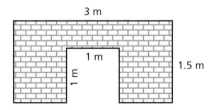
12 m

6 m

4 m   8 m

Grass

Path

2 The frame

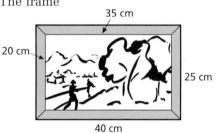
35 cm

20 cm

25 cm

40 cm

3 The brick fireplace

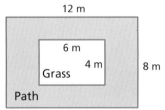
3 m

1 m

1.5 m

1 m

4 The grass

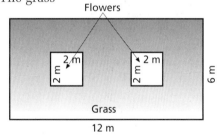
Flowers

2 m

2 m   2 m   2 m

2 m   2 m

Grass

12 m

6 m

5 The side of a chair leg

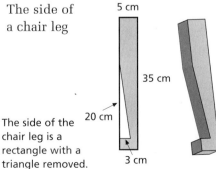
5 cm

35 cm

20 cm

3 cm

The side of the chair leg is a rectangle with a triangle removed.

6 The end of a greenhouse

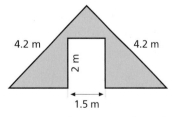
4.2 m   4.2 m

2 m

1.5 m

The end of the greenhouse is a right-angled triangle with a rectangle removed for the doorway.

29

Calculating volume

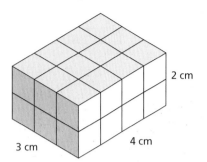

2 cm

3 cm   4 cm

This cuboid measures 4 cm by 3 cm by 2 cm.
We can see it is made up of 2 layers, each
with 4 rows of 3 cubes.
To count the cubes quickly, we can say:
Volume = 4 × 3 × 2
       = 24 cubic centimetres (24 cm^3)

In short, the volume of a cuboid = length × breadth × height.

Volume = $l \times b \times h$

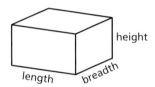

height

length   breadth

EXERCISE 5

Use the above formula to calculate the volume of these cubes and cuboids.

1

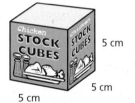

5 cm

5 cm

5 cm

2

15 cm

7 cm   10 cm

3

7 m

3 m

10 m

4

3 cm

3 cm   3 cm

5

3 cm

0.5 cm →

6 cm

EXERCISE 6

1 Computer components are packed in small boxes.
   Each box is a cube of side 6 cm.
   a Calculate the volume of each cube.

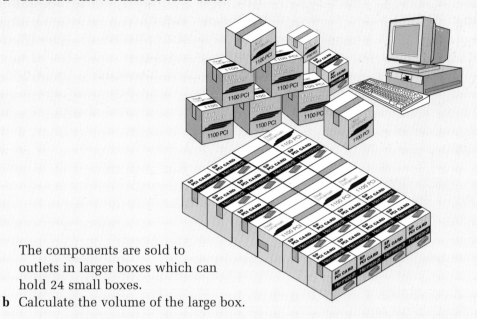

   The components are sold to
   outlets in larger boxes which can
   hold 24 small boxes.
   b Calculate the volume of the large box.

2 The makers of two types of juice each claim they sell the
   carton which holds more juice.
   Quenshy's carton measures
   6 cm × 4 cm × 3 cm.
   Zing's carton measures
   5 cm × 5 cm × 3 cm.
   Calculate how much juice each carton
   holds, and decide who is right.

3 A child's paddling pool is 10 m long, 7 m broad and 0.5 m deep.
   a How many cubic metres of water can it hold?
   b A cubic metre of water weighs a tonne.
      What weight of water is in the pool when it is half full?

4 An oil tank is in the shape of a cuboid.
   It measures 2.5 m by 2 m by 1.5 m.
   a Calculate the volume of the tank.
   b One cubic metre holds 1000 litres.
      How many litres does this tank hold?

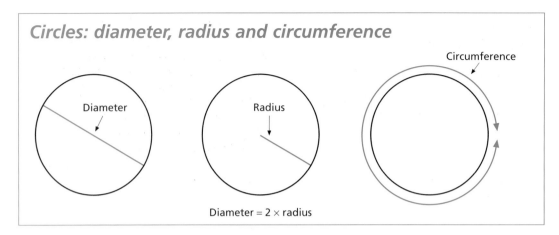

Circles: diameter, radius and circumference

Diameter = 2 × radius

EXERCISE 7

1 Find some circular objects.
   Measure the diameter and circumference of each.
   Record your results in a table like the one below.
   Use a calculator to work out 3 × diameter.

Object	Diameter	Circumference	3 × diameter

> You should have discovered that the circumference is slightly more
> than 3 × diameter.
>
> $$C \approx 3 \times D$$
>
> *Example*
> If the diameter is 12 cm, then $C \approx 3 \times 12$
> $$\approx 36 \text{ cm}$$

2 Estimate the circumference of a circle with:
   a diameter 10 cm   **b** diameter 7 m   **c** diameter 40 cm   **d** diameter 15 mm

3 Work out the diameter and then estimate the circumference of a circle with:
   a radius 3 cm   **b** radius 6 cm   **c** radius 11 cm   **d** radius 25 cm

4 A circular pie dish has a circumference of 36 cm.
   a Divide by 3 to estimate the diameter of the dish.
   b Repeat this for dishes with circumference: **(i)** 24 cm **(ii)** 30 cm **(iii)** 18 cm.

5 Estimate the radius of a circle with circumference:
   a 12 cm   **b** 3 cm   **c** 3.6 cm.

To find a circumference more accurately, we can use:

Circumference = $\pi \times$ diameter

$C = \pi \times d$

π (pronounced pi) is a Greek letter. We use it to stand for the number 3.141 592 653 589 793 238 462 643 383 279 502 884 197 169 399 375 105 820 974 944 592 307 816 406 286 208 998 628 034 825 342 117 067 9 ... and that is just the first 100 decimal places.

When we do a calculation we usually use 3.14 to stand for π, or we use the button on the calculator.

Examples

1 Calculate the circumference of a circle with diameter 14 cm.

Circumference = $\pi \times$ diameter

$3.14 \times 14 = 43.96$

Circumference = 43.96 cm

2 Calculate the circumference of a circle with radius 4.7 m.

Diameter = 2 $\times$ radius

$2 \times 4.7 = 9.4$

Diameter = 9.4 m

Circumference = $\pi \times$ diameter

$3.14 \times 9.4 = 29.516$

Circumference = 29.516 m

EXERCISE 8

Remember to show your working properly. Give your answers to 1 decimal place.

1 Calculate the circumference of a circle with diameter:
   a 4 cm   **b** 1.7 m   **c** 11 mm   **d** 6.3 cm.

2 Calculate the circumference of a circle with radius:
   a 5 cm   **b** 9 mm   **c** 6 m   **d** 0.8 m.

3 The top of a can of soup has a diameter of 12 cm.
   What is the circumference of the can?

4 A circular boating pond is 100 m in diameter. How far is it round the pond?

5 A compact disc has a radius of 6 cm.
   Calculate its circumference.

6 Louise wants to put braid around the top and bottom of a lampshade.
   The top is a circle of diameter 15 cm, and the bottom has a diameter of 20 cm.
   Calculate the length of braid she needs.

7 A bicycle wheel has a radius of 40 cm.
   What distance does the bicycle travel when the wheel makes one turn?

Area of circles

1 Work out the approximate area of each circle by counting the squares.
   Count any part that is half a square or more as one square.
   Ignore any part less than half a square.

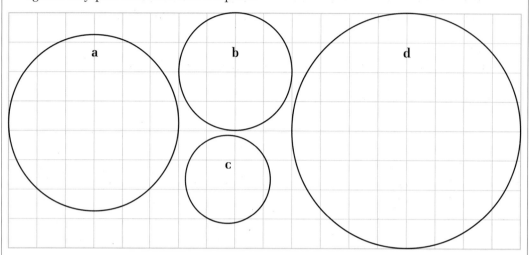

2 Find five circular objects.
   Place the objects on centimetre squared paper and draw round them.
   Copy the table below and fill in your results as you:
   a measure the diameter of each circle
   b count the squares to estimate the area of each circle
   c work out the values for the other columns.
   The first row of the table has been filled in as an example for you to follow.
   Study the answers in the last column. Comment on anything you notice.

Object	Diameter	Counted area	Radius	Radius^2	$\pi \times$ Radius^2
Tin can	6 cm	28 cm^2	3	$3^2 = 3 \times 3 = 9$	$\pi \times 9 = 28.3$

You should find that the area of a circle is roughly 3 times the radius squared.
To be more accurate: **Area of a circle = πr^2.**

Example   A drum has a diameter of 50 cm. What is the area of the drumskin?
   Diameter = 50 cm
      50 ÷ 2 = 25
   Radius = 25 cm
   $\pi \times 25^2 = 1963.5$ (correct to 1 decimal place)
      Area = 1963.5 cm^2

EXERCISE 9

1 Work out the area of a circle with radius:

   a 6 cm   **b** 8 cm   **c** 4.5 cm, correct to 1 decimal place.

2 Work out **(i)** the radius **(ii)** the area of a circle with diameter:

   a 10 cm   **b** 29 cm   **c** 11 cm, correct to 1 decimal place.

3 Work out the area of a circle with:

   a radius 6.4 cm   **b** diameter 1.6 m, correct to 1 decimal place.

4 Calculate the area of these circles.

  a   **b**   **c**   **d**

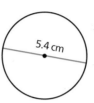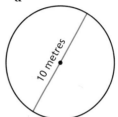

5 A clock has a circular metal face of diameter 13 cm.
   Calculate the area of the clock face.

6 This table shows the diameters of a selection of British coins.

Coin	1p	2p	5p	10p	£1
Diameter	20 mm	26 mm	18 mm	24 mm	22 mm

   Calculate the radius and then work out the area of each coin.

7 A circular table mat has a radius of 15 cm.
   Calculate the area of the table mat.

8 A button has a radius of 7 mm.
   What is the area of the button?

9 A circular rug has a diameter of 3.5 metres.
   a What is the area of the rug?

   The rug is placed in a room measuring 5 metres by 4.2 metres.
   b Calculate the area of the floor.
   c What area of floor is not covered by the rug?

EXERCISE 10

1 An angle measurer is semicircular (half of a circle).
Its radius is 6.5 cm.
Calculate its area.

2 Each wooden shelf is in the shape of a quarter
circle, as shown.
Calculate the area
of each shelf.

20 cm

20 cm

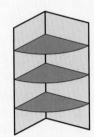

3 A lighthouse has five circular windows.
Each window has a diameter of 3 m.
Calculate the total area of the windows.

4 The brim of a witch's hat is made by cutting a
small circle out of the middle of a larger
circle.
  a Calculate the area of the larger
    circle (with radius 15 cm).
  b Calculate the area of the smaller circle
    (with radius 7 cm).
  c By subtracting, calculate the area of the brim.

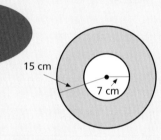

15 cm

7 cm

5

This compact disc has a diameter of 12 cm.
The inner circle has a diameter of 4.4 cm.
Calculate the area of the playing surface of the disc.

6 An archway is in the shape of a semicircle on top of a rectangle.
Calculate the area of:
  a the semicircle
  b the rectangle
  c the archway.

5 m

2 m

7 The side of a breadbin is in the shape of a quarter circle fixed to a rectangle, as
shown.
Calculate the area of:
  a the quarter circle
  b the rectangle
  c the side of the breadbin.

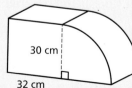

30 cm

32 cm

CHAPTER 3 REVIEW

1 Calculate the area of this garden.

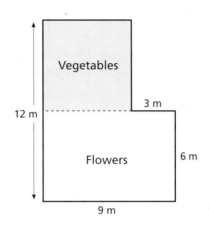

2 Calculate the volume of a cube
with side 3 cm.

3 Calculate the volume of this room.

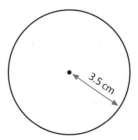

4 Calculate the circumference of each circle.

a   **b**

5 Calculate the area of this circle.

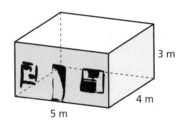

6 A plate stand has a side which is a rectangle
with a right-angled triangle removed.
Calculate the area of:
a the rectangle
b the triangle
c the side.

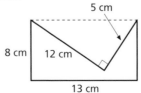 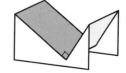

4 Formulae

> **Reminder**
> ab means $a \times b$
> $3a$ means $3 \times a$

Example
If $a = 5$ and $b = 6$
then $ab = 5 \times 6 = 30$
   $3a = 3 \times 5 = 15$

STARTING POINTS

1 Find the missing number in each machine.

a IN 4 × 3 OUT ?

b IN 6 ÷ 2 OUT ?

c IN ? × 6 OUT 18

d IN ? ÷ 4 OUT 10

2 The temperature outside is 5 °C less than the temperature inside.

Complete the table. IN − 5 OUT

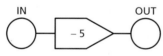

Inside	10 °C	15 °C	23 °C			
Outside				0 °C	8 °C	12 °C

3 When $a = 2$ and $b = 7$, find the value of:
   a $a + b$ **b** ab **c** $5a$ **d** $b - a$ **e** $3a + 2b$

4 Use this machine to help you complete the table below.

IN × 3 − 2 OUT

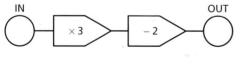

In number	1	5	2.8	1000		
Out number					28	100

Formulae in words

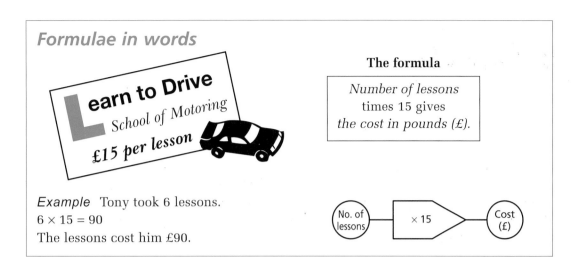

The formula

*Number of lessons
times 15 gives
the cost in pounds (£).*

Example Tony took 6 lessons.
$6 \times 15 = 90$
The lessons cost him £90.

EXERCISE 1

1 Use the formula above to find the cost of:
   a 2 lessons   **b** 5 lessons   **c** 10 lessons   **d** 15 lessons.

2 A lorry driver reads his mileometer at the
start of a week and again at the end.
With the help of a formula he can work
out the distance travelled.
Find the distance travelled in each
case.

*Second reading minus first reading
gives
miles travelled.*

	First reading	Second reading
a	1 520	1 820
b	12 315	15 215
c	28 000	31 320
d	54 527	55 888
e	123 150	130 019

3

*The total cost
divided by
the number of items
gives
the cost of one item.*

Use this formula to calculate the cost of one item:
a 5 loaves costing £4
b 10 apples costing £3
c 4 litres of milk costing £5.

4

*The total cost
divided by
the cost of one item
gives
the number of items.*

Use the formula to work out how many items are
being bought in each case.
a Total cost is 175p.
    The cost of one is 35p.
b Total cost is £91.20.

Two-step formulae

This formula shows how charges for using an Internet terminal are calculated.

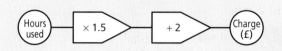

> *Number of hours used*
> *times £1.50*
> *plus*
> *a connecting charge of £2*
> *gives*
> *the charge in pounds (£).*

Example 1 3 hours of use on the terminal would be charged as:
$3 \times £1.50 + £2 = £6.50$

Example 2 8 hours of use would be charged as:
$8 \times £1.50 + £2 = £14$

EXERCISE 2

1 a Use the above formula to complete this table.

Number of hours	1	2	3	4	5	6	7	8
Charge (£)			6.50					14.00

b Mrs Robertson used the terminal for 2 hours on Monday and 3 hours on Wednesday.
She was charged a total of £12.50.
Was this charge correct? (Working must be shown.)

2 Hiring a minibus costs £54 plus £2 per person.

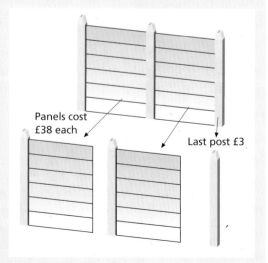

Work out the cost of hiring a minibus for:
a 3 people   **b** 6 people   **c** 13 people.

3 The Fast Fencing Company works out the cost of fencing as follows:

> *The number of panels*
> *times 38*
> *plus 3*
> *gives*
> *the cost in pounds (£).*

Panels cost £38 each

Last post £3

a Use the rule to find the cost of a 3-panel fence.
b Find the cost of fences with:
   (i) 10 panels   **(ii)** 13 panels
   (iii) 45 panels.

4

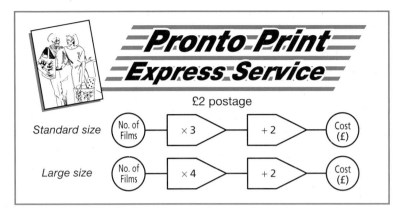

a Susan had five films developed at standard size. How much did she pay?

b Helen wants three films developed at large size. How much will this cost?

Substitution

Letters in expressions stand for numbers.

When we know what the numbers are we can work out the expression.

Example 1 ab stands for $a \times b$.

When $a = 2$ and $b = 3$ then $ab = a \times b = 2 \times 3 = 6$.

Example 2 a^2 stands for $a \times a$.

When $a = 5$ then $a^2 = a \times a = 5 \times 5 = 25$.

Example 3 $3a - b$ stands for $3 \times a - b$.

When $a = 7$ and $b = 11$ then $3a - b = 3 \times a - b = 3 \times 7 - 11 = 10$.

EXERCISE 3

1 For $a = 2$ and $b = 5$ calculate:

a $3a$	**b** $2b$	**c** $5a$	**d** $10b$	**e** $a + b$
f $b - a$	**g** $5a - 2$	**h** $7 + 3a$	**i** $10 + 2b$	**j** ab
k $8 - 3a$	**l** $15 - 3b$	**m** $20 - 5a$	**n** $2b - a$	**o** $2b + 3a$
p $3b + 2$	**q** a^2	**r** b^2	**s** $b^2 + 1$	**t** $a^2 - 1$

2 For $k = 4$ and $p = 7$ calculate:

a $6p$	**b** $4k$	**c** $2 + 3k$	**d** kp	**e** $p - k$
f $7k$	**g** $15p$	**h** $3p + 1$	**i** $10k - 2$	**j** $10 - p$
k p^2	**l** k^2	**m** $k^2 + 5$	**n** $p^2 - 19$	**o** pk
p $50 - p^2$	**q** $17 - k^2$	**r** $100 - kp$		

3 For $g = 5$ and $h = 3$ calculate:

a $2g + 3h$	**b** $g + 5h$	**c** $7g + h$	**d** $4g - 2h$	**e** $g - h$
f $2g - 3h$	**g** $4g + 3h$	**h** $2g - 2h + 1$	**i** $3g + h - 2$	

Things you find in expressions   ... and on the calculator

Example 1 $2a^2 = 2 \times a^2$

When $a = 3$ then $2a^2 = 2 \times 3 \times 3 = 18$

$$\boxed{x^2}$$

Example 2 $\dfrac{a}{b} = a \div b$

When $a = 8$ and $b = 2$ then $\dfrac{a}{b} = \dfrac{8}{2} = 4$

$$\boxed{\div}$$

Example 3

π is special. You will find it on your calculator.
It is approximately 3.14.

$2\pi R = 2 \times \pi \times R$

When R is 4 then

$2\pi R = 2 \times \pi \times 4 = 25.13$

$$\boxed{\pi}$$

Example 4

$\sqrt{a}$ ... what number times itself gives a?
When $a = 25$ then $\sqrt{a} = \sqrt{25} = 5$ ... $(5 \times 5 = 25)$

$$\boxed{\sqrt{}}$$

EXERCISE 4

1 For $m = 2$, $n = 4$ and $p = 8$, evaluate:

a m^2	**b** $5m^2$	**c** n^2	**d** $3n^2$	**e** p^2	**f** $2p^2$
g $\dfrac{n}{m}$	**h** $\dfrac{m}{n}$	**i** $\dfrac{p}{m}$	**j** $\dfrac{p}{n}$	**k** $\dfrac{n}{p}$	**l** $\dfrac{m}{p}$

2 For $a = 7$, $b = 3$ and $c = 2$, evaluate:

a abc **b** $a + b + c$ **c** $a - b - c$ **d** $a^2 + b$ **e** $a + b^2$

3 Using $\pi = 3.14$ (or the π button) calculate the following, correct to 1 decimal place:

a 2π **b** $\pi \times 3 \times 3$ **c** $2\pi \times 7$ **d** $3\pi + 8$

e $2\pi \times 5$ **f** $\pi \times 1.5 \times 1.5$ **g** $36 \div \pi$ **h** $\pi \div \pi$

4 When $a = 5$, $b = 3$ and $c = 10$, calculate to 1 decimal place:

a $2\pi a$ **b** πb^2 **c** πa^2 **d** $\pi a + c$ **e** $b + \pi c$

5 Calculate:

a $\sqrt{x}$ where   **(i)** $x = 16$ **(ii)** $x = 1$ **(iii)** $x = 144$

b $\sqrt{y}$ where   **(i)** $y = 169$ **(ii)** $y = 121$ **(iii)** $y = 196$.

Priorities

In expressions some things must be worked out before others.

Example 1

$$4 + 2 \times 3 =$$

(multiplication) $4 + 6 =$

(addition)   10

Example 2

$$3 \times 4 + 6 \div 2 =$$

(multiplication first) $12 + 6 \div 2 =$

(division) $12 + 3 =$

(addition)   15

Example 3   When $a = 3$ and $b = 2$ find the value of $3(a + b) + b$.

(substitute) $3(3 + 2) + 2 =$

(brackets) $3 \times 5 + 2 =$

(multiplication) $15 + 2 =$

(addition)   17

Example 4   When $p = 2$ and $q = 5$ find the value of $3p + 2q$.

(substitute) $3 \times 2 + 2 \times 5 =$

(multiplication) $6 + 10 =$

(addition)   16

Example 5   Calculate $20 \div 4 \times 5$.

No operation has priority so calculate left to right.

(division) $5 \times 5 =$

(multiplication)   25

Your calculator may work using this set of rules. Check it.

EXERCISE 5

1 Calculate:

  a $3 + 4 \times 2$ **b** $6 + 3 \times 4$ **c** $7 \times 2 + 3 \times 4$ **d** $6 \div 2 - 12 \div 6$ **e** $4 + 5 \times 4 + 2$

  f $5 + 4 \div 2$ **g** $6 \div 3 \times 4$ **h** $3 \times 2 + 2 \times 3$ **i** $12 \div 2 - 8 \div 4$ **j** $3 + 4 \times 2 + 5$

2 Evaluate (remember to do the brackets first):

  a $3 \times (2 + 5)$ **b** $4 \times (1 + 3)$ **c** $5 \times (7 - 3)$ **d** $6 \div (2 + 1)$ **e** $(4 + 5) \times (4 + 2)$

3 Evaluate:

  a $3(a + b)$ when **(i)** $a = 6$, $b = 7$ **(ii)** $a = 4$, $b = 3$ **(iii)** $a = 13$, $b = 27$

  b $x(3y - 2)$ when **(i)** $x = 5$, $y = 6$ **(ii)** $x = 4$, $y = 5$ **(iii)** $x = 1$, $y = 8$ **(iv)** $x = 10$, $y = 30$

Formulae in symbols

Example 1

> Number of lessons
> times 15
> gives
> the cost in pounds (£).

In words: Lessons are £15 each.

Diagram: (No. of lessons) — [× 15] — (Cost (£))

Symbols: $C = 15L$ where L is the number of lessons and C is the cost in pounds (£).

Example 2

> Number of pizzas
> times 3
> plus 1
> gives
> the cost in pounds (£).

In words: Pizzas cost £3 each. There is a delivery charge of £1.

Diagram: (No. of pizzas) — [× 3] — [+ 1] — (Cost (£))

Symbols: $c = 3p + 1$ where p is the number of pizzas and c is the cost in pounds (£).

EXERCISE 6

1 Turn each diagram into a formula using symbols.

a (No. of trips (T)) — [× 25] — (Cost (C))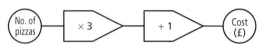

b (No. of guitars (G)) — [× 6] — (No. of strings (S))

c (No. of people (p)) — [+ 1] — (No. of teabags (t))

d (No. of concert tickets (t)) — [× 15] — [+ 5] — (Cost (C))

Tickets at £15 + £5 handling charge

e (No. of spools (s)) — [× 2] — [+ 1] — (Cost in £ of films (f))

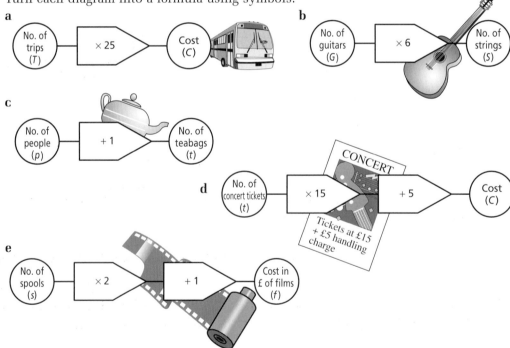

2 It costs £1 to get onto the ski run and £2 every time you use the chairlift.
The cost of a day's skiing can be worked out using the formula:
$C = 2L + 1$ where C is the cost in pounds and
L is the number of times the lift is used.
Evaluate C when L is: **a** 3   **b** 5   **c** 7   **d** 10.

3 The cost of a theatre ticket for an adult is £A.
The cost of a theatre ticket for a child is £C.
The total cost for a party of people is £T.
For a party of 2 adults and 3 children, $T = 2A + 3C$.
Evaluate T when:

a $A = 3$ and $C = 2$ **b** $A = 4$ and $C = 3$.

4 Use these formulae to find: **(i)** the perimeter and **(ii)** the area of each shape below.

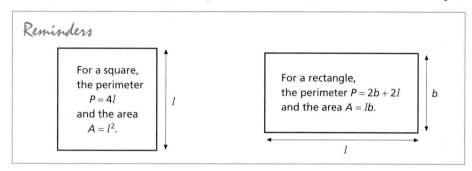

Reminders

For a square, the perimeter $P = 4l$ and the area $A = l^2$.

For a rectangle, the perimeter $P = 2b + 2l$ and the area $A = lb$.

a

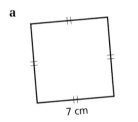

7 cm

b

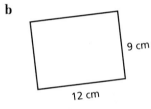

9 cm

12 cm

c

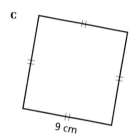

9 cm

d

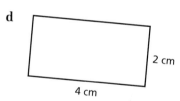

2 cm

4 cm

5 The volume of a room can be calculated using the formula $\boxed{V = ah}$ where a is the area of the floor and h is the height.
Calculate V when:

a $a = 100$ m² and $h = 3$ m   **b** $a = 120$ m² and $h = 4$ m   **c** $a = 90$ m² and $h = 2$ m.

6 The average of a list of numbers can be calculated using the formula $\boxed{A = \dfrac{T}{n}}$ where T is the total of the list and n is the number of items in the list.
Calculate A when:

a $T = 1000$ and $n = 25$ **b** $T = 81$ and $n = 9$ **c** $T = 250$ and $n = 5$.

7 **a** Calculate s where $s = ut + v$ and
    (i) $u = 2, t = 3, v = 5$ **(ii)** $u = 1.2, t = 5, v = 4.5$ **(iii)** $u = 8, t = 1.5, v = 5$.
   b Calculate L where $L = 3a - 2b$ and
    (i) $a = 5, b = 4$ **(ii)** $a = 1.5, b = 0.5$ **(iii)** $a = 7.5, b = 10$.

8

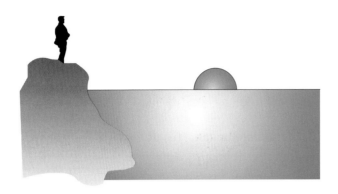

The distance, D km, to the horizon is given by $D = 4\sqrt{h}$
where h is the height, in metres, of the observer.
Find D when: **a** $h = 16$ **b** $h = 49$ **c** $h = 81$.

9 Some volume formulae:

Cylinder $V = \pi r^2 h$

Cuboid $V = lbh$

Cube $V = l^3$

Pyramid $V = \dfrac{Ah}{3}$

Cone $V = \dfrac{\pi r^2 h}{3}$

Find the volume of:
a a pyramid with $A = 26$ cm^2 and $h = 6$ cm
b a cube with $l = 7$ cm
c a cuboid with $l = 2$ cm, $b = 3$ cm and $h = 5$ cm
d a cylinder with $r = 4$ cm and $h = 10$ cm
e a cone with $r = 3$ cm and $h = 20$ cm.

CHAPTER 4 REVIEW

1 A farmer has a herd of 100 cows.
The average amount of milk (in litres) per cow is given by:

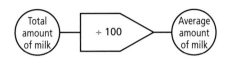

Complete this table:

Total number of litres	1500	3000	6500	6750
Average amount per cow				

2 Livery Stables look after horses.
They charge a £20 booking fee and £12 a day.

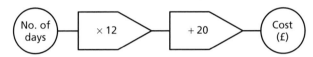

a How much will it cost to keep a horse in the stables for:
(i) 1 day   (ii) 10 days   (iii) a fortnight?
b A trainer keeps two horses at the stables for 30 days.
What is his bill?

3 If $x = 5$ and $y = 7$ evaluate:
   a $2x$ **b** xy **c** $3x + 2$ **d** $20 - 2y$ **e** $5x - 2y$ **f** $100 - x^2$

4 The perimeter, P, of this shape is given
by the formula $P = 4a + 8b$.
Calculate the perimeter, P, when:
a $a = 2$ cm, $b = 3$ cm
b $a = 4$ cm, $b = 2$ cm
c $a = 1$ m, $b = 5$ m.

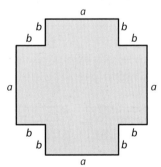

5 The braking distance of a car is worked out from the formula $D = \dfrac{u^2}{20}$

where D is the distance in feet and u is the speed in miles per hour.
What is the braking distance of a car travelling at:
a 30 mph   **b** 50 mph   **c** 70 mph?

5 Calculations in Context

STARTING POINTS

1 Donna buys two CDs which cost £9 each.
How much change does she get from £20?

2 A music store has a special offer.
The full price for a CD is £8.40.
How much will Kazim pay for two CDs?

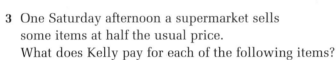

Special offer
Buy one CD
and
get a second
at half price.

3 One Saturday afternoon a supermarket sells
some items at half the usual price.
What does Kelly pay for each of the following items?
a Brown wholemeal loaf   Usual price 68p
b Packet of pancakes   Usual price 84p
c Pack of apple turnovers   Usual price £1.10

Reminder

$5\% = \dfrac{5}{100} = 5 \div 100 = 0.05$

4 Copy and complete this table.

Percentage	5%	10%	1%	25%	50%	20%
Fraction	$\dfrac{5}{100}$					
Decimal	0.05					

5 Megan orders a new coat from a catalogue.
There are three ways to pay.

£5.50 a month
for 24 months

£10 a month
for 12 months

Cash price
£100

a How much does it cost to buy the coat over 24 months?
b How much does it cost to buy it over 12 months?
c How much cheaper is it to pay cash than to pay over 24 months?

6 Jordan put £600 in a bank.
The bank paid 4% interest a year.
Work out 4% of £600 to find how much interest Jordan was paid after a year.

Earning money

People earn their money in different ways.

Some are paid by the year, or month or week.

Some are paid by the hour.

Some are paid by the number of items they make.

Some are paid by the amount they sell.

EXERCISE 1

1 Mary Simpson is a primary school teacher.
   She earns £15 000 a year.
     a She is paid the same amount each month.
        How much does she earn a month?
     b Her annual salary increases by £1200.
        How much does she earn per month now?

2 Jyoti Patel is paid £4.50 per hour.
   He works a 35-hour week.
     a How much does he earn in a week?
     b If he works 50 weeks a year like this, how much does he earn in a year?

3 James Brown is a shop assistant.
   He earns £120 a week.
     a If he works 40 hours a week what does he earn per hour?
     b His wage goes up by £0.50 per hour.
        What is his new weekly wage?

4 Claire Duncan is a self-employed driver. She earns £50 a day.
     a How much did she earn in a week where she worked four days?
     b The following week she worked six days. How much more did she earn that week?

Piecework

This is when people are paid a set amount each time they make or do something.

Example

Phil advertises double glazing by phone. Each phone call he makes earns him 50p.

He makes six calls one evening. How much does he earn?

$6 \times 50 = 300$

He earns £3.

5 Harry Gibson gets a seasonal job wrapping parcels. He is paid 60p per parcel.
   a He wraps 120 parcels one day.
         How much does he earn?
   b How much will he earn if he wraps 300 parcels?

6 TV Broadcasts is a new channel coming on air.
   Stan Green is a TV electrician.
   He makes £2.50 for each system he retunes for the new channel.
   a If he retunes 20 sets, how much does he earn?
   b His friend retunes 28 sets.
         How much more did he earn than Stan?

Commission

When people are paid a percentage of the value of the goods they sell
we say they are paid commission.

Example

Emily Peters works in a bookshop.
She earns 3% commission on her sales.
How much will she earn if she sells £500
worth of books?

3% of 500
= 3 ÷ 100 × 500 = 15
She earns £15 commission.

---

7 Jenny Kline sells advertising space in a newspaper.
   She is paid 8% commission on all her sales.
   a She sells £850 worth of space one day.
         How much does she earn?
   b On a poor day she only sold £120 worth.
         How much did she earn?

8 A booking agency takes 11% commission on every theatre ticket it sells.
   a How much does it earn from sales worth £7500?
   b For an outdoor concert the agency made £25 000 worth of sales.
         Calculate the commission.

Earning extra

People can earn extra cash through bonuses or overtime.

Bonus

A bonus is an extra payment paid for a job well done or as a reward for working harder.

EXERCISE 2

1 A joiner would normally take 7 days to complete a certain task.
He is paid £30 a day.
His employers want the job done in 5 days.
They offer a bonus of £80 if the joiner does this.
   a How much will the joiner be paid if he takes 7 days?
   b How much will he be paid if he does it in 5 days with the bonus?
   c How much more would he earn?

2 Sophie Thomson is employed to address envelopes.
She is paid 1p per envelope.
If she does over 1000 envelopes she gets a bonus of £5.
   a How much is she paid for 999 envelopes?
   b How much will she be paid if she does 1001 envelopes?

3 Abdul Rashid is an electrician who rewires houses.
He gets paid £35 per day to finish the job within 5 days.
If he finishes the job in 3 days he gets a bonus of £80.
   a How much will he get if he does the job:
      (i) in 5 days   **(ii)** in 3 days?
   b How much more does he make if he finishes the job early?

4 Jimmy Bright is a professional footballer.
He earns £200 a week.
He gets a bonus of £60 each time he scores a goal.
   a How much does he earn in a week when he scored
      2 goals?
   b In a 4-week period he scores 7 goals.
      What are his total earnings for this period?

5 Margaret sells shoes. She earns 4% commission on her sales.
If her sales go over £1000 in a week she is paid a bonus of £30.
How much does she earn in a week when her sales are worth:
   a £900   **b** £1010?

Overtime

Overtime is when you work more than your normal hours.
In some jobs this overtime is unpaid but in others you are paid extra.

If you work on a Sunday or a holiday it is common to be paid **double time**.
This means for every one hour that you work you are paid for two hours.

Example
Zoe worked 3 hours of overtime at double time.
She earns £4 per hour normally.
How much does she earn for her overtime?

3 hours at double time would be:
$3 \times 2 = 6$ ... 6 hours' pay
$6 \times 4 = 24$ ... Her overtime pay is £24.

EXERCISE 3

1 Work out how much you would be paid for the following:
   a 3 hours of double time at a basic rate of £3 per hour
   b 2 hours of double time at a basic rate of £5 per hour
   c 6 hours of double time at a basic rate of £3.80 per hour
   d 2.5 hours of double time at a basic rate of £6.10 per hour
   e 8 hours of double time at a basic rate of £4.25 per hour.

2 Martin works 35 hours at a basic rate of £4 an hour.
   a How much does he make for this work?
   b He works 6 hours at double time.
      How much is he paid for this overtime?
   c Calculate his total pay (basic + overtime).

3 Sita works at a petrol station at a basic rate of £3.80 per hour.
   She works 5 hours each day, Monday to Saturday.
   She works 4 hours on Sunday at double time.
   a How much is she paid at the basic rate?
   b How much is she paid for overtime?
   c How much does she earn in the week?

4 Tom Winters is a keeper at the zoo.
   He is paid a basic rate of £4.10 per hour.
   He works 8 hours a day during the week.
   He works 6 hours a day on Saturday and Sunday.
   He is paid double time for the weekend.
   a Calculate his basic pay (Monday to Friday).
   b Calculate his overtime.
   c Calculate his total wage.

5 The time sheets for three workers at an outdoor centre are shown.
Saturdays and Sundays are paid at double time.

Bryan Trent	Hours
Monday	6
Tuesday	7
Wednesday	5
Thursday	6
Friday	4
Saturday	3
Sunday	3

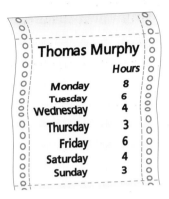

Thomas Murphy	Hours
Monday	8
Tuesday	6
Wednesday	4
Thursday	3
Friday	6
Saturday	4
Sunday	3

Sandra Sinclair	Hours
Monday	4
Tuesday	5
Wednesday	5
Thursday	4
Friday	7
Saturday	2
Sunday	0

a Bryan works for £4.50 per hour.
Calculate his total wage.

b Sandra works for £6 an hour.
Thomas works for £4 an hour.
How much does each person earn?

c Who earns most in the week?

Another common overtime rate is **time and a half**.

Example 1   Jack works 4 hours of overtime at time and a half.
How many hours is this worth at the basic rate?

time	4 hours
plus half the time	2 hours
time and a half	6 hours

4 hours of overtime at time and a half is worth 6 hours at the basic rate.

Example 2   Jenny works for a basic rate of £3.50 an hour.
She works 6 hours at time and a half. How much overtime does
she earn?

time	6 hours
plus half the time	3 hours
time and a half	9 hours

$9 \times 3.50 = 31.50$. Jenny earns £31.50 overtime.

EXERCISE 4

1 Calculate how much overtime is earned, at time and a half, in the following cases:
  a 4 hours of overtime at a basic rate of £4 per hour
  b 6 hours of overtime at a basic rate of £3 per hour
  c 12 hours of overtime at a basic rate of £6 per hour
  d 18 hours of overtime at a basic rate of £4.50 per hour
  e 24 hours of overtime at a basic rate of £3.80 per hour.

2 Tina is a trucker. She earns a basic £4.20 per hour.
   She works 30 hours at the basic rate.
   She works 6 hours on Saturday at time and a half.
   She works 4 hours on Sunday at double time.
   Calculate:
   a her basic earnings
   b her earnings on (**i**) Saturday   (**ii**) Sunday
   c her total earnings for the week.

3 Mike works as a tennis coach.
   He earns a basic £3.50 per hour.
   He works 25 hours at the basic rate.
   He works 4 hours on Saturday at time and a half.
   He works 2 hours on Sunday at double time.
   Calculate:
   a his basic earnings
   b his earnings on (**i**) Saturday   (**ii**) Sunday
   c his total earnings for the week.

4 Susan, Tanith and Harry all work in the transport museum.
   Susan is paid £4 an hour, Tanith £3.80 an hour and Harry £5 an hour.
   Their time sheets for one week are shown.

Susan Jones

	Hours
Monday	4
Tuesday	6
Wednesday	8
Thursday	5
Friday	6
Saturday	4
Sunday	2

Tanith O'Hare

	Hours
Monday	6
Tuesday	7
Wednesday	3
Thursday	6
Friday	6
Saturday	6
Sunday	4

Harry McLean

	Hours
Monday	6
Tuesday	7
Wednesday	7
Thursday	8
Friday	7
Saturday	8
Sunday	0

Saturdays are paid at time and a half.
Sundays are paid at double time.
a Calculate the weekly wage of:
   (**i**) Susan
   (**ii**) Tanith
   (**iii**) Harry.
b Who earned the most in the week?

Pay rises

Prices often increase over time. We need to earn more to pay for these price rises. It is common to have a wage review each year.

Example 1 Theresa earns £160 a week. She is given a pay rise of £10 a week.
160 + 10 = 170
She now earns £170 a week.

Example 2 Samuel earns £160 a week. He is given a pay rise of 10%.
10% of 160 = 10 ÷ 100 × 160 = 16
He now earns 160 + 16 = £176 a week.

EXERCISE 5

1 Calculate the new wage in each of the following cases.
  a Original wage £200 a week; increased by £12 a week.
  b Original wage £25 000 a year; increased by £3000 a year.
  c Original wage £4 an hour; increased by £0.60 an hour.
  d Original wage £300 a week; increased by 8%.
  e Original wage £17 000 a year; increased by 12%.
  f Original wage £4 an hour; increased by 10%.

2 Grace is a filing clerk. She earns £5 an hour.
  a How much does she earn for a 40-hour week?
  b She gets a pay increase of £0.20 an hour. What is her new hourly rate?
  c How much does she now earn for 40 hours of work?

3 Steve works as a tutor at a local golf club.
He earns £17 004 a year. He is paid this in 52 weekly instalments.
  a How much does he earn a week?
  b He is given an annual pay rise of £2080. How much does he now earn a year?
  c How much does he now earn a week?

4 Frank Fisher works as a diver on the rigs.
He earns £25 000 a year. He gets a 6% pay rise.
  a What does he now earn a year?
  b His friend who also works on the rigs earns £18 000.
    What is his annual wage after a 6% pay rise?

5 At a leisure centre, instructors are paid different hourly rates.

Helen £5 per hour   Matthew £4.60 per hour   Tony £6 per hour   Clark £6.50 per hour   Moira £8 per hour

Everyone receives a wage increase of 10%.
  a Calculate the new hourly rate of each instructor.
  b Helen normally works a 40-hour week.
    How much more will she be earning in a week?

Rates of exchange

Example

Louise is off to France for a holiday. She has £500 spending money.

She wants to **exchange** her British pounds for French francs.

Tourist rates		
Country	Currency	Rate (per £)
United States	dollars ($)	1.55
Germany	Deutschmarks (Dm)	2.35
Greece	drachmas (dr)	375.00
Italy	lire (l)	2388.00
Spain	pesetas (pes)	200.00
France	francs (fr)	8.00

Louise checks the tourist exchange rates in a newspaper. She sees she will get 8.00 francs for a pound. How many francs will she get for £500?

500 × 8.00 = 4000

She will get 4000 francs.

EXERCISE 6

1

Use the above rates to convert:

a £200 to francs	**b** £100 to pesetas	**c** £65 to lire
d £1000 to dollars	**e** £30 to Deutschmarks	**f** £3500 to dollars
g £500 to Deutschmarks	**h** £600 to dollars	**i** £560 to francs
j £250 to drachmas	**k** £249 to lire	**l** £750 to drachmas
m £200 to lire	**n** £764 to francs	**o** £200 to Deutschmarks

2 James is going mountaineering in the Alps.
  a He changes £600 into French francs.
     How many francs does he get?
  b He also wants £100 worth of Italian lire.
     Multiply by 2388 to find out how many lire he will get.

3 Copy and complete this table, changing £ sterling into the stated currency.

Amount (£)	Country/ Currency	Amount in foreign currency
£200	France (francs)	
£550	United States (dollars)	
£1000	Italy (lire)	
£780	Spain (pesetas)	
£97	Greece (drachmas)	

4 Three friends go to Venice.

The bank changes their money at the rate of 2400 lire to the pound (£).

Sam has £250, Jane has £500 and Mira has £450.

a How many lire does Sam get?

b How much more does Jane get than Mira?

5 Ryan is going on a European tour.
He changes £100 into French
francs, £150 into Belgian francs
and £300 into German marks.
How much of each type of
currency does he get?

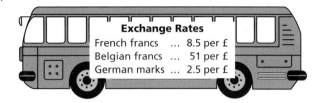

Exchange Rates
French francs ... 8.5 per £
Belgian francs ... 51 per £
German marks ... 2.5 per £

Example

Ryan does not spend all his money on holiday.

He is left with 153 French francs.

To convert his French francs back into pounds he *divides* by the
exchange rate.

153 ÷ 8.5 = 18

His francs are worth £18.

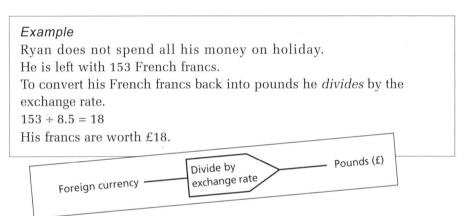

Foreign currency — Divide by exchange rate — Pounds (£)

6 Convert each of the following to pounds, using the exchange rates quoted at the
start of the exercise.

Give your answer to the nearest pound where appropriate.

a 500 francs   **b** 3000 lire   **c** 700 Deutschmarks   **d** 500 dollars

e 8000 pesetas   **f** 340 drachmas   **g** 7500 francs   **h** 425 dollars

i 3981 pesetas   **j** 24 Deutschmarks

7 Laura is on holiday in Canada when the exchange rate is 2.20 Canadian dollars to
the pound.

She looks at some of the prices in the shops. Convert each price to pounds.

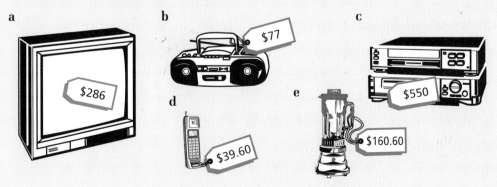

a

$286

b

$77

c

$550

d

$39.60

e

$160.60

8 Lauren books a flight home to France to visit her parents.
The cost of the flight is £99.
She pays in French francs.
(The exchange rate is 8 francs to the pound.)
a How much does she pay in francs?
b Her flight back to Scotland costs her 840 francs.
How much is this in pounds (at the same rate of exchange)?

9 Nikki took a flight from Athens to Gatwick.
It cost her 56 250 drachmas.
A taxi trip costing £14 took her to King's Cross.
A train took her to Berwick upon Tweed at a cost of £64.
a Work out the total cost of Nikki's travel in drachmas.
(Exchange rate: 375 drachmas to the pound.)
b Work out the total cost of her travel in pounds.

Insurance

People take out insurance policies to protect themselves against misfortune.
The most common kinds of insurance cover are:
(i) building   **(ii)** household contents   **(iii)** travel   **(iv)** motor.
In the winter of 1995 many householders were glad they were insured.
The severe weather caused burst pipes and much damage to property.

Building insurance

The payment you make each year is called a premium.
Insurance companies normally quote the cost of insuring each £1000 of value.

Example
Frank wants to insure his house which is
worth £80 000.
The insurance company charges £2 for
each £1000 the house is worth.
What is Frank's premium?

80 000 ÷ 1000 = 80   He wants to insure 80 thousands.
80 × 2 = 160   It will cost him £160 a year.

EXERCISE 7

1 Work out the premium for each of the following.

  a £60 000 house insured at £2 per £1000

  b £80 000 house insured at £3 per £1000

  c £500 000 house insured at £4 per £1000

  d £70 000 house insured at £3 per £1000

  e £75 000 house insured at £4.50 per £1000

  f £84 000 house insured at £2.75 per £1000

2 The Solid as a Rock Insurance Company charges £2.50 per £1000 for house insurance. Calculate the premium on a house worth:

  a £60 000   **b** £90 000   **c** £85 000   **d** £125 000   **e** £87 000.

3 Mike wants to insure his house which is worth £250 000.

House Protect will charge him £2.50 per £1000.

Mammoth Save will charge him £2.49 per £1000.

  a Calculate the premium for **(i)** House Protect   **(ii)** Mammoth Save.

  b What is the difference in **(i)** the charge per £1000   **(ii)** the premium?

4 Al and Lindsey buy a flat in Morningside Road. It costs them £60 000.

The premium for building insurance is £2.50 for every £1000 insured.

  a How many thousands do they want to insure?

  b How much is the annual premium?

5

Modern bungalows for sale at £55 000.
We arrange building insurance.
Only £1.50 per £1000 insured p.a.

Alice Malloy buys one of these bungalows.
How much does it cost to insure it for a year?

6 The Scotts' house is valued at £83 000.

The premium is £1.80 per £1000 insured.

  a How much is their annual premium?

  b They wish to pay monthly. How much is their monthly premium?

7 Copy and complete this table.

House value	Annual premium per £1000	Total annual premium
£69 000	£1.76	
£47 000	£2.00	
£88 000	£1.95	
£100 000	£2.55	

Household contents

It is important to insure the contents of your house.
The premium you pay depends upon:
• the value of the contents
• where you live
• what kind of house you live in.
Here is a typical table produced by insurance companies.
'Extra damage' is a dearer policy which covers all risks.
Premiums are calculated in the same way as building premiums.

Each premium quoted covers £1000 for a year.		
Type of property	**Standard cover**	**Extra damage**
Detached	£2.40	£3.90
Semi-detached	£2.20	£3.60
Terraced house	£2.60	£4.20
Flat	£2.50	£4.10

Example
Janice Napier lives in a terraced house.
She wants standard cover for £12 000 worth of belongings.
How much will it cost?
12 000 ÷ 1000 = 12   She wants to insure 12 thousands.
12 × 2.60 = 31.20   She will pay £31.20 a year.

8 Sam Wood lives in a terraced house. Work out the premium he would have to pay to get standard cover for:
   a £18 000   **b** £20 000   **c** £34 000
   d £12 000   **e** £350 000.

Keep your Contents Safe!

9 Gill Taylor lives in a flat. Work out the premium she would have to pay to get extra damage cover for:
   a £15 000   **b** £24 000   **c** £65 000
   d £76 000   **e** £240 000.

10 Mr Darling lives in a semi-detached house.
   His house contents are worth £16 000.
   How much is his annual premium for standard cover?

11 Marjorie Trainer's house contents are worth £20 000.
   She lives in a flat. She wants an extra damage policy.
   How much is her annual premium?

12 'That will cost you £3.90 for every £1000' says the insurance agent to Mrs Goodfellow.
   a In what kind of house does Mrs Goodfellow live?
   b What kind of policy does she want?

13 How much does Jack Fleming pay for standard cover on contents valued at £18 500? He lives in a detached house.

Holiday and travel insurance

The main reasons for taking out travel insurance are to cover against cancellation or delay, loss of luggage or money, and the need for medical attention.

The table shows a travel insurance company's premiums on different holidays. Prices depend on destination. Prices quoted are per person. There is a 50% reduction for children under 12 and no charge for children under 2.

Area	**Area 1** Great Britain, N. Ireland, Isle of Man, Channel Islands	**Area 2** Europe, Eire, Mediterranean Islands, Morocco, Algeria, Egypt, Israel, Turkey, Madeira, Canary Islands	**Area 3** Rest of world
	1	**2**	**3**
Up to 8 nights	£7	£20.50	£67
9 to 17 nights	£8.50	£25	£78
18 to 23 nights	£9.60	£32	£89
24 to 31 nights	£12.10	£41.60	£96

14 Give a quote for each of these circumstances.
    a One person, 7 nights, area 2   **b** One person, 20 nights, area 3
    c One person, 10 nights, area 1   **d** One person, 30 nights, area 2
    e Two persons, 7 nights, area 1   **f** Two persons, 19 nights, area 3
    g Three persons, 14 nights, area 2   **h** Four persons, 14 nights, area 2

15 Mr and Mrs Fleming go for 7 nights to the
    Channel Islands.
    How much holiday insurance do they pay?

16 Joyce and Jim Thomson are Morocco bound.
    They go for a fortnight's holiday (14 days).
    How much does it cost them for insurance?

17 Ruth and Phil plan a safari in Africa.
    a Which insurance area does this come under?
    b How much does it cost them altogether if they
       go for the month of September (30 days)?

18 Brian Dutch and his wife take their two children aged 7 and 1 on a 15-day
    Mediterranean cruise.
    a How much is the premium per adult?
    b How much does Brian spend on holiday insurance for all the family?

Motor insurance

The cost of motor insurance depends upon:
• the kind of car you own
• where you live
• your age.
An important feature is the
'no claims discount'.
Insurance companies will reduce your
premium if you have not made a claim
in the previous year.
The longer you go without making a
claim, the bigger the discount.

Period without claim	Discount
1 year	30%
2 years	40%
3 years	50%
4 or more years	60%

Example

Grant's car insurance is due for renewal.
The basic premium is £490. He has not claimed for 2 years.
a What is the discount?   **b** What is his premium?

a 2 years without a claim = 40% discount.
     40% of 490 = 40 ÷ 100 × 490 = 196   The discount is £196.
b 490 − 196 = 294   His premium is £294.

EXERCISE 8

1 Work out the premium to be paid in the following cases.
  a Basic premium £300, no claims discount 40%
  b Basic premium £250, no claims discount 60%
  c Basic premium £400, no claims discount 30%
  d Basic premium £199, no claims discount 0%
  e Basic premium £260, period without claim 2 years

2 Marjorie drives a Ford Fiesta. Her premium is £380.
  She has had no claims for 3 years.
  a What percentage discount does she have?
  b Calculate the discount.
  c How much does she pay for her insurance?

3 Karen Craig has made no claims on her insurance for 6 years.
  a What percentage discount will she receive?
  b Her premium is £740 before discount. How much does she actually pay?

4 Balwant Singh's discount on his car insurance is 30%.
  a How many years of no claims does he have?
  b His insurance premium before discount is £480. How much is his discount?
  c How much does he actually pay?

5 Jim Paisley has 10 years of claim-free motoring.
  His premium before discount is £538.
  How much does Jim pay for his motor insurance?

Hire purchase (HP)

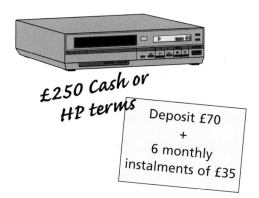

£250 Cash or
HP terms

Deposit £70
+
6 monthly
instalments of £35

Bob Frazer wants to buy a video recorder costing £250.
This is too much for Bob to pay now.
He has two choices.
He could save up for it and buy it later for the cash price.
Or, if he wants it *now*, he can put down a deposit, and pay it up over six months.
He can take it away after paying the deposit but he doesn't own it until the last payment is made.

Six instalments 6 × 35 = 210
Deposit = 70
Total HP price = £280

280 – 250 = 30.

Note that Bob would pay £30 more for the benefit of using HP.

EXERCISE 9

1 Work out the final cost of items bought under the following terms.
  a Deposit £60, 10 instalments of £20   **b** Deposit £45, 12 instalments of £15
  c Deposit £16, 20 instalments of £12   **d** Deposit £24, 6 instalments of £40
  e Deposit £100, 24 instalments of £80

2

£58 cash
or
£10 deposit and
6 instalments
of £9

Calculate:
  a the total cost of the 6 instalments
  b the total HP price
  c the extra paid by buying on hire purchase.

3

£450 cash
or
£80 deposit and
12 instalments
of £35

Calculate:
  a the total cost of the 12 instalments
  b the total HP price
  c the extra paid by buying on hire purchase.

4 The cash price of a car is £12 000.
  Graeme pays a deposit of £3000 and agrees to pay 24 instalments of £400.
  a Calculate the total HP cost of the car.
  b How much cheaper is the cash price?

> The deposit is often given as a percentage of the cash price.
>
> *Example*
> A fishing boat costs £4000.
> The HP terms are:
>   14% deposit + 12 instalments of £300.
> What is the total HP cost?
>
> 14% of 4000 = 14 ÷ 100 × 4000 = 560
> 12 payments of £300 = 12 × 300 = 3600
> Total HP cost = £4160

5 Work out the final cost of items bought under the following terms.
   a Cash price £500, deposit 12%, 10 instalments of £45
   b Cash price £250, deposit 10%, 12 instalments of £20
   c Cash price £1000, deposit 8%, 8 instalments of £120

6

£250 cash
or
12% deposit and
6 instalments
of £38

Calculate:
   a the deposit
   b the total HP price
   c the extra paid by buying on hire
       purchase.

7

£1800 cash
or
15% deposit and
24 instalments
of £65

Calculate:
   a the deposit
   b the total cost of the
       instalments
   c the hire purchase price.

8 A car costs £15 000 cash.
   A deposit of 24% and 12 instalments of £1000 are the HP terms.
   a Calculate the total HP price of the car.
   b How much cheaper is it to pay cash?

CHAPTER 5 REVIEW

1

James Struthers makes soft toys in a factory.
He is paid £15 for each bear and £12 for each mouse.
a How much does he earn when he makes 8 bears?
b How many mice must he make to earn £96?

2 Aziz is paid 8% commission on all sales.
How much commission does he make from £650 worth of sales?

3 Peter is paid £30 a day for a job that would normally take him 7 days.
His firm offers him a bonus of £80 if he does the job in 5 days.
How much will he earn if he does the job in:
a 7 days   **b** 5 days?

4 How much does someone earn for 6 hours at double time when the basic rate is £4
per hour?

5 Holly Macintosh earns £27 000 a year.
She is awarded a 7% pay rise.
What does she earn now in a year?

6 The rate of exchange is £1 = 8.00 francs.
How many French francs will Veronica get for £60?

7 Pamela goes to Spain on a business trip.
She changes £300 for expenses at a rate of 200 pesetas per pound (£).
a How many pesetas does she get?
b Whilst she is there she spends 18 500 pesetas.
How many pesetas does she have left?
c When she gets home she converts her remaining pesetas back to pounds.
How many pounds does she get?

8 Angie owns a flat in Victoria Road.
It is valued at £45 000.
How much does she pay for building insurance if the rate is £1.40 for every £1000
insured?

9 Bill Ferguson's house contents are worth £19 800.
His insurance company quotes him a premium of £2.30 for every £1000.
How much will it cost Bill to insure the contents of his house?

10 This table shows the cost of holiday insurance per person.

Area	1 UK	2 Europe	3 Worldwide
Up to 8 nights	£7.50	£20	£54
9 to 17 nights	£8	£24	£67
18 to 23 nights	£9.20	£31	£78
24 to 31 nights	£11.10	£40.60	£89

a Mr and Mrs Lamb are going to Spain for 14 nights.
How much will they pay for insurance?
b Four friends are going to Africa on safari for 28 nights.
How much will they pay for insurance altogether?

11 A car insurance company quotes the following no claims discount rates.

Number of claim-free years	Discount
1	30%
2	40%
3	50%
4 or more	60%

Sandra Walker is quoted £420 for car insurance.
She has 2 years of no claims.
a What is her percentage discount?
b How much is her discount?
c How much does her insurance premium cost her this year?

12 The cash price of a guitar is £400.
The music shop offers HP terms of a £50 deposit plus 12 payments of £30.
a What is the total HP price?
b How much more than the cash price is this?

13 A designer dress costs £550.
It can be bought on hire purchase by paying a 14%
deposit and 6 instalments of £80.
Calculate the HP price of the dress.

6 Revising Unit 1

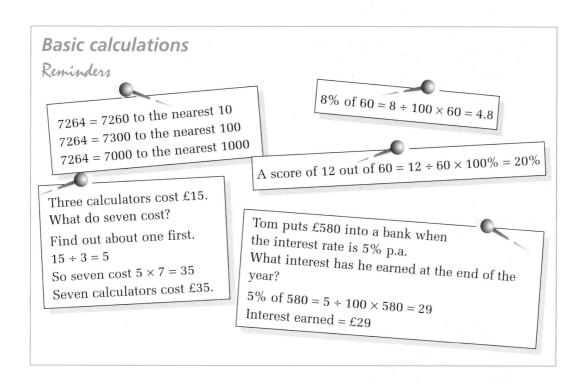

Basic calculations

Reminders

7264 = 7260 to the nearest 10
7264 = 7300 to the nearest 100
7264 = 7000 to the nearest 1000

8% of 60 = 8 ÷ 100 × 60 = 4.8

A score of 12 out of 60 = 12 ÷ 60 × 100% = 20%

Three calculators cost £15.
What do seven cost?

Find out about one first.
15 ÷ 3 = 5
So seven cost 5 × 7 = 35
Seven calculators cost £35.

Tom puts £580 into a bank when the interest rate is 5% p.a.
What interest has he earned at the end of the year?

5% of 580 = 5 ÷ 100 × 580 = 29
Interest earned = £29

EXERCISE 1

1 Write the following numbers to the nearest **(i)** 10 **(ii)** 100.
  a 351 **b** 873 **c** 974 **d** 856 **e** 6745 **f** 9820 **g** 67 431

2 Calculate:
  a 4% of 120 **b** 20% of 300 **c** 8% of 620
  d 75% of 520 **e** 80% of 90 **f** 7% of 65
  g 17.5% of 900 **h** 12.5% of 80 **i** 1% of 350

3 Write the following fractions as percentages.
  a $\frac{7}{10}$ **b** $\frac{12}{48}$ **c** $\frac{25}{75}$ **d** $\frac{20}{80}$ **e** $\frac{65}{70}$ **f** $\frac{21}{42}$

4 Jade scored 14 out of 35 for a biology exam.
  She scored 18 out of 40 for chemistry.
  a Turn both scores into percentages.
  b In which exam did she do better?

5 Three light bulbs cost £3.24.
  a Find the cost of one.
  b Find the cost of eight.

6 Margaret puts £700 in a bank for a year.
The bank pays 6% interest on her account.
How much interest is she paid at the end of the year?

7 Annapurna is one of the highest mountains in the world. It is 8074 m high.
Give its height to the nearest: **a** 10 m   **b** 100 m.

8

Micra Discount Stores
PC with TV and
Internet £1500
+ VAT at 17.5%

Calculate:
a the VAT on this PC
b the total cost of this PC,
giving your answer to
(**i**) the nearest £1
(**ii**) the nearest £10.

9 Eight Choc 'n' crisp bars cost £2.72.
a How much does it cost for five Choc 'n' crisp bars?
b There are special packs of five Choc 'n' crisp for £1.55.
How much do you save buying the pack rather than five individual bars?
c James wants to buy 22 bars at the supermarket.
Describe the cheapest way of buying them.

10 The Blake family put £250 aside for groceries.
They spend 66% of it at the supermarket.
a How much did they spend at the supermarket?
b The supermarket runs a special promotion.
For every £10 spent, the supermarket gives a gift voucher.
How many vouchers do the Blakes collect that week?

11 Ms Hall's flat is valued at £72 000.
Here is part of a table showing council tax charges for her area.

Value	Up to £30 000	£30 000 to £50 000	£50 000 to £75 000	Over £75 000
Tax	£370	£560	£680	£710
Can be paid in ten equal instalments.				

a How much council tax must Ms Hall pay?
b She chooses to pay by instalment. How much is each payment?
c House values rise by 6% that year.
(**i**) What is her flat worth now?
(**ii**) How much tax would she have to pay on the new valuation?

12 Anna is doing a Media Studies course at college.
Here are her marks for two essays she handed in.

Essay 1 $\dfrac{23}{30}$

Essay 2 $\dfrac{28}{35}$

   a Write each mark as a percentage to the nearest whole number.
   b In which essay did she do better?
   c Lecturers give grades according to this table.

A1	A2	B1	B2
90% and above	80% to 89%	70% to 79%	60% to 69%

   What grade did Anne get for **(i)** essay 1   **(ii)** essay 2?

13 Barry is paid £21 a day for working a 5-hour shift in a factory.
One day he is asked to work for 7 hours.
   a How much is he paid an hour?
   b How much is he paid for the 7-hour shift?

14

Vin de Pays
£3.50 per bottle
5% discount on cases
of 12 bottles.
7% discount on cases
of 24 bottles.

   a How much does a case of 12 bottles cost?
   b **(i)** How much does a case of 24 bottles cost?
      (ii) How much do 23 individual bottles cost?
      (iii) Comment on your answers.

15 £500 is put in a bank. The rate of interest is 6% p.a.
   a How much interest is earned in 1 year?
   b How much interest is earned in
      (i)   6 months
      (ii)   1 month
      (iii) 100 days?

Basic geometry

Reminders

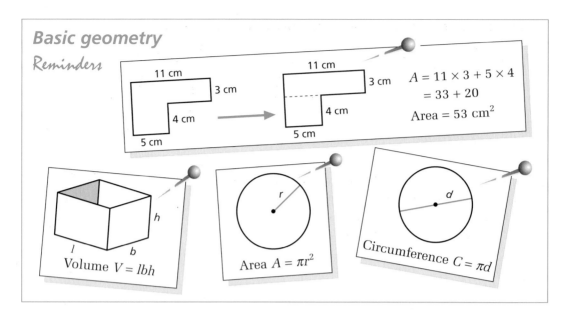

$$A = 11 \times 3 + 5 \times 4$$
$$= 33 + 20$$
$$\text{Area} = 53 \text{ cm}^2$$

Volume $V = lbh$

Area $A = \pi r^2$

Circumference $C = \pi d$

EXERCISE 2

Give answers correct to 2 decimal places where appropriate.

1 Calculate the areas of these rectangles.

a

3 cm

5 cm

b

4 cm

7 cm

c

5.8 cm

3.6 cm

d

3 cm

3 cm

2 Calculate the areas of these shapes.

a

7 cm

4 cm

3 cm

4 cm

b

8.5 cm

3.1 cm

2.1 cm

3.2 cm

c

8 cm

5 cm

3 cm

4 cm

d

9.5 cm

4.2 cm

3.2 cm

3.4 cm

3 Calculate the volumes of these cuboids.

a

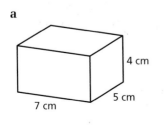

4 cm

5 cm

7 cm

b

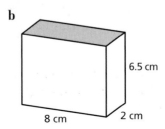

6.5 cm

8 cm

2 cm

c

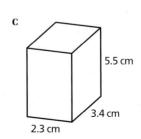

5.5 cm

3.4 cm

2.3 cm

4 Calculate (**i**) the circumference   (**ii**) the area of each circle.

a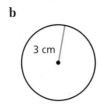

8 cm

b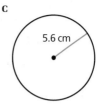

3 cm

c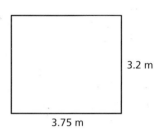

5.6 cm

5 Here is a plan of a living-room floor. It is rectangular.
   a Calculate the area of the floor.
   b Carpet costs £20 per square metre.
      Calculate the cost of carpeting the floor.

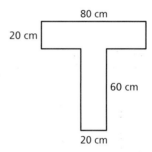

3.2 m

3.75 m

6 Teddy's Tearoom has a large T sign as its logo.
   Sign Design makes the T and paints it gold.
   a Calculate the area of the T.

80 cm

20 cm

60 cm

20 cm

   b The paint comes in small tins. One tin covers 1000 cm².
      How many tins of paint will be needed to paint the T?

7 This garden trough is a cuboid.
   a Calculate the volume of the trough.

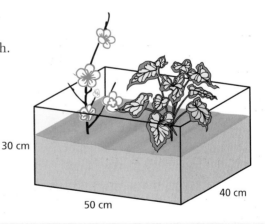

30 cm

50 cm

40 cm

   b A bag of compost fills 25 000 cm³ and costs £2.
      (**i**) How many bags of compost are needed to fill the trough?
      (**ii**) How much will the compost cost?

8 Mrs Fry makes rosettes for the winners at sporting events.
The rosettes are circular with a diameter of 6 cm.
   a What is the circumference of the circle?
   b Round the edge she gathers ribbon.
   She has a rule: the ribbon needed is *3 times* the circumference
   of the circle.
   How much ribbon does she need for a rosette?
   c Will she get two rosettes out of a metre of ribbon?

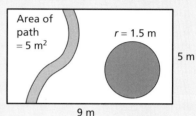

9 A landscape architect redesigns a garden.
The garden has a circular flower bed and a
path. The rest of the garden is to be covered
with grass.
   a Calculate the area of the rectangular garden.
   b The circular bed has a radius of 1.5 metres.
   Calculate its area.
   c The path has an area of 5 square metres.
   Calculate the area of garden covered with grass.

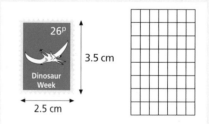

Area of path = 5 m² r = 1.5 m 5 m 9 m

10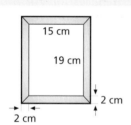

15 cm 19 cm 2 cm 2 cm

A photograph is put in a silver frame.
The length and breadth of the photo are 19 cm
and 15 cm. The frame is 2 cm wide all round.
   a What are the length and breadth of the
   outside of the silver frame?
   b Calculate the area of:
   (i) the photograph   (ii) the silver frame.

11 A postage stamp is rectangular.
A complete sheet of stamps has 8 rows of
7 stamps.
   a What is the area of one stamp?
   b (i) How many stamps are on a sheet?
   (ii) What is the area of a sheet?

26ᵖ Dinosaur Week 3.5 cm 2.5 cm

12 Bottles of wine are packed in a case.
Each bottle is 8 cm in diameter.
   a The width of the case is 48 cm.
   How many bottles of wine will fit
   along the bottom?
   b The case is 32 cm high. How many
   layers of bottles will the case take?
   c How many bottles does the case
   hold altogether?

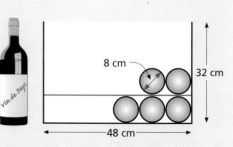

8 cm 32 cm 48 cm

Formulae

Reminder

Formulae can be written as:

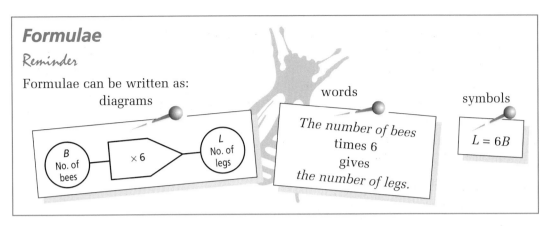

diagrams   words   symbols

The number of bees times 6 gives the number of legs.

$L = 6B$

EXERCISE 3

1 a

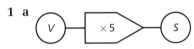

Find *S* when *V* = 5.

b

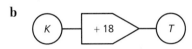

Find *T* when *K* = 7.

c

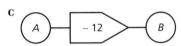

Find *B* when *A* = 19.

d

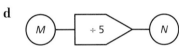

Find *N* when *M* = 1.5.

e

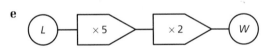

Find *W* when *L* = 4.2.

f

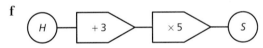

Find *S* when *H* = 5.

2 a

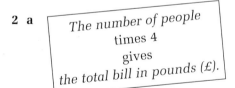

The number of people times 4 gives the total bill in pounds (£).

Work out the bill when there are 6 people.

b

The number of triangles times 180 gives the number of degrees.

How many degrees are there in 10 triangles?

c

The number of hours times 4 plus 2 gives the cost of hire in pounds (£).

What is the cost of hire for 4 hours?

d

The number of tickets times 4 minus 2 gives the total entry cost in pounds (£).

What is the total entry cost when 7 tickets are bought?

3 a $A = 7B$

Calculate A when $B = 3$.

b $C = 3D + 4$

Calculate C when $D = 5$.

c $G = 3M + 2H$

Calculate G when $M = 3$ and $H = 4$.

d $F = 3C^2$

Calculate F when $C = 3$.

4

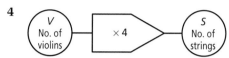

a An orchestra has 20 violins playing at one time.
How many strings are in 20 violins?
b Write the formula given in the above diagram in symbols $(S = ...)$.

5

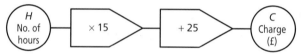

This diagram gives the charges for surfing the Internet.
a What is the charge for: **(i)** 3 hours   **(ii)** 5 hours   **(iii)** 7 hours?
b Write down a formula for the charge for H hours $(C = ...)$.

6 A plumber charges more for being called out at night.
His call-out charges include a £25 standing charge plus £15 per hour of work.

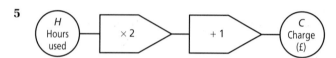

a How much does he charge for a call-out which lasts: **(i)** 1 hour   **(ii)** 2 hours?
b Write down this information in a formula $(C = ...)$.

7 a Write down a formula for the area of this
shape in terms of a, b, x and y.
b Calculate the area when
$a = 7$, $b = 1$, $x = 3$ and $y = 5$.

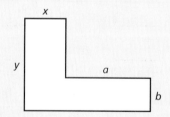

8 A golf shop is having a winter sale.

a Write down a formula to find the sale price, S, when given the cost, C.
b A set of golfing irons normally costs £750.
Work out the sale price.

9 Here is part of a table showing the cost of posting items by registered mail.

Weight up to	Cost
500 g	£4.10
1 kg	£4.40
2 kg	£6.75
10 kg	£14.40
Add 75p for each kilogram over 10 kg.	

  a How much does it cost to send a parcel weighing:
     (i) 700 g   (ii) 3.5 kg   (iii) 11 kg?
  b This formula works out the cost for parcels weighing more than 10 kg:
     $C = 6.9 + 0.75 \times W$ where C = cost (£) and W = weight in kilograms.
     Calculate the cost for a parcel weighing 20 kg.

10 The amount of leather, A cm^2, needed to make a football can be calculated using the formula:

$$A = 4\pi r^2 \text{ where } r \text{ is the radius of the ball.}$$

A manufacturer makes leather footballs with a radius of 12 cm.

  a What area of leather is needed to make a football?
  b How many footballs can be made from 1 m^2 of leather given that
     1 m^2 = 10 000 cm^2?

11 The perimeter of this shape is P cm.

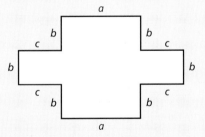

  a Write down a formula for P.
  b Calculate the perimeter when $a = 9$, $b = 4$ and $c = 5$.

Calculations in context

INSURANCE   HIRE PURCHASE

EARNINGS   RATES OF EXCHANGE

EXERCISE 4

1 Mac works at a garage.
He is paid 50p for each tyre he changes.
How much will he earn for changing:
  a 4 tyres   **b** 20 tyres   **c** 60 tyres?

2 Sports Shoes Inc. pay their salesmen 18% commission on all sales.
How much does a salesman earn when his sales are:
  a £1000   **b** £3000   **c** £400?

3 A joiner is paid £45 per day to do a job in 7 days.
If she can finish the job in 6 days she will get a bonus of £45.
  a How much will she get if she does the job in: **(i)** 6 days   **(ii)** 7 days?
  b What is the benefit of doing the job in 6 days?

4 Mary Milligan works for £3.80 per hour.
At the weekend she did 6 hours at double time.
How much did she earn?

5 Rachel Irvine earns £27 000 a year.
She accepts a 2.3% payrise.
How much is she now earning a year?

6 A computer system is valued at £2500.
How much will it cost to insure it if the company charges 85p per £100 insured?

7 When Amir went to France the exchange rate was 8.15 francs to the pound (£).
How many francs did he get for £3400?

8 A bike can be bought for £300 cash or for a deposit of £50 and 12 instalments of £22.
  a How much is the hire purchase price?
  b How much cheaper is it to pay cash?

9 A car costs £12 000 cash or you can pay a deposit of 12% of the cash price and 24 instalments of £450.
  a Calculate the deposit.
  b How much does the car cost under these HP terms?

10 These adverts show two different companies' rates to insure a building.

LOWLAND INSURANCE
House Insurance Rates
£2.75 for each
£1000 insured

HIGHLAND INSURANCE
House Insurance Rates
£3 for each £1000 insured
up to £60 000, then
£1.50 per £1000 thereafter

    a How much does it cost to insure a house valued at £85 000:
       (i) with Lowland
       (ii) with Highland?
    b Which policy is cheaper and by how much?

11 Kenneth More works for £4.10 an hour.
He works 35 hours at the basic rate. On Saturday he does 8 hours at time and a half. On Sunday he does 6 hours at double time.
    a How much does he earn at:
       (i) the basic rate   **(ii)** time and a half   **(iii)** double time?
    b How much does he earn in the week?

12 A catalogue company does not charge extra for its hire purchase terms. They ask for a deposit of 20%. The remainder is paid up over a year in 12 equal instalments. Work out the hire purchase terms for an item costing:
    a £2400   **b** £375   **c** £180.

13 On a trip to France a businesswoman changed £500 into French francs.
The rate of exchange that day was £1 = 8.96 francs.
    a How much did she get in francs?
    b The bank charged 1.5% commission on the money exchanged.
       How much was the bank's commission (to the nearest franc)?
    c How many francs did she receive after the commission was deducted?

14 Here is part of a travel insurance brochure.

Travel Insurance Rates		
Adult 16–64 years		
Cost per person	Destination	
Length of time	UK	Europe
Up to 3 days	£3.50	£6.80
Up to 8 days	£5.40	£13.60
Up to 12 days	£6.00	£16.90
Up to 17 days	£7.30	£18.20
Up to 24 days	£8.30	£20.80

    a Mr and Mrs Murray are going to France for 15 days. Calculate the cost of their insurance.
    b Mr and Mrs Chandra and their 18-year-old daughter are going to London for 3 weeks. How much will they pay for insurance?
    c A football team (11 players, 2 substitutes, a coach and a manager) travel to Berlin for a game. How much is the insurance if they are away for the weekend (3 days)?

7 Using Your Calculator in Unit 2

Try these simple checks to see if your calculator does what you expect it to.

a Check if keying the following gives you the answer 49.

b Which of the following gives you the answer 3?

   or

Positive/negative

 Check whether this goes before or after a number to make it negative.

Example $-3 + (-2) = -5$

3 + 2 = −5   or 3 + 2 = −5

Check by reversing the process.

− 2 = −3   or − 2 = −3

 and

Example $3 \times (4 + 2)$

      ⬛ ⬛ ⎡ 18 ⎤

Check by *repeating* the process.

It is a good idea to clear the memories before repeating

AC 3 × (4 + 2) =   ⎡ 18 ⎤

EXERCISE 1

In this exercise, remember to check by repeating the process.

1 Use the +/− button to work out the following:

    a $-3 + 2$ **b** $-10 - 4$ **c** -10×2 **d** $-12 \div 6$ **e** $-20 + 10$ **f** add −3 and −2

    g subtract −3 from −5   **h** multiply −5 and −3   **i** divide −15 by 5

2 Make use of the bracket buttons to help you calculate:

    a $5 \times (3 + 4)$ **b** $30 \div (3 + 2)$ **c** $10 - (3 + 2)$ **d** $30 - (6 - 1)$

    e $(5 + 1) \times (3 + 4)$ **f** $(7 - 3) \div (3 - 1)$ **g** $(8 - 1) - (9 - 4)$ **h** $(5 - 1) \times (2 + 1)$

3 Use the bracket buttons to help you evaluate:

    a $\sqrt{(3^2 + 4^2)}$ **b** $\sqrt{(5^2 + 12^2)}$ **c** $\sqrt{(45^2 + 108^2)}$ **d** $\sqrt{(12^2 + 35^2)}$

    e $\sqrt{(8^2 + 6^2)}$ **f** $\sqrt{(2^2 + 4.8^2)}$ **g** $\sqrt{(20^2 + 21^2)}$ **h** $\sqrt{(8^2 + 15^2)}$

Some useful buttons

 The square

Example 1
5^2 means '5 multiplied by itself'. $5^2 = 5 \times 5 = 25$

On the calculator, 5 [25]

 The square root

Example 2
$\sqrt{25}$ means 'What number, when multiplied by itself, gives 25?'
$\sqrt{25} = 5$ since $5 \times 5 = 25$

On the calculator, 25 [5] or [√] 25 = [5]

Note that [√] reverses the process of

and x^2 reverses the process of [√].

Example 3 Find the value of 7.2^2.
Estimate	$7.2^2 \approx 7^2 \approx 7 \times 7 = 49$
Calculate	$7.2^2 = 51.84$
Check 1	$51.84 \approx 49$
Check 2	Reverse the process: $\sqrt{51.84} = 7.2$

EXERCISE 2

1 Calculate the following.

   a 1^2 **b** 2^2 **c** 3^2 **d** 4^2 **e** 5^2 **f** 6^2 **g** 7^2 **h** 8^2 **i** 9^2 **j** 10^2

These numbers are the first ten **square** numbers. It is useful to learn them.

2 Work out the following. Estimate, calculate and check as in Example 3.

   a 8.2^2 **b** 19.4^2 **c** 7.5^2 **d** 28.1^2 **e** 9.99^2 **f** 16.8^2 **g** 94.7^2

Example 4 Find the value of $\sqrt{7.84}$.
We use the first ten squares (1, 4, 9, 16, 25, 36, 49, 64, 81, 100) to help us estimate.

Estimate	7.84 lies between 4 and 9, so $\sqrt{7.84}$ lies between $\sqrt{4}$ and $\sqrt{9}$, i.e. between 2 and 3
Calculate	$\sqrt{7.84} = 2.8$
Check 1	2.8 is between 2 and 3
Check 2	Reverse the process: $2.8^2 = 7.84$

3 Work out the following square roots. Remember to estimate, calculate and check.

   a $\sqrt{2.89}$ **b** $\sqrt{7.29}$ **c** $\sqrt{11.56}$ **d** $\sqrt{23.04}$ **e** $\sqrt{34.81}$ **f** $\sqrt{37.21}$ **g** $\sqrt{90.25}$

   h $\sqrt{1.69}$ **i** $\sqrt{6.25}$ **j** $\sqrt{26.01}$ **k** $\sqrt{53.29}$ **l** $\sqrt{70.56}$ **m** $\sqrt{40.96}$ **n** $\sqrt{4.41}$

Handling lists of numbers

You need to be in STAT mode.　MODE　（ • ）　or　MODE　**1**

It is good practice to clear all the memories.　AC

Example　Enter the list of numbers, as shown:

2 M+　3 M+　4 M+　5 M+　5 M+　6 M+　6 M+　7 M+　7 M+

If you now wish to know how many numbers have been entered, press

n　In this example, the display will show 9.

If you wish to know the sum of the list, press

Σx　In this case, the calculator will show 45.

If you wish to know the mean of the list, press

$\bar{x}$　In this example, the answer is 5.

EXERCISE 3

1 a Enter the following lists of numbers and then find:
(i) the sum of the list　**(ii)** the mean of the list.

b As a rough check, use the *n* button to see that you have entered the right amount of data.

(i) 1, 2, 3, 4, 5, 6, 7, 8
(ii) 7, 9, 14, 25, 26, 30, 45, 50
(iii) 2.4, 3.7, 4.5, 6.7, 7.6, 9.8, 12.1, 13.2, 14.5, 20
(iv) 3, 3, 3, 4, 4, 4, 4, 4, 5, 5, 5, 5, 5, 5, 5, 6, 6, 7

2 a Try the following set of button pushes.

3 × 3 M+　4 × 5 M+　5 × 7 M+　6 × 2 M+　7 × 1 M+

(i) Check that the *n* button gives 18.
(ii) Compare your answers for the sum and the mean with those of question **1 b (iv)**.

b Find the sum and the mean of these lists:
(i) 5, 5, 5, 5, 5, 6, 6, 6, 7, 7, 7, 7, 8, 8, 9, 9, 9, 9, 10
(ii) 3, 3, 3, 3, 3, 3, 3, 4, 4, 4, 5, 5, 5, 5, 6, 6, 6, 6, 7, 7

8 Graphs, Charts and Tables

STARTING POINTS

1 Yasmin looks at how often the phone is used in her house.
The **line graph** shows the calls made over ten days.
a How many calls were made on day 6?
b Five calls were made on two different days. Which days?
c On which day were most calls made?
d Calls cost 50p. What was the cost of phoning on day 10?

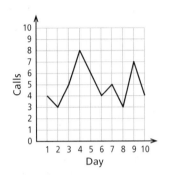

2

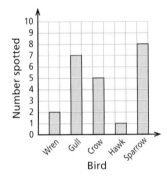

Liam counts the birds he sees in the meadow in one afternoon.
The **bar graph** shows his findings.
a How many gulls did he count?
b Two types of birds were spotted less than 5 times. Which ones were they?
c How many birds did he spot altogether?

3 Georgina records her golf scores in a table.
Later she makes a pie chart. The largest part of the pie chart is labelled B.
The 'pars' occurred most often.
So part B represents the pars.
Say what each of the other parts represents.

Eagles	2
Birdies	3
Pars	9
Bogeys	4

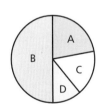

4

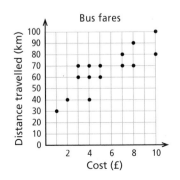

Using a price list, a scatter diagram is made to show distance travelled against cost.
a Use the chart to make a reasonable guess at what a 50 km journey might cost.
b How far would you expect to get for £6?

Bar graphs and line graphs

Graphs can be clearer than tables when you want to make sense of a situation.

Daily Expenses

Day	Mon	Tue	Wed	Thu	Fri
Amount spent	1.80	1.00	0.80	0.60	0.40

Timothy is given £5 to cover minor expenses during the week.

His daily expenditure is shown in the table.

All the information is there but when we look at it in a graph it is clearer that his spending drops every day.

Note that information is lost if you miss out:
- labels
- titles
- scales.

EXERCISE 1

1 The tables give the results of four surveys on teenagers:
- Bedtimes of 13-year-olds
- Film preferences of 14-year-olds
- Favourite sports of 15-year-olds
- Music preferences of 16-year-olds.

Bedtime	8 pm	9 pm	10 pm	11 pm	12 pm
Number	2	7	9	3	1

Film type	Action	Western	Romance	Sci-fi	Fantasy
Number	6	4	5	8	4

Sport	Soccer	Rugby	Swimming	Running	Cricket
Number	8	5	5	4	1

Music	Pop	Classic	Western	Folk	Jazz
Number	9	4	2	6	1

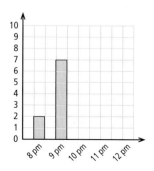

a A bar graph has been started for the bedtime survey.
Copy and complete it using the information above.
(Remember: labels, titles, scales.)

b Using the same basic grid, draw bar graphs to show the results of the other surveys.

2 Students in a class were asked what type of house they lived in. The table shows the results.

House	Semi-detached	Cottage	Tenement	Terraced	Flat
Number	8	12	11	6	4

Draw a bar graph to illustrate the information.

Often a line graph is used instead of a bar graph (especially when you want to highlight the **trend**).
The trend is a rough description of how things are changing.

Examples

After a quick increase ...

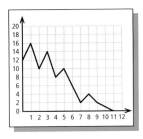

A downward trend

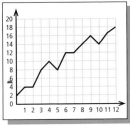

An upward trend

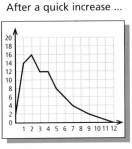

there was a steady downward trend.

---

3 A block of ice is melting.
It is dried and weighed every 2 minutes.

Time (min)	2	4	6	8	10	12
Weight (g)	16	9	6	3	1	0

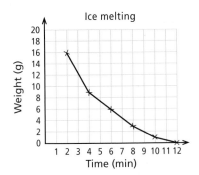

Ice melting

Describe the trend of the graph.

4 A local cinema shows *The House of Horrors* for two weeks.
   A record is kept of the nightly attendance.

Day	Mon	Tue	Wed	Thu	Fri	Sat	Mon	Tue	Wed	Thu	Fri	Sat
Viewers	30	10	20	50	70	90	40	20	30	50	70	80

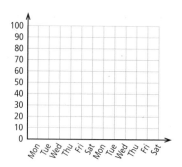

a Using a grid like the one shown, draw a line graph of the cinema attendances.
b Describe any trends you can spot in the graph.

5 Standard Academy has a weather station.
   They keep various records.
   a They record brightness every hour on a scale of 1 (dull) to 10 (bright sun).
      The table shows their findings for one day.

Time	9 am	10 am	11 am	12 noon	1 pm	2 pm	3 pm	4 pm
Brightness	3	5	7	7	8	1	7	6

   (i)   Draw a line graph showing how the brightness changes.
   (ii) Describe the general trend.
   (iii) It becomes cloudy at one point during the day. Suggest when.
   b They record rainfall daily. This is measured in millimetres.
      Here are the results over two weeks.

Time	Mon	Tue	Wed	Thu	Fri	Mon	Tue	Wed	Thu	Fri
Rainfall	1	4	4	5	1	7	8	10	7	6

   (i)   Draw a line graph to show how the rainfall changed over the period.
   (ii) Is there any trend?
   (iii) What is the wettest period?

Stem-and-leaf diagrams

A group of students measured their pulse rates when resting.
The rates were 66, 69, 62, 58, 74, 56, 67, 72, 61, 62, 59.
The data can be shown in a **stem plot** or **stem-and-leaf diagram.**

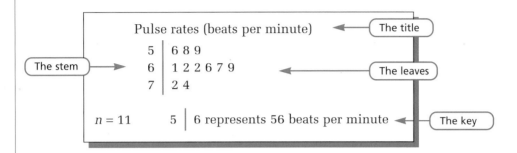

- The figures on the left of the vertical line form the stem.
- Each figure on the right is called a leaf.
- The leaves increase in value outwards from the stem.
- Each row is called a level.
- A title is required at the top.
- A key is required at the bottom.
  This includes the size of the group, *n*, and an example of how the figures should be interpreted. Level 5 should be read as 56 58 59.

EXERCISE 2

1 This stem-and-leaf diagram shows the distances travelled by a cyclist on his practice runs.

```
            Kilometres travelled
         1 | 3 5
         2 | 0 2 5
         3 | 1 2 4 7
         4 | 1

n = 10       2 | 1 represents 21 km
```

a Level 1 should be read as 13 and 15 km.
Write out level 2 in the same way.
b What is the greatest distance recorded in the diagram?
c How many distances are recorded?

2 A batch of watches are all running fast. The stem-and-leaf diagram shows how many seconds each watch has gained in an hour.

```
Seconds gained
    0 | 4 7
    1 | 1 3 8
    2 | 2 5 6 6 9
    3 | 4 6 7 8
    4 | 2

n = 15        3 | 4 represents 34 seconds
```

a Level 0 can be read as 04 seconds and 07 seconds (4 and 7 seconds). Describe level 1 in a similar way.

b List all the seconds gained in order of size, greatest first.

c How many watches are in the batch?

3 The cars in a showroom are all priced. The stem plot shows the figures.

a What is
  (i) the cheapest
  (ii) the dearest cost?

b Which level has the most data?

c Write out level 12 in full.

```
Car costs in a showroom
   10 | 4 5 5 7
   11 | 2 3 6
   12 | 3 5
   13 | 4
   14 | 1

n = 11        10 | 4 represents £10 400
```

4

```
Cholesterol count
   4 | 8 9
   5 | 0 1 3 6 8 8 9
   6 | 1 2 4 7 8
   7 | 3 6
   8 | 1

n = 17        4 | 8 = 4.8 units
```

A health clinic gives people over 45 regular check-ups.
Their cholesterol counts are measured.
The results for one day are given.

a List the counts in order of size, least first.

b A count of 6.0 is considered reasonable.
How many people had a reading higher than that?

c How many people were given a check-up?

5 The speed at which computers send data is measured in kilobytes/second. A survey of various models gives these rates:

24, 43, 16, 12, 32, 25, 19, 20, 28, 30, 32, 25, 20, 18, 28, 48.

Copy and complete this stem-and-leaf diagram.

```
Transmission speeds
   1 |
   2 |
   3 |
   4 |

n = 16        1 | 6 = 16 kps
```

Back-to-back stem-and-leaf diagrams

Sometimes we want to compare sets of figures.
A **back-to-back stem-and-leaf diagram** is useful for this.

Monthly absence figures for Class 4A

Last year		This year
1	3	0 2
1 1	4	2 4 5
6 5 4 4	5	1 3 6
3 2	6	1
1	7	2

$n = 10$ $n = 10$

3 | 0 represents 30 pupils

Note that the leaves still increase in size away from the stem.
Level 3 can be read as:
'Last year there was a month with 31 absences; this year there were months with 30 and 32 absences.'

EXERCISE 3

1 Use the diagram above to answer these questions.
  a What is the total number of absences shown in level 4: **(i)** this year **(ii)** last year?
  b A campaign to cut down absenteeism was started at the end of last year.
    Do you think it was successful? Comment.

2 Ten home owners from two regions are asked about the council tax they pay each month.
  a Level 4 can be read as:
    'Region A £43, £45;
    Region B £41'.
    Write out level 5 in the same way.
  b **(i)** What is the dearest tax recorded?
    (ii) In which region was it?

Council Tax

Region A		Region B
5 3	4	1
6 2	5	4
9 7 4	6	1 3 3
4 4 3	7	2 2 5
	8	2 7

$n = 10$ $n = 10$

5 | 4 represents £54

3 Experiments are carried out to see if a new plant feed works. Some plants are given the feed and some are not. After a while the heights of the plants are measured. The results are tabulated below.

With Feed

9.1	14.2	10.5	13.4	12.6
10.4	11.3	10.6	9.2	11.4
13.7	12.0	12.5	9.2	13.0
11.8	14.3	11.8	12.0	12.6

Without Feed

9.1	10.0	12.0	11.9	13.7
14.3	9.5	11.7	9.3	10.4
12.3	9.5	11.4	12.3	9.7
13.7	13.2	10.6	10.6	11.2

  a Make a back-to-back stem plot to show these results.
  b Is the feed effective? Comment.

Interpreting graphs

When reading graphs always:
- check the title
- examine labels and scales carefully
- check the units used.

A number of people were asked: 'How many flights have you been on this year?'
a How many people said they had been on six flights?
b **(i)** Which number of flights had a frequency of 7?
     (ii) What does that mean?

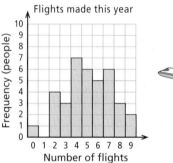

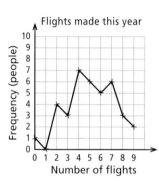

Check both the line graph and the bar graph.
a Five people said they had been on six flights.
b Four flights has a frequency of 7.
     This means that seven people said they had been on four flights.

EXERCISE 4

1 A surveyor examines 20 houses to see how much repair work is necessary.

(i)

a Copy and complete this table for the first graph.

In need of an electrician

Number of jobs										
Number of houses										

(ii)

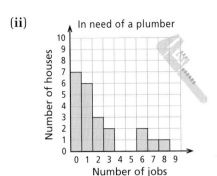

In need of a plumber

(iii)

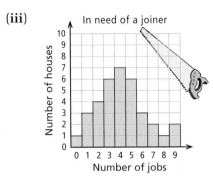

In need of a joiner

b Make similar tables for the second and third graphs.

c How many houses were in need of seven electrical jobs?

d How many plumbing jobs were there in total?

e How many houses needed more than six joinery jobs?

2

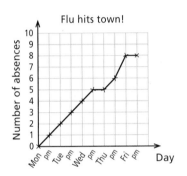

Flu hits town!

The line graph records absences from an office during a flu epidemic.

a How many absences were there on:
 (i) Monday am
 (ii) Thursday pm?

b On which day did the number of absences go over 3?

c Describe the trend.

3 A shopkeeper notes how many pairs of gloves she sells each month.

  a How many pairs were sold in:
 (i) January   **(ii)** June?

  b In which month were there exactly:
 (i) 100 sales   **(ii)** 30?

  c The shopkeeper says that the graph shows a seasonal trend. Explain what she means.

Sales of gloves

4

Sales of ice-cream

A café owner at a holiday resort notes his monthly sales of ice-cream.

a In which months were:
 (i) most sold   **(ii)** least sold?

b What were the total sales for the period January to March?

c Describe the trend.

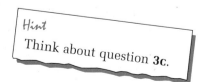

Hint

Think about question **3c**.

Reading pie charts

Newtown Wanderers have played 24 games.
The pie chart shows how they got on.

Newtown Wanderers' Performance

Won
Drawn
Lost

A full circle represents 24 games.

Using a
protractor, we
can measure the
angles...

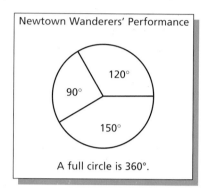

Newtown Wanderers' Performance

120°
90°
150°

A full circle is 360°.

Note that:

The fraction of games they won is $\dfrac{120}{360}$, and $\dfrac{120}{360}$ of 24 = 8. They won 8 games.

The fraction of games they drew is $\dfrac{90}{360}$, and $\dfrac{90}{360}$ of 24 = 6. They drew 6 games.

The fraction of games they lost is $\dfrac{150}{360}$, and $\dfrac{150}{360}$ of 24 = 10. They lost 10 games.

Check that 8 + 6 + 10 = 24 games.

EXERCISE 5

1 The pie chart shows what happened to the school leavers from a local comprehensive.

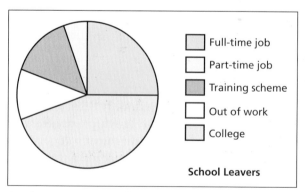

Full-time job
Part-time job
Training scheme
Out of work
College

School Leavers

a Use a protractor to measure the angle of the sector which represents those:
   (i)   in a full-time job
   (ii) in a part-time job
   (iii) on a training scheme
   (iv) out of work
   (v)   at college
b Check that all your answers add up to 360°.

2 There are 60 books on a shelf.

  a Use a protractor to measure the size of each angle to the nearest degree.

  b What fraction of the books are:
  (i) reference books
  (ii) fiction?

  c How many of the books are:
  (i) reference books
  (ii) fiction?

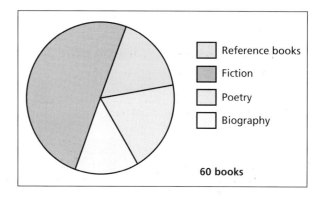

Reference books
Fiction
Poetry
Biography

60 books

3

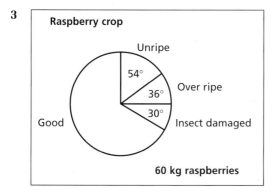

Raspberry crop

Unripe
54°
36° Over ripe
30°
Good   Insect damaged

60 kg raspberries

This pie chart shows what happened to a raspberry crop.

  a What fraction of the crop were:
  (i) over ripe
  (ii) insect damaged?

  b If there were 60 kg of raspberries what weight were:
  (i) over ripe
  (ii) insect damaged
  (iii) under ripe
  (iv) good?

4 A hundred motorists fill their tanks at a local garage. What they bought is shown in the pie chart.

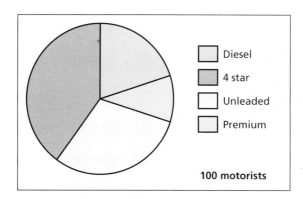

Diesel
4 star
Unleaded
Premium

100 motorists

  a Check that the angles in the pie chart are 144°, 108°, 36° and 72°.
  b What fraction of the motorists use: **(i)** diesel   **(ii)** unleaded?
  c How many motorists use: **(i)** diesel   **(ii)** unleaded?
  d How many motorists use premium?

More interpretation

Features can be added to improve the
appearance of a graph.
Don't let them distract or mislead you.

Graphs can be combined to help
comparisons. Look out for a key.

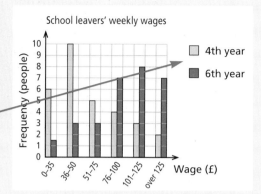

School leavers' weekly wages

EXERCISE 6

1

Change from £1 when buying a loaf

This chart is basically a bar graph.

a How much change did you get
when buying a loaf in January?

b What is the trend in the cost of a
loaf?

c Does this graph mislead the
reader in any way?

2 The members of a fishing club think that
the number of pike in a lake affects the
number of trout. In midsummer each
year the lake is sampled.

a How many trout are in:
  (i) the 1993 sample
  (ii) the 1996 sample?

b Describe the trend in:
  (i) the trout population
  (ii) the pike population.

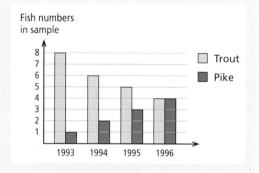

Fish numbers
in sample

3

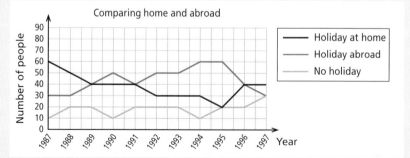

Comparing home and abroad

A hundred people were asked where they had gone on holiday over the past ten
years.

The chart shows the results, giving the number of replies to the nearest 10.
a Describe the trend of home holidaymakers between 1987 to 1995.
b In which years were the numbers holidaying at home and abroad the same?
c What is the connection between the numbers having holidays at home, having holidays abroad and having no holidays?

4 Alongside this chart in a newspaper were the words 'Ridiculous price increase in books'.
   a How much bigger is the picture of the fourth book than the first?
   b What is the actual price increase from 1994 to 1997?
   c Express this increase as a fraction of £1. (Compare this with answer **a**.)
   d How does the graph manage to mislead?

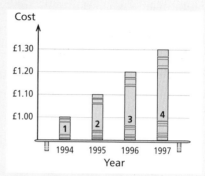

5 The Beagle Bus Company issued this graph with their financial statement at the end of the year. The bigger bus is supposed to show a doubling of the profits.
   a The 1997 bus is two times taller than the 1996 bus. How much wider is it?
   b Count how many rectangles each bus occupies. Comment.

6 'Attendances at our concerts go from strength to strength.'
   This novelty chart seems to show a steady increase in attendance figures at concerts. Transfer each point onto a plain grid. Comment.

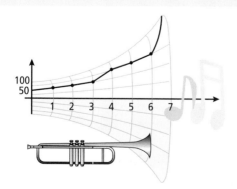

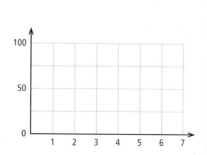

Frequency tables

A television programme examines the deal people get when they buy a bag of chips. The programme makers secretly buy 30 bags and count the number of chips in each. Their survey produces this rather mixed-up set of figures:

32	32	31	34	36	36
33	34	33	34	33	34
30	31	35	36	31	31
31	36	33	36	30	33
31	35	32	35	32	35

With the help of tally marks the results can be better organised in a frequency table.

Note that ||||| stands for 5.

This would enable a suitable graph to be drawn.

Number of chips	Tally	Frequency
30				2
31								6
32						4
33							5
34						4
35						4
36							5

EXERCISE 7

1 A gardener tests a new feed for apple trees.
   She weighs 40 apples from trees which were given the feed and 40 from those which were not.

Given the feed (weight in grams)

181	187	185	181	186	184	185	181
187	186	182	182	187	186	183	184
187	184	187	183	186	184	183	182
182	187	186	185	185	183	185	184
185	184	187	186	185	184	185	184

Not given the feed (weight in grams)

185	186	187	181	181	182	181	187
184	187	186	184	187	186	181	185
185	183	183	182	183	184	181	181
182	182	183	184	182	181	181	183
187	182	185	186	182	181	183	184

Weight (g)	Tally	Frequency
181		
182		
183		
184		
185		
186		
187		

a Make a frequency table like the one shown for each set of figures.
b Do you think the feed is working?

2 A shopkeeper notes the flavours of different ice-lollies he sells: raspberry (R), strawberry (S), lemon (L), apple (A) and vanilla (V).

S	V	A	V	A	R	A	S	S	L
A	R	S	L	R	A	S	L	S	V
V	A	R	R	A	A	S	L	R	S
V	R	R	S	S	R	S	A	R	S
L	L	A	R	R	A	R	S	R	L
L	R	V	A	V	R	V	R	A	R

Flavour	Tally	Frequency
R		
S		
L		
A		
V		

a Make a frequency table to show his sales.
b Draw a bar graph using the table.
c List the flavours in order of popularity.

3 A bus driver kept a record of the type of passenger using his bus between 12 noon and 1 pm and also between 3 pm and 4 pm on one day.
He noted children (C), students (S), adults (A) and old age pensioners (O).

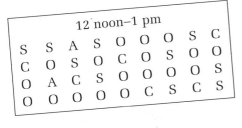

12 noon–1 pm

S	S	A	S	O	O	O	S	C	
C	O	S	O	C	O	S	O	O	
O	A	C	S	O	O	O	O	S	
O	O	O	O	O	C	S	C	S	

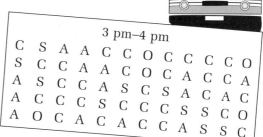

3 pm–4 pm

C	S	A	A	C	C	O	C	C	C	C	O
S	C	C	A	A	C	O	C	A	C	C	A
A	S	C	C	A	S	C	S	A	C	A	C
A	C	C	C	S	C	C	C	S	S	C	O
A	O	C	A	C	A	C	C	A	S	S	C

a Make a frequency table of the bus driver's records for each time.
b How many passengers did he carry between:
   (i) 12 noon and 1 pm   **(ii)** 3 pm and 4 pm?
c How many children did he carry between:
   (i) 12 noon and 1 pm   **(ii)** 3 pm and 4 pm?
d What fraction of the passengers are children between:
   (i) 12 noon and 1 pm   **(ii)** 3 pm and 4 pm?
e Comment on the increase.

4 Pizza Deliveries will deliver to your door if the journey is 10 miles or less.
The driver has to record the mileage of each trip for expenses.
These are the mileages he recorded for one day:

10	9	6	7	4	10
8	8	3	9	7	6
9	10	7	10	5	9
4	8	10	7	8	5
5	9	9	6	10	8

a Organise the data in a frequency table.
b Make a bar graph of the data.

Scatter diagrams

Example 1

A study of bus fares and journeys produces the following table.

Journey	A	B	C	D	E	F	G	H	I	J	K	L	M	N	O
Fare (p)	10	40	30	60	80	30	90	20	40	100	80	40	50	70	70
Distance (km)	4	8	6	8	8	5	8	5	5	10	7	6	7	7	8

There is nothing very obvious in the table, but if you plot the points in a graph you can see that bus fare and distance travelled are what we call **positively correlated**.

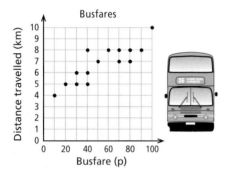

As a rough rule: when the distance *increases,* then the fare *increases.*

Example 2

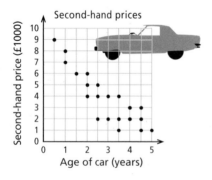

This scatter diagram shows that the age of a car and its second-hand price are **negatively correlated**.

As a rough rule: when the age *increases* the price *decreases.*

EXERCISE 8

1 The French and Spanish exam marks of 20 candidates are recorded.

Candidate	A	B	C	D	E	F	G	H	I	J	K	L	M	N	O	P	Q	R	S	T
French mark	80	70	60	50	30	80	20	20	60	40	40	30	10	20	40	60	10	90	70	50
Spanish mark	90	90	80	80	60	70	50	60	70	70	80	70	40	40	60	90	30	90	80	70

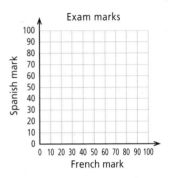

a On a grid like the one shown, plot the points to make a scatter diagram.

b Is the correlation positive or negative?

c Make up a rough rule connecting performance in French and Spanish.

2 The art and maths marks of 20 candidates are also recorded.

Candidate	A	B	C	D	E	F	G	H	I	J	K	L	M	N	O	P	Q	R	S	T
Art mark	40	30	70	50	70	90	20	60	70	10	20	40	80	80	90	50	80	90	10	60
Maths mark	40	60	60	70	90	80	30	50	20	40	90	90	70	50	60	30	30	50	70	60

a On a grid similar to the one shown, plot the points to show that the maths marks and the art marks are not really related.

b Can you suggest pairs of subjects which:
   (i) might be positively correlated
   (ii) are not related?

3 The number of hours of television watched, Monday to Friday, are tabulated along with the maths scores.

Candidate	A	B	C	D	E	F	G	H	I	J
Hours of TV	40	35	28	20	30	15	24	10	10	15
Maths mark	0	10	30	70	10	20	40	70	80	60

a On a suitable grid, make a scatter diagram from the data in the table.

b Is the correlation between 'score' and 'hours of TV' positive or negative?

The best-fitting line

When there is a strong correlation, the points on a scatter diagram lie roughly along a line.

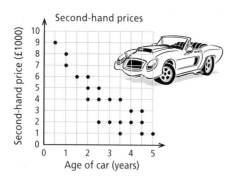

Second-hand prices

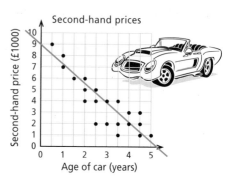

Second-hand prices

We try to draw a line which:

a highlights the trend of the points

b has roughly the same number of points above as below it.

Once we have the line we can use it to estimate values not in the original data.

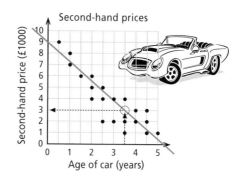

Second-hand prices

Example

Check from the line that a car 3.5 years old will cost about £3000.

EXERCISE 9

1

Petrol consumption

For 20 journeys Steven noted the distance he travelled and the petrol used. The scatter diagram shows his figures.

a Describe the correlation between distance travelled and petrol used.

b Using a clear ruler, or tracing paper, get the best-fitting straight line.

c Use it to estimate:

 (i) how far Steven can go on 17 litres of petrol

 (ii) how much petrol he will need to travel 125 km.

2 In a survey of wasp activity around a school, the number of wasps caught in collecting jars is noted. The date is also noted. The scatter diagram shows what is found.

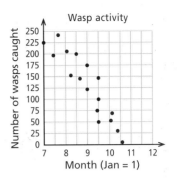

Wasp activity

  a Describe the correlation between the number of wasps and the month.
  b Identify the best-fitting straight line.
  c Use it to estimate how many wasps may be caught on a day in August.
  d 115 wasps are collected one day. Which month is that most likely to be?

3 Ten students with part-time jobs are asked to say how many hours a week they work and how much they earn. The table gives their replies.

Student	A	B	C	D	E	F	G	H	I	J
Hours worked	5	8	8	10	9	6	5	8	6	11
Wage (£)	14	18	14	28	32	16	10	24	12	34

  a With axes similar to those shown, draw a scatter diagram to illustrate the data in the table.
  b Draw the best-fitting straight line on your diagram.
  c Use this line to estimate:
    (i) the wage to expect for 7 hours of work
    (ii) the hours someone would need to work to earn £30.

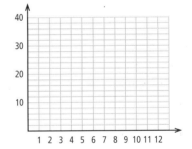

4 The table is a typical record of rainfall and temperature in a warm temperate climate such as Greece throughout one year.

Month	J	F	M	A	M	J	J	A	S	O	N	D
Rainfall (mm)	60	45	40	30	20	20	11	10	25	38	50	62
Temperature (°C)	12	15	16	20	25	30	32	30	28	22	12	10

  a Using suitable axes, draw a scatter diagram to illustrate the data.
  b How are temperature and rainfall related in Greece?
  c Draw the best-fitting straight line on your diagram.
  d Use this line to estimate:
    (i) the rainfall when the temperature is 35 °C
    (ii) the temperature when the rainfall is 45 mm.

CHAPTER 8 REVIEW

1 A claim is made that too much heavy traffic is using a country lane.
A survey is done one day with the following results.

Vehicle	Car	Bus	Bike	HGV	Machinery
Number	9	4	6	5	2

Illustrate the figures on a bar graph.

2 Over a period of 4 hours Jake manages to climb 3000 feet.
Every 30 minutes he notes his height.

Time (hours)	0.5	1	1.5	2	2.5	3	3.5	4
Height so far	500	800	1300	1600	2100	2500	2700	3000

Marking the vertical axis off in hundreds of feet, draw a line graph of the progress of his climb.

3

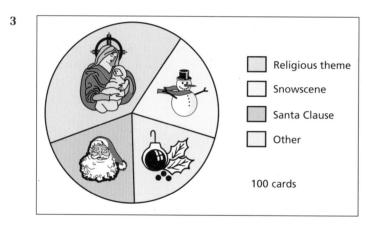

In the run-up to Christmas, the sale of cards is brisk.
The pie chart shows the sales in one shop.
a Use a protractor to measure each angle.
b What fraction of the cards sold are: **(i)** snowscenes **(ii)** religious?
c The pie chart represents 100 cards. How many snowscene cards are sold?

4 The stem-and-leaf diagram shows the number of fish caught per month.
a Level 1 should be read as 12 and
17 fish.
Write out level 2 in the same way.
b What is the greatest number of
catches recorded in the diagram?
c How many fish are recorded?

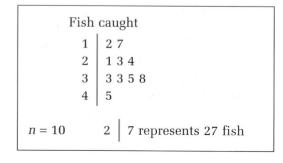

5 The graph shows how the number of customers changes over the year in a new superstore.

a Which month had exactly 400 shoppers?

b In which month did the number of customers first rise above 600?

c Describe the trend in the graph.

Shopping at the superstore

6

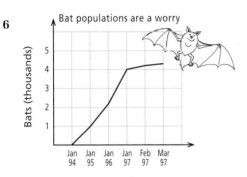

Bat populations are a worry

This chart was produced to back up a claim that the local bat populations were not growing as fast as they used to.

a When does the growth in population seem to slow?

b Comment on what is wrong with the graph.

7

The Grand Cinema   RESTAURANT & BAR

Screen 1 It Happened One Night
Screen 2 I'll Be Back!
Screen 3 Rumpelstiltskin
Screen 4 Macbeth

Forty people were asked which part of the Grand Cinema they had used last (Screen 1, 2, 3, 4 or the restaurant). Here are their answers:

1	3	3	1	4	1	2	3	2	4
1	2	2	4	4	2	3	R	2	R
R	2	3	3	1	3	R	3	R	R
1	1	3	4	3	2	1	3	3	2

a Make a frequency table of the data.

b Illustrate the data in a bar chart.

c Which part is: (i) the most popular   (ii) the least popular?

8 *What Choice* magazine notes how long certain light bulbs last (in hours) and their power (in watts).

Bulb	A	B	C	D	E	F	G	H	I	J	K	L	M	N	O	P
Wattage	40	80	60	100	80	60	110	120	60	40	100	120	110	60	120	60
Lifetime (hours)	100	80	80	70	100	90	80	70	110	110	80	80	70	100	60	90

a On a grid similar to the one shown, plot the points to make a scatter diagram.

b Is the correlation positive or negative?

c Draw the best-fitting straight line.

d Use the line to suggest a reasonable lifetime for a 90 watt bulb.

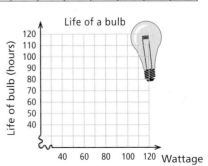

Life of a bulb

9 Time, Distance and Speed

STARTING POINTS

1 Write each of the following as an am or pm time.

  a ten o'clock in the morning
  b half past ten at night
  c a quarter past one in the morning
  d twenty-five to seven in the evening

2 Here are some 24-hour times.
  Write them as 12-hour times using am or pm.
  a 11 00   **b** 06 30   **c** 15 30   **d** 19 15

3 Here are some 12-hour times.
  Write them as 24-hour times.
  a 1 pm   **b** 4 pm   **c** 6.20 am   **d** 11.45 pm

4 a A film lasted from 6.30 pm to 9 pm. How long was the film?
  b Jack was at the hospital from 03 45 to 07 30.
    How long was he there?

5 The senior citizens of
  Cherry Lodge went on a
  coach trip to the seaside.

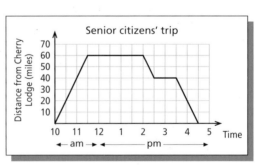

  Use the graph to help you answer the following questions.
  a When did they set off?
  b How far from the sea is Cherry Lodge?
  c When did they arrive?
  d How long did they stay at the sea?
  e On the way home they stopped for tea.
    For how long did they stop?

6 A digger can travel 30 km between sites in one hour.
  How far can it travel in:
  a 2 hours   **b** half an hour   **c** two and a half hours   **d** 15 minutes?

Time intervals

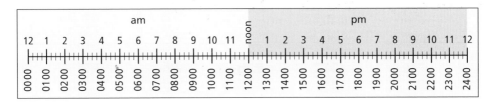

Example 1   A late night movie starts at 11.40 pm and ends at 1.25 am. How long does it last?

$$11.40 \text{ pm to } 12 \text{ (midnight)} = 20 \text{ minutes}$$
$$12 \text{ (midnight) to } 1.25 \text{ am} = \underline{1 \text{ hour } 25 \text{ minutes}}$$
$$\text{Total} = 1 \text{ hour } 45 \text{ minutes}$$

Example 2   Mina's flight is due to leave at 10.35 am. It is delayed until 2.45 pm. How long is the delay?

$$10.35 \text{ am to } 12 \text{ (noon)} = 1 \text{ hour } 25 \text{ minutes}$$
$$12 \text{ (noon) to } 2.45 \text{ pm} = \underline{2 \text{ hours } 45 \text{ minutes}}$$
$$\text{Total} = 3 \text{ hours } \mathbf{70 \text{ minutes}}$$
$$= 4 \text{ hours } 10 \text{ minutes}$$

EXERCISE 1

1 Several people go to the disco and stay until it closes.
   Mike and Zoe get there at 8 pm. So they are at the disco for 4 hours.
   How long do the following people stay at the disco?
   a George and his friends arrive at 9 pm.
   b Cheryl and Tom arrive at 8.45 pm.
   c Sally and Joan enter at 9.40 pm.
   d Ali and Bibi enter at 9.15 pm.
   e Jim and Rob enter at 8.20 pm.

2 Bette started her round of golf at 9.10 am. She finished at noon.
   How long did the round last?

3 Calculate the length of each movie.

Channel 1	Look Back Again	11 pm	till	1 am
Channel 2	The Chase	11.30 pm	till	1 am
Channel 3	The Big Fight	11.45 pm	till	1.30 am
Channel 4	Changing Days	10.50 pm	till	1.15 am
Channel 5	Staying Put	11.05 pm	till	1.50 am

FILMS GALORE!

4 Opening hours!

Calculate the length of time each shop is open.

Newsagent	9 am	until	5 pm
Baker	8.30 am	until	5 pm
Butcher	9.30 am	until	4.30 pm
Grocer	8.45 am	until	5.30 pm
Chemist	8.15 am	until	5.45 pm

5 Mark works on the night shift.

Every night he starts at 10.45 pm and works until 7.30 am the next day.

a How long is a shift?

b How long is it from 7.30 am until he has to go back to work?

EXERCISE 2

1

Name: **Kate Bryson**		
	Start	Stop
Monday	7.23 am	4.11 pm
Tuesday	7.27 am	4.13 pm
Wednesday	7.30 am	4.22 pm

How long did Kate work on:

a Monday   **b** Tuesday   **c** Wednesday?

2 The *Aberdeen Standard* gives the following information in its weather report:

a What is the length of time between high tides?

b How long is the sun up?

c How much time passes between the moon setting and rising?

Aberdeen Standard
High tides:

High tides:	2.30 am and 2.52 pm	
Sunrise:	7.18 am	Sunset: 4.43 pm
Moon sets:	10.16 am	Moon rises: 6.15 pm

3 Ben and Tricia are watching a film on TV. It starts at 10.15 pm and lasts for 1 hour and 40 minutes. At what time does the film finish?

4 Here is part of Gohar's telephone bill. It gives the details of three calls.

	Date	Time	Destination		Duration hours : minutes
a	23 May	11.25 am	Glasgow	0141 12345	0 : 55
b	25 May	11.37 am	Troon	01292 98756	1 : 44
c	26 May	11.41 am	Edinburgh	0131 99897	0 : 37

When did each of these calls end?

5 In 1989 Bill Neal crossed the English Channel in a bath tub.

It took him 13 hours 29 minutes.

He set off at 5.30 am.

When did he arrive at the French shore?

Distance–time graphs

Molly and Matthew drive to their local
supermarket to pick up the week's shopping.
Their outing is shown in the graph.

You can see that after 5 minutes
they were 2 km from home.

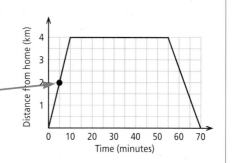

Notice that
after 10 minutes they stopped travelling,
after 55 minutes they started for home,
and after 70 minutes they arrived home.

EXERCISE 3

1 Use Molly and Matthew's graph to answer the following questions.
  a How far did they drive to the supermarket?
  b How long were they away from home?
  c How long were they at the supermarket?
  d How long was the journey home?

2 A saleswoman visited two shops before
  returning to base.
  a How long was the journey to the
    first shop?
  b How long did she stay there?
  c How long did she stay at the
    second shop?
  d How far apart are the two shops?
  e How long was she travelling, was it:
    (i) 1 hour **(ii)** 2 hours or **(iii)** 3 hours?

3

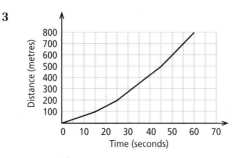

A train pulls out of Irvine Station.
The first 60 seconds of its journey are
shown in the graph.
How far does the train travel in:
a the first 15 seconds
b the first 25 seconds
c the first 45 seconds
d the first 50 seconds
e the *last* 10 seconds?

4 The Kawala family from Troon go on a day trip to the Isle of Arran.
At 8.30 they catch a train to Kilwinning.
They get another train to Ardrossan.
They board the ferry to Arran.
At each stage they have to wait.

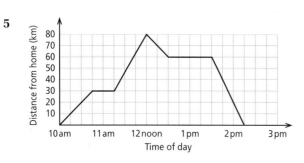

ARRAN
Scotland in miniature

a How long does each train journey take?

b How long is the ferry trip?

c How long is the wait at Kilwinning?

d How long is the wait for the ferry?

e How many kilometres are there between Ardrossan and Arran?

5

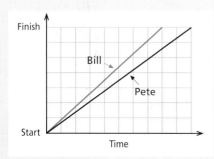

The Wilsons go for a Sunday drive.
Their first stop is for coffee.
Their second stop is a traffic jam.

a How long are they away from home?

b How long is the coffee break?

c How far do they get from home?

d How far do they travel altogether?

Look at the graph of this race between Bill and Pete.
You can see that Bill took less time. He won.
He must have been going faster.

The steeper the line, the faster the journey.

EXERCISE 4

1 Emma travelled from the centre of Glasgow onto the motorway.
She sped along the motorway to Edinburgh.
She then travelled to the centre of Edinburgh.
Which of these graphs is most likely to show her journey?

Reminder
Remember: steeper = faster.

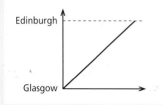

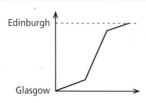

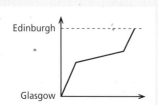

2 Liz enters a competition to find Miss Super Fit.

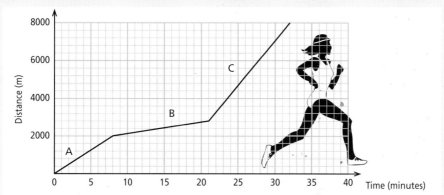

It involves a race with three parts: running, swimming and cycling.
The graph shows Liz's race.

a Identify the part of the graph which shows her:
  (i) running   **(ii)** swimming   **(iii)** cycling.
b How far did she cycle?   **c** For how long was she running?

3 Emir sets out to cycle
to a friend's house at
11 am. He has to
return home when
he remembers he has
forgotten his wallet.
He sets off again and
is unlucky enough to
get a puncture. He
eventually reaches
his friend's house at
2.30 pm.

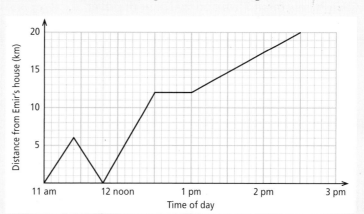

a How far was he from his house when he turned back?
b What time was it when he got the puncture?
c How long did it take to repair the tyre?   **d** When was he travelling fastest?

4 Abe, Bert and Cy
raced over 400 m.
a Write down the
order in which
they crossed the
finishing line.
b How long did
each person take
to finish the race?
c How far ahead
was the winner
when he won?

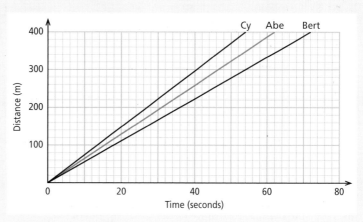

Meeting places

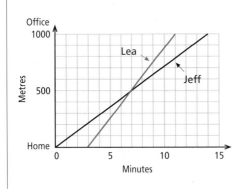

Jeff leaves home for the office first.
Three minutes later Lea leaves running.
She is going faster so she has a steeper graph.
Lea catches up with Jeff 500 metres from home.
(See where the lines cross.)
Lea arrives at the office first.

EXERCISE 5

1 Sandy and her brother John are going fishing.
   Sandy sets off at 7 am and walks to the river.
   John sets off later on his bike.
   a How long after Sandy does John leave?
   b When does John catch up?
   c How far from home are they then?

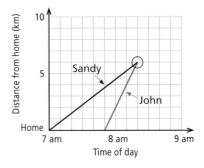

2 A train leaves Glasgow for Edinburgh at 10 am.
   A train leaves Edinburgh for Glasgow at the same time.

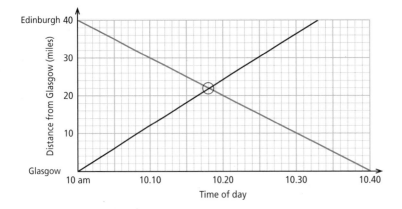

   a How long does each train take?
   b When do the trains pass each other?
   c How far from Glasgow is the passing point?
   d How far from Edinburgh is the passing point?

3 A gorilla escapes from a zoo. Use the graph to answer the questions.

a When did the gorilla escape?

b When did the search party set off?

c How far from the zoo was the gorilla at this time?

d When was the gorilla recaptured?

e How far from the zoo was the gorilla when it was recaptured?

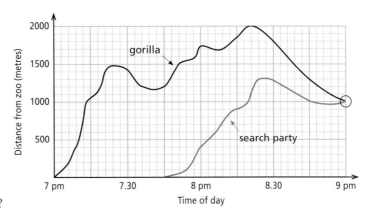

4 Mavis lives in Aberdeen. She travels to Edinburgh, stopping in Perth for lunch. Norah does the same journey but leaves later. She does not stop.

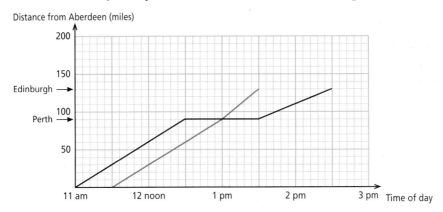

a When does each woman leave Aberdeen?

b Where are they when Norah passes Mavis?

c How long does Mavis stop for lunch?

d When does Norah pass Mavis?   e When does each woman arrive in Edinburgh?

5 Tom walks from Ayr to Prestwick. His friend Arnie walks from Prestwick to Ayr at the same time. When they meet they stop for a chat.

a Whose journey is represented by:
   (i) the broken line
   (ii) the solid line?

b How far from Ayr do they meet?

c How long is their chat?

d For how long does each man actually walk?

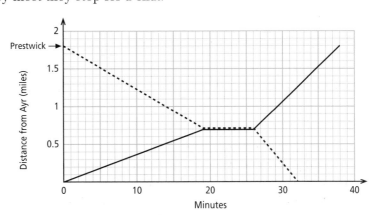

EXERCISE 6

1 A coach leaves Aberdeen heading for Glasgow.
A little later a car makes the same journey.

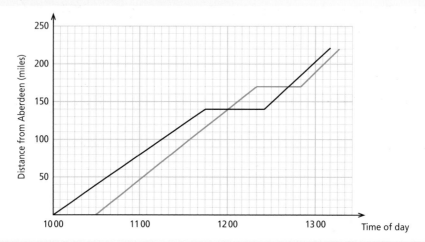

   a When does the car set off?   **b** What is the length of the journey?
   c Describe what happens at 12 noon.   **d** For how long is the car stopped?
   e What happens at 12.40 pm?   **f** Which vehicle arrives first?

2 *Sea Voice* and *Lady Day* had a race. They sail from Tobermory, round a buoy and
then back to Tobermory.

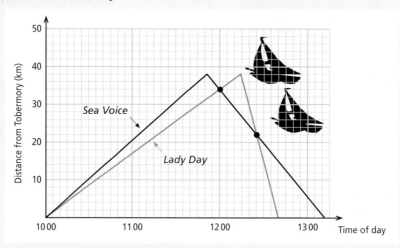

   a How far is the buoy from Tobermory?
   b Give the times that each boat reached this buoy.
   c Who turned first?
   d What happened at 12 noon?
   e What happened 22 km from the finishing line?
   f **(i)** Who won?   **(ii)** By how many minutes?
      (iii) By how many kilometres?

Calculating speed

Neil drove from Glasgow to Penrith (a distance of
100 miles).
He travelled along the A74 at a steady speed.
It took him 2 hours. What was his speed?
If he drove 100 miles in 2 hours, then in 1 hour
he drove

      $100 \div 2 = 50$

     His speed was **50 miles per hour**.
Tony also drove from Glasgow to Penrith but he
used country roads. He could not keep a steady
speed, but he also managed the 100 miles in 2 hours.
We say Tony's **average** speed was 50 miles per hour.

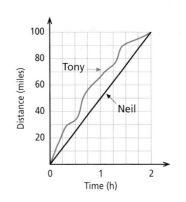

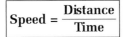

$$\text{Speed} = \frac{\text{Distance}}{\text{Time}}$$

This triangle will help you remember the formula:

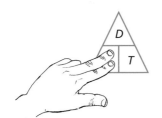

Cover up S with your fingers to disclose the formula
for speed.

$$S = \frac{D}{T}$$

EXERCISE 7

1 Work out the average speed for each of these.
  a A hillwalker covered 20 km in 4 hours.
  b A cyclist managed 144 km in 3 hours.
  c A car travelled 576 km in 6 hours.
  d A jet flew 5570 km in 2 hours.

2 Copy and complete this table. Look at the units.

Distance	450 miles	1760 metres	260 km	26.2 miles	2000 km
Time	9 hours	11 seconds	7 hours	2.25 hours	3.5 hours
Speed	miles/h	m/s	km/h	miles/h	km/h

3 Calculate the speeds involved in the following records.

   a The fastest sprinter: 100 m in 9.9 s

   b The fastest speed cyclist: 1000 m in 58 s

   c The fastest greyhound: 374 m in 20 s

   d The fastest horse: 402 m in 21 s

   e The fastest swimmer 100 m in 48 s

   f The fastest skater: 500 m in 36 s

4

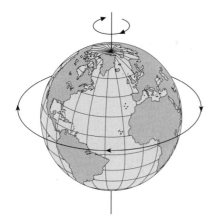

Just standing still you travel 25 992 miles in 24 hours as the earth spins once on its axis.

At what speed are you travelling?

5 Alice cycled 38 km in 4 hours. Bethany cycled 46 km in 5 hours.

   a Whose speed was greater?

   b By how much?

Fractions

Example 1 Write 25 minutes as a fraction of an hour.

To work this out on a calculator enter:

The answer is $\frac{5}{12}$.

Example 2 Graham travelled 50 miles in $6\frac{1}{4}$ hours. What was his speed?

$S = 50 \div 6\frac{1}{4}$

To work this out on a calculator enter:

His speed was 8 miles per hour.

EXERCISE 8

1 Write each of these times as a fraction of an hour.
   a 10 minutes   **b** 20 minutes   **c** 30 minutes   **d** 40 minutes
   e 50 minutes   **f** 12 minutes   **g** 24 minutes   **h** 5 minutes
   i 15 minutes   **j** 18 minutes

2 **a** Lauren walks 100 metres in half a minute. What is her speed in metres per minute?
   b Jack cycles 16 kilometres in half an hour. What is his speed in km/h?

3 **a** Jafar drives 12 km in a quarter of an hour. What is his speed in km/h?
   b A mouse runs 2 metres in a quarter of a minute. What is its speed in m/min?

4 Copy and complete the table.

	Skater	Snail	Bird	Spider	Runner
Distance	12 miles	9 cm	102 m	148 cm	45 km
Time	$\frac{1}{2}$ hour	$1\frac{1}{2}$ min	$8\frac{1}{2}$ s	$9\frac{1}{4}$ s	$2\frac{3}{4}$ h
Speed	miles/h	cm/min	m/s	cm/s	km/h

5 A windsurfer travelled 30 km in 1 hour and 40 minutes.
   a Write 40 minutes as a fraction of an hour.
   b Calculate her speed in km/h.

Finding the distance

A motorist travels at a steady speed of 30 mph.
In one hour he will have travelled 30 miles.
After 4 hours he will have travelled $30 \times 4 = 120$ miles.

Distance = Speed × Time

Using the triangle, cover up the D with your
fingers to disclose the formula for distance.

$D = ST$

EXERCISE 9

1 Use the formula $D = S \times T$ to work out the distance travelled in:
   a 2 hours at 18 km/h
   b 5 hours at 10 miles/h
   c 6 hours at 45 m/h
   d 4 hours at 6.5 km/h
   e 25 minutes at 7 cm/min
   f 17 seconds at 8 m/s

2 John cycled at 18 km/h for 4 hours. Peter cycled at 23 km/h for 3 hours.
   a Who travelled further?
   b By how much?

3 At sea a yachtswoman keeps a note of how far
she has travelled by recording times and speeds.

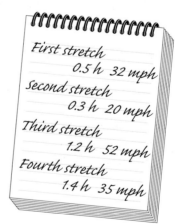

First stretch
   0.5 h 32 mph
Second stretch
   0.3 h 20 mph
Third stretch
   1.2 h 52 mph
Fourth stretch
   1.4 h 35 mph

   a How far does she travel in the first stretch?
   b How far does she travel in the third stretch?
   c How far has she travelled altogether?

EXERCISE 10

1 A motoring organisation issues
this chart.
It gives the estimated journey
times for someone travelling at 50
miles per hour.

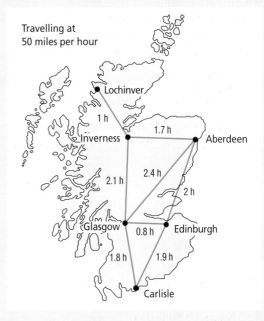

Travelling at
50 miles per hour

a **(i)** How long is a journey from Glasgow to Edinburgh?
(ii) Using the formula $D = S \times T$, work out the distance from Glasgow to
Edinburgh.
b In a similar way work out the distance from:
(i) Glasgow to Aberdeen
(ii) Glasgow to Carlisle
(iii) Edinburgh to Carlisle.
c Helen plans to drive from Glasgow to Lochinver.
(i) How long should the journey take?
(ii) What distance will she travel?

2 **a** What fraction of an hour is:
(i) 15 minutes
(ii) 10 minutes?
b Callum goes jogging at lunchtime. He keeps
up an average speed of 9 km/h.
He jots down his times.
Work out the distance he jogged each day.

Monday 15 minutes

Tuesday 10 minutes

Wednesday
12 minutes

Thursday 5 minutes

Friday no jogging

Finding the time

Travelling 90 miles at 30 miles per hour will take $90 \div 30 = 3$ hours.

Time = Distance ÷ Speed

Using the triangle, cover up the T with your fingers to disclose the formula for time.

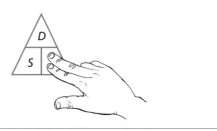

$$T = \frac{D}{S}$$

EXERCISE 11

1 Use the formula $T = \dfrac{D}{S}$ to work out the time for each journey.

  a 90 km at 30 km/h   **b** 240 miles at 60 miles/h   **c** 96 km at 8 km/h

  d 330 miles at 55 miles/h   **e** 108 cm at 9 cm/s   **f** 196 km at 7 km/h

2 Calculate the time taken to make each of these journeys.

  a 260 miles at 65 miles/h

  b 672 km at 96 km/h

  c 135 miles at 45 miles/h

3 a Use the chart to work out these journey times:

    (i) Glasgow to Aberdeen at 47 miles/h

    (ii) Edinburgh to London at 62 miles/h

    (iii) Leeds to Cardiff at 42 miles/h

    (iv) Penzance to Dover at 31 miles/h.

  b Edinburgh to Leeds is a distance of 190 miles. Leeds to London is also 190 miles.

    (i) What is the total distance from Edinburgh to London via Leeds?

    (ii) If you travel at an average speed of 63 miles/h via Leeds, will you beat the time of someone doing the direct journey at 62 miles/h?

Distances by road in miles

141

372

210

341

Aberdeen

Glasgow

Edinburgh

Leeds

Cardiff

London

Dover

Penzance

Decimals and time

Example 1   A hovercraft travelled 24 miles at a speed of 16 mph.
How long did it take?

The calculator gives an answer of 1.5 hours.
The decimal part can be *multiplied by 60* to turn it into minutes.
$0.5 \times 60 = 30$
So the journey time is 1 hour 30 minutes.

Example 2   Change 7.3 hours into hours and minutes.

7.3 hours = 7 hours and 0.3×60 minutes
= 7 hours and 18 minutes

EXERCISE 12

1 Change the following into hours and minutes.
   a 2.1 hours   **b** 3.5 hours   **c** 7.6 hours   **d** 2.25 hours
   e 3.15 hours   **f** 8.45 hours

2 Neil travelled 36 km at 8 km/h. Gavin travelled 48 km at 10 km/h.
   a Whose journey was quicker?
   b By how many minutes?

3 The Inverness to London train averages 60 mph.
   The distance is 570 miles.
   Work out how long the journey takes in hours and minutes.

4 Susie estimates that she can run for hours at a steady rate of 8 mph.
   She enters the marathon, a distance of 26 miles.
   How long should it take her to complete the race? Give your answer in hours and minutes.

5 Mr Dun drives 64.8 km from work at an average speed of 48 km/h.
   Mrs Dun drives 81.2 km from work at an average speed of 58 km/h.
   They both leave work at the same time.
   a Who arrives home first?
   b How many minutes later is it before the second person gets home?

Summary for time, distance and speed

$S = \dfrac{D}{T}$

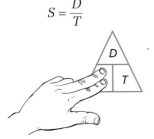

$D = S \times T$

$T = \dfrac{D}{S}$

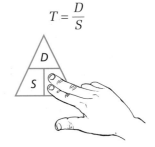

CHAPTER 9 REVIEW

1 How many hours is the surgery open each week?

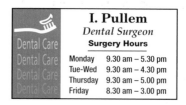

I. Pullem
Dental Surgeon
Surgery Hours

Monday	9.30 am – 5.30 pm
Tue-Wed	9.30 am – 4.30 pm
Thursday	9.30 am – 5.00 pm
Friday	8.30 am – 3.00 pm

2 The graph shows the race between the tortoise and the hare.

  a When did the hare first stop?
  b For how long did he rest?
  c How long did the tortoise take for the race?
  d Who won? By how many minutes?
  e When did the tortoise pass the hare?
  f For how many minutes was the hare actually running?

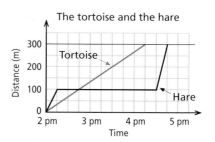

3

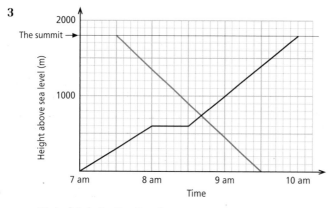

A party of hillwalkers sets off at 7 am to climb Ben McDuff.
A little later another party begins to come down.

  a How high is the Ben?
  b At what time does the second party start to come down?
  c How long does the first party stop for a rest?
  d When do the two parties meet?
  e How high are they when they meet?

4 A river flows at 4 metres per second.
How far will driftwood in the river travel in 30 seconds?

5 Jamila drives to an appointment in Manchester, 280 miles away.
She averages 56 miles an hour. How long will it take her to drive there?

6 Bill's go-cart has a maximum speed of 25 km/h. Calculate his time for a 100 km race if he stays at maximum speed throughout the race.

7 The Earth takes one year to go round the sun. The distance travelled is 584 million miles. There are 365 days in a year.
At what speed is the Earth going (in millions of miles per day)?

10 The Theorem of Pythagoras

STARTING POINTS

Using the $\boxed{x^2}$ button

1 Copy and complete the table.

Number	5	7	3	8	12	20	2.5	3.4
Number squared	5×5 $= 25$	7×7						

2 Find the area of each of the following squares.

Reminder
$A = l^2$

a

4 cm

b
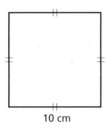
10 cm

c
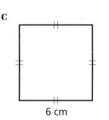
6 cm

d

1.3 cm

3 Measure the length of these squares to the nearest millimetre.
Copy and complete the table.

a

①

b

②

c

③

Square	Length of side	Area
①		
②		
③		

4 Calculate each of the following.
  a 8^2 **b** 9^2 **c** 30^2 **d** 11^2 **e** 2.6^2

Using the $\sqrt{}$ button

> *Example* What number, when squared, gives 81?
>
> $\sqrt{81} = 9 \quad (9^2 = 81)$

5 Answer the following in a similar way.
  a What number, when squared, gives 1?
  b What number, when squared, gives 16?
  c What number, when squared, gives 25?
  d What number, when squared, gives 9?
  e What number, when squared, gives 36?
  f What number, when squared, gives 2.25?

6 Calculate each of the following.
  a $\sqrt{64}$ **b** $\sqrt{144}$ **c** $\sqrt{49}$ **d** $\sqrt{1600}$ **e** $\sqrt{1.44}$

7 This square is made up of 25 tiles (5 × 5). There are $\sqrt{25} = 5$ tiles along each side.

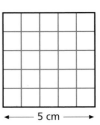

5 cm

Work out the number of tiles along the side of each of these squares.

  a   **b**   **c**

Area = 16 cm^2

Area = 36 cm^2

Area = 49 cm^2

EXERCISE 1

Calculate each of the following. $\boxed{x^2}$

1 a 9^2 **b** 13^2 **c** 6.5^2 **d** 0.5^2 **e** 25^2

2 a $3^2 + 4^2$ **b** $7^2 + 9^2$ **c** $13^2 - 12^2$ **d** $10^2 - 8^2$

3 a 0.6^2 **b** 0.3^2 **c** 2.5^2 **d** 1.2^2 **e** 1.5^2

4 a $1.5^2 + 0.4^2$ **b** $2.4^2 + 0.7^2$ **c** $2.9^2 + 2.1^2$ **d** $2^2 - 1.2^2$

5 A carpet fitter lays square carpet tiles in a *square* room. He lays 7 along one wall.
How many tiles will he lay altogether?

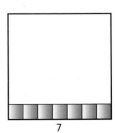

7

6 A chess board has 8 squares along each side.
  a How many squares cover the board?
  b If each square is 3 cm long, what is the area of the chess board?

Calculate each of the following.

7 a $\sqrt{100}$ **b** $\sqrt{289}$ **c** $\sqrt{0.36}$ **d** $\sqrt{0.49}$ **e** $\sqrt{0.0025}$

8 a $\sqrt{9 + 16}$ **b** $\sqrt{49 + 576}$ **c** $\sqrt{0.36 + 0.64}$ **d** $\sqrt{25 - 16}$

9 a $\sqrt{5^2 + 12^2}$ **b** $\sqrt{7^2 + 24^2}$ **c** $\sqrt{21^2 + 20^2}$ **d** $\sqrt{41^2 - 9^2}$

Example
The area of this square is 49 cm^2.
How long is each side?
$\sqrt{49} = 7$
Each side is 7 cm long.

---

10 For each of the following squares find the length of a side.

a
Area = 225 cm^2

b
Area = 361 cm^2

c
Area = 169 cm^2

d
Area = 10 000 cm^2

11 A washing machine has a square-shaped top. This top has an area of 2304 cm^2.
The space into which it must fit is 50 cm wide.
Is there enough room to fit in the washing machine?

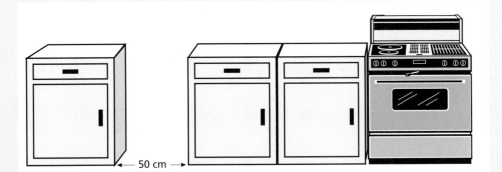

50 cm

12 Andy wants to put fencing around the sides of his rose garden.
The garden has an area of 400 m^2 and is square shaped.
What length of fencing does he need to go round the rose garden?

The Theorem of Pythagoras

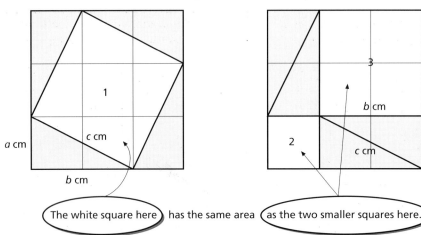

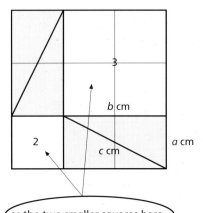

The white square here has the same area as the two smaller squares here.

$$\text{Area 1} = \text{Area 2} + \text{Area 3}$$

since the white area in each diagram is equal to
the area of the large square less the area of the four shaded triangles.

If we look at one of the right-angled triangles,

Area 1 = c^2

Area 2 = a^2

Area 3 = b^2

so we have $c^2 = a^2 + b^2$

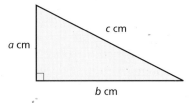

Around 543 BC a Greek philosopher called Pythagoras discovered this connection
between the sides of a right-angled triangle. It is called **The Theorem of Pythagoras**.
The side of the triangle opposite the right angle is known as the **hypotenuse**.
The theorem states:

In any right-angled triangle,
the square on the hypotenuse
is equal to
the sum of the squares on the other two sides.

$$c^2 = a^2 + b^2$$

This can be used to find the length of the hypotenuse when the other two sides are
known.

Example The hypotenuse is x cm long.
The theorem tells us that:

$x^2 = 5^2 + 12^2$

$x^2 = 25 + 144$

$x^2 = 169$

$x = \sqrt{169}$ (What number, when squared, gives us 169?)

$x = 13$

The hypotenuse is 13 cm long.

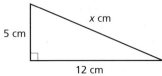

EXERCISE 2

1 Copy and complete the working to find the length of the hypotenuse in each case.

a The hypotenuse is x cm long.
The theorem tells us that:

x cm
4 cm
3 cm

$$x^2 = 3^2 + 4^2$$
$$x^2 = 9 + \dots$$
$$x^2 = \dots$$
$$x = \sqrt{\dots}$$
$$x = \dots$$

The hypotenuse is ... cm long.

b The hypotenuse is x cm long.
The theorem tells us that:

x cm
12 cm
9 cm

$$x^2 = 9^2 + 12^2$$
$$x^2 = 81 + \dots$$
$$x^2 = \dots$$
$$x = \sqrt{\dots}$$
$$x = \dots$$

The hypotenuse is ... cm long.

c The hypotenuse is x cm long.
The theorem tells us that:

x cm
15 cm
8 cm

$$x^2 = 8^2 + 15^2$$
$$x^2 =$$

d The hypotenuse is x cm long.
The theorem tells us that:

x cm
16 cm
12 cm

$$x^2 =$$
$$x^2 =$$

2 Find the length of the hypotenuse in each case. (The diagrams are *not* to scale.)

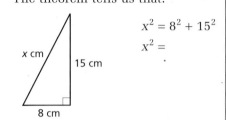

a x cm, 24 cm, 7 cm

b x cm, 10 cm, 24 cm

c x cm, 20 cm, 21 cm

d x cm, 30 cm, 16 cm

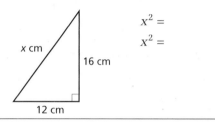

e x cm, 40 cm, 9 cm

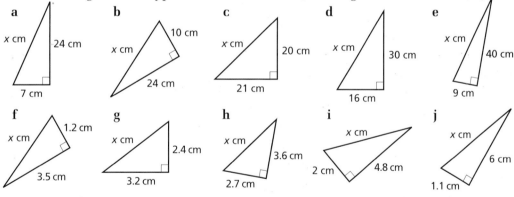

f x cm, 1.2 cm, 3.5 cm

g x cm, 2.4 cm, 3.2 cm

h x cm, 3.6 cm, 2.7 cm

i x cm, 2 cm, 4.8 cm

j x cm, 6 cm, 1.1 cm

3 Engineers are making a model of Tower Bridge.
The supporting chains form a right-angle triangle
with the tower and the ground as shown.
Calculate the length of the chain.

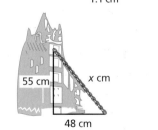

55 cm, x cm, 48 cm

4 A wire helps to support the wing of the old plane.
   a What does the Theorem of Pythagoras tell us
      about the right-angled triangle in the sketch?
   b Calculate the length of the supporting wire.

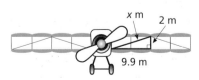

x m, 2 m, 9.9 m

123

The answer does not always work out exactly.

Example

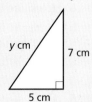

$y^2 = 7^2 + 5^2$

$y^2 = 49 + 25$

$y^2 = 74$

$y = \sqrt{74} = 8.602\,325$

$\cdot\ y = 8.60$ (to 2 decimal places)

EXERCISE 3

In this exercise give your answers to 2 decimal places.

1 Find the length of the hypotenuse in each triangle.

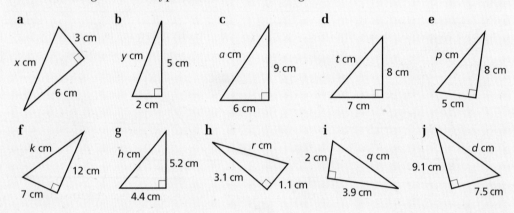

2 A guy rope is fixed from the top of a tent pole to the ground. Using the measurements shown, calculate the length of the rope.

3 The diagram shows part of a house's roof space. Calculate the length of the sloping roof.

4 m Slope 5 m

4 A rectangular park is 155 m long and 200 m wide. How far is it from corner to corner?

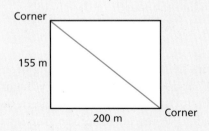

Corner

155 m

200 m

Corner

Finding a shorter side

Example

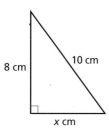

The hypotenuse is 10 cm long.
The Theorem of Pythagoras tells us that:

$$10^2 = 8^2 + x^2$$
$$x^2 = 10^2 - 8^2$$
$$x^2 = 100 - 64$$
$$x^2 = 36$$
$$x = \sqrt{36}$$
$$x = 6$$

EXERCISE 4

1 Copy and complete the working to find x in each triangle.

a

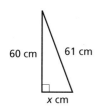

$$61^2 = 60^2 + x^2$$
$$x^2 = 61^2 - 60^2$$
$$x^2 = \ldots$$
$$x^2 = \ldots$$
$$x = \sqrt{\ldots}$$
$$x = \ldots$$

b

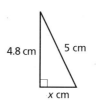

$$5^2 = 4.8^2 + x^2$$
$$x^2 = 5^2 - \ldots$$
$$x^2 = \ldots$$
$$x^2 = \ldots$$
$$x = \ldots$$
$$x = \ldots$$

c

$$15^2 = 12^2 + x^2$$
$$x^2 = \ldots$$

d

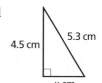

$$5.3^2 = 4.5^2 + x^2$$

2 Calculate the unknown length in each of the following.

a

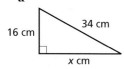

b

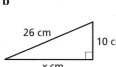

c

d

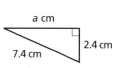

3 Calculate the unknown length in each triangle, correct to 2 decimal places.

a

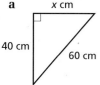

b

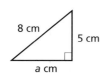

c

d

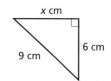

EXERCISE 5

Work where necessary to 2 decimal places.

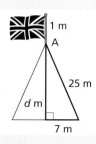

1 A flagpole is supported by ropes.
   a Calculate the height of the point, A, where the ropes meet.
   b The length of the pole above the ropes is 1 m.
      What is the *total* height of the pole?

2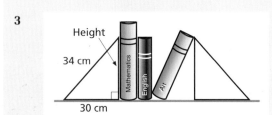

   Calculate the length of this 5-bar gate.
   (Consider the right-angled triangle marked.)

3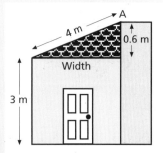

   This bookend is in the shape of a
   right-angled triangle.
   Calculate its height.

4 A telephone pole is held up by a wire stay 8 m long.
   The wire is fixed to the ground 5 m from the foot of
   the pole. How high up the pole is the wire fixed?

   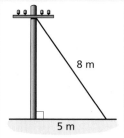

5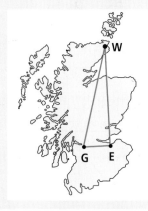

   This house extension has a roof as shown. It
   is a right-angled triangle. The slope is 4 m
   long. The height of the roof space is 0.6 m.
   a Calculate the width of the extension.
   b From the ground to the roof is a height of
      3 m. What is the height of the point A
      above the ground?

6 On the map Glasgow, Edinburgh and Wick form a
   right-angled triangle with the right angle at Edinburgh.
   The distance from Glasgow to Wick is 288 km.
   The distance from Edinburgh to Wick is 280 km.
   What is the distance from Glasgow to Edinburgh?

Finding any side

Always check which side is the hypotenuse.

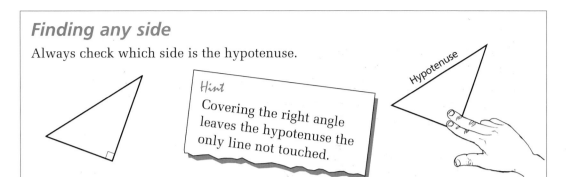

Hint

Covering the right angle leaves the hypotenuse the only line not touched.

Hypotenuse

EXERCISE 6

Work to 2 decimal places where necessary.

1 Calculate x in each triangle.

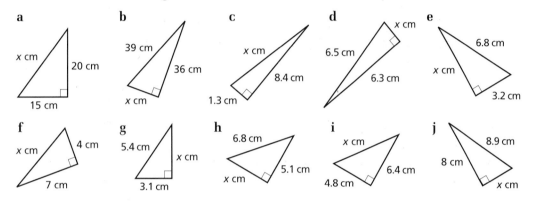

a x cm, 20 cm, 15 cm

b 39 cm, 36 cm, x cm

c x cm, 8.4 cm, 1.3 cm

d x cm, 6.5 cm, 6.3 cm

e 6.8 cm, x cm, 3.2 cm

f x cm, 4 cm, 7 cm

g 5.4 cm, x cm, 3.1 cm

h 6.8 cm, x cm, 5.1 cm

i x cm, 6.4 cm, 4.8 cm

j 8.9 cm, 8 cm, x cm

2 The roof of a house is in the shape of a right-angled triangle.
Each slope is 4 m long.
Calculate the width of the house.

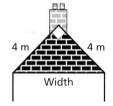

4 m   4 m   Width

3

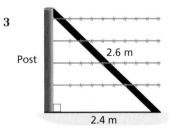

Post   2.6 m   2.4 m

A fence post is supported by a stay which is 2.6 m long.
The post and stay make a right-angled triangle with the ground.
Calculate the height of the post.

4 The jib of a crane is 24 m long.
The end of the load is 11 m from the cabin as shown.
Calculate the length of the cable.

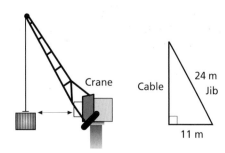

Crane   Cable   24 m   Jib   11 m

5 How far along the ground is it from A to B?

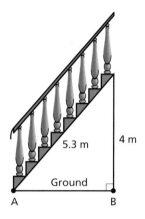

5.3 m   4 m

Ground

A   B

EXERCISE 7

1 The strain on a suspension bridge is taken by steel hawsers.
The hawser is attached to the tower 209 m up and to the ground 120 m from the foot of the tower.
Calculate the length of the hawser.

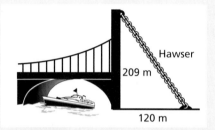

Hawser

209 m

120 m

2 A wildlife research team fixes radio beacons to two rhinos.
After a few days one rhino is detected 7.5 km due north of the base.
The other rhino is 7.5 km due east.
How far apart are the rhinos?

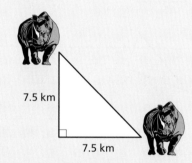

7.5 km

7.5 km

3

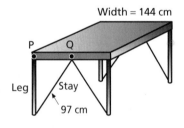

Width = 144 cm

P   Q

Leg   Stay

97 cm

The width of the folding table is 144 cm.
Q is the midpoint of the edge of the table.
The length of the stay is 97 cm.
a What is the distance PQ?
b Calculate the length of the legs of the table.

4 On this escalator the banister rail is the same length as the stringer.
The height of the stringer is 2.4 m. The distance along the ground is 4.2 m.
Calculate the length of the banister rail correct to 2 decimal places.

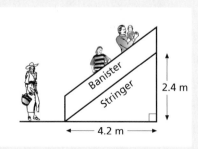

Banister

Stringer

2.4 m

4.2 m

CHAPTER 10 REVIEW

1 Calculate the length of the unknown side in each triangle.

a

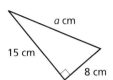

15 cm, a cm, 8 cm

b

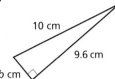

10 cm, 9.6 cm, b cm

2 Calculate the length of the unknown side in each triangle correct to 2 decimal places.

a

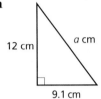

12 cm, a cm, 9.1 cm

b

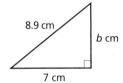

8.9 cm, b cm, 7 cm

3 A boat sets out from the harbour. It sails north for 8 km. It then sails east for another 12 km.
How far is the boat from the harbour?

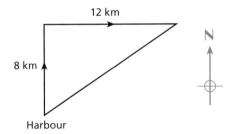

12 km

8 km

Harbour

N

4 The mast of a sailing ship is 25 m long. The boom at the bows is 10 m long. The rigging, AB, connecting the mast to the boom completes a right-angled triangle as shown. Calculate, to 2 decimal places, the length of the rigging.

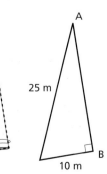

A

25 m

B

10 m

11 Integers

STARTING POINTS

1 The position of point A is given by the coordinates (4, 2).
Write down the coordinates of B, C and D.

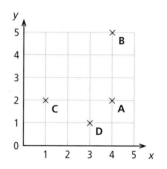

2 a Draw a coordinate diagram like the one in question **1**.
   b Clearly plot the positions of each of these points:
   P(5, 1), Q(3, 4), R(2, 2), S(0, 2), T(4, 0).
   Make sure you put the letter beside the cross marking the point.

Reminder

Along (the x-direction) then *up* (the y-direction).

3   Temperatures around the world

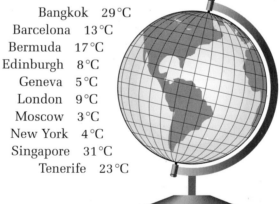

Bangkok	29 °C
Barcelona	13 °C
Bermuda	17 °C
Edinburgh	8 °C
Geneva	5 °C
London	9 °C
Moscow	3 °C
New York	4 °C
Singapore	31 °C
Tenerife	23 °C

   a Which place is warmest?
   b Which place is coldest?
   c What is the difference in temperature between the warmest and coldest places?
   d What is the difference in temperature between Edinburgh and Tenerife?
   e At night the temperature in Bangkok falls by 12 degrees.
   What is the night-time temperature in Bangkok?

4 The temperatures at midday in Inverness one week were:
9 °C, 12 °C, 11 °C, 14 °C, 10 °C, 7 °C, 14 °C.
Calculate the average temperature.

Temperatures below zero

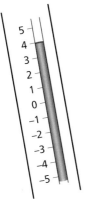

Zero degrees Celsius (0 °C) is the temperature at which water freezes to ice.

On a cold day the temperature can fall below zero. Four degrees *below* zero is written as – 4 °C. We read – 4 °C as 'minus 4 °C' or 'negative 4 °C' or simply '4 degrees below zero'.
Four degrees *above* zero is written as 4 °C.

EXERCISE 1

1 Write down the temperatures shown on these thermometers.

a   **b**   **c**   **d**   **e**

2 Put the temperatures in question **1** in order, coldest first.

3 Here are the temperatures around Britain one day in winter.

Aberdeen	5 °C	Glasgow	−3 °C
Brighton	2 °C	Inverness	−9 °C
Dover	4 °C	Liverpool	0 °C
Dumfries	−3 °C	London	1 °C
Edinburgh	−2 °C		

Warmer
5
4
3
2
1
0
−1
−2
−3
−4
−5
−6
−7
−8
−9
−10
Colder

a Re-write this list in order of temperature. Start with the warmest.
b How many degrees warmer than Liverpool is Dover?
c How many degrees colder than Liverpool is Edinburgh?
d Note in the scale opposite that −2 °C is 5 below 3 °C.
  How much below 3 °C is:
  (i) 1 °C   **(ii)** −3 °C   **(iii)** – 10 °C   **(iv)** −7 °C?
e How far below 4 °C is −9 °C?

4 The temperature is recorded every two hours one day at Prestwick weather centre.
   The results are shown in the line graph.

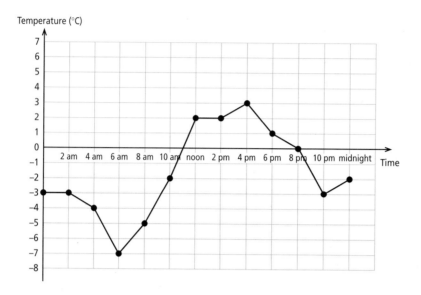

a When was Prestwick at its coldest?
b What was its highest temperature?
c Between 6 pm and 8 pm the temperature fell 1 °C.
   What happened to the temperature between:
   (i)   4 pm and 6 pm
   (ii)   2 pm and 4 pm
   (iii) 8 pm and 10 pm
   (iv)   noon and 2 pm
   (v)   6 am and 8 am
   (vi)   8 am and noon?
d For how many readings was the temperature below zero?

Negative coordinates

Reminder

Any point P(*x*, *y*) has two coordinates:
- an *x* coordinate (directions for right or left)
- a *y* coordinate (directions for up or down).

The point O (0, 0), is called the **origin.**
Follow the *x* instructions first.

Examples   P(1, 3)   P is the point 1 to the *right* and 3 *up* from O.
             Q(–4, 1)   Q is the point 4 to the *left* and 1 *up* from O.
             R(–2, –3)   R is the point 2 to the *left* and 3 *down* from O.
             S(4, –2)   S is the point 4 to the *right* and 2 *down* from O.

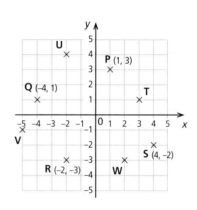

EXERCISE 2

1 For the coordinate diagram above:
  a Check that the coordinates of P, Q, R and S are correct.
  b Write down the coordinates of T, U, V and W (in the form T(,)).

2 The grid below represents the plan of a park.

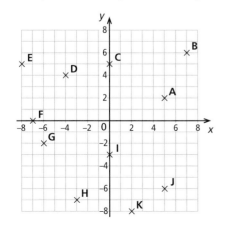

The crosses are where trees have to be planted.
Write down the coordinates of the points A, B, C, D, ..., K.

3 a Draw a coordinate diagram.
   Number the axes from −10 to 10.
   b Plot the points D(−8, 3), E(−3, −5), F(−2, 7), G(6, 1), H(−5, −7), I(6, −4),
   J(−5, 1), K(2, −5), L(−3, −1), M(9, −7), N(−4, 9).

4 Write down the coordinates of the corners of the
square PQRS.

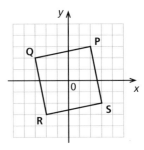

5

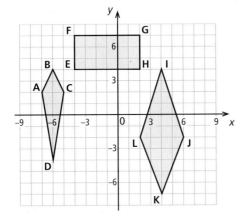

Write down the coordinates of the
corners of these three shapes.

EXERCISE 3

1

   a A honeycomb looks like a tiling of hexagons.
   On a coordinate diagram plot the following points, joining them up to form a
   hexagon:
   P(5, 2), Q(2, 5), R(−1, 2), S(−1, −3), T(2, −6), U(5, −3), P(5, 2).
   This represents hexagon A.
   b Draw hexagon B on the same diagram.
   Give the coordinates of its corners.
   c Write down the coordinates of hexagon C.

2 This map of Scotland has its origin at Edinburgh.

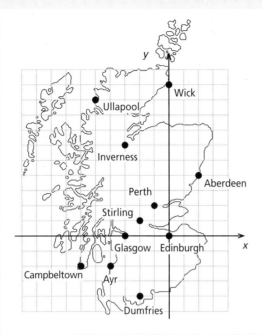

a Make a list of the places marked on the map.
Mark their coordinates beside them.

b The people in Perth have the same map but with the origin at Perth.
Write down what the coordinates of all the places will be on the Perth map.

3 An artist wishes to make the design shown.
ABCD is a square.
A(−5, 2) and B(4, 2) are two corners of the square.

a Plot A and B on a suitable grid.

b Plot the points C and D to complete the square.
Give the coordinates of C and D.

c The centre of the circle is where the diagonals
of the square meet.
What are the coordinates of this point?

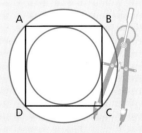

4 On a hike Jessica passes through points A(−7, −3), B(−5,−2) and C(−3, −1).

a Plot these points on a suitable grid and draw the path Jessica takes.

b At the same time Henry passes through P(3, −4), Q(2, −3) and R(1, −2), also
walking in a straight line.
Draw his route.

c They plan to meet at a point M. Give the coordinates of this point.

d Patrick walks through (−5, 3), (−4, 2) and (−3, 1).
Will his route pass through M?

Number lines in context

EXERCISE 4

Temperatures

1 The temperature at Aviemore is 4 °C.
   Write down the temperature at Aviemore if it falls from 4 °C by:

   a 3 degrees   **b** 4 degrees   **c** 5 degrees
   d 6 degrees   **e** 8 degrees   **f** 10 degrees.

2 The temperature at Stornoway is –1 °C.
   Write down the temperature at Stornoway if it falls from –1 °C
   by:

   a 1 degree   **b** 2 degrees   **c** 4 degrees
   d 6 degrees   **e** 8 degrees   **f** 10 degrees.

3 The temperature at Lerwick is –3 °C.
   Write down the temperature at Lerwick if it rises
   from –3 °C by:

   a 1 degree   **b** 3 degrees   **c** 4 degrees
   d 6 degrees   **e** 7 degrees   **f** 10 degrees.

4 Here is an extract from a weather report in a newspaper. How many degrees is:

   a London warmer than Manchester
   b Manchester warmer than Inverness
   c Edinburgh colder than London
   d Dumfries colder than Inverness
   e London warmer than Dumfries?

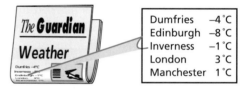

Dumfries	–4 °C
Edinburgh	–8 °C
Inverness	–1 °C
London	3 °C
Manchester	1 °C

Sea-level

5

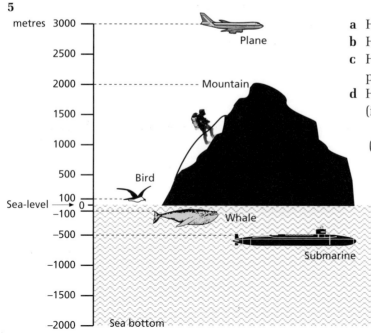

a How high is the mountain?
b How deep is the sea?
c How much higher is the plane than the bird?
d How far is it from:
   (i) the plane to the bottom of the sea
   (ii) the top of the mountain to the bottom of the sea
   (iii) the whale to the bird
   (iv) the submarine to the bottom of the sea
   (v) the whale to the submarine?

The air temperature at sea-level is 7 °C.
The temperature drops 1 °C for every 200 m of height.

e What is the temperature at:
   (i) the top of the mountain
   (ii) the height of the aeroplane
   (iii) the mountaineer's height of 1400 m?

Profit and loss

6 Bart's Bakery sometimes makes a profit and sometimes makes a loss.
The bar graph shows the 'profit' made by the bakery each month last year.
A 'negative profit' is a loss.

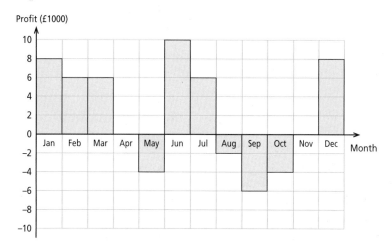

a For how many months did the bakery make a profit?
b For how many months did it make a loss?
c In January the bakery makes a profit of £8000.
   What happened in:
   (i) February
   (ii) April
   (iii) October?
d Did the bakery make an overall profit or loss for the year? Calculate the amount.

Adding using the number line

You have been adding and subtracting integers that crop up in real-life situations.
It is important that you learn to add and subtract integers quickly.
An addition combines two numbers:
3 + 2 combines 3 and 2; 3 + (−2) combines 3 and −2.
Treat an addition as a set of instructions.

Example 1

3 + 2 = ...   Start at 3 and move 2 to the right.

3 + 2 = 5

Example 2

3 + (−2) = ...   Start at 3 and move 2 to the left.

3 + (−2) = 1

Example 3

−3 + (−2) = ...   Start at −3 and move 2 to the left.

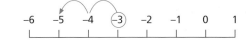

−3 + (−2) = −5

Start at the first number and take whatever steps the second number suggests.

EXERCISE 5

1 Use a number line to help you with these additions.
   a 1 + 8   **b** −2 + 3   **c** −6 + 8   **d** −3 + 5   **e** −4 + 0
   f −8 + 3   **g** −3 + 3   **h** −1 + 8   **i** −5 + 4

2 Now try these. Use a number line again to help you.
   a 7 + (− 2)   **b** 7 + (−5)   **c** 7 + (−7)   **d** 7 + (−8)   **e** 2 + (−3)
   f 0 + (−3)   **g** −2 + (−1)   **h** −3 + (−2)   **i** −4 + (−4)   **j** −3 + (−6)

3 Write down the answers to these.
   a −1 + 3   **b** −2 + (−5)   **c** 4 + (−7)   **d** −3 + (−1)   **e** −4 + 2
   f −4 + 6   **g** −9 + 6   **h** −5 + 5   **i** 2 + (−5)   **j** −4 + (−1)

4 Tacitus was born in 23 BC and died when he was 47.
   a Calculate −23 + 47.
   b In which year did Tacitus die?
   c In a similar way, find the year when:
      (i) Julius, born in 55 BC, died at the age of 60
      (ii) Caius, born in 72 BC, died at the age of 46
      (iii) Brutus, born in 12 BC, died at the age of 56.

5 A pin is put in at the point (–2, –5).

It is then moved 5 units to the right and 6 units down.

  a Calculate: **(i)** $-2 + 5$ **(ii)** $-5 + (-6)$.

  b Write down its new coordinates.

  c In a similar way, find the new positions of these pins:

    (i)   starts at (–2, 1), moves 3 units right and
        2 units up

    (ii) starts at (–5, –3), moves 2 units left and 4 units up

    (iii) starts at (–4, –5), moves 4 units right and 4 units down.

6 It's mid-winter in Aviemore!

The temperature is taken at noon each day for a week:

–4 °C, –1 °C, 3 °C, 3 °C, 1 °C, –3 °C, 1 °C.

Calculate the average temperature.

Subtracting integers

Study this pattern of numbers: Compare it with this pattern:

$$4 - 4 = 0 \qquad\qquad 4 + (-4) = 0$$
$$4 - 3 = 1 \qquad\qquad 4 + (-3) = 1$$
$$4 - 2 = 2 \qquad\qquad 4 + (-2) = 2$$
$$4 - 1 = 3 \qquad\qquad 4 + (-1) = 3$$
$$4 - 0 = 4 \qquad\qquad 4 + 0 = 4$$

We can continue the pattern:
$$\qquad\qquad\qquad\qquad 4 + 1 = 5$$
$$4 - (-1) = 5 \qquad\qquad 4 + 2 = 6$$
$$4 - (-2) = 6 \qquad\qquad 4 + 3 = 7$$
$$4 - (-3) = 7$$

Subtracting a number is the same as adding its negative.

Check these examples on a number line.
$$5 - 7 = 5 + (-7) = -2$$
$$-4 - 6 = -4 + (-6) = -10$$
$$-5 - (-3) = -5 + (3) = -2$$
$$5 - (-3) = 5 + (3) = 8$$

EXERCISE 6

1 Turn each of these subtractions into an addition, for example: $1 - 6 = 1 + (-6)$.

  a $1 - 2$ **b** $6 - 2$ **c** $8 - 1$ **d** $5 - 7$ **e** $4 - 5$ **f** $0 - 2$

2 Write down the answers to these.

  a $3 - 4$ **b** $4 - 8$ **c** $6 - 9$ **d** $1 - 4$ **e** $4 - 5$ **f** $2 - 12$

  g $2 - 8$ **h** $7 - 2$ **i** $7 - 9$ **j** $5 - 7$ **k** $12 - 15$ **l** $6 - 18$

  m $0 - 7$ **n** $1 - 9$

EXERCISE 7

1 Write down the answers to these.

a 4 – (–4)   **b** 4 – (–5)   **c** 7 – (–5)   **d** 8 – (–1)   **e** 0 – (–4)   **f** 1 – (–1)

g 1 – (–3)   **h** 3 – (–4)   **i** 2 – (–5)   **j** –1 – (–2)   **k** –3 – (–2)   **l** –5 – (–5)

2 Now try these.

a 3 – 7   **b** 4 – 5   **c** –1 – 6   **d** 3 – (–5)   **e** 2– (–9)   **f** –3 + (–4)

g –1 – 3   **h** –2 – 5   **i** 1 – (–6)   **j** –4 + (–1)   **k** –6 – 6   **l** –4 – 6

m –7 – 3   **n** –9 – (–6)

3 Calculate:

a 5 – (–4)   **b** 1 – (–5)   **c** 7 – (–3)   **d** 2 – (–3)   **e** 0 – (–10)   **f** –3 – (–4)

g –1 – (–5)   **h** –4 – (–6)   **i** –3 – (–4)   **j** –2 – (–1)   **k** –7 – (–3)   **l** –6 – (–5)

m –8 – (–4)   **n** 6 – (–6)   **o** –7 – (–7)

4 a The temperature in Wick one morning is 4 °C.
The temperature in Ullapool is –3 °C.
What is the difference in temperature?

b The temperature in Stranraer one evening is –2 °C.
The temperature in Eyemouth is –5 °C.
What is the difference in temperature? (Show all your working.)

5 The diagram shows the heights of various objects.

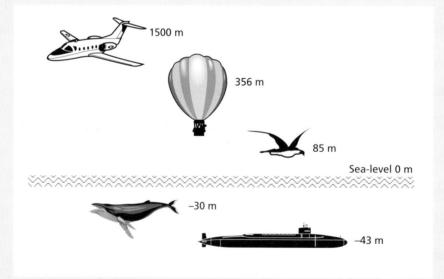

What is the difference in height between:
a the plane and the whale
b the balloon and the submarine
c the gull and the plane
d the whale and the submarine?

Multiplying and dividing integers

×	5	4	3	2	1	0	–1	–2	–3	–4
5	25	20	15	10	5	0				
4	20	16	12	8	4	0				
3	15	12	9	6	3	0				
2	10	8	6	4	2	0				
1	5	4	3	2	1	0				
0	0	0	0	0	0	0				
–1										
–2										
–3										
–4										

Area A

Area B

Look at row 1. It shows the 5 times table.

$$5 \times 5 = 25$$
$$5 \times 4 = 20$$
$$5 \times 3 = 15$$
$$5 \times 2 = 10$$
$$5 \times 1 = 5$$
$$5 \times 0 = 0$$

Notice each entry is 5 less than the previous entry.

Continue the pattern to complete the row.

$$5 \times (-1) = -5$$
$$5 \times (-2) = -10$$
$$5 \times (-3) = -15$$
$$5 \times (-4) = -20$$

Task 1 Use the same method as above to help you complete area A of the table.

Task 2 Look at column 1.

$$5 \times 5 = 25$$
$$4 \times 5 = 20$$
$$3 \times 5 = 15$$
$$2 \times 5 = 10$$
$$1 \times 5 = 5$$
$$0 \times 5 = 0$$

Continuing the pattern, 25, 20, 15, 10, 5, 0, ... (subtracting 5 each time), lets us complete the column:

$$-1 \times 5 = -5$$
$$-2 \times 5 = -10$$
$$-3 \times 5 = -15$$
$$-4 \times 5 = -20$$

Use this method to help you complete area B of the table.

Multiplying a *positive number* by a *negative number* results in a *negative answer*.
Multiplying a *negative number* by a *positive number* results in a *negative answer*.
The rules are the same for division. (Work the table backwards.)

Examples $3 \times (-6) = -18$ $-3 \times 6 = -18$ $-18 \div 6 = -3$

EXERCISE 8

1 Multiply these integers.

a $2 \times (-3)$ b $4 \times (-5)$ c $6 \times (-1)$ d $0 \times (-5)$ e $(-1) \times 3$ f $(-8) \times 2$

g $(-2) \times 5$ h $(-1) \times 0$ i 6×3 j $(-2) \times 6$ k $7 \times (-1)$ l $(-10) \times 10$

2 Divide these.

a $6 \div (-3)$ b $10 \div (-5)$ c $0 \div (-1)$ d $4 \div (-4)$ e $(-3) \div 1$

f $(-15) \div 5$ g $(-6) \div 6$ h $(-16) \div 8$ i $18 \div (-9)$ j $24 \div (-8)$

k $100 \div (-10)$ l $14 \div (-2)$ m $(-18) \div 3$

3 Divide again.

a $\dfrac{-6}{2}$ **b** $\dfrac{-25}{5}$ **c** $\dfrac{-4}{1}$ **d** $\dfrac{-30}{6}$ **e** $\dfrac{-24}{12}$ **f** $\dfrac{-32}{8}$

g $\dfrac{-34}{2}$ **h** $\dfrac{-81}{3}$ **i** $\dfrac{-100}{25}$ **j** $\dfrac{0}{5}$ **k** $\dfrac{-6}{6}$

4 a The temperatures at midnight one week in Glencoe were:
$-3\,°C, -1\,°C, -6\,°C, -7\,°C, -9\,°C, -10\,°C, -6\,°C$.
Calculate the average temperature.

b The following week the temperatures were:
$-2\,°C, -1\,°C, -1\,°C, -1\,°C, -1\,°C, -1\,°C, 0\,°C$.
Calculate this week's average temperature.

5 a Give the coordinates of the points A, B, C and D.

b A rectangle twice as big as ABCD can be made by multiplying each coordinate by 2.
Work out these coordinates.

c Plot the points to check that each side of the rectangle is twice a big.

d Find, by division, the coordinates of a rectangle half as big.

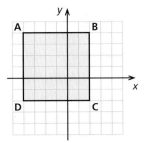

6

×	5	4	3	2	1	0	−1	−2	−3	−4
5	25	20	15	10	5	0	−5	−10	−15	−20
4	20	16	12	8	4	0	−4	−8	−12	−16
3	15	12	9	6	3	0	−3	−6	−9	−12
2	10	8	6	4	2	0	−2	−4	−6	−8
1	5	4	3	2	1	0	−1	−2	−3	−4
0	0	0	0	0	0	0	0	0	0	0
−1	−5	−4	−3	−2	−1	0				
−2	−10	−8	−6	−4	−2	0				
−3	−15	−12	−9	−6	−3	0				
−4	−20	−16	−12	−8	−4	0				

Look at the seventh row:

$-1 \times 5 = -5$
$-1 \times 4 = -4$
$-1 \times 3 = -3$
$-1 \times 2 = -2$
$-1 \times 1 = -1$
$-1 \times 0 = 0$

Continuing the pattern, we can complete the row: $-1 \times -1 = 1$
$-1 \times -2 = 2$
$-1 \times -3 = 3$
$-1 \times -4 = 4$

In a similar fashion complete the last three rows.

You should have noticed that:
   multiplying a *negative number* by a *negative number* results in a *positive answer*.
So now we know: signs the same, positive answer,
                         signs different, negative answer,
                  … and the same rules apply for division.

Examples $5 \times 9 = 45$ (signs the same, positive answer)
               $-5 \times (-9) = 45$ (signs the same, positive answer)
               $5 \times (-9) = -45$ (signs different, negative answer)
               $-45 \div (-9) = 5$ (signs the same, positive answer)
               $45 \div (-9) = -5$ (signs different, negative answer)

EXERCISE 9

1 Work out:

  a $-2 \times (-2)$ **b** $-5 \times (-4)$ **c** $-7 \times (-2)$ **d** $-5 \times (-1)$ **e** $12 \times (-2)$

  f -6×9 **g** $-8 \times (-5)$ **h** $7 \times (-5)$ **i** $-12 \times (-10)$ **j** $4 \times (-3)$

  k -9×7 **l** $25 \times (-4)$ **m** $-11 \times (-8)$ **n** $14 \times (-2)$ **o** -13×3

2 Evaluate:

  a $-6 \div (-2)$ **b** $-9 \div (-3)$ **c** $-20 \div (-4)$ **d** $-11 \div (-1)$ **e** $-8 \div (-8)$

  f $8 \div (-4)$ **g** $-36 \div 12$ **h** $-24 \div (-6)$ **i** $-21 \div (-1)$ **j** $36 \div (-6)$

3 Write down the value of:

  a $\dfrac{-25}{-5}$ **b** $\dfrac{-34}{-17}$ **c** $\dfrac{-30}{-6}$ **d** $\dfrac{-144}{-9}$ **e** $\dfrac{120}{-10}$ **f** $\dfrac{-40}{8}$ **g** $\dfrac{-49}{-7}$

  h $\dfrac{52}{4}$ **i** $\dfrac{72}{-3}$ **j** $\dfrac{-24}{-4}$ **k** $\dfrac{-45}{-9}$ **l** $\dfrac{36}{-2}$ **m** $\dfrac{96}{-3}$ **n** $\dfrac{-21}{-3}$

If you have a string of multiplications to do, take them two at a time.

Example 1 $-2 \times (-3) \times (-4)$ *Example 2* $2 \times (-3) \times (-4)$

    $= \quad 6 \quad\quad \times (-4)$ $= \quad -6 \quad\quad \times (-4)$

    $= \quad\quad -24$ $= \quad\quad 24$

---

4 Calculate:

  a $3 \times 1 \times 5$ **b** $-3 \times 1 \times 5$ **c** $-3 \times 1 \times (-5)$ **d** $-1 \times (-2) \times (-3)$

  e $-5 \times (-8) \times 0$ **f** $4 \times (-2) \times 5$ **g** $3 \times (-3) \times (-2)$ **h** $-1 \times (-1) \times (-1)$

  i $2 \times (-5) \times (-4)$ **j** $6 \times (-1) \times 3$ **k** $-7 \times 5 \times (-1)$ **l** $-10 \times (-2) \times (-3)$

5 $4^3 = 4 \times 4 \times 4 = 64$. In a similar way evaluate:

  a $(-2)^3$ **b** $(-1)^4$ **c** $(-3)^3$ **d** $(-2)^4$

EXERCISE 10

Try these without a calculator, then use your calculator to check your answers.

1 $7 - 8$ **2** $-4 + 9$ **3** $-1 - 6$ **4** $3 + (-7)$

5 $-5 + (-2)$ **6** $5 \times (-4)$ **7** $10 \div (-2)$ **8** -3×2

9 $-10 + (-4)$ **10** $3 - 11$ **11** -4×5 **12** $-1 + 10$

13 $3 + (-12)$ **14** $-45 \div 9$ **15** $-20 + (-1)$ **16** $20 \div (-10)$

17 $15 \times (-1)$ **18** $-5 + 7$ **19** $3 + (-9)$ **20** $-7 + 6$

21 -9×2 **22** $21 \div (-3)$ **23** $-4 - 9$ **24** $8 + (-12)$

25 $-5 \div (-5)$ **26** $2 - (-4)$ **27** $-3 \times (-8)$ **28** $-10 \div (-5)$

29 $-4 - (-10)$ **30** $-35 \div (-7)$ **31** $-10 \times (-100)$ **32** $-6 - (-5)$

33 $-3 \times (-7) \times (-2)$ **34** $-5 \times 4 \times (-3)$ **35** $(-2)^5$ **36** $(-1)^6$

CHAPTER 11 REVIEW

1 Make a list of the places marked on this diagram and their coordinates.

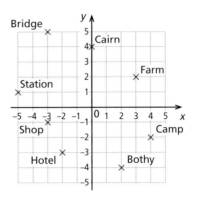

2 On a coordinate diagram plot the points A(0, 3), B(−2, 0), C(2, 6) and D(−4, −3).
   a What do you notice about these four points?
   b The point (−6, y) is part of the pattern. What is the value of y?
   c The point (x, −9) is part of the pattern. What is the value of x?

3 The temperature in Banff at midnight was −3 °C. By 6 am it had fallen 2 degrees. In the following six hours it rose 8 degrees.
   Write down the temperatures at:
   a 6 am
   b noon.

4 A diver is 25 m below sea-level.
   a A wreck lies at the bottom of the sea 65 m below the diver.
     How deep is the sea?
   b A helicopter hovers at a height of 30 m. It is directly above the diver.
     What is the distance between the helicopter and (i) the diver   (ii) the wreck?

5 Jeremiah was born in 37 BC and lived until he was 62 years old.
   In what year did he die?

6 Calculate the average of these temperatures:
   −7 °C, −5 °C, 3 °C, 0 °C, 2 °C, −4 °C, −3 °C.

7 Calculate:
   a $1 - 7$ b $5 + (-3)$ c $6 \times (-3)$ d $-9 + (-4)$ e $-4 + 3$

   f $-6 + 8$ g -3×7 h $-20 \div 4$ i $-10 - 11$ j $16 \div (-2)$

   k $2 + (-10)$ l $7 \times (-1)$ m $-5 - 4$ n $\dfrac{-60}{10}$ o $\dfrac{30}{-6}$

12 Statistics

STARTING POINTS

1 The shoe sizes of a group of students are:

  8 9 7 8 7 8 8 6 8 7

Shoe size	Tally	Total
6		
7		
8		
9		

  a Copy and complete the table.
  b Which size is the most common?
  c How many students are in the survey?

2

  180 cm   178 cm   182 cm   184 cm   178 cm   179 cm   175 cm

  a List these students' heights in order of size, smallest first.
  b Which is the **(i)** tallest   **(ii)** smallest height?

3 Calculate the difference between the maximum and minimum temperatures on each
  day.

  a Saturday

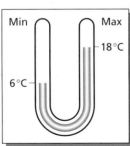

  b Sunday

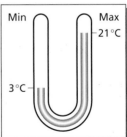

4 For the students in your group:
  a What is the typical age?
  b What is the most typical hair colour?
  c Guess the average height.
  d Guess the average shoe size.

The mean

Mean = total ÷ number of items

Example 1
Joan earns a total of £80 over 4 days.
Her mean earnings = £80 ÷ 4 = £20.

Example 2
Bashir records the time he waits for the bus over a week.

Mon	Tue	Wed	Thu	Fri
10 min	12 min	7 min	6 min	10 min

Total time = 10 + 12 + 7 + 6 + 10 = 45 minutes
Number of days = 5
Mean waiting time = 45 ÷ 5 = 9 minutes

EXERCISE 1

1 Three melons weigh a total of 6 kg. What is the mean weight?

2 a What is the total weight of the three parcels?
b Calculate the mean weight.

3

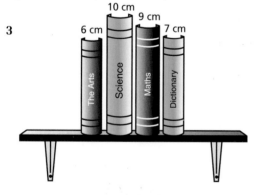

    a What is the total width of the books?
    b How many books are there?
    c Calculate the mean width.

4 Mrs Marks records the number of absentees in the office over a week.

Mon	Tue	Wed	Thu	Fri
4	2	0	3	6

Calculate:
a the total number of absentees for the week
b the mean number of absentees for the week.

5 These are Laura's scores in a golf tournament: 76, 68, 74, 66.
   a Calculate her mean score.
   b By how much is her highest score above the mean?

6 Martin is a part-time taxi driver.
   He draws a graph to show how many
   kilometres he travels each evening.
   a Calculate the mean.
   b **(i)** On which day did he drive the
       furthest?
     (ii) How much above the mean did he
       drive on this day?

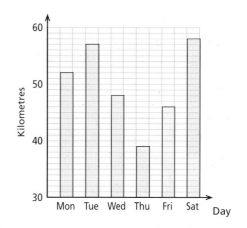

EXERCISE 2

1 The engine sizes of the company cars in a small business are listed:
   2.0 L, 1.7 L, 2.5 L, 4.0 L, 3.2 L, 1.1 L, 2.3 L.
   a Calculate the mean engine size.
   b Is the greatest engine size much more than the mean?

2 Two students, Kanti and Sue compare
   their marks in a set of maths tests.
   a Calculate the mean score for each
       student.
   b Who has the higher mean? By how
       many?

Test	1	2	3	4	5
Kanti	64	76	78	58	64
Sue	70	72	68	54	61

3 Tim and Sarah compare their scores in a computer game.
   Tim's scores are 140, 200, 180, 170, 250, 260.
   Sarah, who has played one game less, scores 150, 190, 210, 280, 220.
   a Calculate the mean score for each player.
   b Who is the better player?

4 The weights (in kilograms) of two rowing crews are:

   a Which is the heavier crew?
   b Calculate the mean weight of each crew.
   c By how many kilograms is one mean greater than the other?

The range

Example 1

For yeast to grow when making wine, the temperature
should be not less than 30 °C and not more than 50 °C.
50 – 30 = 20
The range is 20 °C.

Example 2

Hours of sunshine are recorded for a week.
The number of hours are 2.8, 8.4, 6.2, 3.6, 1.8, 2
and 3.7.
The range = greatest – least
8.4 – 1.8 = 6.6
The range is 6.6 hours.

Range = greatest – least

EXERCISE 3

1 **a** Pupils at Parkside High are aged from 11 to 18. What is the range?
   b The ages of pupils at East Moor Primary range from 5 to 12 years.
       Students at Moorside College have ages ranging from 16 to 45 years.
       (i) Find the range of each place.
       (ii) Which has the bigger range in ages?

2 The Clyde Tunnel has a maximum speed limit of 30 mph and a minimum speed
   limit of 8 mph. Calculate the range in speeds.

3 The lengths of the holes at a 9-hole golf course are:
   480, 358, 190, 456, 330, 120, 394, 288 and 475 yards.
   a What is the length of: **(i)** the longest hole   **(ii)** the shortest hole?
   b Calculate the range.

4 Mr White lists the wattage of all the light bulbs in his house:
   100 W, 40 W, 100 W, 150 W, 250 W, 200 W, 60 W and 100 W.
   Calculate the range.

5 The final scores in a local soccer league are: 2–0, 3–3, 0–1, 2–1, 5–0, 1–1, 3–0, 0–4.
   a Work out the total number of goals scored at each match.
   b What is the **(i)** greatest   **(ii)** least total number of goals scored in a match?
   c Calculate the range of total goals scored in a match.

6 Two machines fill boxes with thumb tacks. There are supposed to be 50 tacks per
   box. Six boxes from each machine are checked.

   | Machine A | 51 | 47 | 53 | 50 | 49 | 50 |
   | Machine B | 46 | 50 | 48 | 50 | 54 | 52 |

   a Work out the range for each machine.
   b Which machine seems to be more reliable?

EXERCISE 4

1 The heights of a group of students are:
   1.72 m, 1.81 m, 1.69 m, 1.75 m, 1.74 m, 1.70 m, 1.64 m and 1.78 m.
   Calculate the range of heights.

2 In a 4×400 m relay race the winning team's times (in seconds) for each part are:
   63 s, 59 s, 63 s and 57 s.
   a Calculate **(i)** the range **(ii)** the mean time.
   b The second team had times of 60 s, 61 s, 59 s and 60 s.
      (i) Calculate the range of this team's times.
      (ii) Which team had the more consistent set of runners?

3 A building company orders kitchen units from two suppliers.
   A note is kept of the number of weeks it takes for an order to arrive.

   Here are the figures for eight different orders.

   | Fine Fittings | 6 8 8 3 4 12 7 16 |
   | Kosy Kitchens | 8 7 9 8 6 7 6 9 |

   a Calculate **(i)** the mean number of weeks and
      (ii) the range of weeks for each supplier.
   b Which supplier would you advise the company to use in future? Give two reasons.

4 An engineering company plans to buy chains.
   They measure the breaking point of six samples from two different companies.
   On a scale of 1 to 15, the bigger the breaking point the better the chain.

   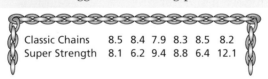

   | Classic Chains | 8.5 8.4 7.9 8.3 8.5 8.2 |
   | Super Strength | 8.1 6.2 9.4 8.8 6.4 12.1 |

   a Calculate the mean and range of the breaking points.
   b Which would you recommend? Give your reasons.

5 Here are descriptions of four darts players in a tournament.

   Debbie:
   brilliant at darts, always gets a high score.

   Mike:
   terrible at darts, but sometimes is very lucky.

   Sarah:
   very good at darts, but occasionally misses the board.

   Trevor:
   can hardly hit the board, never gets a good score.

   Match each player with one of these statistics:

A	B	C	D
Mean is high	Mean is low	Mean is high	Mean is low
Range is low	Range is low	Range is high	Range is high

The mode

The mode is the most frequent value. It is possible to have more than one mode.

Example 1
In this diagram there are more triangles
than any other shape.
The triangle is the mode.

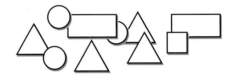

Example 2
1, 1, 2, 2, 2, 3, 3, 3, 3, 4, 4, 4, 4, 5, 6.
In this list, 3 and 4 occur more often than any other score.
The modes are 3 and 4.

Example 3
The shoe sizes of a group of students are:

8, 7, 7, 8, 9, 6, 9, 8, 8, 7,
6, 5, 9, 8, 7, 8, 9, 6, 5, 8.

When there are a lot of data it helps to make
a frequency table.

The size that occurs most is 8. The mode is 8.

Shoe size	Tally	Frequency
5	||	2
6	|||	3
7	||||	4
8	ＨＨ ||	7
9	|||| ·	4

EXERCISE 5

1 Here are the scores from nine rolls of the dice:
  3, 6, 1, 2, 5, 3, 3, 3, 6.
  a Which score is the mode?
  b State the range in scores.

2 Kate looks at her report grades:
  B, A, B, C, D, B, A, B.
  a Which grade is the mode? **b** Does the range have any meaning here?

3 At her market stall Mrs Malik records the sizes of
  T-shirts sold one day:
  M, S, L, M, L, S, M, M, S, S, M,
  L, L, M, M, S, L, L, S, L, M, M.
  a Copy and complete the table.
  b Which size is the mode?

Size	Tally	Frequency
S		
M		
L		

4 This table shows the pars for the holes at Sandside Golf Course.

Hole	1	2	3	4	5	6	7	8	9	10	11	12	13	14	15	16	17	18
Par	4	3	3	4	3	3	5	3	4	4	3	3	5	3	4	4	3	4

  a Copy and complete the table.
  b Which par is the mode?

Par	Tally	Frequency
3		
4		
5		

5 The waist size for men's trousers is usually given in inches.
   Sam's waist is 32 inches.
   His friends' sizes are: 34, 28, 32, 32, 30, 30, 36, 34, 32, 30, 28, 32, 30.
   a State the range of the sizes.
   b Make a frequency table of Sam's friends' waist sizes.
   c What is the mode (or modes)?
   d How does Sam compare?

EXERCISE 6

1 A store sells milk in 1 litre, 2 litre and 4 litre packs.
   Its sales for one morning are shown in the diagram.

   a Make a frequency table.
   b What is the mode?
   c Calculate the mean.
   d Is the mode or the mean more typical?

Milk Sales
1, 2, 1, 1, 2,
2, 4, 2, 2, 4,
4, 4, 2, 1, 4,
4, 2, 2, 2, 2

2 John and Ben are strikers for rival soccer teams.
   Here are their scoring records for the games they have played this season.

Game	1	2	3	4	5	6	7	8	9	10	11	12
John	0	3	3	0	0	0	0	3	0	0	0	3
Ben	1	2	1	1	1	1	2	1	1	0	0	1

   a Find the mode for each player.
   b Is it fair to judge them by their modes? Explain.

3 The judges in an ice-skating competition give Emma these scores.

   | 5.6 | 5.8 | 6.0 | 5.6 | 5.6 | 5.9 | 6.0 | 5.9 | 6.0 | 5.6 |

   a Find the mode.
   b Calculate the mean.
   c Which of these averages gives the fairer picture of her performance?

4 The makers of a TV holiday programme decide to compare two seaside resorts.
   They record the hours of sunshine each day in July for both resorts.

Seaside resorts	Mode	Range
Sandy Bay	3	8
Rockton-on-Sea	8	3

   Which do you think had the better weather? Why?

151

The median

The median is a score which splits a list into two equal parts.

To find the median:

- list the items in order of size
- if there is an odd number of items, find the middle one
- if there is an even number of items, take the mean of the middle two.

Example 1

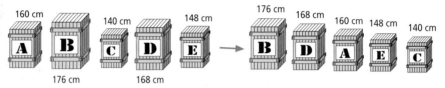

Five crates sit in a warehouse. They are put in order, biggest first.

Crate A is the middle one. Its height is 160 cm.

160 cm is the median height.

Example 2

Crate C is removed, leaving four crates.

Now the middle lies between crates D and A.

$(168 + 160) \div 2 = 164$

164 cm is the median height.

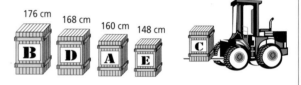

EXERCISE 7

1 Work out the median of each of the following lists:

   a 1, 2, 3, 4, 4, 5, 8   **b** 1, 4, 5, 10, 20, 99, 101, 111, 123

   c 2, 5, 7, 3   **d** 9, 12, 34, 51, 66, 14, 1, 5, 3

2 Five different-sized toothpaste tubes are on sale in a shop.

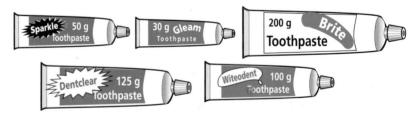

   a List them in order, smallest size first.

   b Which is the median size?

3 a List Yvonne's grades in order.

   b What is her median grade?

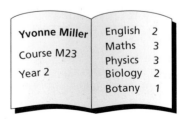

Yvonne Miller	English	2
Course M23	Maths	3
	Physics	3
Year 2	Biology	2
	Botany	1

4 Find the mean of:
  a 10 and 20   **b** 63 and 69   **c** 16 and 16   **d** 49 and 54   **e** 220 and 294.

5 Four friends go on a Club 18–30 holiday. Their ages are 25, 28, 19 and 21.
  a List their ages in order, youngest first.
  b Calculate the median age.

6 A perfume is sold in different-sized bottles:
  20 ml, 10 ml, 24 ml, 80 ml, 30 ml and 50 ml.
  a List these sizes in order.
  b Calculate the median size.

7 Gary makes these scores when playing darts:
  26, 80, 61, 5, 100, 26, 45 and 65.
  a Find the median.
  b His next score is 120. What is the new median?

EXERCISE 8

1 Here are Natasha's scores in a women's gymnastics competition:
  Beam 9.4   Assymetric bars 9.9   Floor 9.4   Vault 9.8.
  a What is the mode?
  b Find the median.
  c Does the mode or the median give the better idea of her overall performance?

2 In the men's competition Uri's scores are:
  Floor 9.3   Rings 9.7   Vault 9.9   Parallel bars 9.5
  Pommels 9.9   Horizontal bar 8.1.
  a Find the median.
  b Calculate the mean.
  c Which gives the better idea of his overall performance?

3 The number of days that patients take to recover after an operation are recorded as:
  10   6   4   3   5   10   3   10   4   5
  5   10   5   3   10   6   4   3   10   4
  a What is the mode?
  b Find the median.
  c Calculate the mean.
  d Which of the averages is the least typical?
  e Which would you use as the most typical?

4 Jill's phone bill lists the cost of calls over 10 minutes.
  £0.40   £0.65   £3.85   £0.57   £0.48
  £0.52   £0.71   £0.42   £0.55   £0.86
  £0.29   £0.77   £7.63   £0.50   £0.59
  a Why is the mode no use here?
  b Find **(i)** the mean   **(ii)** the median.
  c Why is the median more typical than the mean?

Frequency tables

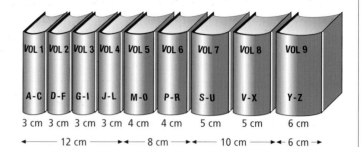

The widths of the books
can be shown in a
frequency table:

Width (cm)	Frequency	Width × frequency
3	4	3 × 4 = 12
4	2	4 × 2 = 8
5	2	5 × 2 = 10
6	1	6 × 1 = 6
Total 9		36

Total of widths (cm)

Total number of books

36 ÷ 9 = 4

The mean is 4 cm. The mode (most common) is 3 cm.

The median is 4 cm (out of nine books the middle one is the fifth).

EXERCISE 9

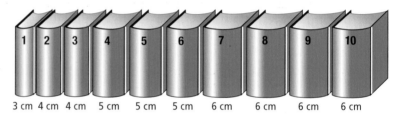

1 a Copy and
complete the
table for
these books.

Thickness (cm)	Frequency	Thickness × frequency
3	1	3 × 1 =
4	2	4 × 2 =
5		
6		
Total		

b Mean = total thickness ÷ number of books. Calculate the mean.

c What is the mode?

2 Sixteen people hire skates at the
ice-rink. The sizes are:

6, 6, 6, 6, 6, 6, 6, 6,

6, 6, 8, 8, 9, 9, 9, 9.

a Copy and complete the table.

b Calculate the mean skate size.

c What is the mode?

d Is the mean or the mode better to use for this group of skaters?

Skate size	Frequency	Size × frequency
6	10	6 × 10 =
8		
9		
Total		

3 A market gardener counts the peas in a sample of pods.

a Copy and complete the table.

b Calculate the mean number of peas per pod.

c What is the mode?

d Is the mode or the mean the more typical value?

No. of peas Score	No. of pods Frequency	Score × frequency
1	6	1 × 6 =
2	8	
3	6	
4	4	
5	2	
6	4	
Total		

4 The amounts won by competitors in the Gala Day races are:

£1, £1, £10, £5, £1, £1, £1, £10, £10, £20, £1, £1, £10, £20, £1, £1, £1, £5, £10, £10.

Amount (£)	Tally	Frequency	Amount × frequency
£1	⊬⊬ ⊬⊬	10	£1 × 10 =
£5			
£10			
£20			
Total			

a Copy and complete the table.   b Calculate the mean amount won.

c What is the mode?

d Is the mean or the mode more typical of the amount won?

e What is the range of the amounts won?

5 The table shows the annual wages of all the staff in a factory.

a Copy and complete the table.

b Calculate the mean wage.

c What is the mode?

d Calculate the range.

e Is the mode or the mean more typical?

Wages (in £1000 s)	Frequency	Wages × frequency
10	5	
15	2	
20	2	
80	1	
Total		

Summary

Mean = total (sum) ÷ number of items

Range = greatest value – least value

Mode = most frequent value

Median = the middle value when put in order.

Note: when there are two middle values, find halfway between them.

Probability

If you go bird spotting around town,

| you won't see a dodo | you're unlikely to see an owl | there's a fair chance of seeing a blue tit | you'll very likely spot a gull | you're almost certain to spot a starling. |

In mathematics we measure likelihood on a scale of 0 to 1.

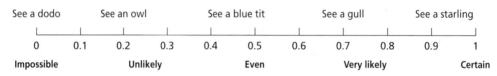

'0' stands for **impossible** and '1' for **certain**.
You can calculate or estimate the likelihood or **probability**, as it is called, in different ways.

1 Theoretical

$$\text{Probability} = \frac{\text{Number of favourable outcomes}}{\text{Number of possible outcomes}}$$

Example 1   What is the probability of a coin landing head up when you spin it?

There is only one head. There are two possible outcomes (a head or a tail).
So the probability of getting a head is $\frac{1}{2} = 0.5$.

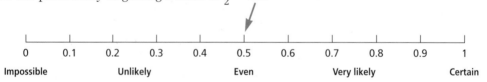

2 Experimental

$$\text{Probability} = \frac{\text{Number of successful trials}}{\text{Number of observed trials}}$$

Example 2   Jeff observed 80 birds. 64 were gulls. Estimate the probability of seeing a gull.

The probability of seeing a gull is $\frac{64}{80} = 0.8$.

EXERCISE 10

Work to 2 decimal places where appropriate.

1

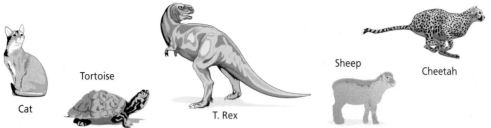

Tortoise

Cat

T. Rex

Sheep

Cheetah

Which of these animals is a person living in town likely to see next?
Draw a likelihood line.
Show (roughly) the likelihood of a person living in town seeing each of the animals.

2 A dice is rolled.
  a **(i)** List all the possible outcomes.
    (ii) List the even numbers.
    (iii) What is the probability of rolling an even number?
  b **(i)** List the outcomes less than 3.
    (ii) What is the probability of rolling a number less than 3?
  c What is the probability of rolling: **(i)** a 5   **(ii)** more than 5   **(iii)** less than 5?

3 A pack contains the usual 52 cards. One card is picked at random.
  a **(i)** How many are red?
    (ii) What is the probability that the card is red?
  b **(i)** How many hearts are there?
    (ii) What is the probability that the card is a heart?
  c **(i)** How many queens are there?
    (ii) Calculate the probability that the card is a queen.
  d What is the probability that the card is the ace of spades?

4

1 2 3
4 5 6
7 8 9
* 0 #

The diagram shows the key pad of a phone.
A button is pushed without looking.
  a **(i)** How many buttons are there?
    (ii) How many contain a digit less than 6?
    (iii) What is the probability that the button is
        a digit less than 6?

  b **(i)** How many buttons contain a digit greater than 6?
    (ii) What is the probability that the button pushed is a digit greater than 6?
  c To 2 decimal places, what is the probability that the button pushed is a 6?

5 A basket contains 16 eggs. Four are brown and the rest are white.
Five are cracked. One is bad.
Calculate the probability that an egg picked at random will be:
  a brown
  b bad
  c not cracked.

6 The table shows the number of each type of tree in a park.

Type	Number
Oak	8
Elm	12
Chestnut	16
Beech	24

a How many trees are there?

b Someone reports that one tree has been damaged. Use the table to help you estimate the probability that the damaged tree is: **(i)** an oak **(ii)** a beech tree.

7 A shopowner keeps a note of the size of her customers' shopping bills to the nearest £10.

Size of bill	Number of bills
£10	12
£20	15
£30	25
£40	20
£50	10
more	18

a How many bills were recorded?

b Use the table to help you estimate the probability that the next customer will spend:
(i) £10 **(ii)** £30 **(iii)** more than £50 **(iv)** more than £40.

8 The Card Shop notes the different types of Christmas cards they sell.

Type	Number of cards
Religious	50
Snow Scene	36
Santa	46
Candles/Holly	57
Toys	23
Other	64

a How many cards were sold?

b Use the table to help you estimate the probability that the next card sold will have:
(i) a religious theme
(ii) a Santa theme
(iii) a toy theme
(iv) other.

CHAPTER 12 REVIEW

1   Ahmed scores a total of 180 runs over six cricket matches.
    Calculate his mean score.

2   Michelle writes down the number of lectures she has each
    week in each subject.
    What number of lectures is the mode?

Maths	6
English	6
Languages	8
Technology	4
Science	6
Geography	4

3   Four friends form a pop group. They buy drums at £600,
    a bass guitar at £450, a rhythm guitar at £500 and a synthesizer at £800.
    a Calculate the mean cost of their instruments.
    b A singer joins them and shares the cost. Calculate the new mean cost.

4   The heights, to the nearest 10 m, of the hills known as the Five Sisters of Kintail, are:
    1030 m, 990 m, 1070 m, 930 m, 1000 m.
    a Calculate the range.
    b Find the median.

5   These are the competitors' times (in seconds) in a 400 m race:
    54 s, 48 s, 46 s, 57 s, 52 s and 45 s.
    a Find the median.
    b By how much does the winner beat the median time?

6   This table gives data about the frequency of students' visits to the cinema in a
    month.

Number of visits	Frequency	Number × frequency
0	15	
1	10	
2	5	
3	8	
4	6	
5	4	
6	2	
Total		

    a What is the range?
    b Calculate the mean.
    c What is the mode?
    d Is the mode or the mean the most typical? Why?

7

a (i) How many numbers are on the spinner?
  (ii) How many even numbers are on the spinner?
  (iii) What is the probability that the spinner will land on an even number?
b What is the probability that the spinner will stop at 3?

8 A survey on favourite ball sports produced the following table.

Favourite sport	Number of votes
Tennis	12
Rugby	16
Cricket	8
Soccer	24
Golf	16
Other	4

a (i) How many votes were cast?
  (ii) How many voted for rugby?
  (iii) Use the table to estimate the probability that a person picked at random will chose rugby as their favourite ball sport.
b Estimate the probability that a person picked at random will chose cricket as their favourite ball sport.

13 Revising Unit 2

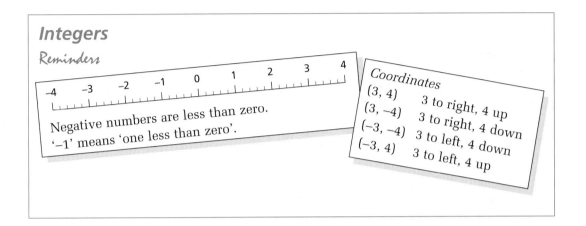

Integers

Reminders

Negative numbers are less than zero.
'−1' means 'one less than zero'.

Coordinates
(3, 4)   3 to right, 4 up
(3, −4)   3 to right, 4 down
(−3, −4)   3 to left, 4 down
(−3, 4)   3 to left, 4 up

EXERCISE 1

1 The coordinates of the point A are
(1, 3).
Write down the coordinates of the
points B, C, D, ... J.

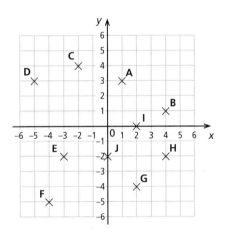

2 Plot the following points on a coordinate diagram:
K(3, 5), L(6, 2), M(−3, 5), N(−5, 1), O(0, 0), P(−6, −2), Q(−3, −4), R(0, −3), S(3, −6),
T(5, −1), U(3, 0).

3 Each of these temperatures falls by 4 degrees. Write down the new temperatures.
   a 7 °C   **b** 4 °C   **c** 2 °C   **d** 0 °C   **e** −3 °C

4 Each of these temperatures rises by 5 degrees. Write down the new temperatures.
   a 0 °C   **b** −2 °C   **c** −4 °C   **d** −8 °C   **e** −11 °C

5

	Aberdeen	Edinburgh	Glasgow	London	Torquay
Temperature at midnight	−1 °C	0 °C	1 °C	2 °C	4 °C
Temperature at 6 am	−3 °C	−6 °C	−5 °C	−3 °C	−1 °C
Temperature at noon	5 °C	−3 °C	−1 °C	8 °C	9 °C

a What happened to the temperature in each place between midnight and 6 am?
b What happened to the temperatures between 6 am and noon?

6 Calculate:
    a −3 + 4   **b** −2 + 8   **c** −5 + 9   **d** 4 + (−3)   **e** 6 + (−2)   **f** 5 + (−6)
    g −3 + (−3)   **h** −4 + (−1)   **i** −6 + (−2)   **j** −8 + (−3)   **k** 4 + (−4)   **l** 3 + (−3)

7 Calculate:
    a −3 − 5   **b** −2 − 3   **c** −6 − 1   **d** 2 − 7   **e** 9 − 12   **f** 5 − 6
    g −3 − (−3)   **h** −5 − (−2)   **i** −4 − (−9)   **j** −1 − (−3)   **k** 6 − (−6)   **l** 7 − (−1)

8 Calculate:
    a 3 × (−4)   **b** (−2) × 7   **c** (−8) ÷ 1   **d** −30 ÷ 10   **e** −20 ÷ 2   **f** (−8) × 2
    g (−6) ÷ 3   **h** 6 × (−7)   **i** (−10) × 10   **j** −12 ÷ 1   **k** −36 ÷ 4   **l** (−1) × 0

9 Plot the points P(2, 4), Q(6, −6), R(−2, −8) and S(−6, 2) on a coordinate diagram.
    a What shape is PQRS?
    b What are the coordinates of the point where the diagonals meet?

10

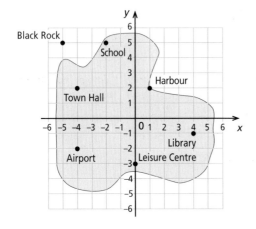

    a Make a list of the places marked on the map.
    b Beside each place in your list write its coordinates.
    c A new map is drawn with the origin at the harbour.
        Write down the new coordinates of:
        (i) the town hall
        (ii) the airport
        (iii) the school
        (iv) the leisure centre.

11 The city of Rome was founded in the year 753 BC. How old is it now?

12 The rows, columns and two diagonals of the square all add up to the same number.
    a What is the number?
    b Calculate the values of A, B and C.

−1	−6	1
0	C	B
−5	A	−3

13 The table shows the 'profit' made by the company 'Ed's Beds' in the first six months of last year.

Month	Jan	Feb	Mar	Apr	May	Jun
Profit (£100s)	−4	2	3	−4	1	5

   a What does a negative profit mean?

   b How did the company do in **(i)** February   **(ii)** April?

   c What was the total profit over **(i)** January and February
      (ii) March, April and May?

   d Calculate the total profit over the six months.

14 Mick and Monty play a new darts game.
Each person throws ten darts and then works out his total score.

Mick's darts are shown by ×.

Monty's darts are shown by **O**.

   a Calculate each player's total score.

   b Who has the higher score? How much higher?

   c Molly has a turn. Her ten throws produce these scores:
     −2, 1, 3, −4, −2, 5, 3, 1, −4, 3.
     Calculate Molly's total score.

   d How much higher is it than **(i)** Mick's   **(ii)** Monty's?

   e Now it's Mae's turn. Her first nine throws produce these scores:
     3, −2, −2, 1, −4, 5, 1, −2, −2.
     Can Mae beat Molly? Give a reason for your answer.

15 A survey was carried out of the arrival times of ten trains at Waverley Station.
The table shows the results.
The first train was 8 minutes late. This was written as +8.
The tenth train was 5 minutes early. This was written as −5.

Train	1	2	3	4	5	6	7	8	9	10
Time	+8	+3	−1	−12	+4	−3	−5	+7	−6	−5

   a Which train was nearest to being on time?

   b Calculate the average time for the ten trains.

   c Is a train more likely to be early or late? By how many minutes?

16 Calculate:

   a 6 − (−3)   **b** −3 − (−5)   **c** 8 + (−4)   **d** −7 + (−5)

   e −1 − (−3)   **f** −6 − (−4)   **g** −5 − (−1)   **h** −8 − (−9)

   i (−4) × (−3)   **j** (−20) × (−2)   **k** (−8) ÷ (−2)   **l** (−6) ÷ (−6)

17 Calculate:

   a 3 × (−2) × 4   **b** (−5) × (−4) × (−3)   **c** (−4) × 3 × (−5)

Speed, distance and time

$S = \dfrac{D}{T}$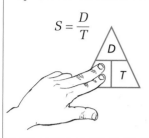

$D = S \times T$

$T = \dfrac{D}{S}$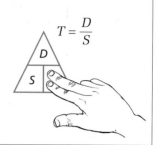

EXERCISE 2

1

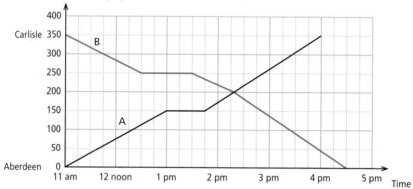

Distance from Aberdeen (km)

The distance/time graph shows the journey of a car travelling from Aberdeen to Carlisle (A) and a car travelling from Carlisle to Aberdeen (B).

a How far is it from Aberdeen to Carlisle?

b How long did it take car A to travel from Aberdeen to Carlisle?

c How long did the journey take car B from Carlisle to Aberdeen?

d How long did car A stop?

e When did the cars pass each other?

f Approximately how far from Aberdeen were they when they passed each other?

g When did car B reach Aberdeen?

2 This distance/time graph shows the race between two greyhounds, 'At the Double' and 'Fleetfoot'.

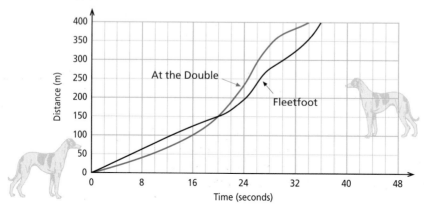

a Which greyhound went into the lead at the beginning of the race?
b What happened after 150 m? How long had the dogs been running then?
c Which dog won the race?
d Estimate the time each dog took to cover the 400 m.

3

	Clock-in	Clock-out
Monday	8.15 am	4.15 pm
Tuesday	8.20 am	4.10 pm
Wednesday	8.17 am	3.02 pm
Thursday	8.28 am	4.45 pm
Friday	8.45 am	4.10 pm

Part of Sal's timesheet is shown.
a How long is she at work each day?
b How long is she at work altogether over the five days?

4 a A girl cycles for 3 hours at an average speed of 40 km/h.
What distance does she travel?
b A train has an average speed of 30 mph for 240 miles.
How long does the journey take?
c A car travels 540 km in 6 hours.
What is its average speed in km/h?
d An athlete runs 100 m in 10.6 seconds.
What is her average speed in m/s?

5 Ali and Tariq race to the top of Ben Lawers and down again.

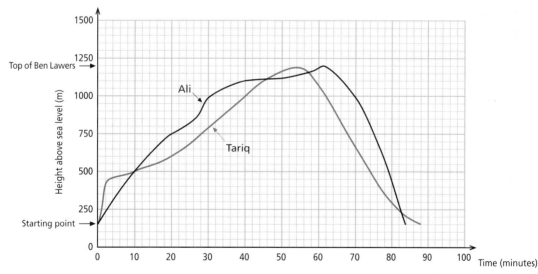

a What is the height of Ben Lawers?
b What was the winning time?
c What happened 500 m up the mountain? When was this?
d Who was first to the top of the Ben? How long did it take him?
e How long did it take Tariq to run down the mountain?
f Describe what happened after 58 minutes of the race.

6 The table shows part of a bus timetable.

Place	Time
Crosbie (dep.)	11 17
Darley	11 35
Fullarton	12 14
Lothian (arr.)	13 17

a How long is the journey from Crosbie to Fullarton?

b The distance from Crosbie to Lothian is 196 km.
What is the average speed for this journey?

c The distance from Crosbie to Fullarton is 90 km.
Is the average speed for this journey more or less than 90 km/h? Explain your answer.

7

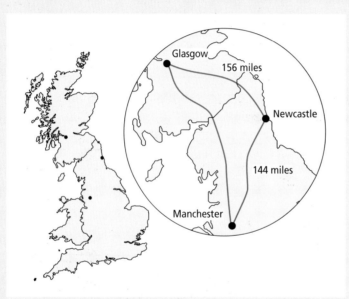

a Sinita drives from Glasgow to Newcastle at an average speed of 48 mph.
How long does the journey take her? (Answer in hours and minutes.)

b It takes her $2\frac{1}{2}$ hours to drive from Newcastle to Manchester.
Calculate her average speed for the journey.

c Driving at an average speed of 60 mph, it takes Sinita $3\frac{2}{3}$ hours to drive home to Glasgow from Manchester.
How far is the drive from Manchester to Glasgow?

The Theorem of Pythagoras

Reminders

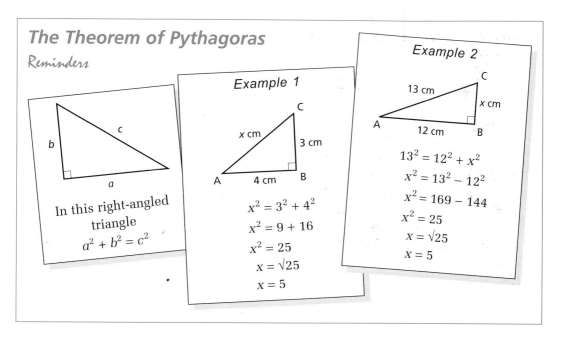

In this right-angled triangle
$$a^2 + b^2 = c^2$$

Example 1

$$x^2 = 3^2 + 4^2$$
$$x^2 = 9 + 16$$
$$x^2 = 25$$
$$x = \sqrt{25}$$
$$x = 5$$

Example 2

$$13^2 = 12^2 + x^2$$
$$x^2 = 13^2 - 12^2$$
$$x^2 = 169 - 144$$
$$x^2 = 25$$
$$x = \sqrt{25}$$
$$x = 5$$

EXERCISE 3

Where appropriate, give answers correct to 1 decimal place.

1 Calculate the length of AC in each triangle.

a 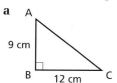   **b** 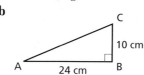   **c**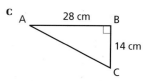

2 Calculate the length of PQ in each triangle.

a 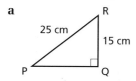   **b** 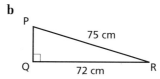   **c**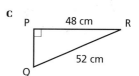

3 Calculate the length of the unknown side in each triangle.

a 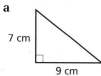   **b**   **c**

4 Each shape below is either a rectangle or a square.
Calculate the length of each diagonal.

a 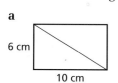   **b**   **c** 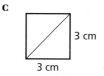   **d**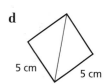

5 Calculate the length of the escalator rail, JK.

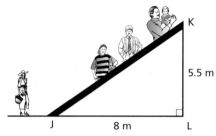

6

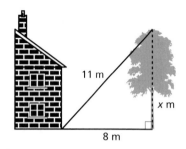

The tree is rotten and about to fall over.
When it falls, will it hit the house? Explain your answer.

7 A garden is in the shape of a right-angled triangle.
New fencing is being erected right round the garden.
Calculate the length of fencing required.

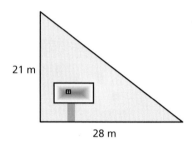

8 Ken needs to fix the roof of his house.
His ladder is 5.6 m long and needs to reach 5.2 m up the wall.
The ground is horizontal.
Ken places the foot of the ladder 3 m from the foot of the wall.
Will the ladder reach?

9

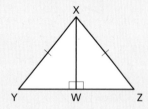

a Triangle XYZ is isosceles with XY = XZ.
YZ = 10 cm and XW = 9 cm.
Find the lengths of the two equal sides.

b ABCD is a kite.
Calculate the lengths of the diagonals AC and BD.

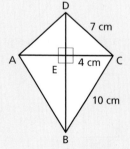

10 **a** A is the point (1, 3) and B is the point (7, 5).
   (i) Draw the line AB on a coordinate diagram.
   (ii) Use Pythagoras to find the length of the line AB.
   b Repeat **a** for the line CD where C is the point (−4, 6) and D is the point (−2, 2).

11 The diagram shows a road from A to B
passing through C and D.
A new, more direct, road is to be built.
It is shown by the dotted lines in the
diagram.
Calculate the length of the new road.

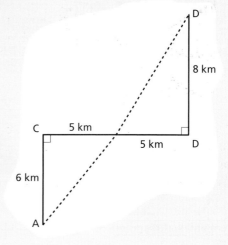

12

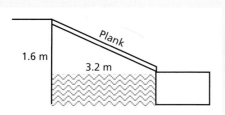

a What length of plank is needed
to cross the stream?

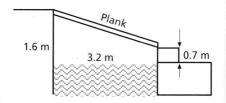

b What length of plank is needed
now to cross the stream?

Graphs, charts and tables
Reminders

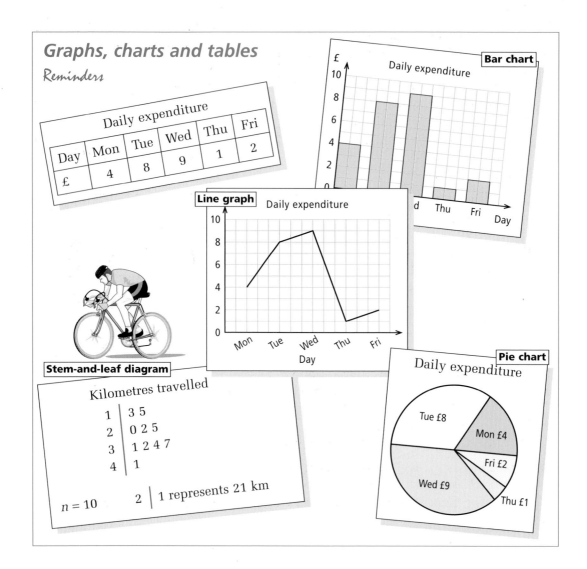

Daily expenditure

Day	Mon	Tue	Wed	Thu	Fri
£	4	8	9	1	2

Bar chart

Daily expenditure

Line graph — Daily expenditure

Stem-and-leaf diagram

Kilometres travelled

```
1 | 3 5
2 | 0 2 5
3 | 1 2 4 7
4 | 1
```

n = 10   2 | 1 represents 21 km

Pie chart

Daily expenditure

Tue £8 Mon £4 Fri £2 Thu £1 Wed £9

EXERCISE 4

The graphs for questions 1, 2 and 5 could be drawn on 5 mm squared paper.
The other graphs should be drawn on 2 mm graph paper.

1 A survey to discover how workers travelled to a factory produced these figures.

Transport	Bus	Train	Car	Cycle	Motorbike	Walk
Number of workers	18	8	24	6	4	9

Show this information in a bar graph.

2 Approximate unemployment figures for Craigend are shown below.

Year	1993	1994	1995	1996	1997	1998
Number of unemployed	160	130	120	115	105	110

Draw a line graph for these statistics.

3 The stem-and-leaf diagram shows the distances travelled by a salesman over ten working days.

   a List all the journeys he made which are less than 25 km long.
   b What is the total distance travelled?
   c He is given 30p per kilometre travelling expenses. How much is that in total?

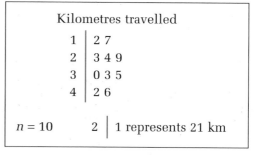

Kilometres travelled	
1	2 7
2	3 4 9
3	0 3 5
4	2 6

$n = 10$ 2 | 1 represents 21 km

4 A leisure centre had 720 visitors one weekend. The pie chart shows how they were made up.

   a **(i)** What fraction of the visitors were men?
      (ii) How many men visited?
   b **(i)** What fraction of the visitors were children?
      (ii) How many children visited?
   c 80 pensioners visited. How many women visitors were there?

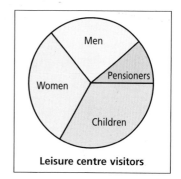

Leisure centre visitors

5 Square Wheel Car Sales sell second-hand cars.
   Last month they sold cars with these registration letters:
   L, P, L, K, J, K, M, L, N, P, M, G, H, M, L, H, N, L, K, M, M, L.
   a Make a frequency table of the data.
   b Draw a bar graph using the frequency table.

6 Tamara is a sales representative for a cosmetics company.
   She drives all over the country.
   The bar graph shows the distance she drove each day over the last four working weeks.

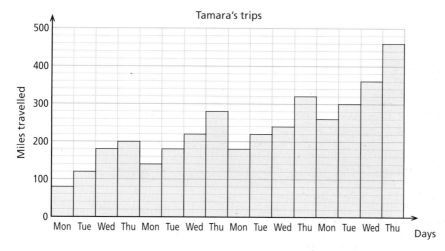

   a How far did she drive in each of the four weeks?
   b Describe the weekly trend.
   c Describe the overall trend.

7 Thirty-six thousand people voted in an election.
The pie chart shows how the five candidates
shared the vote.
  a Who won the election?
  b Calculate the number of votes received
    by each candidate.

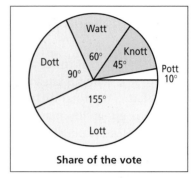

Share of the vote

8 The temperature in a greenhouse was recorded every
2 hours over a 24-hour period. The line graph shows the results.

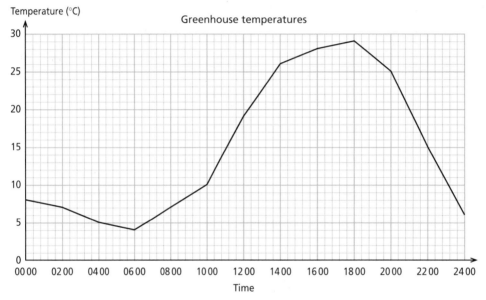

  a When was the temperature at its lowest? What was the lowest temperature?
  b Estimate the temperature at (i) 9 am (ii) 1 pm (iii) 9 pm.
  c Between which two hours did the temperature (i) rise the most (ii) fall the most?
  d For how long was the temperature above 20 °C?
  e For how long was the temperature below 10 °C?

9 A member of a health club was asked to perform 'sit-ups'.
The increase in his pulse rate was noted throughout.
The results are shown in the table.

Number of sit-ups	10	20	30	40	50	60	70	80
Increase in pulse rate	3	8	12	19	21	29	33	38

  a Plot the points to form a scatter graph.
  b What correlation do you notice between the increase in his pulse rate and the
    number of sit-ups?

c Draw a line of best-fit on your scatter graph.

d What increase in pulse rate would you expect from the member after he had done 55 sit-ups?

10 Staff at a large menswear shop note the number of pairs of gloves they sell each week and the average noon temperature for the week.
The results are shown in the table.

	Week 1	Week 2	Week 3	Week 4	Week 5	Week 6	Week 7	Week 8
Temperature (°C)	8	5	3	9	2	12	14	18
Pairs of gloves sold	12	15	16	12	18	7	6	3

a Draw a scatter graph of the data in the table.

b Write down the correlation you notice from your scatter graph.

c Draw a line of best-fit on your scatter graph.

d How many pairs of gloves would the store staff expect to sell in a week with an average noon temperature of 10 °C?

11 The line graph shows the amount of coal sold from Penny Veenie mine every two months over the last three years.

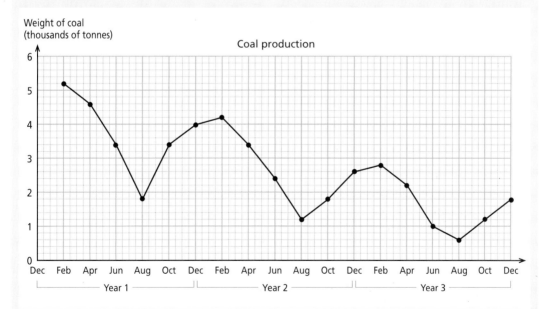

a Describe the trend in the sale of coal over the first year.

b Describe the overall trend of sales of coal over the three years.

c **(i)** What was the lowest weight of coal sold in a two-month period over the three years?

    (ii) When was this?

d How much coal was sold in January and February of year 2?

e How much coal was sold in each of the three years?

12 The stem-and-leaf diagram gives the lengths of the tracks on a CD.

Track times

1	49 53 57
2	35 47 49 56 58
3	24 31 43 52 56 59
4	05 12

$n = 16$ 1 │ 49 represents 1 minute
                              49 seconds

a What is the range of times?
b What is the median time?
c Calculate the mean time correct to the nearest second.

13 The graph shows the sales of leaded and unleaded petrol from a large filling station over the years 1990 to 1997.

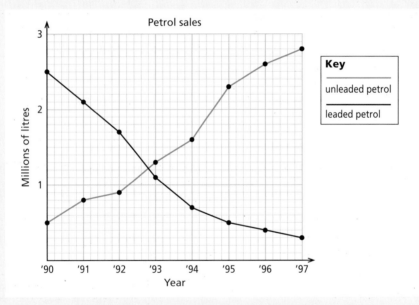

a How much of each kind of petrol was sold in 1990?
b How much of each kind of petrol was sold in 1997?
c In which year was the greatest amount of petrol sold? How much was sold?
d Describe the trend in sales of both kinds of petrol.

Statistics

Reminders

Range = highest score – lowest score

Mean = sum of scores ÷ number of scores

The mode is the most common score.

The median is the middle score when the scores are put in order.

EXERCISE 5

1 Attendances at the George Cinema over one fortnight were:
83, 78, 65, 67, 42, 128, 103, 75, 93, 58, 65, 53, 114, 96.
a Calculate the mean.
b What was the median attendance?
c What was the range of the attendances?

2 The age distribution of the members of the Young
Farmers' Club is shown in the frequency table.
a What is the range of ages of the members?
b Calculate (i) the mean   (ii) the median
(iii) the mode of the members' ages.
c How many members are below the mean age?

Age	Frequency
17	9
18	23
19	12
20	8
21	16
22	22
Total	90

3 The weekly wages of the employees of Fox's Furniture Store (to the nearest £1) are:
£230, £145, £145, £360, £145, £116, £94, £145, £145, £116, £116.
a Calculate (i) the mean wage   (ii) the median wage
(iii) the mode   (iv) the range of wages at the store.
b How many of the employees earn less than the mean wage?
c Compare the wages of £360 and £94 with the mean wage.

4 Fifty people were asked how many hours were in
their basic working week.
The replies are given in the frequency table.
a Calculate the mean number of hours in a basic
week.
b What is the median number of hours worked?
c What is the mode?

No. of hours	Frequency
35	4
36	0
37	9
38	13
39	10
40	4
41	4
42	6
Total	50

5

In a game of Scrabble this word is worth 11 points.
The tiles are put in a bag and one is selected without looking.
What is the probability that the selected tile is:

a an N

b worth 2 points

c a vowel?

6 A registry office noted the ages of the last 12 couples married.
The ages are given in the table.

	Age (years)											
Bride	32	28	21	17	27	24	23	30	32	18	35	22
Bridegroom	35	27	24	18	36	26	23	32	29	18	44	23

a Calculate the mean age of **(i)** the brides **(ii)** the bridegrooms.

b What is the mode for **(i)** the brides **(ii)** the bridegrooms?

c Find the median age of **(i)** the brides **(ii)** the bridegrooms.

d What is the range of ages of **(i)** the brides **(ii)** the bridegrooms?

e Compare the mean ages of the brides and the bridegrooms.

f Compare the ranges of the ages.

7 These temperatures were taken at midnight at ten weather centres:
0 °C, –1 °C, 1 °C, –2 °C, 0 °C, –4 °C, –2 °C, 1 °C, –2 °C, –1 °C.
Find:

a the mean

b the median

c the mode

d the range of these temperatures.

8

(i) 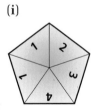 **(ii)** **(iii)** **(iv)**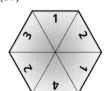

a Work out the probability of scoring a 2 on each spinner.

b Which spinner offers the best opportunity of scoring a 1?

c Which two spinners offer the same chance of scoring a 4?

14 Basic Algebra

Reminders

5x means $5 \times x$

x^2 means $x \times x$

If $x = 4$ then

$3x + 1 = 3 \times 4 + 1$

$= 13$

'<' means 'less than'

'>' means 'more than'

'≤' means 'less than or equal to'

'≥' means 'more than or equal to'

STARTING POINTS

1 What number is hidden in each problem?

  a ■ + 1 = 9   **b** ■ − 2 = 8   **c** $3 \times$ ■ = 36

2 If $x = 3$ find the value of:

  a 5x   **b** $x + 4$ **c** $x − 3$ **d** $2x + 7$

3 Simplify:

  a $2x + 3x$ **b** $5m − 2m$ **c** $5a + b − 2a + 3b$

4 Which of the following are true?

  a $2 < 3$ **b** $2 > 3$ **c** $2 ≤ 2$ **d** $−2 < 1$ **e** $−2 > −1$ **f** $3 ≥ 1$

5 $6 = 2 \times 3$ so 2 and 3 are factors of 6.

Copy and complete:

  a $8 = 2 \times 4$ so … and … are factors of 8.

  b $35 = … \times …$ so … and … are factors of ….

  c $ab = a \times b$ so … and … are factors of ….

6 Find the value, correct to 2 decimal places, of:

  a $\sqrt{2}$

  b $\sqrt{(2 + 3)}$

  c $\sqrt{(10 + x)}$ where $x = 7$

  d $x^2 + 3$ where $x = 5$

  e $\sqrt{(a^2 + b^2)}$ where $a = 2.1$, $b = 5.3$

Evaluating expressions

Reminder

In expressions some calculations must be done before others.

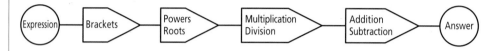

Example 1

Evaluate $m^2 + 3n$ when $m = 4$ and $n = 5$.

$$m^2 + 3n = 4^2 + 3 \times 5 \qquad \text{(Substitute.)}$$
$$= 16 + 15 \qquad \text{(Work out the parts in the correct order.)}$$
$$= 31$$

$m^2 + 3n$ has the value 31.

Reminder

π is a number. It is roughly 3.14.

Example 2 Evaluate πD when $D = 4$.

$$\pi D = \pi \times 4 \qquad \text{(Substitute and use the } \pi \text{ button.)}$$
$$= 12.57 \qquad \text{(Round to 2 decimal places.)}$$

EXERCISE 1

1 Evaluate when $a = 2$ and $b = 4$:

   a $2a$ **b** $5b$ **c** $7a$ **d** $3 + a$ **e** $5 - b$ **f** ab

   g $2ab$ **h** $3 + 2b$ **i** $b + a$ **j** $5a - 2b$ **k** ab **l** a^2

2 For $a = 7$, $b = 3$ and $c = 6$, find:

   a $2a$ **b** $2a - b$ **c** $a - b + c$ **d** $3c$ **e** $3a - 2b$ **f** $3a + c$

   g $5a + 1$ **h** $a - 2b + c$ **i** $3a - 2c$ **j** $6bc$ **k** $10 - b^2$ **l** $3 + a^2$

3 For $a = 3$, $b = 1$ and $c = 4$, find:

   a $4a - b$ **b** $5c - b + 2a$ **c** $\sqrt{b}$ **d** $5abc$ **e** $12 - 2b$ **f** $1 + a^2$

   g $2a - 2b$ **h** $3c + b - a$ **i** $\sqrt{c}$ **j** $2ac + 1$ **k** $3bc - 6$ **l** $2a + b^2$

4 For $a = 2$, $b = 5$ and $c = 0$, find:

   a $5a^2$ **b** $b^2 - a^2$ **c** $bc + ab$ **d** abc **e** $b - c$ **f** $1 - c^2$

   g $a^2 + c^2$ **h** $b^2 + a^2$ **i** $ac + bc$ **j** $a + bc$ **k** $2b - 4a + c$ **l** $3 + 2c^2$

5 When $x = 3$ and $y = 4$, which expression gives the greatest and which the least value?

   a $2x^2$ **b** $3y^2$ **c** $5xy$ **d** $2x + 3y$

6 Calculate:

   a $\sqrt{a}$ when $a = 49$

   b $\sqrt{b} + 2$ when $b = 81$

   c $\sqrt{a} + \sqrt{b}$ when $a = 16$, $b = 9$

   d $\sqrt{(a + b)}$ when $a = 20$, $b = 5$

7 Evaluate each expression (correct to 1 decimal place):

   a $2\pi r$ where $r = 8.2$

   b πb^2 where $b = 1.6$

   c $\pi a + c$ where $a = 2.8$ and $c = 8.3$

   d $2a^2 - b$ where $a = 6.5$ and $b = 9.26$

Formulae

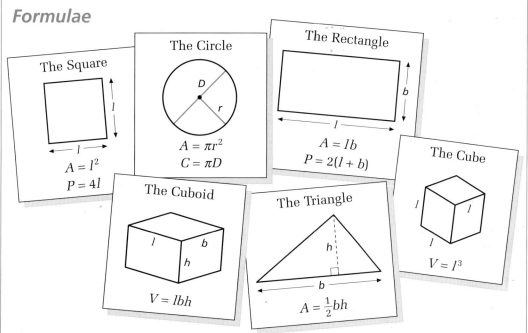

Formulae are like recipes.

They show you how to work out an unknown quantity using quantities that are known.

Example   What is the area of the rectangle?

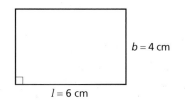

The length (l) and breadth (b) are known.

Area (A) is not known.

The formula: $A = lb$

                       gives $A = 6 \times 4$

                          Area $= 24$ cm^2

EXERCISE 2

Work to 2 decimal places where necessary.

1 Use the formulae on page 179 to help you work out the following.

a

3 cm
10 cm

b
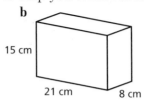
15 cm
21 cm
8 cm

c

2 cm

(i) The perimeter of the rectangle

(ii) The area of the rectangle

The volume of the cuboid

The volume of the cube

d

13 cm

e

7 cm

f
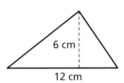
6 cm
12 cm

The circumference of the circle

The area of the circle

The area of the triangle

2 a $K = C + 273$. Find K when $C = 100$.

b $S = 2R + 4$. Find S when $R = 6$.

c $Q = 12 - 2B$. Find Q when $B = 3$.

d $A = 2B + 2C$. Find A when $B = 1$ and $C = 10$.

e $P = 2g + f$. Find P when $g = 5$ and $f = 8$.

f $F = 2DE$. Find F when $D = 5$ and $E = 6$.

g $W = \dfrac{J}{S}$. Find W when $J = 215$ and $S = 5$.

h $K = \dfrac{C}{D}$. Find K when $C = 72$ and $D = 9$.

3 The cost, £T, of a group going to the cinema can be worked out using the formula $T = 4a + 3c$, where a is the number of adults and c is the number of children in the group.

Calculate the value of T when:

a $a = 4$ and $c = 5$ **b** $a = 1$ and $c = 3$ **c** $a = 0$ and $c = 2$.

4 a A motorist drives at 35 km/h (S) for 5 hours (T). How far does he travel?

b A train covers 300 km in 6 hours. What is its average speed?

c How long will it take to travel 125 km at a speed of 25 km/h?

d A cyclist travels at 30 miles per hour for 3.5 hours. What distance does she cover?

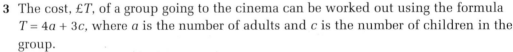

Reminder

The formulae for distance, speed and time:

$D = ST$ $S = \dfrac{D}{T}$ $T = \dfrac{D}{S}$

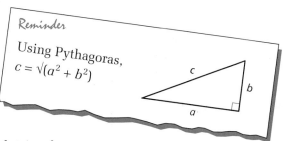

Reminder

Using Pythagoras,
$c = \sqrt{(a^2 + b^2)}$

5 Calculate c in each triangle.

a
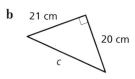

5 cm

c

12 cm

b 21 cm
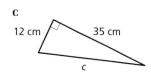

20 cm

c

c
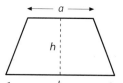

12 cm

35 cm

c

EXERCISE 3

The formula for the area of a trapezium is:

$A = \frac{1}{2}h(a + b)$

Example When $a = 3$, $b = 5$ and $h = 4$,

$A = \frac{1}{2} \times 4 \times (3 + 5)$

$= \frac{1}{2} \times 4 \times 8$

$= \frac{1}{2} \times 32$

Area = 16 cm²

1 Find the area, A, of a trapezium if:
  a $a = 2$, $b = 3$ and $h = 6$ **b** $a = 3$, $b = 6$ and $h = 2$.
    (All units are in centimetres.)

2 A shopkeeper calculates her percentage profit, P, using the formula: $P = \dfrac{100(S - B)}{B}$
  S is her selling price in pounds. B is her buying price in pounds.
  Calculate her percentage profit for these.

a A television set
   Selling price £300
   Buying price £200

b A plug
   Selling price £3.50
   Buying price £2.00

c A packet of fuses
   Selling price £2.40
   Buying price £1.80

The cylinder

A piece of paper is curled to make a cylinder.

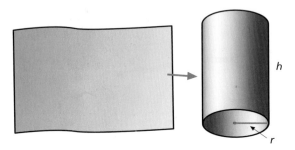

Area of paper and curved surface of cylinder, $S = 2\pi rh$

Total area of cylinder including ends, $A = 2\pi r(r + h)$

Volume of cylinder, $V = \pi r^2 h$

3 Find:
  a S if $r = 1$ and $h = 3$
  b A if $r = 3$ and $h = 5$
  c V if $r = 2$ and $h = 4$.
     (All units are in centimetres.)

4

The speed of a wave can be worked out from its length.

$$S = 2.2 \times \sqrt{\left(\frac{L}{\pi}\right)}$$

Calculate the speed, S m/s, of a wave when its length is:
  a 200 m
  b 400 m.

Simplifying

Examples

1 Collecting *like terms*:

$x + x + x = 3x$

$8m - 3m = 5m$

$2c + d - c + 3d = c + 4d$

$8 + 4n - 2 = 6 + 4n$

$y^2 + y^2 = 2y^2$

2 Multiplying:

$8 \times n = 8n$

$y \times 3 = 3y$

$t \times t = t^2$

$2a \times a = 2a^2$

$3q \times 2q = 6q^2$

EXERCISE 4

Simplify in questions **1** to **4**.

1
a $a + a$
b $x + x + x$
c $1 + 1 + 1 + 1$
d $b + b + b$
e $x - x + x$
f $1 + 1 - 1 + 1$
g $y + y + y + y$
h $t + 2t + 3t - t$
i $3k + 2k - 5k + 4k$
j $2b + 2b + c + c$
k $x - y + x + y$
l $2y + 3x + 4y - x$
m $p + 2q - 3p$
n $4h + 2n - 6n + 3h$
o $f + 2g - f - g$
p $x^2 - y^2 + x^2 + y^2$

2
a $m \times m$
b $3 \times n$
c $a \times a$
d $p \times p$
e $5 \times k$
f $7 \times b$
g $x \times 5$
h $b \times 6$
i $r \times r \times 4$
j $x \times 3 \times 2$
k $3 \times b \times 2$
l $3r \times 4$
m $p \times p \times 5$
n $a \times b$
o $p \times q \times 5$
p $f \times 3 \times g$
q $4 \times k \times k$
r $7t \times 2r$

3
a $y + 2y$
b $2y \times y$
c $a \times 2a$
d $5y - 2y$
e $7q \times 3q$
f $6p \times 2p$
g $3a + 2a$
h $3x \times 5y$
i $3m + m$
j $12a + 3a - 4a$
k $4x \times 5x \times 2y$
l $7m - m$

4
a $x^2 + 2x^2$
b $5x^2 - 2x^2$
c $7x^2 + 3x^2 - 3x^2$
d $2x + y + x$
e $2a + 3 - a$
f $6x + 7 - 4x$
g $5 + 3c - c$
h $6 - 3c + 7c$
i $2a^2 - 3 + a^2$
j $5y^2 - 3y^2 + 6y^2$
k $k^2 + 2l^2 + k^2 - l^2$

5 In each case **(i)** simplify and **(ii)** calculate the value of the expression when
$x = 7$ and $y = 4$.

a $2x + x$
b $3x + y - x$
c $3x - 2x + y + y$
d $3y + y$
e $4x + 2y - x + y$
f $x - 2y + y + 4y$
g $4y + x - 3y + 3x$
h $x + x + 2x + 2y$
i $4y + x - y$
j $6y + y - 3y + 3y$
k $3x + 2x + 2y$
l $7y - x - y$
m $3x + 2y + 2x - y$
n $6x + 3y - y + x$
o $3x^2 - 2x^2 + y^2 + y^2$
p $7x^2 - x^2 + 4y^2 + y^2$

Removing brackets

The area of the front of the CD cover can be worked out in two ways.

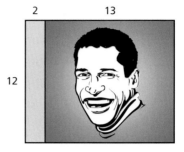

Method 1
Length = (2 + 13)
Breadth = 12
$A = lb$
$A = 12 \times (2 + 13)$
   = 180

Method 2
Area of spine = 2 × 12
          = 24
Area of picture = 12 × 13
              = 156
$A = 24 + 156 = 180$

Note that 12 × (2 + 13) = 12 × 2 + 12 × 13

This always works. You can remove brackets by multiplying each term inside the brackets by the number outside.

Example 1
$3 \times (4 + 5)$
$= 3 \times 4 + 3 \times 5$
Check:
$3 \times (4 + 5) = 3 \times 9 = 27$
$3 \times 4 + 3 \times 5 = 12 + 15 = 27$

Example 2
$4 \times (3 - 1)$
$= 4 \times 3 - 4 \times 1$
Check:
$4 \times (3 - 1) = 4 \times 2 = 8$
$4 \times 3 - 4 \times 1 = 12 - 4 = 8$

Example 3
$a\,(b + 2)$
$= a \times b + a \times 2$
$= ab + 2a$

EXERCISE 5

1 (i) Remove the brackets as in Example 1 and then **(ii)** do the check.

    a $3 \times (4 + 6)$ **b** $2 \times (5 + 1)$ **c** $6 \times (8 - 3)$ **d** $5 \times (6 - 4)$

> *Example* $4(x + 3)$
> $= 4x + 4 \times 3$
> $= 4x + 12$

2 Write these without brackets.

    a $3(y + 2)$ **b** $2(x - 3)$ **c** $3(a + 3)$ **d** $2(y - 1)$
    e $7(x + 3)$ **f** $5(t - 2)$ **g** $2(y + 5)$ **h** $9(m - 1)$
    i $3(y + 2)$ **j** $8(k + 5)$ **k** $3(b + 7)$ **l** $2(b - 7)$
    m $5(d - 3)$ **n** $6(g + 1)$ **o** $8(l + 2)$ **p** $6(x - 1)$

> *Example* $5(3 - x)$
> $= 5 \times 3 - 5x$
> $= 15 - 5x$

3 Remove the brackets.

    a $2(1 + x)$ **b** $3(2 - y)$ **c** $7(3 + t)$ **d** $3(8 - u)$
    e $5(9 + v)$ **f** $2(2 - y)$ **g** $5(x - y)$ **h** $8(x + y)$
    i $7(a - b)$ **j** $8(m + n)$ **k** $2(7 - m)$ **l** $4(y - 2)$
    m $10(10 + k)$ **n** $12(a - b)$ **o** $7(10 - c)$ **p** $5(14 - a)$

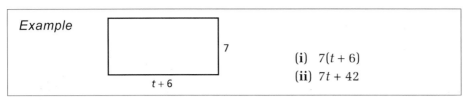

Example

7

(i) $7(t + 6)$

(ii) $7t + 42$

$t + 6$

4 Write down the area of each rectangle **(i)** with the brackets **(ii)** without the brackets.

a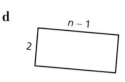
$x + 4$

6

b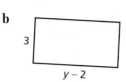

3

$y - 2$

c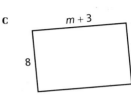
$m + 3$

8

d
$n - 1$

2

e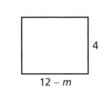

4

$12 - m$

f

6

$10 - x$

5 Write these without brackets.

a $2(3x + 1)$ **b** $7(3y - 1)$ **c** $2(3b + 1)$ **d** $7(3b - 2)$

e $6(3d + 2)$ **f** $3(2x - 3)$ **g** $7(2m - 1)$ **h** $3(6k - 1)$

i $3(a + 2b)$ **j** $7(2a - 3b)$ **k** $8(3x - 2y)$ **l** $7(3l + 5m)$

Example

$d(3a - 2b)$

$= 3d^2 - 2ab$

---

6 Remove the brackets.

a $a(2a - 3)$ **b** $x(x - 2)$ **c** $m(m + n)$ **d** $b(3b + c)$

e $y(y - x)$ **f** $x(5x - y)$ **g** $n(2 + 5n)$ **h** $2x(x - 3)$

i $5y(2 + y)$ **j** $2x(3y - 5x)$ **k** $5r(2r + 3s)$ **l** $x(5x + 6y)$

Removing brackets and then simplifying

Example 1

$2(x + 3) + 4$

$= 2x + 6 + 4$

$= 2x + 10$

Example 2

$3(4y + 5z) - 10z$

$= 12y + 15z - 10z$

$= 12y + 5z$

Example 3

$2(x + 3) + 3(x + 5)$

$= 2x + 6 + 3x + 15$

$= 5x + 21$

EXERCISE 6

1 Remove the brackets and then simplify.

a $2(x + 1) + 3$ **b** $2(y - 1) + 10$ **c** $10(10 - m) + 10$

d $5(k - 1) + 18$ **e** $3(2 + x) - 5$ **f** $3(7 - y) + 5$

g $6(p + 2) - 3$ **h** $5(1 + r) - 1$ **i** $5(2 - f) + 6$

j $7(c + 1) - 3$ k $10 + 9(1 + x)$ l $1 + 3(2 + p)$

m $3(x + 1) + 2x$ n $4(y - 3) + 2y$ o $2(1 - m) + 6m$

p $3(k - 2) + 5k$ q $6(3 + x) - 2x$ r $5(1 - y) + 7y$

s $3(c + 2) - 3c$ t $8x + 7(3 + x)$ u $p + 2(7 + p)$

2 Simplify.

a $2(3x + 2) + 4x$ b $6(2y + 4) - 12$ c $7(2 + 3m) + 5m$

d $2(5k - 1) - 6k$ e $3(4 + 3x) - 8$ f $4(5 + 3y) + 7y$

g $5(2c - 3) - 9c$ h $6 + 2(2 + 8x)$ i $3p + 4(1 + 2p)$

j $3(2x + y) + 3x$ k $2(2y + 3z) - 3z$ l $4(3n + 5m) + 6m$

m $3(4k - p) + 8p$ n $5(2w + 7x) - 6w$ o $7(3x + 4y) + 5y$

p $9(4c - 2d) - 20c$ q $8q + 6(3p + 2q)$ r $5p + (r + 3p)$

3 Simplify.

a $2(x - 1) + 3(x + 1)$ b $5(y - 3) + 3(y + 5)$ c $3(z - 3) + 4(z + 3)$

d $5(2 + p) + 2(1 - p)$ e $3(1 - t) + 4(1 + t)$ f $6(2m + 4) + 2(3m - 5)$

g $2(4k - 3) + 2(3k + 4)$ h $5(2 - 3x) + 4(1 + 4x)$ i $3(5s + 2t) + 2(4s - t)$

6 Using the example as a guide, find an expression for the area of each shape.

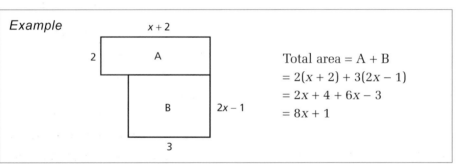

Example

Total area = A + B
$$= 2(x + 2) + 3(2x - 1)$$
$$= 2x + 4 + 6x - 3$$
$$= 8x + 1$$

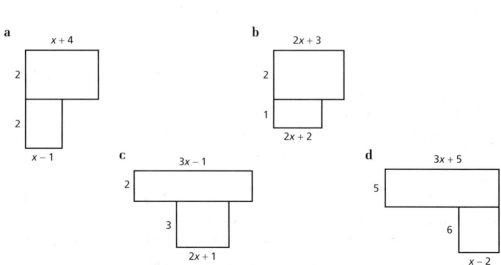

Factors

When two integers are multiplied to make a third integer, then they are called **factors** of the third.

Example 1

$3 \times 2 = 6$ 3 and 2 are factors of 6.

$1 \times 6 = 6$ 1 and 6 are factors of 6.

1, 2, 3 and 6 are all the factors of 6.

Example 2

$1 \times 9 = 9$ 1 and 9 are factors of 9.

$3 \times 3 = 9$ 3 is a factor of 9.

1, 3 and 9 are all the factors of 9.

Note that 1 and 3 belong to both lists. 1 and 3 are **common factors** of 6 and 9. 3 is the **highest common factor** of 6 and 9.

In algebra, when two expressions multiply to make a third expression, they are called **factors** of the third.

Example 1   **$3xy$**

$1 \times 3xy = 3xy$ 1 and $3xy$ are factors of $3xy$.

$3x \times y = 3xy$ $3x$ and y are factors of $3xy$.

$3 \times xy = 3xy$ 3 and xy are factors of $3xy$.

$3y \times x = 3xy$ $3y$ and x are factors of $3xy$.

1, 3, x, y, xy, $3x$, $3y$ and $3xy$ are all the factors of $3xy$.

Example 2   **$9x^2$**

$1 \times 9x^2 = 9x^2$ 1 and $9x^2$ are factors of $9x^2$.

$3 \times 3x^2 = 9x^2$ 3 and $3x^2$ are factors of $9x^2$.

$9 \times x^2 = 9x^2$ 9 and x^2 are factors of $9x^2$.

$3x \times 3x = 9x^2$ $3x$ is a factor of $9x^2$.

$9x \times x = 9x^2$ $9x$ and x are factors of $9x^2$.

1, 3, 9, x, $3x$, $9x$, x^2, $3x^2$ and $9x^2$ are all the factors of $9x^2$.

Note that 1, 3, x and $3x$ belong to both lists. 1, 3, x and $3x$ are **common factors** of $3xy$ and $9x^2$. $3x$ is called the **highest common factor** of $3xy$ and $9x^2$.

EXERCISE 7

1 List all the factors of: **a** 8   **b** 18   **c** 36   **d** 5   **e** 20   **f** 25   **g** 30

2 List the common factors of each pair of numbers:
   a 8, 10   **b** 18, 36   **c** 36, 32   **d** 56, 72   **e** 5, 23

3 Find the highest common factor of each pair of numbers:
   a 9, 24   **b** 40, 36   **c** 18, 72   **d** 63, 40   **e** 7, 41

4 List all the factors of:
   a xy **b** ab **c** $2a$ **d** $6a$ **e** $2ab$ **f** $8pq$ **g** $5x^2$ **h** $6a^2$

5 List the common factors of each pair of expressions:
   a xy, $4x$ **b** $2pq$, $6qr$ **c** $6ab$, $15b$ **d** $3km$, m^2 **e** $8fg$, $2g^2$

6 Find the highest common factor of each pair of expressions:
   a $3xy$, $6x$ **b** $8ab$, $36b$ **c** $18pq$, $6pr$ **d** $9k$, $3k^2$ **e** $12a^2$, $42ab$

Factorising using common factors

If $3(x + 4) = 3x + 12$
then obviously
$3x + 12 = 3(x + 4)$.

We can see that 3 and $(x + 4)$ are factors of $3(x + 4)$ and hence factors of $3x + 12$.
Putting the brackets back is called **factorising**.

Example 1 $3x + 6$

Recognising 3 is the highest common factor of $3x$ and 6 gives $3(x + 2)$

Check by reversing the process:
$3 \times x + 3 \times 2 = 3x + 6$

Example 2 $20x + 28y$

Recognising 4 is the highest common factor of $20x$ and $28y$ gives $4(5x + 7y)$

Check by reversing the process:
$4 \times 5x + 4 \times 7y = 20x + 28y$

Example 3 $6x^2 + 2x$
Recognising $2x$ is the highest common factor of $6x^2$ and $2x$ gives $2x(3x + 1)$

Check by reversing the process:
$2x \times 3x + 2x \times 1 = 6x^2 + 2x$

EXERCISE 8

1 Copy and complete each of the following:

a $9x + 6 = 3(3x + ...)$ b $4x + 8 = 4(x + ...)$ c $14x - 21 = 7(2x - ...)$

d $10x + 15 = 5(... + ...)$ e $24x + 18 = 6(... + ...)$ f $56x + 16 = 8(... + ...)$

g $14 - 10x = 2(... - ...)$ h $21 + 33x = 3(... + ...)$ i $30x + 35 = ...(... + ...)$

j $36x + 44 = ...(... + ...)$ k $12 - 24x = ...(... - ...)$ l $16 + 40x = ...(... + ...)$

m $2x + xy = x(... + ...)$ n $4x + 18xy = 2x(... + ...)$ o $2x - 2x^2 = 2x(... - ...)$

2 Factorise (remembering to check your answers):

a $4x - 2$ b $6y + 3$ c $3x - 3$ d $5m + 5$ e $6x - 18$ f $4y + 8$

g $9x - 6$ h $2m + 10$ i $7x - 14$ j $8y + 12$ k $15x - 5$ l $18m + 12$

m $36x - 12$ n $8y + 6$ o $4x - 4$ p $10m + 25$ q $6m + 8$ r $10t - 15$

s $2ab + 2$ t $6 - 3ab$ u $8pq + 2$

3 Factorise:

a $ab + 2a$ b $d - cd$ c $14yx - 7x$ d $6k + 9hk$ e $pq + 4q$

f $6d - 12cd$ g $8jk - 4k$ h $6yg + 24g$ i $5a - ab$ j $2ab + b$

k $3kl - 2k$ l $5mn - 7n$ m $9e + 7ef$ n $4pq - 2q$ o $2ab + 4a$

p $8rs - 12r$ q $8gh + 28h$ r $42ts - 12s$

4 Factorise fully:

a $a^2 - 3a$ b $y^2 + 4y$ c $6m - m^2$ d $2n - n^2$ e $3t^2 + 2t$

f $4c - c^2$ g $2x^2 + 4x$ h $5xy + y^2$ i $2ab + 3b^2$ j $4p^2 - 2p$

k $6q + 3q^2$ l $5m^2 + 15n^2$ m $5n^2 - 15n$ n $18x^2 - 12x$ o $16y + 20y^2$

Solving equations

Example 'Solve $3x + 7 = 22$' means 'what number does x represent?'.

One way is to use the 'cover up' method.

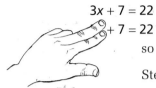

Step 1

$3x + 7 = 22$

$+ 7 = 22$ $15 + 7 = 22$

so $3x = 15$

Step 2

$3 \times \quad = 15$ $3 \times 5 = 15$

$x = 5$

Check: $3 \times 5 + 7 = 22$

We usually write: $3x + 7 = 22$

so $3x = 15$

so $x = 5$

EXERCISE 9

1 Solve these equations. (Remember to check your solutions.)

a $y - 2 = 10$ **b** $x + 3 = 4$ **c** $8 = 10 - x$
d $14 - y = 12$ **e** $5x = 15$ **f** $3t = 30$
g $2m = 8$ **h** $7r = 35$ **i** $2x + 1 = 7$
j $3 + 4x = 7$ **k** $3n + 2 = 8$ **l** $2r + 6 = 18$

2 Solve these equations.

a $8c - 2 = 30$ **b** $14 + 5k = 14$ **c** $8 = 3m + 8$
d $7k + 10 = 10$ **e** $10 - 3d = 10$ **f** $14 - 2x = 6$
g $0 = 12 - 3n$ **h** $3 = 18 - 5l$ **i** $10l - 7 = 43$
j $8q + 12 = 52$ **k** $43 = 8 + 7w$ **l** $83 = 9x - 7$

Example $2(x + 3) = 8$

$\Rightarrow 2x + 6 = 8$

$\Rightarrow 2x = 2$

$\Rightarrow x = 1$

Reminder

'$\Rightarrow$' means 'therefore'.

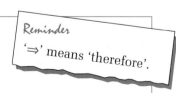

3 Solve each equation by first removing brackets.

a $3(x + 1) = 9$ **b** $5(y + 2) = 10$ **c** $7(m - 2) = 21$
d $3(t - 3) = 3$ **e** $9(n + 5) = 63$ **f** $10(c - 5) = 20$
g $12(2 + y) = 24$ **h** $6(8 - x) = 36$

Balancing

Example 1 Solve $5x = x + 8$.

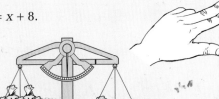

Here the 'cover up' method does not work.

Imagine a balance.

$5x = x + 8$

Taking x off both sides keeps the balance.

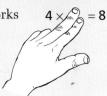

$4x = 8$

Now the cover up method works

$4 \times \square = 8$

$x = 2$

Check: $5 \times 2 = 2 + 8$

Example 2 $6m + 4 = 2m + 12$

$4m + 4 = 12$
$4m = 8$
$m = 2$

Take $2m$ from both sides,

then use the cover up.

Check: $2 + 4 = 2 \times 2 + 12$

Example 3 $12 - x = 3x$

$12 - x + x = 3x + x$
$12 = 4x$
$x = 3$

Add x to both sides,

then use the cover up.

Check: $12 - 3 = 3 \times 3$

EXERCISE 10

1 Solve these equations with the help of the hint given.
  a $3x = x + 8$ (Hint: take x from both sides.)
  b $7x = 4x + 12$ (Hint: take $4x$ from both sides.)
  c $6x - 4 = 3x + 2$ (Hint: take $3x$ from both sides.)
  d $2x + 3 = x + 17$ (Hint: take x from both sides.)
  e $8 - x = 3x$ (Hint: add x to both sides.)
  f $5x = 12 - x$ (Hint: add x to both sides.)
  g $6x + 2 = 10 - 2x$ (Hint: add $2x$ to both sides.)
  h $3m - 5 = m + 9$ (Hint: take m from both sides.)

2 Solve (and check your solutions).

a $4y = 3y + 5$	**b** $6x = x + 10$	**c** $2m = m + 3$
d $2x = 9 - x$	**e** $5 - k = 4k$	**f** $3y = 12 - y$
g $3w + 6 = 5w$	**h** $3t + 21 = 10t$	**i** $5c = 3c + 6$
j $5u = 20 + u$	**k** $2y + 1 = y + 7$	**l** $6n - 2 = 5n + 10$
m $3a - 1 = a + 7$	**n** $5e - 3 = 2e + 6$	**o** $4x + 5 = x + 8$

3 The lengths of each pair of planks are equal. All measurements are in metres.
For each pair:
(i) form an equation
(ii) solve it for x
(iii) work out the length of each plank.

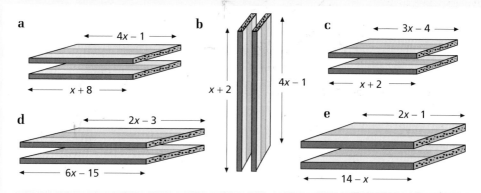

a $4x - 1$, $x + 8$
b $x + 2$, $4x - 1$
c $3x - 4$, $x + 2$
d $2x - 3$, $6x - 15$
e $2x - 1$, $14 - x$

Inequalities

Do you remember these signs?

< 'is less than'

> 'is greater than'

≤ 'is less than or equal to'

≥ 'is greater than or equal to'

Here are some examples of their use (with whole numbers):

$3 < 5$ means 3 is less than 5

$7 > 3$ means 7 is greater than 3

$x \le 2$ means x is less than or equal to 2,
$x = 0, 1, 2$

$x \ge 2$ means x is greater than or equal to 2,
$x = 2, 3, 4, \dots$

Note that the sign always points to the smaller side.

Example   Choosing from {1, 2, 3, 4, 5, 6} find the solutions of $3x - 4 < 8$.

$3 \times 6 - 4 = 14$	(not less than 8)
$3 \times 5 - 4 = 11$	(not less than 8)
$3 \times 4 - 4 = 8$	(not less than 8)
$3 \times 3 - 4 = 5$	(yes, less than 8)
$3 \times 2 - 4 = 2$	(yes, less than 8)
$3 \times 1 - 4 = -1$	(yes, less than 8)

So the solutions are {1, 2, 3}.

EXERCISE 11

1 In a built-up area a motorist must not travel faster than 30 mph.
  This can be written as:
  '$s \leq 30$ where s is the speed of the car in miles per hour.'
  Write out the following in a similar way.
  a A lift can hold no more than 8 persons. (Use p for the number of persons.)
  b A box can hold no more than 6 eggs. (Use e for the number of eggs.)
  c You must have more than £4 to go to the cinema.
     (Use m for the number of pounds.)
  d A taxi can only carry parties of less than 5 people.
     (Use p for the number of persons.)
  e A football stadium has capacity for 10 000 people.
     (Use p for the number of persons.)
  f James has less than 36 exposures left in his camera.
     (Use e for the number of exposures.)

2 Put either '<' or '>' between each pair of numbers to make a true statement.
a 3 ... 4	**b** 6 ... 3	**c** 10 ... 8	**d** 0 ... 2
e 2 ... 1	**f** 5 ... 6	**g** 13 ... 3	**h** 0 ... 6
i 19 ... 2	**j** 1 ... 3	**k** 4 ... 2	**l** 7 ... 6
m −2 ... 0	**n** 0 ... −1	**o** −4 ... −6	**p** −5 ... −4

3 Peter is throwing a dice. In each case x stands for one of his scores.
  So we must choose replacements from {1, 2, 3, 4, 5, 6}.
  Find all the solutions of:
a $x > 3$	**b** $x < 2$	**c** $x < 4$	**d** $x > 4$
e $x + 2 > 5$	**f** $x + 2 > 4$	**g** $x + 2 < 4$	**h** $x − 1 > 2$
i $2x > 8$	**j** $5x < 15$	**k** $2x − 1 < 7$	**l** $3x − 2 > 7$

```
  −5 −4 −3 −2 −1  0  1  2  3  4  5
  |  |  |  |  |  |  |  |  |  |  |
```

> **Reminder**
> Negative numbers are less than zero.

4 Are these true or false? Use the number line to help you.
a $−1 < 4$	**b** $−3 > −2$	**c** $−4 \geq 2$	**d** $−2 < −1$
e $−2 \leq −1$	**f** $−3 < −4$	**g** $2 > −3$	**h** $2 \leq −3$

5 Put $<, >, \leq$ or $\geq$ between each pair of numbers to make a true statement.
a $−1$ ... 3	**b** 0 ... −4	**c** $−3$ ... −4	**d** 8 ... −9
e $−2$ ... 0	**f** $−1$ ... −2	**g** $−2$ ... 1	**h** 7 ... −9

6 Choosing replacements from {0, 1, 2, 3, 4}, find all the solutions of:
a $x − 3 < 0$	**b** $y − 6 > −3$	**c** $2 − x > 0$
d $1 > 3 − x$	**e** $3 − 2x < −1$	**f** $5 − 3x \leq −4$
g $−1 \leq 1 − 2x$	**h** $−6 \leq 3x − 12$	**i** $x \geq 2x − 2$

Solving inequalities

In the same way that it helped you solve equations, 'balancing' can be used to solve inequalities.

'x is a whole number' means 'x comes from the list 0, 1, 2, 3, 4, 5, 6, 7, ...'.

<table>
<tr><td>

Example 1

x is a whole number and $\quad 4x > 2x + 8$

Subtract $2x$ from
both sides $\qquad\qquad 2x > 8$

Divide both sides by 2 $\qquad x > 4$

$\qquad\qquad$ Solution: $\quad x > 4$

$x = 5, 6, 7, 8, ...$

</td><td>

Example 2

x is a whole number and $\quad x \geq 3x - 8$

Subtract x from both sides $\quad 0 \geq 2x - 8$

Add 8 to both sides $\qquad\quad 8 \geq 2x$

Divide both sides by 2 $\qquad 4 \geq x$

$\qquad\qquad$ Solution: $\quad x \leq 4$

$x = 0, 1, 2, 3, 4$

</td></tr>
</table>

EXERCISE 12

1 Solve these inequalities (x is a whole number).

a $x + 1 > 2$ (Hint: subtract 1.)   **b** $y + 3 \leq 5$ (Hint: subtract 3.)

c $m - 3 < 6$ (Hint: add 3.)   **d** $2x \geq x + 8$ (Hint: subtract x.)

e $2n - 2 < 8$ (Hint: add 2.)   **f** $3x + 4 \geq 7$ (Hint: subtract 4.)

g $6y + 1 > 13$ (Hint: subtract 1.)   **h** $4x - 2 \geq 10$ (Hint: add 2.)

i $8c - 3 < 5$ (Hint: add 3.)   **j** $p + 5 > 7$ (Hint: subtract 5.)

k $q + 7 \leq 9$ (Hint: subtract 7.)   **l** $h - 1 < 9$ (Hint: add 1.)

2 Solve these inequalities.

a $m + 6 > 9$ **b** $x + 2 < 8$

c $8 + y \leq 10$ **d** $4 + k \geq 4$

e $k + 8 > 22$ **f** $h + 5 < 7$

g $9 + f \leq 20$ **h** $1 + y \geq 4$

i $2x < x + 11$ **j** $4y \geq 3y + 7$

k $6t > 5t + 3$ **l** $4y \leq 2y + 4$

3 Solve these inequalities where the solutions are whole numbers.

a $4n < n + 12$ **b** $3n - 2 > n + 8$

c $8k + 1 \leq 3k + 16$ **d** $4l - 6 \geq l + 21$

e $2x - 1 > 11 - x$ **f** $4y - 6 \leq 14 - y$

g $3x - 6 \geq x + 2$ **h** $2x - 1 \leq x + 3$

i $5x - 3 \leq 3x + 7$

CHAPTER 14 REVIEW

1 Find the value of:
   a $3a + 2b$ when $a = 5$ and $b = 2$
   b $12 - ab$ when $a = 3$ and $b = 1$.

2 The temperature can be estimated from the number of 'chirps' a cricket makes in 1 minute.
   $C = 5(n + 20) \div 36$, where C is the temperature and n is the number of chirps.
   Estimate the temperature when the number of chirps is:
   a 52   b 34   c 25

3 Simplify:
   a $5b - 6 + 2b$ b $2a + 3b + 4a + 5b$ c $x \times x$
   d $r \times r \times r$ e $t \times 2t$ f $(4 \times 6m) + 3$

4 Write without brackets:
   a $5(m + 6)$ b $4(7 + x)$ c $3(2n - 5m)$
   d $a(a + 1)$ e $x(2y - x)$ f $6(2 - 3k)$

5 Simplify:
   a $2(x + 3) - 2$ b $14(1 + y) - 3y$ c $3x + 2(x - 1)$

6 Factorise:
   a $6m + 3$ b $3ab - 9b$ c $16x^2 - 12x^2a$ d $m^2 - m$

7 Solve these equations:
   a $2x - 1 = 9$ b $17 - 2y = 11$ c $3(m - 2) = 15$ d $5k = 4k + 3$

8 These pieces of wood are the same length.
   Measurements are in metres.
   a Form an equation.
   b Solve it to find n.
   c Calculate the length of the pieces.

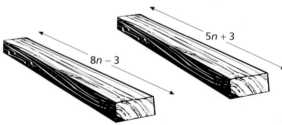

$5n + 3$

$8n - 3$

9 Solve these inequalities:
   a $m + 3 < 9$ b $5m + 2 < 17$ c $2x - 6 < 10$

15 Graphical Relationships

STARTING POINTS

1

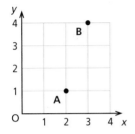

a The coordinates of A are (2, 1).
Which is the x-coordinate?
b What is the y-coordinate of B?
c Give the coordinates of B.

2 Copy the x and y axes.
Plot and label the points:

a P(1, 2) b Q(3, 1)
c R(0, 2) d S(2, 0)
e T(−1, 2) f U(2, −2)

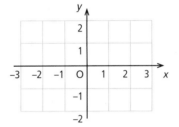

3 Copy and complete the table where y = 3x + 2.

x	0	1	2	3	4
y	2	5			

4 The point (4, 6) lies on this graph.
a Does the point (2, 3) lie on it?
b Give the coordinates of three different
points that lie on this graph.

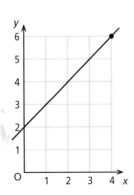

Plotting points and naming lines

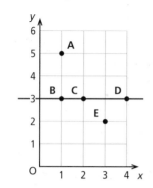

A has coordinates (1, 5). It is above the heavy line.

E has coordinates (3, 2). It is below the heavy line.

B(1, **3**), C(2, **3**) and D(4, **3**) are on the line.

Notice that all points on the line have a *y*-coordinate of 3.

This line is usually referred to as **$y = 3$**.

$y = 3$ is known as the **equation of the line**.

EXERCISE 1

1

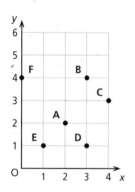

a Name the points with:
   (i) an *x*-coordinate of 3 $(x = 3)$
   (ii) a *y*-coordinate of 4 $(y = 4)$
   (iii) an *x*-coordinate of 2 $(x = 2)$
   (iv) an *x*-coordinate the same
    as the *y*-coordinate $(x = y)$
b (i) What do B and F have in common?
   (ii) What do B and D have in common?

2 Which of the labelled points have:
   a $x = 2$ **b** $y = 4$
   c $y = 0$ **d** $x = 3$
   e $x = 0$ **f** $y = 2$
   g $y = x$ **h** $x = -1$
   i $y = -2$

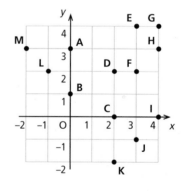

3

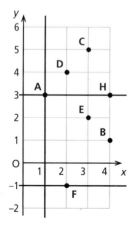

The point A sits on the line $x = 1$ and the line $y = 3$.
   a On which two lines does B sit?
   b Is C to the right or left of $x = 2$?
   c D is on $y = 4$. On what other line is it?
   d E is on $x = 3$. On what other line is it?
   e F is on $y = -1$. On what other line is it?

4 a Give the coordinates of three different points on the line labelled:

  (i) $x = 1$ **(ii)** $y = 3$ **(iii)** $y = 1$.

b Give the coordinates of the point where the lines $x = 1$ and $y = 3$ cross.

c Which two lines cross at (1, 1)?

d Which two lines cross at (1, −2)?

e The diagram is not big enough to show the line $y = 10$.
   Which of these points are on the line $y = 10$?

  (i) (10, 4)   **(ii)** (12, 10)   **(iii)** (3, 5)
  (iv) (3, 10)   **(v)** (10, 1)

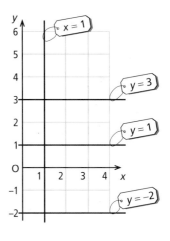

5 What equation goes on each label?

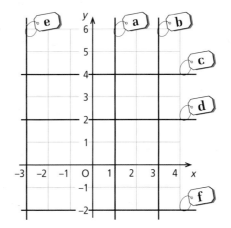

6 For each set of points below,
  (i) plot the points
  (ii) give the equation of the line that passes through them.

  a (2, 4), (2, 6) and (2, 8)
  b (3, 1), (5, 1) and (9, 1)
  c (5, 1) and (5, 7)
  d (4, 3) and (4, 4)
  e (−1, 3) and (−1, 6)
  f (0, −6) and (3, −6)

7 Draw a diagram to help you decide whether:
  a A(2, 3) is above or below the line $y = 2$
  b B(1, 4) is left or right of $x = 2$
  c C(3, 5) is above or below $y = 4$
  d D(2, 0) is left or right of $x = 1$.

8 An artist working at a computer can draw a shape by telling the machine the lines which form its outline.

Example

The lines

$y = 5$,

$y = 1$,

$x = 1$ and $x = 4$

form the shaded rectangle.

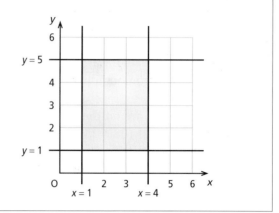

a Name the lines which form these shapes.

(i)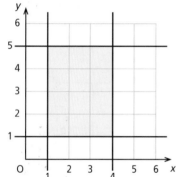

(ii)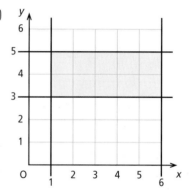

(iii)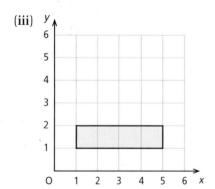

b Draw the shapes which will be formed by these lines.

(i) $x = 4$, $x = 6$, $y = 4$, $y = 5$ (ii) $x = 1$, $x = 5$, $y = 0$, $y = 2$

(iii) $x = 0$, $x = 4$, $y = 3$, $y = 4$ (iv) $x = -4$, $x = 6$, $y = -1$, $y = 3$

(v) $x = -2$, $x = 0$, $y = -1$, $y = 1$ (vi) $x = 3$, $x = -2$, $y = 1$, $y = -3$

Graphed relations

A coach speeds along a motorway at 2 kilometres per minute.
The table shows a period of 3 minutes.

Minutes (x)	0	1	2	3
Kilometres (y)	0	2	4	6

This information can be graphed.
Notice that distance = 2 × time.
The y-coordinate is 2 times the x-coordinate.

$$y = 2x$$

This is the equation of the line.

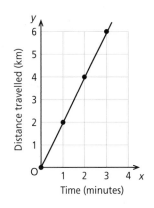

EXERCISE 2

1 A DIY store sells glass at £3 per square metre.
  a Copy and complete the table.

Glass in m² (x)	0	1	2	3	4
Cost in £ (y)	0	3	6		

  b **(i)** Plot the points on a grid.
  (ii) Draw a line through the points.
  c Write down the equation of the line (y = ?x).

2 A plane is climbing at a rate of 9 metres per second.
  a Copy and complete the table.

Time in s (x)	0	1	2	3	4
Height in m (y)	0	9			

  b Draw a graph from the table.
  c Write down the equation of the line.

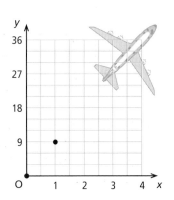

3 The falcons in a district are being studied.
Their numbers are going up by five a year.

  a Copy and complete the table.

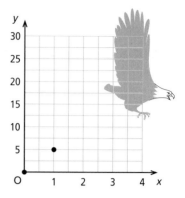

Years (x)	0	1	2	3	4
Falcons (y)	0	5			

  b Draw a graph from the table.
  c Write down the equation of the line.

4 Complete a table and draw a graph for each equation.

  a $y = 5x$ **b** $y = 2x$ **c** $y = 4x$
  d $y = 1.5x$ **e** $y = 2.5x$ **f** $y = 3x$

5 Lines which go through the origin have an equation of the form $y = ax$.

  a **(i)**   On the line $y = 5x$, what is the value of y when $x = 1$?
     (ii) On the line $y = 2x$, what is the value of y when $x = 1$?
    (iii) On the line $y = 6x$, what is the value of y when $x = 1$?
    (iv) On the line $y = ax$, what is the value of y when $x = 1$?

  b Give the equations of each of these lines.

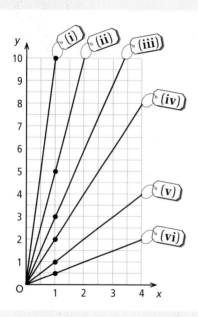

6 The equations of these three lines are:

$$y = -2x$$
$$y = -3x$$
$$y = -\frac{1}{2}x$$

Which is which?

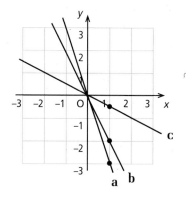

7 Copy and complete the table for each equation.

a $y = -4x$ **b** $y = -5x$ **c** $y = -1.5x$ **d** $y = -2.5x$

x	−3	−2	−1	0	1	2	3
y							

Draw a graph for each equation.

Challenge

Try this investigation if you have a Graph Drawing package.

Task 1
Draw: $y = x$, $y = 2x$, $y = 3x$, $y = 4x$, $y = 5x$
What effect does increasing the number in front of x have on the graph?

Task 2
Draw: $y = -x$, $y = -2x$, $y = -3x$, $y = -4x$, $y = -5x$
What effect does changing the number in front of x have on the graph?

Task 3
Draw: $y = x$, $y = \frac{1}{2}x$, $y = \frac{1}{3}x$, $y = \frac{1}{4}x$, $y = \frac{1}{5}x$
What effect does changing the fraction in front of x have on the graph?

Lines not passing through the origin

Look at the equation $y = 2x + 3$

Make a table of values.

x	−3	−2	−1	0	1	2	3	4
y	−3	−1	1	3	5	7	9	11

Plot the points and draw a
line through them to give
the graph of $y = 2x + 3$.

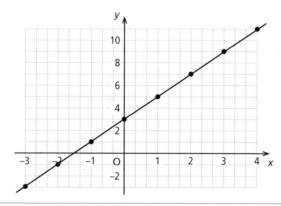

EXERCISE 3

1 Find the value of:

   a $3x + 2$ when $x = 4$

   b $12 - 2x$ when $x = 3$

   c $3x + 5$ when $x = -2$

   d $15 - 6x$ when $x = 2$

   e $13 - 5x$ when $x = 0$.

2 Copy and complete the table for
each equation below.
Plot the points and draw a line
through them to give the graph of
each equation.

x	−3	−2	−1	0	1	2	3	4
y								

   a $y = 2x + 1$ **b** $y = x + 4$ **c** $y = x - 5$ **d** $y = 2x - 7$

3 In each case use the equation to complete
a table and draw its graph.

   a $y = 12 - x$ **b** $y = 3 - 2x$

   c $y = 5 - x$ **d** $y = 3 + 2x$

Hint

It is easier if you don't use
negative values for x.

x	0	1	2	3	4
y					

4 Stephen's phone charge card has a value of £10.
His calls are charged at £2 per hour.
The formula $y = 10 - 2x$ gives the value of the
card, £y, after x hours of phone calls.

   a Copy and complete the table.

   b Plot the points and draw a line through
them to give the graph of the equation.

x	0	1	2	3	4
y					

5 On a diagram like this, draw graphs of:

   a $y = 10x - 5$ **b** $y = 5x + 5$

   c $y = 5x + 30$ **d** $y = 30 - 5x$

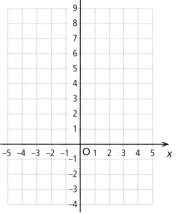

6 Find the value of:

   a $2x + 1$ when $x = -1$

   b $5x - 8$ when $x = 1$

   c $3x + 4$ when $x = -3$

   d $x + 8$ when $x = -2$

   e $2x - 1$ when $x = 0$.

7 Copy and complete the table, then draw graphs for:

   a $y = x + 2$ **b** $y = 2x - 1$

   c $y = x - 3$ **d** $y = 2x + 1$

x	−3	−2	−1	0	1	2	3
y							

8 Lines have an equation of the form

$$y = ax + b.$$

   a **(i)** On the line $y = 2x + 5$ what is the value of y when $x = 0$?

      (ii) On the line $y = 3x + 7$ what is the value of y when $x = 0$?

     (iii) On the line $y = x + 2$ what is the value of y when $x = 0$?

     (iv) On the line $y = 2x + 10$ what is the value of y when $x = 0$?

      (v) On the line $y = ax + b$ what is the value of y when $x = 0$?

   b Match each graph opposite to one of these equations:

      (i) $y = 10 - 2x$

      (ii) $y = x + 13$

     (iii) $y = 5 - x$

     (iv) $y = x + 16$

      (v) $y = 12 - x$

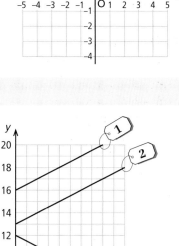

How to find the equation of this graph

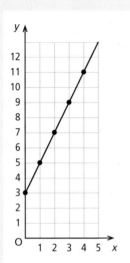

1. Make a table of values.

x	0	1	2	3	4
y	3	5	7	9	11

2. The y-values go up in twos. Consider 2x.

x	0	1	2	3	4
y	0	2	4	6	8

3. Compare these with the actual y-values.

y	3	5	7	9	11

This suggests 2x + 3.
The equation is $y = 2x + 3$. Check it!

EXERCISE 4

1

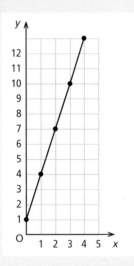

a Make a table of values:

x	0	1	2	3	4
y					

b The y-values go up in threes. Consider 3x.

x	0	1	2	3	4
3x					

c Compare these with the actual y-values and write down the equation of the line.

2 Find the equations of these graphs.

a
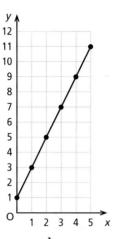

b
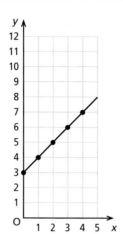

c
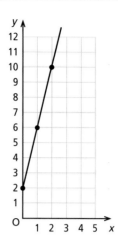

d
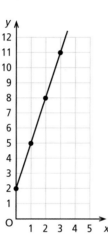

e
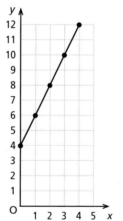

3 Find the equations of these lines.

a
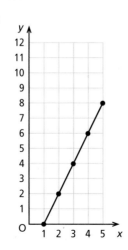

b
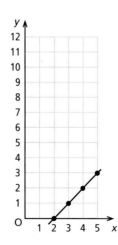

c

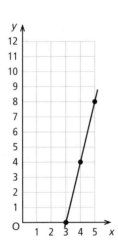

d

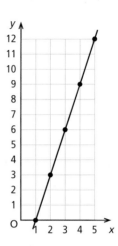

4 An engineering firm makes screws of different lengths.

The graph gives the length (y) when the number of turns on the thread (x) is known.

a Copy and complete the table.

x	10	11	12	13	14
y					

b Write down an equation connecting length of screw (y) and number of turns (x).

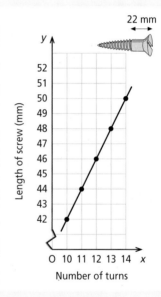

5

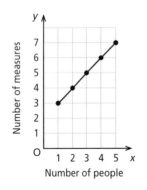

A manufacturer provides a measuring spoon with each box of tea sold.
They also issue a ready reckoner.

a Copy and complete the table.

x	1	2	3	4	5
y					

b Write down an equation connecting the number of measures (y) and number of people (x).

CHAPTER 15 REVIEW

1 Give the equation of each of the three lines.

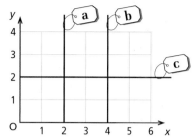

2 Give the equation of the line passing through:
   a (2, 5) and (2, 10)   **b** (1, 3) and (7, 3).

3 **a** Given $y = x$, copy and complete the table.
   Plot the points and draw the graph $y = x$.

x	−3	−2	−1	0	1	2	3
y							

   b Copy and complete the table for $y = -x$.
   Plot the points and draw the graph $y = -x$.

x	0	1	2	3
y				

   c Given $y = 3x$, copy and complete the table.
   Plot the points and draw the graph $y = 3x$.

x	−3	−2	−1	0	1	2	3
y							

   d Copy and complete the table for $y = 2x + 3$.
   Plot the points and draw the graph $y = 2x + 3$.

x	−3	−2	−1	0	1	2	3
y							

4 On a diagram like this draw graphs of:
   a $y = 2x + 4$
   b $y = 4x + 1$
   c $y = 10 - 2x$
   d $y = 8 - x$.

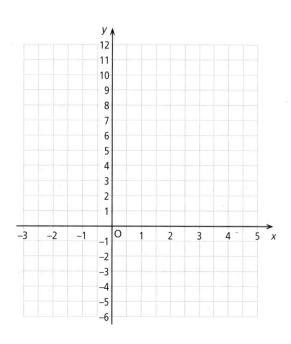

16 Basic Trigonometry

The study of triangles is important in:

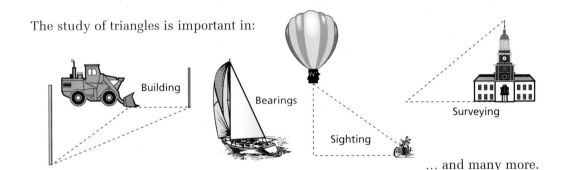

Building

Bearings

Sighting

Surveying

… and many more.

STARTING POINTS

1 Copy these triangles and write 'H' on the side known as the **hypotenuse**.

a **b** **c** **d**

2 Round each of these numbers to **(i)** 1 decimal place   **(ii)** 2 decimal places.
   a 43.7248   **b** 5.683 52   **c** 0.358 201   **d** 27.9836

3 **a** Use the formula $P = AB$ to calculate P when $A = 12$ and $B = 5.3$.

   b Use the formula $M = \dfrac{X}{Y}$ to calculate M when $X = 45$ and $Y = 0.9$.

4 Here is the triangle which helps you remember the speed, distance and time formulae.

State the formula being hinted at in each picture below.

a

$T =$

b

c

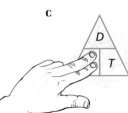

In this right-angled triangle, the right angle and an angle of size $x°$ have been marked.

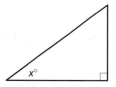

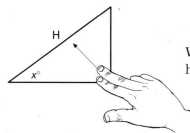

We call the side opposite the right angle the hypotenuse (H).

We refer to the other two sides as:

(i) the side **opposite** $x°$ (O)

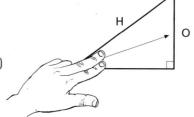

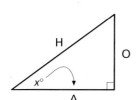

(ii) the side **adjacent** to $x°$ (A). 'Adjacent' means 'next to'.

EXERCISE 1

1 Copy the following triangles and label the sides hypotenuse (H), opposite (O) and adjacent (A), with respect to the angle marked $x°$.

a 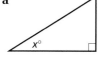   **b**   **c**

d 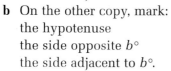   **e**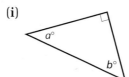

2 Make two copies of each of these triangles.
  a On one copy, mark:
  the hypotenuse
  the side opposite $a°$
  the side adjacent to $a°$.
  b On the other copy, mark:
  the hypotenuse
  the side opposite $b°$
  the side adjacent to $b°$.

(i)   **(ii)**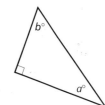

3 A surveyor stands 26 m from a steeple.
He measures an angle of 35° as shown.
How can he find the height of the steeple?

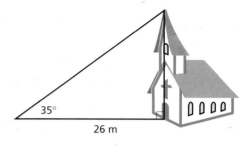

26 m

a Draw an angle of 35°
($\angle BAC$).

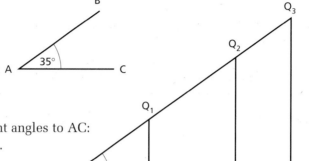

b Draw three lines at right angles to AC:
P_1Q_1, P_2Q_2 and P_3Q_3.

c Measuring as accurately as you can with a ruler, complete a table similar to the
one shown.

position	opposite PQ	adjacent AP	opp ÷ adj PQ ÷ AP
1	1.7	2.3	0.7
2	2.2	3	0.7
3	2.7	3.7	0.7

d Compare your answers with other students.
Notice that you should all have the same answer in the last column even although
you were measuring different lengths.

e Repeat the above example for angles of:
(i) 40° **(ii)** 45° **(iii)** 50°.

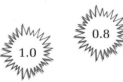

For any particular angle, $x°$, the ratio of the opposite side to the adjacent side is a fixed number.

For 35°, opposite side ÷ adjacent side = 0.7.

Historically this number has been called the **tangent of $x°$** (shortened to **tan $x°$**).

For 35°: tan 35° = 0.7

In the not so distant past you could look up the tangent of each angle in a printed table.

Nowadays this table is programmed into your calculator.
Check your calculator.

Either   or

should give you 0.700 207 5.
Unless otherwise stated we will work to 3 d.p. (tan 35° = 0.700).
Check your display reads 'DEG'.

Using [2nd F] we can reverse the process.

With 0.700 207 5 in the display [2nd F] [TAN] [=] gives 35.0°.
(Give angles to 1 d.p.)
This means 'the angle which has 0.700 207 5 for a tangent is 35.0°'.

This triangle will help you remember:

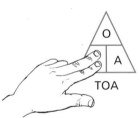

$$\tan x° = \frac{\text{opposite}}{\text{adjacent}}$$

Example 1

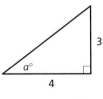

$\tan a° = \dfrac{3}{4}$

$= 3 ÷ 4 = 0.75$

Example 2

If $x = 56$

then tan $x° = 1.483$

(3 d.p.)

Example 3

If tan $x° = 0.35$

then $x° = 19.3°$

(1 d.p.)

EXERCISE 2

1 Write down the tangent of each labelled angle. (Take care in **d**.)

a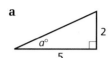

b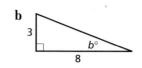

c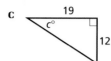

d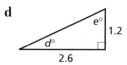

2 Calculate, to 3 decimal places:

   a tan 20°   **b** tan 67°   **c** tan 36.8°   **d** tan 78.3°   **e** tan 6.4°.

3 Use your calculator to work out the size of the angle
  (to 1 d.p.), given that:

   a tan $x°$ = 0.578   **b** tan $x°$ = 1.25

   c tan $x°$ = 0.896   **d** tan $x°$ = 1.

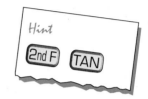

Using tangent to find the size of an angle in a triangle

Example
Calculate the size of the angle marked $x°$.

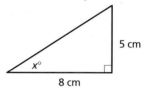

Copy the triangle.
Label the sides.

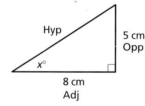

Remember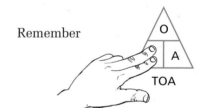

$$\tan x° = \frac{\text{opposite}}{\text{adjacent}}$$

Substitute. $\tan x° = \dfrac{5}{8} = 5 \div 8$

              $\tan x° = 0.625$

Using the calculator [2nd F] [TAN] we get $x° = 32.0°$ (to 1 d.p.)

EXERCISE 3

Give each angle correct to 1 decimal place.

1 Calculate the size of the angle marked $x°$ in each triangle.
  Be careful when labelling 'opposite' and 'adjacent'.

   a $\tan x° = \dfrac{4}{\ldots} = 4 \div \ldots$

      $\tan x° = \ldots$

        $x° = \ldots$ (to 1 d.p.)

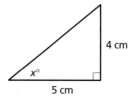

b $\tan x° = \dfrac{...}{6} = ... \div 6$

   $\tan x° = ...$

     $x° = ...$ (to 1 d.p.)

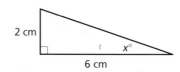

2 cm

6 cm

c

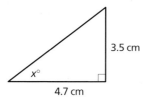

3.5 cm

4.7 cm

d

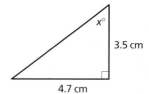

$x°$

3.5 cm

4.7 cm

e

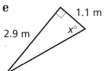

1.1 m

2.9 m

$x°$

f

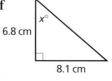

$x°$

6.8 cm

8.1 cm

g

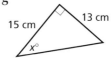

13 cm

15 cm

$x°$

h

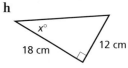

$x°$

18 cm

12 cm

2 A flagpole is 4.5 m high.
A wire is attached from the top of the pole to the
ground, 2.7 m from the foot of the pole.
What angle does the wire make with the ground?

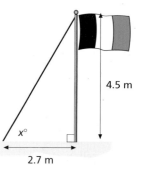

4.5 m

$x°$

2.7 m

3 A submarine dives.
After 100 m it is at a depth of 17.6 m.
What is its angle of dive?

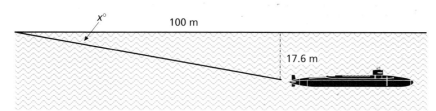

$x°$

100 m

17.6 m

The sine of an angle

In this triangle we are told the lengths of the opposite side and the hypotenuse but not the adjacent side.

We cannot use the tangent.

To cope with this, another ratio has been invented.

The ratio $\dfrac{\text{opposite side}}{\text{hypotenuse}}$ is called the **sine of the angle**.

In the above triangle the sine of $x°$ is $\dfrac{6}{10}$.

We write: $\sin x° = \dfrac{6}{10} = 0.6$.

This triangle will help you remember:

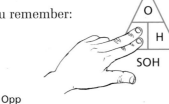

SOH

$$\sin x° = \frac{\text{opposite}}{\text{hypotenuse}}$$

Example 1

$$\sin x° = \frac{5}{6} = 0.833$$

Example 2

 SIN

If $x = 56$
then $\sin x° = 0.829$
(3 d.p.)

Example 3

 2nd F   SIN

If $\sin x° = 0.35$
then $x° = 20.5°$
(1 d.p.)

EXERCISE 4

1 Work out the sine of each angle marked $x°$ (to 3 d.p.).

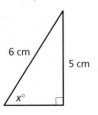   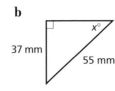   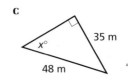   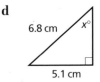

2 Use the SIN button to find the value of each of the following (to 3 d.p.):

   a $\sin 45°$ **b** $\sin 0°$ **c** $\sin 86°$ **d** $\sin 90°$

   e $\sin 46.4°$ **f** $\sin 79.8°$ **g** $\sin 21.6°$

3 Use the SIN and 2nd F buttons to find the value of each angle (to 1 d.p.):

   a $\sin a° = 0.876$ **b** $\sin b° = 0.137$ **c** $\sin c° = 0.500$ **d** $\sin d° = 0.401$.

4 Find sin $x°$. Hence find x in each triangle.

a

6 cm, 3 cm, $x°$

b
17 cm, 21 cm, $x°$

c
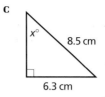
$x°$, 8.5 cm, 6.3 cm

d
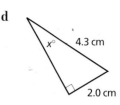
$x°$, 4.3 cm, 2.0 cm

5 A plank of wood is leaning against a wall.
The plank is 3 m long.
The top of the plank reaches 1.7 m up the wall.
Calculate the angle the plank makes with the ground.

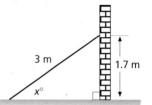
3 m, 1.7 m, $x°$

6
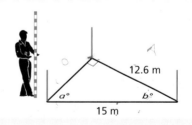

An observation balloon is tethered
120 m above the ground.
It is held by a rope 150 m long.
What angle does the rope make with the ground?

150 m, 120 m, $x°$

7 A vintage plane takes off at an air show.
After flying 325 m it is 60 m off the
ground.
What is its angle of climb?

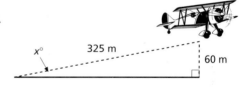
$x°$, 325 m, 60 m

8 A surveyor marks out a triangular patch of
ground with a right angle as shown.
  a Calculate the size of the angle
    marked $a°$.
  b Hence calculate the size of the angle
    marked $b°$.

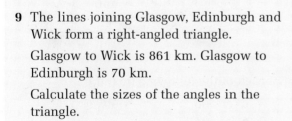
12.6 m, $a°$, $b°$, 15 m

9 The lines joining Glasgow, Edinburgh and
Wick form a right-angled triangle.

Glasgow to Wick is 861 km. Glasgow to
Edinburgh is 70 km.

Calculate the sizes of the angles in the
triangle.

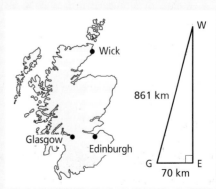
Wick, W, 861 km, Glasgow, Edinburgh, G, E, 70 km

The cosine of an angle

A third ratio is needed in examples where the lengths of the adjacent side and the hypotenuse are used.

The ratio $\dfrac{\text{adjacent side}}{\text{hypotenuse}}$ is called the **cosine of the angle**.

In this triangle the cosine of $x°$ is $\dfrac{3}{5}$.

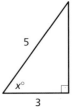

We write: $\cos x° = \dfrac{3}{5} = 0.6$.

Use this triangle to help you remember:

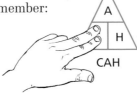

CAH

CAH

$$\cos x° = \frac{\text{adjacent}}{\text{hypotenuse}}$$

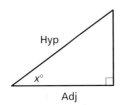

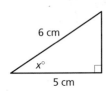

Example 1

$\cos x° = \dfrac{5}{6} = 0.833$

Example 2

If $x = 56$
then $\cos x° = 0.559$
(3 d.p.)

Example 3

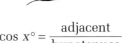

If $\cos x° = 0.35$
then $x° = 69.5°$
(1 d.p.)

EXERCISE 5

1 Work out the cosine of each angle marked $x°$ (to 3 d.p.).

a 16 cm, 12 cm

b 24 mm, 43 mm, $x°$

c 6.1 m, $x°$, 8.6 m

d 9.9 cm, $x°$, 3.6 cm

2 Use the [COS] button to find the value of each of the following (to 3 d.p.):

  a $\cos 45°$ **b** $\cos 0°$ **c** $\cos 90°$ **d** $\cos 12°$

  e $\cos 49.4$ **f** $\cos 33.8°$ **g** $\cos 84.1°$.

3 Use the [COS] and [2nd F] buttons to find the value of each angle (to 1 d.p.):

  a $\cos a° = 1$ **b** $\cos b° = 0$ **c** $\cos c° = 0.500$ **d** $\cos d° = 0.321$.

4 Find cos $x°$ and hence the value of x in each triangle.

a

7 cm
6 cm
$x°$

b

20 cm
15 cm
$x°$

c

7.4 cm
8.9 cm
$x°$

d

34 mm
25 mm
$x°$

5 A ladder is propped up against a wall.
The ladder is 3.5 m long.
The foot of the ladder is 1.2 m from the wall.
Calculate the angle the ladder makes with the
ground.

3.5 m
$x°$
1.2 m

6 A 'wall of death' is supported by
triangular struts as shown.
  a What angle does the wall make
  with the ground?
  b What angle does the wall make
  with the vertical support?

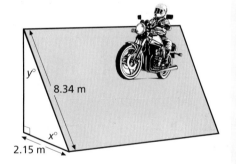

$y°$
8.34 m
$x°$
2.15 m

7 On a model of Tower Bridge, Michael measures:
  • the height of the tower as 20 cm
  • the distance from the top of one tower to the bottom of the other as 40 cm.
Calculate the sizes of the angles in the triangle shown.

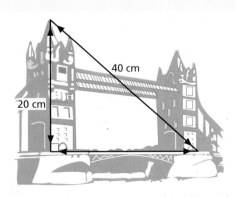

40 cm
20 cm

Picking the ratio

Remember the triangles:

SIN
COS
TAN

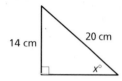

O
S | H
SOH

A
C | H
CAH

O
T | A
TOA

Hyp   Opp

$x°$

Adj

Example 1   Find the size of x.

14 cm   20 cm

$x°$

Label the sides involved.

Hyp
20 cm

14 cm
Opp

$x°$

Spot the ratio.

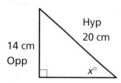

Two ticks — (SOH)   CAH   TOA

O
H
SOH

$$\sin x° = \frac{\text{opposite}}{\text{hypotenuse}} = \frac{14}{20} = 0.7$$

$$x° = 44.4°$$

Example 2   Find the size of x.

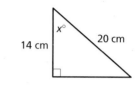

$x°$ 20 cm

14 cm

Label the sides involved.

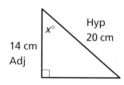

Hyp
20 cm

14 cm
Adj

$x°$

Spot the ratio.

SOH   (CAH)   TOA

Two ticks

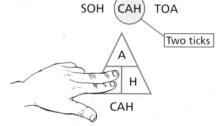

A
H
CAH

$$\cos x° = \frac{\text{adjacent}}{\text{hypotenuse}} = \frac{14}{20} = 0.7$$

$$x° = 45.6°$$

EXERCISE 6

1 Work out the size of the angle marked $x°$ in each triangle.

a
3 cm

$x°$
8 cm

b
16 cm
12 cm
$x°$

c
$x°$
24 cm
31 cm

d
7.2 cm
$x°$
5.5 cm

e
0.9 m   1.3 m
$x°$

f

1.3 m
$x°$
0.9 m

g
4.7 cm
$x°$
4.2 cm

h
130 cm
$x°$
100 cm

Finding the length of a side: using tan

Example
Calculate x.

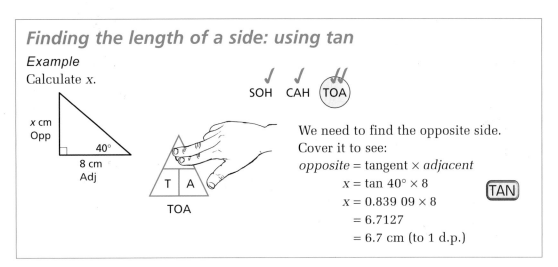

SOH CAH TOA

We need to find the opposite side.
Cover it to see:

opposite = tangent × *adjacent*

$$x = \tan 40° × 8$$
$$x = 0.839\,09 × 8$$
$$= 6.7127$$
$$= 6.7 \text{ cm (to 1 d.p.)}$$

TAN

EXERCISE 7

Find each length correct to 1 decimal place.

1 Calculate the length of the side marked x in each triangle.

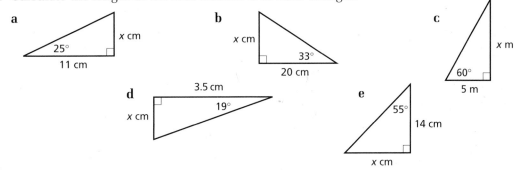

a 25° 11 cm x cm

b x cm 33° 20 cm

c x m 60° 5 m

d 3.5 cm 19° x cm

e 55° 14 cm x cm

2 A helicopter on a rescue mission hovers
near a cliff as shown.
The person needing rescued is 50 m
down the cliff.
The rope makes an angle of 35° with
the cliff.
Calculate how far from the cliff the
helicopter is hovering.

3 A jet takes off from an airport at a
steady climb of 21°.
How high is the aircraft when it is
1000 m from the airport?

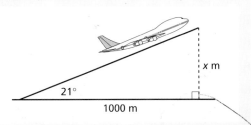

Finding the length of a side: using sine

Example
Calculate *x*.

(SOH) CAH TOA

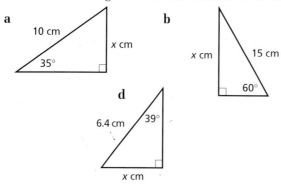

We need to find the opposite side.
Cover it to see:

opposite = sine × *hypotenuse*

$$x = \sin 28° \times 14$$
$$x = 0.469\ 47 \times 14$$
$$= 6.5726$$
$$= 6.6 \text{ cm (to 1 d.p.)}$$

SIN

EXERCISE 8

Find each length correct to 1 decimal place.

1 Calculate the length of the side marked *x* in each triangle.

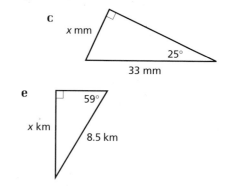

a 10 cm, *x* cm, 35°

b *x* cm, 15 cm, 60°

c *x* mm, 25°, 33 mm

d 6.4 cm, 39°, *x* cm

e 59°, *x* km, 8.5 km

2 The slope of the roof of this house is 2.3 m long.
The roof slopes at an angle of 51°.
What is the headroom in the attic (*x* m)?

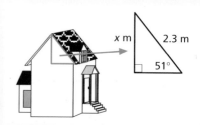

3 A skier goes down a constant slope of 19° for 150 m.
How much height did she lose?

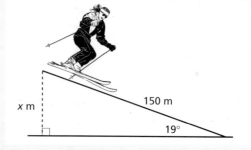

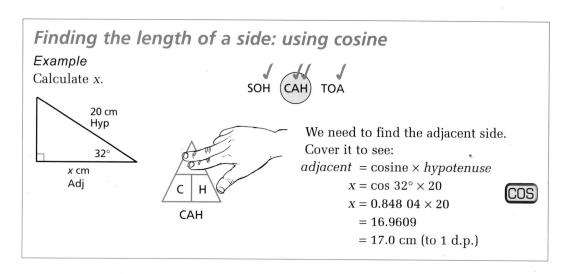

Finding the length of a side: using cosine

Example
Calculate x.

SOH (CAH) TOA

20 cm
Hyp

32°

x cm
Adj

C | H

CAH

We need to find the adjacent side.
Cover it to see:
adjacent $= cosine \times hypotenuse$

$$x = \cos 32° \times 20$$
$$x = 0.848\ 04 \times 20$$
$$= 16.9609$$
$$= 17.0 \text{ cm (to 1 d.p.)}$$

COS

EXERCISE 9

Find each length correct to 1 decimal place.

1 Calculate the length of the side marked x in each triangle.

a

11 cm

53°

x cm

b

66°   8.5 cm

x cm

c

x cm

35 cm   17°

d

24°

30 km

x km

e

x cm

47°

51 cm

2

N

x km

56°   8 km

A yacht sailed for 8 km at an angle of 56° to the north.
Calculate the value of x to see how far north of the start it is.

Finding the length of a side: mixed examples

Reminder

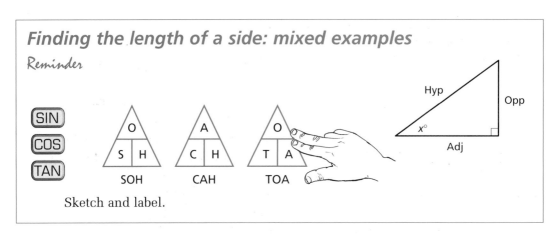

SIN
COS
TAN

O / S H — SOH
A / C H — CAH
O / T A — TOA

Hyp
Opp
$x°$
Adj

Sketch and label.

EXERCISE 10

1 Calculate x in each triangle.

a
20°
x cm
5.7 cm

b
x cm
15 cm
47°

c
24 cm
35°
x cm

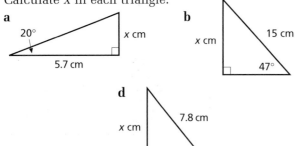

d
7.8 cm
x cm
50°

e
x cm
33 cm
12°

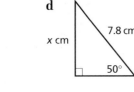
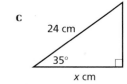
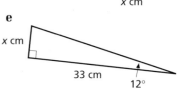

f
x cm
5.2 cm
30°

g
8.5 cm
66°
x cm

h
x cm
3.4 cm
38°

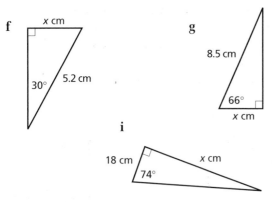
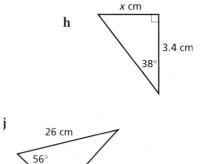

i
18 cm
74°
x cm

j
26 cm
56°
x cm

2 A 6 m ladder reaches the top of a wall.
The ladder makes an angle of 70° with the ground.
How far is the foot of the ladder from the wall?

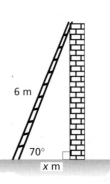

6 m
70°
x m

3 The string on a weather balloon is 40 m long.
The angle between the string and the ground is 65°.
Calculate the height of the balloon above the ground.

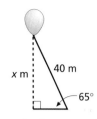
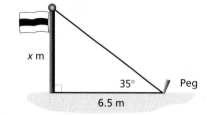

4

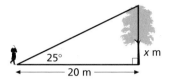

Grant is standing 20 m from the bottom of a tree.
He measures the angle to the top of the tree. It
measures 25°. Calculate the height of the tree.

5 A flagpole is held in place by a wire as shown.
The wire makes an angle of 35° with the ground.
The distance from the peg holding the wire to the
base of the flagpole is 6.5 m.
How high is the flagpole?

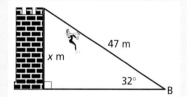

EXERCISE 11

1 A 'death-slide' wire 47 m long is attached from the
top of a tower to the ground at B.
The wire makes an angle of 32° with the ground.
  a How high is the tower?
  b How far is B from the foot of the tower?

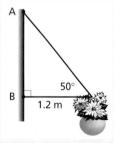

2

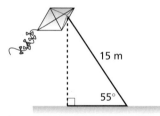

A kite is held by 15 m of string. The angle
between the string and the ground is 55°.
  a Calculate the height of the kite.
  b The string stays the same length but the
  angle drops to 30°.
  How high is the kite now?

3 A hanging basket of plants is supported by two pieces of
wrought iron, as shown. One piece of metal is horizontal
and is 1.2 m long. The other is at an angle of 50° to the
horizontal.
  a Screws are attached at A and B. How far apart are the
  screws?
  b Calculate the length of the sloping support using Pythagoras.

6

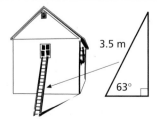

A 3.5 m ladder is leaning against the wall of a
house. The ladder is at an angle of 63° to the
ground.
  a How far from the wall is the base of the ladder?
  b The top of the ladder reaches a window.
  How high above the ground is the window?

5 A see-saw has a 0.75 m high pivot in the middle.
The see-saw is 3 m long.
Calculate the angle it makes with the ground.

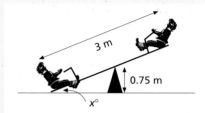

6

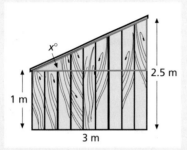

The diagram shows the side view of a shed.
Calculate the angle the roof makes with the horizontal.

7 Two poles (of different heights) are 20 m apart.
A wire is strung between the poles.
The wire makes an angle of 15° to the horizontal.
If the smaller pole is 6 m high, how high is the larger one?

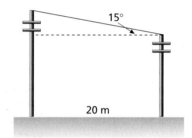

8 A brainstormer!
An observer in a balloon has to look down through 32° to look at a lorry at L.
He has to look down through 57° to see a cyclist at C.
The balloon is 324 m up.
How far apart are the lorry and cyclist?

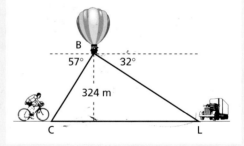

Summary

$$\sin x° = \frac{\text{opposite side}}{\text{hypotenuse}}$$

SOH

$$\cos x° = \frac{\text{adjacent side}}{\text{hypotenuse}}$$

CAH

$$\tan x° = \frac{\text{opposite side}}{\text{adjacent side}}$$

TOA

CHAPTER 16 REVIEW

1 Calculate the angle marked $x°$ in each of these right-angled triangles.

a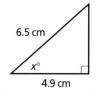

6.5 cm

4.9 cm

$x°$

b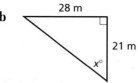

28 m

21 m

$x°$

c

$x°$

70 mm

54 mm

2 Calculate the length of the side marked x in each triangle.

a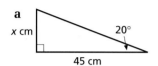

x cm

20°

45 cm

b

x cm

5.4 cm

81°

c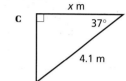

x m

37°

4.1 m

3

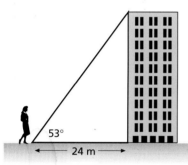

53°

24 m

Indira is standing 24 m from a tall building.
The angle of elevation to the top of the building from where she is standing is 53°.
Calculate the height of the building (to 1 d.p.).

4 A radio mast is 30 m high.
It is held in place by a wire 40 m
long, as shown in the diagram.
Calculate the angle the wire makes
with the ground.

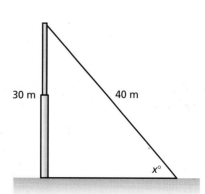

30 m

40 m

$x°$

17 Standard Form

Reminder

$$4^5 = 4 \times 4 \times 4 \times 4 \times 4 = 1024$$

On a calculator: 1024

STARTING POINTS

1 a $10^7 = 10 \times 10 \times 10 \times 10 \times 10 \times 10 \times 10 = 10\,000\,000$
Make similar statements about:
(i) 10^6 **(ii)** 10^5 **(iii)** 10^4 **(iv)** 10^3 **(v)** 10^2

b 10^7 means that seven zeros follow the 1.
Make similar statements about:
(i) 10^6 **(ii)** 10^5 **(iii)** 10^4 **(iv)** 10^3 **(v)** 10^2

c Look at the patterns above.
Can you suggest a meaning for: **(i)** 10^1 **(ii)** 10^0?

2 Can your calculator work out a million times a million?
Write down what your calculator displays when you enter:
$1\,000\,000 \times 1\,000\,000 =$

3 Use your calculator to find:
a 2×93 **b** 2×93 m **c** 2×93 kg

Working with big numbers

Scientists often have to work with big numbers.
Example The distance the earth travels in one orbit is $6 \times 93\,000\,000$ miles.

$6 \times 93\,000\,000 = 6 \times 93 \times 1\,000\,000$
$\qquad\qquad\qquad = 558 \times 1\,000\,000$
$\qquad\qquad\qquad = 558\,000\,000$

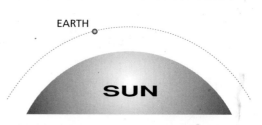

EXERCISE 1

1 93 000 000 = 93 × 1 000 000. Write the following in a similar manner:

    a 1200   **b** 275 000 000   **c** 34 000   **d** 300   **e** 9 740 000   **f** 80

2 84 × 100 = 8400. Calculate:

    a 23 × 100   **b** 456 × 1000   **c** 4 × 1 000 000

    d 78 × 10   **e** 3.1 × 100   **f** 6.75 × 1000

3 Calculate the following using the method shown in the example at the start of this exercise.

    a 16 × 75 000 000   **b** 8 × 127 000 000

    c 9 × 578 000 000 000   **d** 244 × 98 100 000

4 Fish first appeared in the Silurian period. This period lasted 40 000 000 years. Dinosaurs ruled the earth in the Jurassic period. This period was 1.2 times as long. Calculate the length of the Jurassic period.

5 Calculate:

    a 3.14 × 100   **b** 6.29 × 1000   **c** 8.41 × 10 000

    d 7.21 × 1000 000   **e** 1.45 × 1 000 000 000   **f** 9.79 × 10

6 845 000 can be written as 8.45 × 100 000.

450 can be written as 4.5 × 100.

Write these numbers in the same way. Remember to put the decimal point after the first digit.

    a 94 200   **b** 841 000   **c** 214   **d** 616 000 000   **e** 92

Scientists use the above ideas to help them express all numbers in a **standard form** (sometimes referred to as **scientific notation**). Look at these examples.

$$7500 = 7.5 \times 1000 = 7.5 \times 10^3$$
$$75\,000 = 7.5 \times 10\,000 = 7.5 \times 10^4$$
$$7\,500\,000 = 7.5 \times 1\,000\,000 = 7.5 \times 10^6$$
$$750 = 7.5 \times 100 = 7.5 \times 10^2$$
$$75 = 7.5 \times 10 = 7.5 \times 10^1$$
$$7.5 = 7.5 \times 1 = 7.5 \times 10^0$$

Note that:

- the decimal point is always after the first digit
- the index tells you how many places to move the decimal point to get the normal form of the number. (By 'normal' we mean the usual way of writing numbers.)

Example   Write 4.56×10^5 in normal form.

Step 1 List the digits.   4 5 6

Step 2 Move point 5 places to the right.   4 5 6 0 0 0

So $4.56 \times 10^5 = 456\,000$ 5 places

Add zeros as required

EXERCISE 2

1 Write these numbers in **normal form**.

   a 4.56×10^6 **b** 8.41×10^3 **c** 2.96×10^1 **d** 4.11×10^0 **e** 5.46×10^5

   f 7.19×10^2 **g** 8.82×10^1 **h** 6.17×10^0 **i** 8.9×10^4 **j** 2.3×10^3

2 Write these in **standard form**.

   a 321   **b** 4726   **c** 52.1   **d** 5.12   **e** 49.6

   f 596.4   **g** 396 000 **h** 45 600 000 **i** 13 000   **j** 17

   k 2   **l** 425   **m** 14 000 000 **n** 800 000 **o** 250 000 000

   p 610 000 **q** 201 000 000 **r** 5 622 000

3

> Look at these two examples.
>
> *Example 1*
> $$5 \times 164\,000\,000$$
> $$= 5 \times (1.64 \times 10^8)$$
> $$= (5 \times 1.64) \times 10^8$$
> $$= 8.2 \times 10^8$$
> $$= 820\,000\,000$$
>
> *Example 2*
> $$3.2 \times 2\,100\,000$$
> $$= 3.2 \times (2.1 \times 10^6)$$
> $$= (3.2 \times 2.1) \times 10^6$$
> $$= 6.72 \times 10^6$$
> $$= 6\,720\,000$$

Do the following in the same way.

   a $4 \times 124\,000$ **b** $2 \times 445\,000$ **c** $3 \times 241\,000\,000$

   d $5 \times 110\,000\,000$ **e** $3.14 \times 23\,700\,000$ **f** $4.15 \times 125\,000\,000$

4 Saturn is 1 425 000 000 km from the sun.
To go round the sun once, it must travel 6.28
times this distance.
Calculate how far this is. Use standard form.

Very small numbers

We can work with very small numbers in a similar way.
Here are two examples.

      $1.63 \times 0.001 = 0.001\,63$ Note the decimal point moves 3 places to the left.

  $2.41 \times 10^{-3} = 0.002\,41$ Note the decimal point moves 3 places to the left.

EXERCISE 3

1 a Calculate these and comment on the movement of the decimal point.

     (i) 1.4×0.1 **(ii)** 1.4×0.01 **(iii)** 1.4×0.001

     (iv) 1.4×0.0001 **(v)** $1.4 \times 0.000\,01$ **(vi)** $1.4 \times 0.000\,001$

b Use the $\boxed{10^x}$ button on your calculator to work out these.

  (i) 10^{-1} **(ii)** 10^{-2} **(iii)** 10^{-3} **(iv)** 10^{-4} **(v)** 10^{-5}

c Here are two more examples.

$$0.0052 = 5.2 \times 0.001$$
$$0.000\,36 = 3.6 \times 0.0001$$

Check them by reversing the process on your calculator.

Now express these numbers in a similar fashion, placing the decimal point after the first digit.

  (i) 0.062 **(ii)** 0.857 **(iii)** 0.000 045 6 **(iv)** 0.000 091
  (v) 0.000 000 000 238 **(vi)** 0.035 **(vii)** 0.021 **(viii)** 0.0004
  (ix) 0.000 078 **(x)** 0.000 000 916

d Look at these two examples.

$$0.0052 = 5.2 \times 0.001 = 5.2 \times 10^{-3}$$
$$0.000\,36 = 3.6 \times 0.0001 = 3.6 \times 10^{-4}$$

Again check them by reversing the process on your calculator.

Now do the same with these numbers.

  (i) 0.062 **(ii)** 0.857 **(iii)** 0.000 045 6 **(iv)** 0.000 091 **(v)** 0.000 238

2

Example Write 5.2×10^{-3} in normal form.

Step 1 List the digits. $\qquad\qquad\qquad\qquad$ 5 2

Step 2 Move the point 3 places to the left $\quad$ 0 . 0 0 5 2
  (adding zeros as needed).

So $5.2 \times 10^{-3} = 0.0052$

Write these numbers in normal form.

a 7.21×10^{-1} **b** 3.85×10^{-3} **c** 6.11×10^{-5} **d** 1.27×10^{-7}

e 8.89×10^{-2} **f** 7.49×10^{-1} **g** 4×10^{-4} **h** 5×10^{-6}

3 Express these small numbers in standard form.
  a 0.01 **b** 0.0034 **c** 0.000 005 41 **d** 0.000 093 **e** 0.0461 **f** 0.9

4

Example

$$3.2 \times 0.000\,0152$$
$$= 3.2 \times (1.52 \times 10^{-5})$$
$$= (3.2 \times 1.52) \times 10^{-5}$$
$$= 4.864 \times 10^{-5}$$
$$= 0.000\,048\,64$$

Calculate these in the same way.
  a 4.1×0.0125 **b** $2.14 \times 0.000\,022$ **c** $1.41 \times 0.000\,000\,314$
  d $3.14 \times 0.001\,56$ **e** $2.9 \times 0.000\,000\,000\,21$ **f** $1.09 \times 0.000\,000\,53$
  g $5.4 \times 0.000\,000\,000\,124$

Using calculators

Although the numbers you have been working with have too many digits to enter into your calculator, you can still use it to come up with the answer. This is because your calculator is equipped to handle numbers in standard form.

$\boxed{\text{Exp}}$

Example 1

To calculate 4.12×10^4, enter $\boxed{4}$ $\boxed{\cdot}$ $\boxed{1}$ $\boxed{2}$ $\boxed{\text{Exp}}$ $\boxed{4}$ $\boxed{=}$

Different calculators will display the answer in different ways, but they all mean the same thing. Your calculator may display the answer in one of these forms:

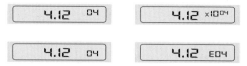

$4.12 \quad 04$	4.12×10^{04}
$4.12 \quad 04$	$4.12 \quad E04$

Your calculator can work all the time in SCI mode (standard form) if you wish. Remember to return to NORM mode (normal form) when you are finished.
Note that it is only the form of the numbers which has changed. Once the numbers are in the calculator's memory, it can manipulate them as it has always done. (Don't be afraid to experiment.)

Example 2

To calculate $7 \times (6.37 \times 10^5)$,

enter $\boxed{7}$ $\boxed{\times}$ $\boxed{6}$ $\boxed{\cdot}$ $\boxed{3}$ $\boxed{7}$ $\boxed{\text{Exp}}$ $\boxed{5}$ $\boxed{=}$

The answer is 4.459×10^6.
The brackets exist in the written form for the sake of clarity.
They are optional on the calculator.

EXERCISE 4

1 Interpret these calculator displays.

a $\boxed{4.6 \quad -05}$ **b** $\boxed{4.2 \quad E04}$ **c** $\boxed{2.9 \quad E07}$

d $\boxed{6.51 \quad 04}$ **e** $\boxed{2.017 \times 10^{09}}$ **f** $\boxed{1.15 \quad E-04}$

g $\boxed{3.2 \quad -07}$ **h** $\boxed{7.13 \quad 08}$ **i** $\boxed{7.61 \times 10^{07}}$

2 Work out the following, leaving your answer in standard form.

a $6 \times (4.12 \times 10^5)$ **b** $8 \times (3.79 \times 10^8)$

c $2.15 \times (3 \times 10^{10})$ **d** $8.21 \times (3.5 \times 10^4)$

e $3.14 \times (6 \times 10^{-3})$ **f** $2 \times (5.66 \times 10^{-8})$

g $6.71 \times (8.6 \times 10^{-9})$ **h** $3.52 \times (8.99 \times 10^{-6})$

Hint
Make use of the $\boxed{\text{Exp}}$ button to enter a negative index.

3

> *Example*
>
> Calculate $(3.78 \times 10^7) \div 4.3$.
>
> Enter 3 • 7 8 Exp 7 ÷ 4 • 3 =
>
> The display will show 8.790697674 ^{06}
>
> We can round off some of the digits if we wish.
>
> We say the answer is 8.79×10^6 correct to **3 significant figures** or 8.791×10^6 correct to **4 significant figures**.

Work out the following, rounding to 3 significant figures where necessary.

a $(3.4 \times 10^4) \div 2$

b $(6.4 \times 10^6) \div 3$

c $(8.14 \times 10^3) \div 4.7$

d $(8.94 \times 10^5) \div 3.6$

e $5 \div (4.44 \times 10^3)$

f $9 \div (4 \times 10^7)$

g $3.14 \div (7.1 \times 10^{-4})$

h $4.97 \div (1.03 \times 10^{-7})$

4 Adding and subtracting is also possible. Try these.

a $(2.7 \times 10^2) + 25$

b $(1.04 \times 10^0) + 37$

c $(7.89 \times 10^2) - 84$

d $(9.97\times 10^{-1)} - 0.35$

e $18 + (2.04 \times 10^{-1)})$

f $87 + (3 \times 10^2)$

g $873 - (8 \times 10^2)$

h $0.761 - (6.1 \times 10^{-2})$

5 Both numbers in a calculation can be in standard form.
Work out each of the following, leaving your answer in standard form.

a $(1.26 \times 10^5) + (3.19 \times 10^4)$

b $(3.61 \times 10^7) \times (2.46 \times 10^5)$

c $(4.976 \times 10^9) - (8.54 \times 10^9)$

d $(7.91 \times 10^9) \div (5.55 \times 10^2)$

Challenge

Something for you to explore!

a Can you square a number in standard form?
Does the calculator give the same answer for:
$[(7.9 \times 10^5)]^2$ and $(7.9 \times 10^5) \times (7.9 \times 10^5)$?

b Can you find the square root of a number in standard form? How would you check it?

Standard form in context

Any of the mathematics you have learned could contain very large or very small numbers.

Example 1

The lottery jackpot was £7.5×10^6.
It was to be shared equally among five winners.
What is $(7.5 \times 10^5) \div 5$?

$(7.5 \times 10^6) \div 5 = 1.5 \times 10^6$
   Each share = £$1\,500\,000$

Example 2

A large company made £3.5×10^7 profit one year.
The next year they made five times that.
What is 5 times (3.5×10^7)?

$5 \times (3.5 \times 10^7) = 1.75 \times 10^8$
   Profit = £$175\,000\,000$

EXERCISE 5

Express each answer in standard form.

1 Time

   a There are 8.64×10^4 seconds in one day.
   How many seconds are there in 365 days?

   b There are 3.156×10^7 seconds in a solar year.
   How many seconds are there in 4 solar years?

   c There are 2.778×10^{-4} hours in one second.
   How many hours are there in 60 seconds?

   d There are 1.90×10^{-6} years in a minute.
   How many years are there in 60 minutes?

2 Astronomy

   a Pluto has a diameter of 3.1×10^3 km. Neptune is 1.5 times bigger.
   What is the diameter of Neptune?

   b Saturn has a diameter of 1.2×10^5 km. Earth is 9.4 times smaller.
   Divide by 9.4 to find the diameter of Earth.

   c Venus is a mean distance of 1.08×10^8 km from the sun. Jupiter is 7.2 times as far.
   How far is Jupiter from the sun?

   d The distance from the sun to Neptune is 4.497×10^9 km. The distance to Uranus is 1.6 times smaller. Divide by 1.6 to find this distance.

3 Chemistry

   a A carbon atom weighs 2.03×10^{-23} g. An oxygen atom is 1.33 times as heavy.
   What does one oxygen atom weigh?

   b An atom of lead weighs 3.49×10^{-22} g. It is 207 times as heavy as a hydrogen atom. Divide by 207 to find the weight of a hydrogen atom.

   c An electron weighs 9.11×10^{-28} g. A proton is 1800 times as heavy.
   What does one proton weigh?

d A carbon atom weighs 2.03×10^{-23} g. A kilogram is 1000 g.

Divide 1000 by (2.03×10^{-23}) to estimate how many atoms are in a kilogram of carbon.

Example Calculate $(4.12 \times 10^4) \times (5.6 \times 10^7)$.

$$\boxed{4}\ \boxed{\cdot}\ \boxed{1}\ \boxed{2}\ \boxed{\text{Exp}}\ \boxed{4}\ \boxed{\times}\ \boxed{5}\ \boxed{\cdot}\ \boxed{6}\ \boxed{\text{Exp}}\ \boxed{7}$$

$$\boxed{=}\qquad \boxed{2.3072\ {}^{12}}$$

The answer is 2.3072×10^{12},
or 2 307 200 000 000, although we usually leave it in standard form.

EXERCISE 6

1 The circumference of a circle is worked out using the formula $C = 2\pi r$.

Assume planets move in circular orbits.

a Mercury has an orbit of radius 3.6×10^6.
Calculate the following to work out the orbit's circumference:
$C = 2 \times \pi \times (3.6 \times 10^6)$.

b Pluto has an orbit of radius 3.67×10^9.
Work out the circumference of Pluto's orbit.

2 Light travels at a speed of 3.00×10^5 km/s.
There are 3.2×10^7 seconds in a year.

a Use the formula $D = S \times T$ to find out how far light travels in a year.

b The sun is (1.49×10^8) km from Earth.
Use the formula $T = D \div S$ to find out how long the light from the sun takes to get here.

3 The Triassic period when reptiles flourished lasted for (4.5×10^7) years.
The Cambrian period during which life began lasted (1.00×10^8) years.
Work out $(1.00 \times 10^8) \div (4.5 \times 10^7)$ to see by what factor the Cambrian is the longer time.

4 A large square in space is surveyed.
Its side is (8.2×10^5) km.
Work out $(8.2 \times 10^5)^2$ to find its area.

8.2×10^5 km

CHAPTER 15 REVIEW

1 $1000 = 10^3$. Express these numbers in a similar way.

   a 10 000   **b** 1 000 000   **c** 0.0001   **d** 0.000 0001   **e** 10   **f** 1

2 Write the following in standard form.

   a 3245   **b** 34.1   **c** 34 000 000   **d** 0.0073   **e** 4.56

3 Express these in normal form.

   a 3.14×10^4 **b** 6.24×10^2 **c** 4.15×10^0 **d** 9.56×10^7

   e 8.02×10^{-4} **f** 7×10^{-3} **g** 6.11×10^{-7}

4 Do these calculations on your calculator and give your answers in normal form.

   a 2 000 000 × 1 200 000   **b** 0.000 000 1 ÷ 2 000 000

5 Interpret these displays:

   a $\boxed{\text{3.81 \quad 03}}$ **b** $\boxed{\text{8.09 \quad ×10^{04}}}$

   c $\boxed{\text{7.45 \quad -04}}$ **d** $\boxed{\text{7.90 \quad E-6}}$

6 Calculate, leaving your answer in standard form.

   a $(6.54 \times 10^4) \times 7.21$ **b** $(8 \times 10^4) \div 4.02$

   c $(7.2 \times 10^{-5}) \times 1.9$ **d** $(2.1 \times 10^{-6}) \div 5.4$

   e $3.14 \times (8.9 \times 10^3)$ **f** $6 \div (8 \times 10^4)$

7 Answer each of the following in standard form.

   a Canada's population is 2.18×10^6 people.

      The population of the USA is four times as big.

      What is the population of the USA?

   b Light travels at 3×10^{10} cm per second.

      There are 86 400 seconds in a day.

      Multiply these figures to find how far light travels in a day.

   c The population of the UK is 5.5×10^7 people.

      The area of the UK is 244 000 km².

      Divide the population by the area to find how many people there are per square kilometre.

   d The age of the Earth is 4.6×10^9 years.

      The first life appeared 6×10^8 years ago.

      Subtract these two times to find out how long the Earth was lifeless.

18 Revising Unit 3

Basic algebra

Reminders

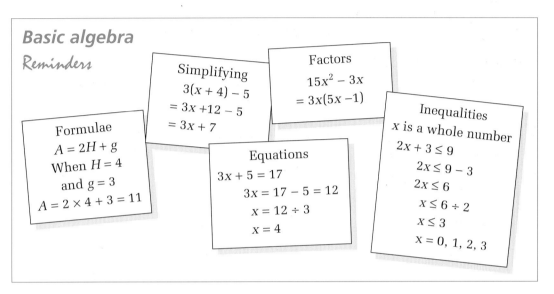

Simplifying
$3(x + 4) - 5$
$= 3x + 12 - 5$
$= 3x + 7$

Factors
$15x^2 - 3x$
$= 3x(5x - 1)$

Inequalities
x is a whole number
$2x + 3 \leq 9$
$2x \leq 9 - 3$
$2x \leq 6$
$x \leq 6 \div 2$
$x \leq 3$
$x = 0, 1, 2, 3$

Formulae
$A = 2H + g$
When $H = 4$
and $g = 3$
$A = 2 \times 4 + 3 = 11$

Equations
$3x + 5 = 17$
$3x = 17 - 5 = 12$
$x = 12 \div 3$
$x = 4$

EXERCISE 1

1 When $a = 6$ and $b = 7$ find:

   a $a + 2b$ **b** $5a - 3b$ **c** $7a^2$ **d** $b^2 + a^2$

2 Use the formulae to calculate the volume of each shape.

   a

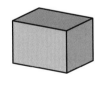

      $l = 12$ cm
      $b = 6$ cm
      $h = 8$ cm

     $V = lbh$

   b

      $r = 6$ cm
      $h = 12$ cm

     $V = \pi r^2 h$

3 The number of triangles in this pattern can be calculated using the formula
$T = 2(S + 1)$, where T is the number of triangles and S is the number of squares.

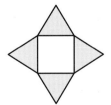
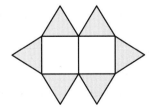
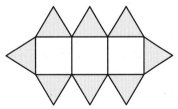

   a How many triangles would be needed for 6 squares?
   b How many triangles would be needed for 50 squares?

4 Simplify these expressions.

   a $3a + b + 2a + 3b$ **b** $6x^2 - 2x^2$

   c $5x + 2y - 3x - 4y$ **d** $c + 4d + d - c + 2c$

5 Factorise the following.

   a $3x + 12$ **b** $x - 6x^2$ **c** $10y + 5$ **d** $2xy - 3x$

6 Solve the following equations.

   a $3x + 4 = 25$ **b** $5x - 6 = 29$ **c** $12 - 2x = 4$

7 a Copy and complete the table if $y = 2x + 3$.

x	0	1	2	3	4	5
y						

   b Draw the line $y = 2x + 3$.

8 Solve the following inequalities where x is a whole number.

   a $3x + 1 < 13$ **b** $2x - 5 > 29$

   c $4x - 16 \leq 0$ **d** $12 + 3x \geq 36$

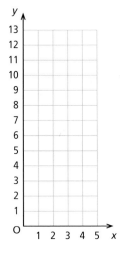

9 Solve $7x + 1 = 4x + 28$.

10 a Find a formula for the area of rectangle: **(i)** A   **(ii)** B   **(iii)** C.

   b What is the formula for the total surface area of this net of a cuboid?

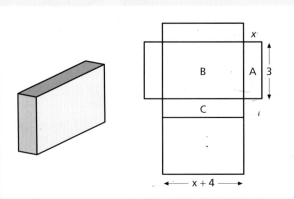

11 The maximum weight a delivery van can carry is given by the formula $M = 0.85C$, where M is the maximum weight and C is the weight of the van.

   a Is it safe for a van weighing 920 kg to carry 780 kg?
      Show your working to explain your answer.

   b A van weighing 1000 kg is carrying a 500 kg load.
      The depot wants it to take some more.
      How much *more weight* can it safely carry?

12 a Solve this inequality: $4x + 5 \geq 3x + 8$.

  b If x is a whole number less than 10 what are the possible values of x?

13 Solve this inequality: $2(x + 3) < 18$.

14 How long will it take to travel 980 km at an average speed of 75 km/h?

> Reminder
>
> $T = \dfrac{D}{S}$

15

(i)	x is a whole number
(ii)	x is a perfect square
(iii)	x is an even number
(iv)	$4x + 8 > 3x + 20$
(v)	$5x + 10 < 2x + 100$

  a List five whole numbers which fit each clue.

  b What value of x fits all the clues?

Graphical relationships

Reminders

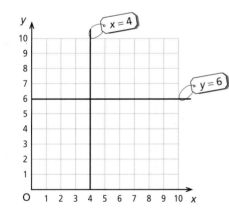

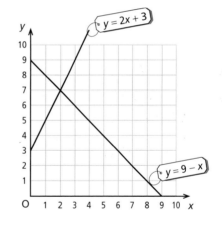

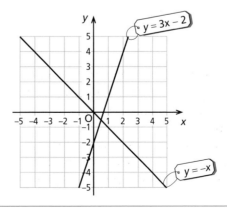

EXERCISE 2

1 For each equation below:

    (i) copy and complete the table

x	−3	−2	−1	0	1	2	3
y							

    (ii) draw the graph of the equation.

  a $y = 2$ **b** $y = x$ **c** $y = 2x$

  d $y = 2x + 1$ **e** $y = -x + 1$ **f** $y = 3 - 2x$

2 a Draw the line $y = 2x + 3$.

  b Is the point (3, 4) above or below the line?

3 a Draw the line $y = 3x + 1$.

  b On the same diagram draw the line $y = 4x$.

  c Give the coordinates of the point where they cross.

4 a On the same diagram, draw the lines: **(i)** $x = 3$ **(ii)** $y = 6$ **(iii)** $y = 6 - 2x$.

  b Calculate the area of the triangle they form.

5

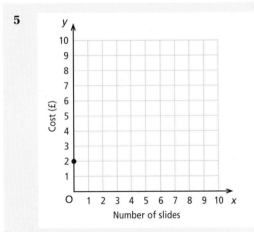

It cost £2 to develop a film and then £0.50 to mount each slide. So, the number of slides, x, and the cost, y, are related by the formula $y = 0.5x + 2$.

  a Copy and complete the table.

Number of slides (x)	0	2	4	6	8	10
Cost (y)	2					

  b Copy and complete the graph.

6 A theatre charges a party of theatregoers a £2 booking fee and then £3 per ticket. The number of tickets, x, and the total charge, y, are related by the formula $y = 3x + 2$.

  a Copy and complete the table.

Number of tickets (x)	1	2	3	4	5	6
Charge (y)	5	8				

  b Draw a graph of the formula.

7 During trials, 10 litres of fuel were
put in the tank of a motorbike.
The engine was then run for 5 hours.
The bike used up 2 litres each hour.
This is modelled by the equation
$y = 10 - 2x$, where y is the fuel left
and x is the number of hours for
which the bike has been running.

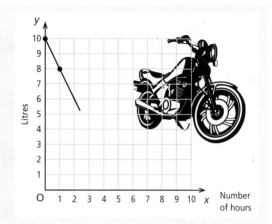

a Copy and complete
the table.

b Copy and complete
the graph.

Number of hours (x)	0	1	2	3	4	5
Litres of fuel left (y)	10	8				

Basic trigonometry

Reminder

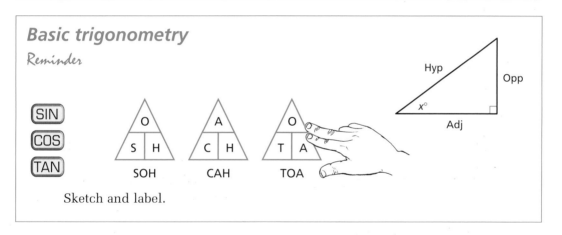

SIN COS TAN

SOH   CAH   TOA

Sketch and label.

EXERCISE 3

Give your answers to 1 decimal place were necessary.

1 Calculate x in each triangle.

a
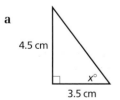
4.5 cm
3.5 cm
$x°$

b
15 m
25 m
$x°$

c
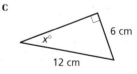
6 cm
12 cm
$x°$

2 Calculate the lengths of a, b and c.

a
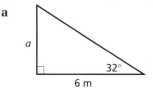
a
$32°$
6 m

b
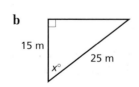
b
5 cm
$70°$

c
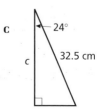
$24°$
32.5 cm
c

3 A ladder is placed against a wall.
The ladder is 3 m long.
The foot of the ladder is 1.4 m from the foot of the wall.
Calculate the angle the ladder makes with the ground.

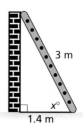

4 A plane is coming in to land. It is 500 m high as it flies over a beacon.
The beacon is 7000 m from the landing point.
The correct flightpath makes an angle of between 3° and 4° with the ground.
Is the aircraft on the correct flightpath?

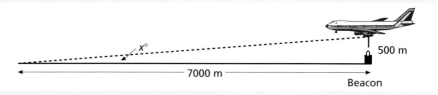

5 A straight road runs due north. Michael sets off, from point A, to walk across country on a bearing of 040° for 3.7 km.
What is the shortest distance he will have to walk to rejoin the road?

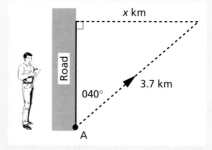

6

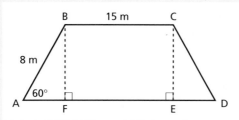

This trapezium is symmetrical.
Calculate:
a the length of AF
b the length of ED
c the perimeter of the trapezium.

7 Two ships are at A, 5 km from a lighthouse, L.
They set off in different directions.
One takes the route AB to end up north of the lighthouse;
the other travels from A to C to end up south of the lighthouse.
Calculate:
a the distance BL
b the distance CL
c how far apart the two ships are at the end.

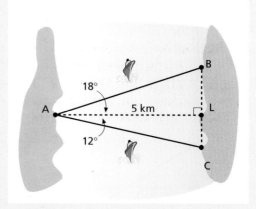

Standard form

Reminders

$3.14 \times 10^5 = 314\,000$ $3.14 \times 10^{-5} = 0.000\,031\,4$

$3.14 \times 10^0 = 3.14$

EXERCISE 4

1 Write these numbers in standard form.

   a 3140   **b** 6.28   **c** 0.0456

   d 2 134 000   **e** 7   **f** 0.4

   g 5 200 000 000 000   **h** 64 000 000 000   **i** 444 440 000 000

   j 0.000 009 3   **k** 0.000 000 000 006

2 Write each of these calculator displays: **(i)** in standard form   **(ii)** in normal form.

   a

               `3.9  -02`

   b

               `6.3  EOS`

   c

               `8.47  03`

   d

               `1.309  x10⁰⁴`

3 Perform each of these calculations, leaving your answer in standard form.

   a $4.1 \times (3.25 \times 10^5)$ **b** $(1.07 \times 10^3) \times 17$

   c $(4.5 \times 10^5) \div 3.6$ **d** $37 \div (4 \times 10^8)$

   e $(2.6 \times 10^{-3}) \times 6$ **f** $8.1 \times (3.65 \times 10^{-5})$

   g $(3.2 \times 10^{-5}) \div 5$ **h** $64 \div (8 \times 10^{-1})$

4 A manufacturer makes (3.65×10^6) screws.

   He puts them in packets of 50.

   Divide (3.65×10^6) by 50 to find out how many packets he makes.

5 How many seconds are there in a century? (Ignore leap years.)

   Give your answer in standard form.

6 A headline reads 'Stolen painting worth £2.3 million'.

   a Write this number out in full.

   b Write it in standard form.

   c The insurance company offers a reward of one eighth of its value.

      Divide by 8 to work out the reward in standard form.

7 In 1987 there were (8.91×10^7) homes in the USA which had a TV set.

In 1989 there were (9.04×10^7).

Subtract these two figures to find out the number of extra homes in the USA with a TV.

8 Write these fractions **(i)** in normal form **(ii)** in standard form.

> *Example*
>
> $\dfrac{1}{200}$ ... $1 \div 200 = 0.005 = 5 \times 10^{-3}$

a $\dfrac{1}{400}$ **b** $\dfrac{1}{250}$ **c** $\dfrac{1}{5000}$ **d** $\dfrac{1}{2000}$

9 The nearest star is 5×10^{13} km from the Earth.

Light travels at 3×10^5 km per second.

How long will it take light from the star to reach Earth?

10 It costs £10 for an adult to get into the National Garden Show and £5 for a child. During the month of June, 3 500 000 adults and 750 000 children visited the exhibition.

    a Express, in standard form, the number of:

       (i) adult visitors

       (ii) child visitors.

    b Calculate the total ticket sales for June, leaving your answer in standard form.

11 Dinosaurs ruled the Earth during the Mesozoic era.

This lasted from 2.48×10^8 years ago until 6.5×10^7 years ago.

    a Find, by subtraction, how long the Mesozoic era lasted.

    b Part of this time was the Jurassic period which lasted from 1.44×10^8 years ago until 2.13×10^7 years ago.

      For how long did the Jurassic period last?

    c By dividing answer **b** by answer **a**, find what fraction of the Mesozoic the Jurassic period is.

19 Calculations in a Social Context

Wages and loans

Reminders

$6\% = \frac{6}{100} = 6 \div 100 = 0.06$ 6% of £80 $= 6 \div 100 \times 80 = £4.80$

STARTING POINTS

1 Match each word with its description.

Bonus

Piecework

Overtime

Commission

a A person is paid a percentage of the value of the goods he sells.

b A person is paid a set amount for each item she makes.

c An extra payment for a job well done or as a reward for working harder.

d A person works more than her normal hours.

2 Nicola works 34 hours a week as a shop assistant. She earns £3.75 an hour. Calculate her weekly wage.

3 Alastair earns £320 per week. He works 50 weeks a year. How much does he earn in a year?

4 Louise earns £210 per week as a veterinary assistant. The week before Christmas she is given a bonus of £25. What is her total wage for that week?

5 Callum sells double glazing. He is paid 9% commission on all his sales. One week he sells windows worth £2100. How much commission does he earn?

6 Khatum works as a secretary. Her basic pay is £5.00 per hour. When she works overtime she is paid **double time**. How much does she earn for 3 hours of overtime?

7 Change the following into decimal fractions.
   a 2%   **b** 13%   **c** 2.2%   **d** 1.95%

8 Calculate: **a** 5% of £1000   **b** 6% of £3500.

9 A store charges 6% extra for goods bought on hire purchase.

   a A settee costs £600. How much extra is paid when it is bought on hire purchase?

   b What is the total cost of the settee?

   c The total cost is divided into 12 equal instalments. How much is each instalment?

DISCUSSION

Look at this selection of job advertisements.

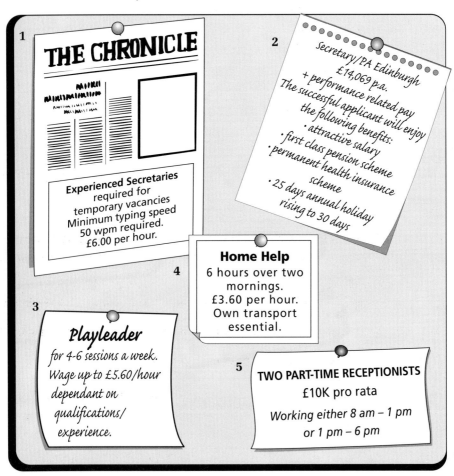

   a What type of jobs quote an hourly rate?

   b Why do some jobs give a range for the salary?

   c What does **£10K** mean in advert 5?

   d What does **p.a.** mean in advert 2?

   e What does **pro rata** mean in advert 5?

Do you know the meaning of the other abbreviations in the adverts?

Look up job advertisements in your local paper.

What sorts of jobs are available in your area?

Are the wages quoted as an annual amount or as an hourly rate?

How would you be paid in the job of your choice?

Overtime

You are familiar with working out overtime at double time.
Some employers pay overtime at **time and a half**.
This means for every one hour that you work you are paid for an hour and a half at the basic rate.

Example
Samantha works 6 hours of overtime at time and a half.
Her basic rate of pay is £4.40 per hour.
How much does she earn for her overtime?

6 hours at time and a half means
$6 + \frac{1}{2}$ of $6 = 6 + 3 = 9$
She is paid for 9 hours.
$9 \times 4.40 = 39.60$
She earns £39.60.

EXERCISE 1

1 How many hours of basic pay do you get when you work at time and a half for:
   a 8 hours   **b** 10 hours   **c** 5 hours   **d** 7 hours   **e** 18 hours   **f** 24 hours?

2 The basic rate of pay is £5. How much do you earn at time and a half for:
   a 4 hours   **b** 6 hours   **c** 10 hours   **d** 3 hours   **e** 9 hours   **f** 12 hours?

3 The basic rate of pay is £4.50. How much do you earn for 8 hours at time and a half?

4 Anthony works a basic 34-hour week at a rate of £5 per hour.
   a Calculate his basic weekly wage.
   b He works 4 hours of overtime at time and a half. How much is he paid for the overtime?
   c Calculate his total pay for the week.

5 Angela Martin is a part-time care assistant. She works 28 hours a week at £3.85 per hour.
   a Calculate her basic weekly wage.
   b One week she worked 6 hours of overtime at time and a half.
   Calculate her total wage for that week.

6 Erin O'Donnell is paid £4.66 per hour for a basic 35-hour week.
   a Calculate her basic weekly wage.
   b She does 4 hours of overtime on Saturday at time and a half.
   Calculate her overtime pay for Saturday.
   c She does 5 hours of overtime on Sunday at double time.
   Calculate her pay for working on Sunday.
   d What is her total wage for the week?

7 Asha Wood works as a ranger at a nature reserve.

A normal week's work is 33 hours. Her basic rate is £5.25 per hour.

One week Asha works 4 hours at time and a half and 3 hours at double time.

a Calculate her basic wage.

b How much is she paid for 4 hours at time and a half?

c How much is she paid for 3 hours at double time?

d What is her total wage for this week?

e The next week Asha again worked 4 hours at time and a half.

She also did 5 hours at double time.

Calculate her total wage for this week.

8 Joe works in a knitwear factory. He does a basic 7 hours a day, Monday to Friday. Any hours above this are considered overtime. Overtime worked Monday to Saturday is paid at time and a half. Overtime on Sunday is paid at double time. Work out Joe's earnings from his timesheet. (Note that he works overtime on Wednesday.)

Joseph McGregor	
Monday	7 hours
Tuesday	7 hours
Wednesday	9 hours
Thursday	7 hours
Friday	7 hours
Saturday	4 hours
Sunday	2 hours
Basic rate = £4.50 per hour.	

Annual salary

This is the amount earned in a year.

Examples

Emily earns £224 per week.

Her annual salary is £224 × 52, i.e. £11 648.

Ronald has an annual salary of £21 450.

His monthly salary is £21 450 ÷ 12, i.e. £1787.50.

EXERCISE 2

1 Robert Clark earns £110 per week as a trainee painter and decorator.
He works 49 weeks a year. Calculate his annual salary.

2 Sarah Tullie is an accountant. She is paid £2100 per month.
Calculate her annual salary.

3 Lorna Shaw has an annual salary of £18 312. She is paid an equal amount each month.
What is her monthly salary?

4 Nazir Khan works 35 hours a week. He earns £4.40 per hour.
a Calculate his weekly wage.
b Nazir works 48 weeks a year. Calculate his annual salary.

5 Ali Aslam earns a basic salary of £350 per month.
   He is paid 5% commission on all his sales.
   In one year his sales totalled £45 000.
   Calculate his annual income that year.

6 Winston Jones works as an electrician. His
   employer pays him £262 a week.
   He is paid for 52 weeks in the year
   although he only works for 48 weeks.
   The extra is called **holiday pay**.
   Calculate:
   a Winston's annual salary
   b his holiday pay.

Pay slip	
Name: Mrs S. Alam	
Gross Pay	£208.00

The longer you work for some
employers the more holiday pay you
can expect.

7 Kiera Williams works in a shop. She is paid £118.50 a week.
   She works for 49 weeks of the year. She is on holiday for the other three weeks.
   Her employers pay £75 per week holiday pay.
   Calculate Kiera's annual salary.

8 Suzi Telfer is new to her job. She is not entitled to holiday pay.
   She works for 49 weeks for £192 per week. At Christmas she is given a £10 bonus.
   Calculate her annual income.

Gross pay

This is the total of what you earn before any deductions.

Examples

Thomas Warwick has a basic
pay of £180 per week.
He earns a bonus of £35.
His gross pay for that week is
      £180 + £35 = £215.

Chloe Esslemont has a basic
salary of £840 per month.
She earns £252 in overtime.
Her gross monthly salary is
      £840 + £252 = £1092.

EXERCISE 3

1 Michael Lerwick has a basic pay of £270 per week. He earns £357 overtime.
   Calculate his gross pay for that week.

2 Sally Peters has a basic salary of £935 per month. She earns £421 in overtime.
   She also gets travelling expenses of £80. What is her gross monthly pay?

3 Eve Adamson is a receptionist. Her basic monthly salary is £752.
   a Calculate her basic annual salary.
   b In one year she earned £1378 in overtime and was given a Christmas bonus
        of £25.
        Calculate her gross annual salary that year.

4 Rachel Crosby has a part-time job as a waitress in a restaurant. She earns £4.76 per hour. One evening Rachel worked for four and a half hours. Her customers gave her tips totalling £17.32. Calculate her gross wage for that evening.

5 Iain McGregor makes paperweights. He has a basic pay of £75 a week.
He is also paid £1.00 for each paperweight he makes.
One week his company has an urgent order for 250 paperweights.
They offer Iain a bonus of £30 if he can complete the order within the week.
If he does, what will his gross wage be for the week?

6 Andrew Brogan is a car salesman. He has a basic monthly salary of £400.
He is also paid commission of 3% on all his sales. One month Andrew sells cars worth £38 000. Calculate his gross salary for that month.

7 Azar Jarmine is a supervisor in a carpet factory.
His gross annual salary for one year was £12 452.
£3087 of that amount was for overtime. The rest was his basic salary.
Calculate his basic annual salary for the year.

8 Here are extracts from five wageslips. Calculate each person's gross wage.

a

Name: **Alex Taylor**		Week No. 17
		Employee No. 032518
Basic Wage	£182.46	HRS. O/T @
Overtime	£43.85	HRS. O/T @
		HRS. O/T @
Gross Wage		OTHER...............

b

Name: **Mary Whyte**		Week No. 03
		Employee No. 0007123
Basic Wage	£197.50	HRS. O/T @
Overtime	£87.50	HRS. O/T @
Bonus	£125.00	HRS. O/T @ OTHER...............
Gross Wage		BONUS, HOLIDAY, SICK PAY,S.S.P. S.M.P.

c

Name	S Hutchings			**Pay Advice**
Employee No. 250897		Month 04		

Basic	Overtime	Bonus	Travel Expenses	Gross Pay
£1047.28	£154.60	£0.00	£27.34	

d

Week No. 17	
Name: **Caroline Anderson**	
Employee No. 055671	
Basic: 35 hours at £4.40 per hour	
Overtime (Double Time): 4 hours	£35.20
Gross Wage	

e

Month 05	
Name: **Timothy Fletcher**	
Employee No. 152763	
Basic:	£742
Commission: 3% of £21 200	
Salesman of the Month Bonus	£50
Gross Wage	

9 Marjorie Maxwell is a representative for a publishing company. She has a basic monthly salary of £380. She is paid 7% commission on all her orders, and is also paid travelling expenses. One month her orders totalled £5214.
  a Calculate her commission for that month.
  b Her travelling expenses amounted to £94.50 that month. Calculate her gross wage.

Deductions

This is the term used for money taken off your earnings to pay for various things.

If you earn more than a set amount each year you *must* pay:
- **income tax** (a percentage of your salary which is used to help run the country, paying for health, education, defence, etc.)
- **National Insurance** (a percentage of your salary which goes towards paying for the National Health Service, pensions and unemployment benefit).

Whatever you earn, you may choose to pay:
- **superannuation** or **AVCs** (extra pension payments)
- **union dues** (membership fees to belong to a union)
- **a charity donation** (some employees offer to pay an amount towards a charity each week)
- **a contribution to a social fund** (some employees save each week towards social events).

You may also have to pay:
- **professional insurance** (in case you are held responsible for damage caused through work).

EXERCISE 4

1 One week, Tara Smith paid £42.20 in income tax, £13.47 in National Insurance and £0.50 towards her company's charity fund.
Calculate the total amount to be deducted from her salary.

2 Ailidh Dunlop pays £310.64 in income tax, £149.70 in National Insurance, £114.38 in superannuation and £4 to her company's social fund.
Calculate her total deductions.

3 Jeff Simpson doesn't earn enough to be required to pay income tax.
However, each week he pays £1.24 in National Insurance and £0.83 for professional insurance. Calculate his total deductions.

4 These are extracts from the wageslips of three people.
Calculate the total deductions each will pay.

a

Name: **Simon Mungall**	PAYSLIP
Income Tax	£96.15
National Insurance	£31.87
Superannuation	£24.03
Total Deductions	

b

Name: **Benny King**	PAYSLIP
Income Tax	£26.55
National Insurance	£8.43
Union Fee	£0.46
Charity	£0.25
Total Deductions	

c

Name	Amir Iqbal				Pay Advice
Employee No.					
Income Tax	National Insurance	Superannuation	AVC	Charity	Total Deductions
£427.00	£195.40	£76.41	£25.33	£0.00	

5 How much income tax did Steve pay this week?

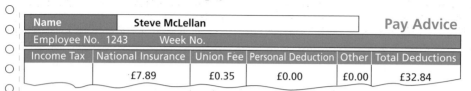

Name	Steve McLellan					Pay Advice
Employee No. 1243		Week No.				
Income Tax	National Insurance	Union Fee	Personal Deduction	Other	Total Deductions	
	£7.89	£0.35	£0.00	£0.00	£32.84	

Challenge

Find the answers to the following questions.

a What is the Budget?
b How much can you earn before tax?
c What are the current rates of income tax?
d Does the job you want to do have a superannuation scheme?

Net wage

This is your pay after deductions.

Gross Pay – Total Deductions = Net Pay

Example
Bejal has a basic weekly wage of £176.40. One week he earns £52.64 in overtime.
He pays £31.27 in income tax and £9.88 for National Insurance.
Calculate his net pay for that week.

Gross Pay:

$$
\begin{array}{r}
£176.40 \\
+ \quad £52.64 \\
\hline
£229.04
\end{array}
$$

Total deductions:

$$
\begin{array}{r}
£31.27 \\
+ \quad £9.88 \\
\hline
£41.15
\end{array}
$$

Net Pay = Gross Pay – Total Deductions
= £229.04 – £41.15
= £187.89

EXERCISE 5

1 Copy and complete these calculations.

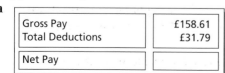

a

Gross Pay	£158.61
Total Deductions	£31.79
Net Pay	

b

Gross Pay	£1347.28
Total Deductions	£405.94
Net Pay	

c

Gross Annual Salary	£19 667.00
Total Deductions	£4 056.85
Net Annual Salary	

d

Gross Annual Salary	£22 668.00
Total Deductions	£6 394.80
Net Annual Salary	

2 These wageslips give details of people's wages and deductions.
Calculate the gross wage, total deductions and the net wage for each one.

a

Basic Wage	Overtime	Bonus	Expenses	Gross Wage
£309.67	£49.36	£0.00	£5.60	
Income Tax	Nat. Ins.	Superannuation	Other	Total Deductions
£43.52	£14.88	£0.00	£0.85	
			Net Wage:	

b

Basic Wage	Overtime	Bonus	Expenses	Gross Wage
£853.56	£0.00	£50.00	£34.10	
Income Tax	Nat. Ins.	Charity	Other	Total Deductions
£100.58	£37.22	£0.00	£0.00	
			Net Wage:	

c

Basic Wage	Overtime	Bonus	Expenses	Gross Wage
£1889.00				
Income Tax	Nat. Ins.	Charity	Other	Total Deductions
£365.00	£167.90			
			Net Wage:	

3 Copy and complete a payslip like this for each of the following:

Basic Wage	Overtime	Bonus	Expenses	Gross Wage
Income Tax	Nat. Ins.	Charity	Other	Total Deductions
			Net Wage:	

a Ben Turner earns a basic £1500, makes £400 in overtime and is given a bonus of £50. He is paid £18 in expenses.
He pays £325 tax, £92 National Insurance and a pension contribution of £83.

b Moll Fleming earns a basic £1825, makes £354 in overtime. She gets £35 expenses.
She pays £415 tax, £101 National Insurance and a £94 pension contribution.

c Annette Curtin earns a basic £325 a week, makes £75 in overtime and is given a bonus of £20.
She pays £82 tax, £19 National Insurance and a £22 pension contribution.

EXERCISE 6

1 Rangan Chattergee manages a burger bar.
  He is paid £6.14 per hour for a basic 35-hour week.
  One week he worked 7 hours of overtime, paid at time and a half.
  He paid £26.82 in income tax and £8.70 in National Insurance.
  Calculate his net pay for that week.

2 Matt Tucker works as a computer operator. He works **flexitime** (he chooses which hours he wants to work, as long as he does a set number of hours).
  This is a copy of his timesheet and salary slip. Copy and complete it.

Name __Matt Tucker__

	In	Out	In	Out	No. of hours
Mon	8 am	12 noon	1 pm	4 pm	
Tue	8.30 am	12 noon	1 pm	4.30 pm	
Wed	8 am	12 noon	1 pm	5 pm	
Thu	8 am	12 noon	1 pm	5 pm	
Fri	7 am	12 noon	1 pm	3 pm	
Sat	8 am	12 noon			
Sun	8.30 am	12 noon			

Basic Pay: 35 hours at £5.70   = ...
Overtime:
(Mon to Sat) ... hours at time and a half = ...
(Sunday)   ... hours at double time   = ...

                    Gross Pay = [   ]

Deductions:
Income Tax   =   £40.56
National Insurance   =   £13.33
Charity   =   £1.00

Total Deductions = [   ]

Net Pay   = [   ]

3 Copy and complete this wageslip.

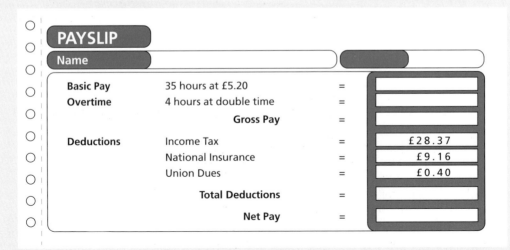

PAYSLIP

Name

Basic Pay	35 hours at £5.20	=	
Overtime	4 hours at double time	=	
	Gross Pay	=	
Deductions	Income Tax	=	£28.37
	National Insurance	=	£9.16
	Union Dues	=	£0.40
	Total Deductions	=	
	Net Pay	=	

19 Calculations in a Social Context

·U·N·I·T·4·

Borrowing money

Why do we borrow money?

To buy things when we don't have the ready cash.

Who can we borrow it from?

Banks, building societies, even the shops themselves.

But remember, when we put money in a bank we receive interest, when we borrow money we pay interest.

Anyone who lends money should tell you:
• their **monthly rate** of interest and
• their **annual percentage rate** (APR).

Example

> ## Bank of Scotia
> ### Home Improvement Loans
> **Monthly rate: 2.2%**
> **APR: 30%**

James borrows £2000 to do up his kitchen.

a How much interest is owed after a month?

b How much money is owed after the first month?

c How much interest is owed after a year?

a 2.2% of £2000
= 2.2 ÷ 100 × 2000
= 44
He owes £44 interest after the first month.

b Amount owed after 1 month = debt plus interest
= 2000 + 44
= 2044
He owes £2044 after 1 month.

c APR = 30%
30% of £2000
= 30 ÷ 100 × 2000
= 600
He owes £600 interest after 1 year.

EXERCISE 7

1 For each of the following calculate:
  (i) the interest after one month   **(ii)** the amount owed at the end of the month.

	Amount borrowed (£)	Monthly rate of interest
a	1000	2.5%
b	670	2.3%
c	3500	1.8%
d	2450	2.1%
e	800	1.95%

2 The table shows the interest rates charged by four credit card companies.

Credit card	Bank of Scotia 12 345 678	Southern Gold 43 567 987	Advanta 900 7654 12	Albion Gold 12345 678
Monthly rate	2.2%	1.3%	1.67%	1.14%
APR	30%	17.9%	23.2%	14.5%

a (i) How much is Southern Gold's monthly rate of interest?
  (ii) How much interest would you owe at the end of the first month on a loan of £1600 from Southern Gold?
b (i) How much is the APR with Advanta?
  (ii) How much interest is paid in a year on a loan of £3000 from Advanta?
c How much more than Albion Gold is Bank of Scotia's APR?
d Calculate: (i) 17.9% of £500   (ii) 23.2% of £400.
e Which of the above cards gives the most favourable rate of monthly interest? (Most favourable means smallest.)
f Peter Brown borrows £3000 from the Bank of Scotia.
  He promises to repay £324 per month.
  Copy and complete the following.

After one month the interest is: $2.2 \div 100 \times 3000 = £66$
So at the start of the second month he owes: $3000 + 66 - 324 = £2742$
After the second month the interest is: $2.2 \div 100 \times 2742 = £\ldots$
So at the start of the third month he owes: $2742 + \ldots - 324 = £\ldots$
After the third month the interest is: $2.2 \div 100 \times \ldots = £\ldots$
So at the start of the fourth month he owes: $\ldots + \ldots - 324 = £\ldots$

Loan repayment tables

This table shows the monthly repayments on a loan of £1000.

Period of loan in months	Annual interest rate				
	8%	9%	10%	11%	12%
12	£87	£87.50	£88.00	£88.50	£89
18	£59	£59.50	£60.00	£60.50	£61
24 (2 years)	£45	£45.50	£46.00	£46.50	£47
36 (3 years)	£31	£31.50	£32.00	£32.50	£33
48 (4 years)	£24	£24.80	£25.30	£25.80	£26
60 (5 years)	£20	£20.70	£21.25	£21.70	£22

Example 1   For a loan of £1000 taken over 36 months at 9% calculate:

     a the monthly repayment

     b the total repayment

     c the cost of the loan.

Period of loan in months	Annual interest rate				
	8%	9%	10%	11%	12%
12	£87	£87.50	£88.00	£88.50	£89
18	£59	£59.50	£60.00	£60.50	£61
24 (2 years)	£45	£45.50	£46.00	£46.50	£47
36 (3 years)	£31	£31.50	£32.00	£32.50	£33
48 (4 years)	£24	£24.80	£25.30	£25.80	£26
60 (5 years)	£20	£20.70	£21.25	£21.70	£22

a the '36 month' row and the '9%' column cross at £31.50.
The monthly repayment is £31.50.

b The total repayment is 36 monthly repayments:
$36 \times 31.50 = 1134$
The total repayment is £1134.

c £1000 was borrowed. £1134 was paid back.
$1134 - 1000 = 134$
The cost of the loan is £134.

Example 2   What is the monthly repayment on a loan of £3500 repayable over 24 months at 11%?

How many thousands are borrowed?
$\frac{3500}{1000} = 3.5$ thousands
The table shows £46.50 per thousand.
So the monthly repayment is $3.5 \times 46.50 = £162.75$.

EXERCISE 8

Use the above table to answer the questions in this exercise.

1 On each of the following loans, calculate:

    (i) the monthly repayment **(ii)** the total repayment **(iii)** the cost of the loan.

	Period of loan in months	Annual interest rate	Loan
a	12	10%	£1000
b	36	8%	£1000
c	18	11%	£5000
d	60	9%	£2000
e	48	12%	£3500

2 Nicola Green asks for a loan of £5000 to help to buy a car.
   She agrees to repay the loan over 48 months. The rate of interest is 8%.
   a What is the monthly repayment?
   b What is the total repayment?
   c How much does the loan cost Nicola?

3 Mike Lee is building a conservatory onto his house.
   He is given a bank loan of £6500. The rate of interest is 12% over 60 months.
   a What is the monthly repayment?
   b What is the total repayment?
   c How much does the loan cost Mike?

Loan protection

You can pay a little extra each month for **loan protection**. This means that in the event of illness, accident or redundancy your monthly repayments will be taken care of for a certain period of time. In the event of death the loan will be fully paid up.

These tables compare the costs with and without loan protection.

With Loan Protection

Period of loan	APR	Amount of loan	Total repayable	Monthly repayment
12 months	36.8%	£2000	£2360.64	£196.72
12 months	36.3%	£3000	£3534.36	£294.53
24 months	28.7%	£2000	£2573.52	£107.23
24 months	28.2%	£3000	£3844.80	£160.20
36 months	25.7%	£3000	£4184.64	£116.24

Without Loan Protection

Period of loan	APR	Amount of loan	Total repayable	Monthly repayment
12 months	16.6%	£2000	£2171.40	£180.95
12 months	16.2%	£3000	£3251.16	£270.93
24 months	15.8%	£2000	£2322.96	£96.79
24 months	15.4%	£3000	£3472.32	£144.68
36 months	14.9%	£3000	£3693.24	£102.59

EXERCISE 9

1 Use the tables to answer the following questions.
   a With loan protection, what is the monthly repayment on a loan of £2000 over 12 months?
   b Without loan protection, what is the monthly repayment on a loan of £2000 over 12 months?

c How much extra is the monthly repayment on such a loan with protection?

d How much more is the APR on a loan of £3000 over 12 months with loan protection than without?

e How much is the monthly repayment on a loan of £3000 over 36 months:
  (i) with protection **(ii)** without protection?

f What is the total amount repayable on a loan of £2000 payable over 24 months:
  (i) with protection **(ii)** without protection?

2

Amount of loan £	Repayment term									
	5 years		4 years		3 years		2 years		1 year	
	With	Without	With	Without	With	Without	With	Without	With	Without
500	15.35	13.00	17.10	15.00	20.55	18.35	27.65	25.25	49.35	46.10
1000	30.80	26.02	34.25	30.00	41.15	36.75	55.35	50.50	98.77	92.23
3000	92.40	78.10	102.70	89.95	123.45	110.20	166.10	151.50	296.30	276.70
5000	154.10	130.20	171.15	149.95	205.78	183.70	276.80	252.45	493.80	461.20
7000	215.70	182.20	239.60	209.90	288.10	257.15	387.55	353.40	691.35	645.65
10 000	308.16	260.30	342.30	299.85	411.50	367.40	553.65	504.90	987.65	922.40

Use the above table showing monthly repayments to calculate:

a the monthly repayment on a 5 year loan of £3000 with protection

b the monthly repayment on a 3 year loan of £7000 without protection

c the *total* repayment on a 2 year loan of £500 with protection.

3 The Martins take out a £10 000 loan for a truck.
They wish to repay the loan over 4 years. They want to protect the loan.
a What are their monthly payments?
b What is the total repayment?
c Calculate the cost of the loan.

4 The Sutherlands take out a £5000 loan for home improvements.
They wish to repay the loan over 5 years. They want to protect the loan.
a What are their monthly payments?
b What is the total repayment?
c Calculate the cost of the loan.

5 Malcolm wants to take out a £3000 loan for diving gear.
He wants to repay it over 3 years.
He wants to know how much loan protection would cost.
a What is his monthly repayment: **(i)** without protection **(ii)** with protection?
b How much extra per month will he pay for protection?
c Over the 3 years how much extra would he pay for protection?

6 A garage owner wants to borrow £10 000 to help buy a new truck.
He considers a 1 year payback without protection or a 2 year repayment with protection.
Work out which of the two plans works out cheaper.

CHAPTER 19 REVIEW

1 Tamar earns £734 per month. He is given a bonus of £250 before Christmas. Calculate his total annual salary.

2 Margaret works 35 hours a week for £5.75 per hour. She does 4 hours of overtime at double time. Calculate her total wage for the week.

3 Jake works 32.5 hours a week at a basic rate of £6.12 per hour. He also works 5 hours of overtime at time and a half. Calculate his gross wage for the week.

4 Copy and complete Selina's wageslip.

Basic Wage	Overtime	Bonus	Expenses	Gross Wage
£568.20	£46.92	£10.00	£0.00	
Income Tax	Nat. Ins.	Superannuation	Other	Total Deductions
£67.66	£25.40	£0.00	£0.40	
			Net Wage:	

5 A bank lends £2000 to a customer. Interest is charged at a monthly rate of 2.2%. Calculate:
   a the interest charged for the first month   b the amount owed after a month.

6 Here is part of a table showing the monthly repayments for a loan of £1000. For a loan of £3000 at 9% for 36 months, calculate:
   a the monthly repayment
   b the total repayment
   c the cost of the loan.

	Annual interest rate	
Period of loan in months	9%	10%
24	£47.50	£49.00
36	£32.20	£34.50
48	£24.50	£26.30

7 This table shows the monthly repayments for various loans, over different periods, with and without loan protection.

Amount of loan £	Repayment term									
	5 years		4 years		3 years		2 years		1 year	
	With	Without	With	Without	With	Without	With	Without	With	Without
500	14.05	12.10	15.90	14.10	19.45	17.50	26.65	24.42	48.45	45.30
1000	28.15	24.20	31.84	28.25	38.95	35.05	53.35	48.85	96.90	90.65
3000	84.40	72.60	95.50	84.70	116.85	105.15	160.00	146.55	290.65	271.90
5000	140.60	121.00	159.15	141.10	194.74	175.25	266.70	244.30	484.40	453.15
7000	196.89	169.40	222.80	197.60	272.65	245.35	373.35	342.00	678.90	634.40
10 000	281.25	242.00	318.35	282.28	390.00	350.50	533.38	488.60	968.75	906.30

   a What is the monthly repayment on £3000 taken over 5 years with loan protection?
   b What is the total repayment on £1000 taken over 2 years without protection?

20 Logic Diagrams

STARTING POINTS

1 This table gives details on chests of drawers in a furniture catalogue.

E16	×✓				
	A	**B**	**C**	**D**	**E**	**F**
1	Code	No. of drawers	Width (mm)	Depth (mm)	Height (mm)	Price
2	B45	2	457	406	457	£59.00
3	C38	3	457	406	559	£75.00
4	D27	3	508	457	660	£78.00
5	E52	4	559	457	711	£114.00
6	E55	4	559	508	762	£122.00

  a The word **Code** is in position A1 in the table.
What is in position: **(i)** D1   **(ii)** E2   **(iii)** A5   **(iv)** F5?
  b Give the codes for the chests of drawers which cost less than £100.
  c What is the cost of two chests of drawers of type D27?

2 Calculate this bill.

Item	No. of items	Cost per item	Total
Munch Bars	3	£0.63	
Milk Shakes	4	£0.82	
Cool Kola	2	£0.51	
		Grand total	

3 **a** Calculate the 'average' of 2, 8, 3, 5, 7 and 2.
  b What is the cost of hiring a car for 6 days if the deposit is £35 and the daily charge is £22?
  c Iain travelled 200 km and used 8 litres of petrol.
On average how far did he travel per litre of petrol?
  d Calculate 5% of £60.

4 This map shows part of South Ayrshire.
The numbers give the miles between
the places.
  a How far is it from Ballantrae to Barrhill?
  b How far is it from Barr to Ballantrae?
  c Compared with the direct route, how much
further is it to go from Girvan to
Ballantrae via Pinmore?
  d What is the total length of all the
roads shown on the map?

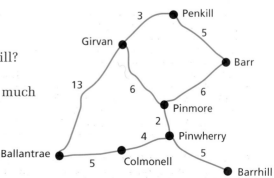

Spreadsheets

A spreadsheet is opened on a computer. The display shows a grid like the one below. Each box in the grid is called a **cell**.

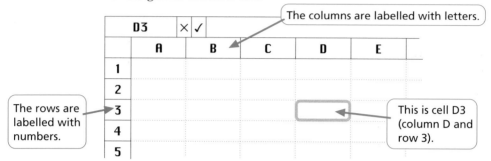

The columns are labelled with letters.

The rows are labelled with numbers.

This is cell D3 (column D and row 3).

When the pointer (usually shaped ⊹ in a spreadsheet) is over cell B2 and clicked,

the cell B2 is selected.

Any typing done will appear in the **Edit bar** at the top of the spreadsheet.

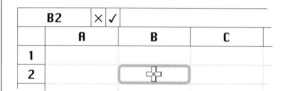

Pressing the 'Return' key makes the typing appear in cell B2. The highlighted cell moves down to B3.

Pressing the 'Tab' key instead makes the highlighted cell move to the right to C2.

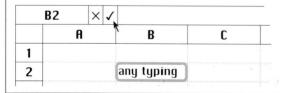

Clicking the tick in the Edit bar keeps the highlighting at B2.

EXERCISE 1

1 a Name the cell containing:
  (i) 3 **(ii)** 7
  (iii) 15 **(iv)** 12
  (v) 13 **(vi)** 5
  (vii) 4 **(viii)** 9.

C3	×✓				
	A	B	C	D	E	F
1						
2	15			3	4	5
3		7		12		
4				13	11	
5		9				

b Which cell is highlighted?

c Which column has no entries?

d Which row has no entries?

e Why does C3 appear in the Edit bar?

2 Look at these Edit bars.

a | D5 | ×✓ | 135 |

b | B3 | ×✓ | Peter |

c | D7 | ×✓ | = D8+C4 |

d | A3 | ×✓ | A15 |

For each say: **(i)** which cell is selected at the moment
(ii) which cell will be selected if 'Return' is pressed
(iii) which cell will be selected if 'Tab' is pressed.

3 If you are working at the computer now, open a new spreadsheet page.
  a These Edit bars tell you which cells to select and what to type.
    After each one press 'Return' or 'Tab' to enter the typing into the cell.

(i) | A1 | ×✓ | Ian |

(ii) | A2 | ×✓ | 135 |

(iii) | C2 | ×✓ | 145 |

(iv) | E2 | ×✓ | 139 |

(v) | B1 | ×✓ | Amer |

(vi) | C1 | ×✓ | Helen |

(vii) | E1 | ×✓ | Peter |

(viii) | D1 | ×✓ | Thomas |

(ix) | B2 | ×✓ | 172 |

(x) | D2 | ×✓ | 160 |

b You should have a spreadsheet like this:

D2	×✓	160		
	A	B	C	D	E
1	Ian	Amer	Helen	Thomas	Peter
2	135	172	145	160	139

It gives the heights in centimetres of five students.
(i) How tall is Thomas? **(ii)** Who is the shortest?
(iii) Who is the tallest? **(iv)** Who is 12 cm taller than Thomas?

Try this.
Select a cell, then go to Format menu and choose Alignment with option Centre. This alters the way the typing is displayed in the cell. There are other options in the Format menu.
Alter the format of cells in your spreadsheet to improve the presentation of the information.

	A	B
1	Ian	Aligned
2	135	right
3	135	left
4	135	centre

4 Each arrow key ⬇ → ← ⬆ moves the highlighted cell in the direction of the arrow. Name the next selected cell when:

a C2 is highlighted and ⬆ is pressed   b B2 is highlighted and → is pressed

c A2 is highlighted and ⬇ is pressed   d E5 is highlighted and ← is pressed.

5

	A	B	C	D	E	F
1		Rainfall	in	June (cm)		
2	Place	Week 1	Week 2	Week 3	Week 4	Monthly total
3	Thurso	0.9	3	2.6	1.1	7.6
4	Wick	0.1	4.5	3.9	1	9.5
5	Stornoway	1.2	4.3	4.1	4.2	13.8
6	Inverness	1.3	8.2	2.1	0	11.6
7	Aberdeen	2.1	5.7	0.4	1.7	

This spreadsheet shows the rainfall in June for various places in Scotland.
Note how **bold**, *italics,* right, left and centre are used to make the format clearer.
a The monthly total is the sum of the four weeks.
   What number should appear in F7?
b The entry in cell B3 is wrong. It should read 1.1.
   To overwrite the 0.9 entry:
   • select B3
   • type 1.1
   • press 'Return'.
   The total for row 3 will now be wrong. What should it be?
c If you are at the computer now:
   (i) make up the spreadsheet
   (ii) make the corrections.

Entering formulae

Totals

Here is part of a spreadsheet that shows daily absentees at a school:

| D5 | ×|✓ | = D2+D3+D4 |

	A	B	C	D	
1	Year	Monday	Tuesday	Wednesday	Th
2	1st	25	12	8	
3	2nd	12	11	11	
4	3rd	14	15	20	
5	Total	51	38	39	

The total of the three cells is displayed but the cell contains a formula.

Cell D5 is highlighted.
It contains a **formula**. Look at the Edit bar.
It contains the formula = D2 + D3 + D4.
Note that a formula always starts with '='.
This formula can be entered as follows:

| D5 | ×|✓ | = D2+D3+D4 |

• select cell D5
• type =
• now click on each cell you wish included in the total
• press 'Return'.

EXERCISE 2

1 If you are at the computer then create the spreadsheet shown above.
    You can use it in the following questions.
    a You select cell C2, type 20 and press 'Return'.
       What happens in (i) cell C2   (ii) cell C5?
    b You change the contents of cell B2 to 15. What happens in cell C5?
    c You change Wednesday's third year absentees to 18.
       What is the new Wednesday total?

2 Extending the spreadsheet for the whole week gives us:

| G2 | ×|✓ | = B2+C2+D2+E2+F2 |

	A	B	C	D	E	F	G
1	Year	Monday	Tuesday	Wednesday	Thursday	Friday	Weekly total
2	1st	25	12	8	7	15	
3	2nd	12	11	11	10	16	
4	3rd	14	15	20	23	39	
5	Total	51	38	39	40	70	

    a Cell G2 contains the formula = B2 + C2 + D2 + E2 + F2. This is the weekly total of
       first year absences. What value will appear in cell G2?
    b What formula will be in (i) G3   (ii) G4?
    c What formula could be in cell G5?

3 When the total of a group of cells is wanted, we can make use of the = SUM( ) formula.

Example 1   To find the first year weekly total:

G2	×✓	= SUM(B2..F2				
	A	**B**	**C**	**D**	**E**	**F**	**G**
1	Year	Monday	Tuesday	Wednesday	Thursday	Friday	Total
2	1st	25	12	8	7	15	

- type = SUM(
- hold down the button on the mouse and drag the pointer from B2 to F2
- type)
- press 'Return'
- check the formula reads = SUM(B2..F2).

Example 2   To find the Monday total:

G2	×✓	= SUM(B2..B4	
	A	**B**	**C**
1	Year	Monday	Tuesday	We
2	1st	25	12
3	2nd	12	11
4	3rd	14	15
5	Total		38

- type = SUM(
- hold down the button on the mouse and drag the pointer from B2 to B4
- type)
- press 'Return'
- check the formula reads = SUM(B2..B4).

Example 3   To put the grand total for the week in cell G5:

G5	×✓	= SUM(B2..F4				
	A	**B**	**C**	**D**	**E**	**F**	**G**
1	Year	Monday	Tuesday	Wednesday	Thursday	Friday	Total
2	1st	25	12	8	7	15	67
3	2nd	12	11	11	10	16	60
4	3rd	14	15	20	23	39	111
5	Total	51	38	39	40	70	238

- select G5
- type = SUM(
- drag the pointer from B2 to F4
- type)
- press 'Return'
- check the formula reads = SUM(B2..F4).

---

a By this method B5 contains the formula = SUM(B2..B4).
What formula is in **(i)** C5   **(ii)** E5?
b G2 contains the formula = SUM(B2..F2). What formula is in **(i)** G3   **(ii)** G4?

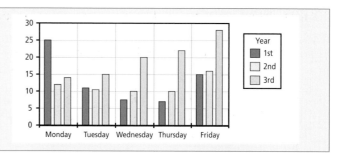

Challenge

Explore how to make charts of the data from Exercise 2.

Other formulae

You now have to use these special signs:

+ denotes   add (+)
− denotes   subtract (−)
* denotes   multiply (×)
/ denotes   divide (÷)

Examples

By taking the distance travelled away from the length of the journey you find the distance left to go.

C3 = A3 − B3

C3	× ✓	= A3-B3	
	A	**B**	**C**
1	Length of	Distance	Distance
2	journey	travelled	left
3	300	40	260
4	186	94	92

C2	× ✓	= A2*B2	
	A	**B**	**C**
1	Speed	Time	Distance
2	30	4	120
3	25	6	150

Multiplying speed by time gives the distance travelled.

C2 = A2 * B2

Dividing the size of the prize by the number of winners gives the share each winner receives.

C2 = A2/B2

C2	× ✓	= A2/B2	
	A	**B**	**C**
1	Amount	No. of winners	Share
2	10000	4	2500
3	3000	6	500

B3	× ✓	= A3-0.1*A3
	A	**B**
1	Price before	Price after
2	discount	10% discount
3	£300.00	£270.00
4	£186.00	£167.40

The signs can be mixed to produce many formulae, for example working out a sale price:

B3 = A3 − 0.1*A3

EXERCISE 3

If you are at a computer you should construct each spreadsheet.

1

B5	✕	✓	= SUM(B2..B4)		
	A	**B**	**C**	**D**	**E**	**F**

	A	B	C	D	E	F
1		Ian	John	David	Alison	Yvonne
2	Round 1	120	430	200	520	70
3	Round 2	0	100	50	0	150
4	Round 3	250	10	50	0	60
5	Total	370				

The scores in a card game are shown.
a What formula would you put in: **(i)** C5 **(ii)** D5 **(iii)** E5 **(iv)** F5?
b What values will appear in the cells?

2 Net pay is gross pay less deductions.

D2	✕	✓	= B2-C2

	A	B	C	D
1	Employee	Gross pay (£)	Deductions (£)	Net pay (£)
2	S.Thomson	150	40.55	
3	K.Dillon	234.74	63.18	
4	H.Peters	198.55	53.46	

a What formula goes into: **(i)** D2 **(ii)** D3 **(iii)** D4?
b What value will appear in these cells?

3 This spreadsheet shows the number of nails in stock in a hardware store.
The number of nails of type B is 150 × 18 = 2700.

B5	✕	✓	= B1*B2

	A	B	C	D
1	Number in tub	150	250	350
2	Number of tubs	18	45	35
3	Total nails	2700		

a What formula goes into:
(i) C3 **(ii)** D3?
b What value will appear in each cell?

4 A bus company has a fleet of buses. They keep an eye on the number of kilometres each bus travels on one litre of fuel.

D2	✕	✓	= B2/C2

	A	B	C	D
1	Vehicle	Distance	Fuel	km/l
2	Bus 1	280	40	7
3	Bus 2	308	35	
4	Bus 3	441	42	

a Examine the Edit bar. What calculation has produced the 7 km/l in D2?
b What formula should be entered in: **(i)** D3 **(ii)** D4?
c What values will appear in these cells?

More format ideas

The number 12.345 has been entered in each cell in the A column.

The Format menu allows you to pick how the number should be displayed.

If you choose **fixed** then you should also choose **precision** to show the number of decimal places you want fixed.

If you choose **currency** then a £ sign appears (*do not type it in*) and the precision is fixed at 2 automatically.

To format a cell, or block of cells, you must first select them by dragging.

Try to format the cells for a professional look.

A1	×✓	Useful formats	
	A	**B**	**C**
1		Format	Precision
2	12.345	general	
3	12	fixed	0
4	12.3	fixed	1
5	12.35	fixed	2
6	12.345	fixed	3
7	£12.35	currency	2 forced
8	1235%	per cent	0 forced

5 In this spreadsheet columns B and D have been formatted for currency.

a What formula is entered in cell:
  (i) D2   **(ii)** D3
  (iii) D4   **(iv)** D5
  (v) D6
      (check Edit bar)
  (vi) D7?

D6	×✓	= D5*0.175		
	A	**B**	**C**	**D**
1	Item	Unit cost	Quantity	Cost
2	Soup	£1.60	4	£6.40
3	Main course	£6.90	3	£20.70
4	Sweet	£2.30	5	£11.50
5			Total	£38.60
6			VAT at 17.5%	£6.76
7			Bill	£45.36

b If you are working at the computer use the spreadsheet to calculate the bill for:
  (i) 8 soups, 7 main courses and 5 sweets
  (ii) 12 soups, 11 main courses and 13 sweets
  (iii) 27 soups, 27 main courses and 27 sweets.

6 This spreadsheet calculates the area of a rectangle.

B4	×✓	= B2*B3		
	A	**B**	**C**	**D**
1		Rectangle 1	Rectangle 2	Rectangle 3
2	length	1.45		
3	breadth	2.54		
4	area	3.683		

a What formula has been entered in B4? Check that the value shown is correct.

b **(i)** Fixed, precision 2 format is selected. What does the entry in B4 read now?
  (ii) Fixed, precision 1 format is selected. What shows in B4?
  (iii) Fixed, precision 0 format is selected. State the entry in B4.

7 Study this spreadsheet. Note that π is written as PI( ).

B5	× ✓	= PI()*B3*B3		
	A	**B**	**C**	**D**
1		*Circle 1*	*Circle 2*	*Circle 3*
2	diameter	5	10	12
3	radius	2.5	5	6
4	circumference	15.71	31.42	37.70
5	area	19.63	78.54	113.10

a The diameters of three circles are given.
What formula is entered in: **(i)** B3 **(ii)** C3 **(iii)** D3?
b The circumference of a circle is given by $C = \pi D$.
What formula is entered in: **(i)** B4 **(ii)** C4 **(iii)** D4?
c What precision has been fixed?
d The area of a circle is given by $A = \pi r^2$.
For cell B5 we enter = PI( )*B3*B3 (see Edit bar).
What formula is entered in: **(i)** C5 **(ii)** D5?

Copying and pasting formulae

D2	× ✓	= B2+C2	
	A	**B**	**C**	**D**
1		*Basic wage*	*Overtime*	*Earnings*
2	T.Jones	£125.00	£67.00	£192.00
3	B.Smith	£163.00	£54.00	
4	G.Townsend	£267.00	£78.00	

Cell D2 contains the formula
= B2 + C2
T. Jones earnings =
his basic wage + *his* overtime

We can copy this formula to suit B. Smith.
Step 1 Select D2 (where the formula is).
Step 2 Copy the formula (go to the Edit menu and choose Copy).
Step 3 Select cell D3 (where the copy is to go).
Step 4 Paste in the formula (go to the Edit menu and choose Paste).

D3	× ✓	= B3+C3	
	A	**B**	**C**	**D**
1		*Basic wage*	*Overtime*	*Earnings*
2	T.Jones	£125.00	£67.00	£192.00
3	B.Smith	£163.00	£54.00	£217.00
4	G.Townsend	£267.00	£78.00	

Notice how the formula has changed:
D2 = B2 + C2
has copied as
D3 = B3 + C3

Similarly, when the formula is copied into D4 it becomes = B4 + C4
The formula can be pasted into blocks of cells at the same time if at step 3 the blocks of cells are selected by dragging.

EXERCISE 4

If you are at a computer you should construct each spreadsheet.

1

A2	X ✓	= A1+1		
	A	B	C	D	E
1	1	1	100	1024	2
2	2	2	99	512	3
3					
4					

a A2 contains the formula = A1 + 1.
It is copied into A3 to A6.
What formula is in cell
  (i) A3
  (ii) A4?
  (iii) What numbers appear in each cell?

b B2 contains the formula = B1*2.
It is copied into B3 to B6.
What formula is in cell
  (i) B3
  (ii) B4?
  (iii) What numbers appear in each cell?

c C2 contains the formula = C1 − 1.
It is copied into C3 to C6.
What formula is in cell
  (i) C3
  (ii) C4?
  (iii) What numbers appear in each cell?

d D2 contains the formula = D1/2.
It is copied into D3 to D6.
What formula is in cell
  (i) D3
  (ii) D4?
  (iii) What numbers appear in each cell?

e E2 contains the formula = 2*E1 − 1.
It is copied into E3 to E6.
What formula is in cell
  (i) E3
  (ii) E4?
  (iii) What numbers appear in each cell?

2

A2	X ✓	= A1+2	
	A	B	C	D
1	1	1	1	1
2	3	3	0.5	3
3	5	9	0.25	7
4	7	27	0.125	15
5	9	81	0.0625	31
6	11	243	0.03125	63

'1' has been entered into each cell in row 1.

a A formula has been put in A2. The formula has been copied into the rest of the A column. What is the formula?

b A formula has been put in B2. The formula has been copied into the rest of the B column. What is the formula?

c Identify the formula which has created **(i)** column C   **(ii)** column D.

d Keeping the formula the same, A1 is changed to 6.
What does the rest of the column now show?

e Keeping the formula the same, C1 is changed to 32.
What does the rest of the column now show?

Finding the mean

A spreadsheet uses the term **average** for the mean.
= AVERAGE(D2..D6) is a formula for the mean of the numbers from D2 to D6.

EXERCISE 5

If you are at a computer you should construct each spreadsheet.

1

B7	× ✓	= AVERAGE(B2..B6)	
	A	**B**	**C**	**D**
1		Test 1	Test 2	Total
2	Yvonne	23	47	70
3	Siobhan	43	49	92
4	Michael	37	38	75
5	Peter	31	36	67
6	John	15	12	27
7	Mean	29.8	36.4	66.2

This spreadsheet gives the marks of five students over two tests.

a What formula goes into cell D2 to work out Yvonne's total?

b The formula is copied into cells D3 to D6. What formula is in cell D6?

c Cell B7 holds the formula for calculating the mean mark of test 1, namely = AVERAGE(B2..B6).
  (i) What formula goes into C7 to do a similar job for test 2?
  (ii) What formula goes into D7 to calculate the mean of column D?

d Who scored **(i)** above **(ii)** below average?

2 A motorist constructs a petrol consumption spreadsheet.

a What formula is in C2? (Look at the Edit bar.)

b This formula is pasted into cells C3 to C6. Write down the formula in C5.

c The answers should be correct to 2 decimal places. What format should be picked?

C2	× ✓	= A2/B2	
	A	**B**	**C**
1	Journey (km)	litres used	km per litre
2	285	12	23.75
3	312	15	
4	487	25	
5	912	43	
6	110	5	

d Cell C7 is to hold the mean petrol consumption. What formula should be entered into C7?

e In which journeys was the petrol consumption above average?

3 A shop advertises its prices for photocopies as shown. Design a spreadsheet which calculates the cost of photocopying when the number of A4, A3 and A2 size sheets is entered. Use the spreadsheet to calculate these bills:

a 78 copies of A4 and 25 copies of A3

b 150 copies of A4, 200 copies of A3 and 50 copies of A2

c 250 copies of each size.

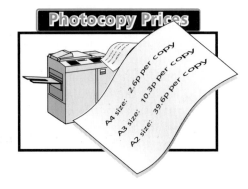

Photocopy Prices

A4 size: 2.6p per copy
A3 size: 10.3p per copy
A2 size: 39.6p per copy

Network diagrams

This map shows some of the roads in part of Fife. Distances are shown in miles.

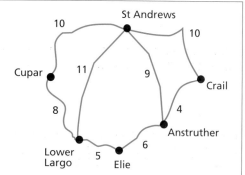

If all we need to know is which town is connected to which and how far apart they are, then a simplified map or **network** can be used.
This network has six vertices (the dots) and eight arcs or edges (the lines joining the dots).

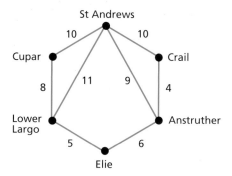

Other networks give the same information.

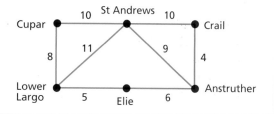

EXERCISE 6

1 a This network diagram also represents the map above.
Copy it and complete the labelling of the vertices and arcs.

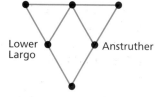

b Here are some different examples of the Fife network. Copy them and label the vertices and arcs correctly.

(i) 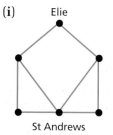   **(ii)** 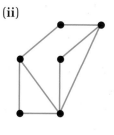   **(iii)**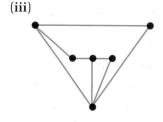

c Find the shortest route from St Andrews to Elie. How long is it?

d The 'St Andrews' vertex has degree 4 since four arcs meet at it.
Find the degree of each of the other five vertices.

> **Hint**
> St Andrews has four roads leaving it.

2 When the degree of a vertex (or node) is even we call it an even vertex.
When the degree of a vertex (or node) is odd we call it an odd vertex.

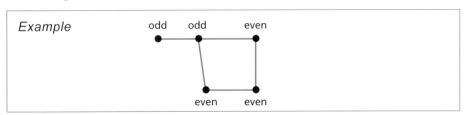

Example odd odd even even even

For each network below state the number of: **(i)** vertices **(ii)** arcs **(iii)** odd vertices.

a

b

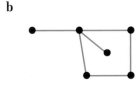

c

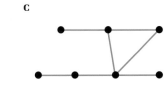

3 This map shows some of the roads on the island of Mull.

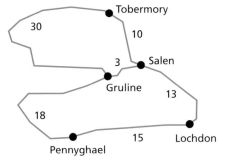

Tobermory
30
10
3 Salen
Gruline
13
18
15 Lochdon
Pennyghael

a Copy each of these network diagrams. Label the vertices and arcs so that they represent this map. (Hint: How many roads leave Salen?)

(i)

(ii)

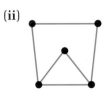

b Give the degree of each vertex in the network.

> The network can be redrawn as a TREE diagram when we wish to find the longest or shortest route. e.g. What is the longest route between Tobermory and Pennyghael?
>
>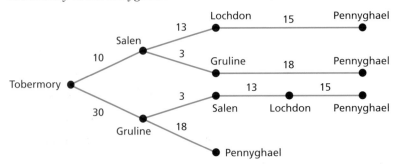
>
> Lochdon 15 Pennyghael
> 13
> Salen
> 10 3
> Gruline 18 Pennyghael
> Tobermory
> 13 15
> 3
> 30 Salen Lochdon Pennyghael
> Gruline 18
> Pennyghael
>
> We can see that the longest route is Tobermory, Gruline, Salen, Lochdon, Pennyghael, a distance of 61 miles.

c Find the shortest route from Tobermory to Pennyghael. How long is it?

4 a Draw a network to represent each of these maps.
Label the vertices to show the places. Label the arcs to show the distances.

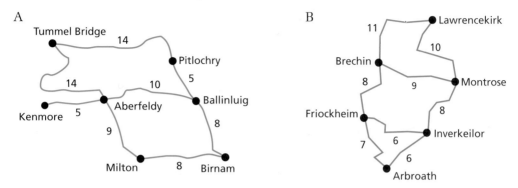

A

Tummel Bridge 14 Pitlochry
14 10 5
Kenmore Aberfeldy Ballinluig
5
9 8
Milton 8 Birnam

B

11 Lawrencekirk
10
Brechin Montrose
8 9
Friockheim 8
7 6 Inverkeilor
6
Arbroath

b (i) Copy and complete this
tree diagram by entering the
mileage between towns.
(ii) Use the tree to identify the
longest and shortest
routes between
Kenmore and Birnam.
(iii) Draw a tree diagram
which will help you find the
longest and shortest routes between
Pitlochry and Milton.

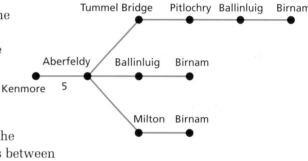

Tummel Bridge Pitlochry Ballinluig Birnam

Aberfeldy Ballinluig Birnam

Kenmore 5

Milton Birnam

c From Lawrencekirk there are eight ways of getting to Arbroath without going
through the same town twice.
(i) Copy and complete the tree diagram to help you find all eight routes.
(ii) Identify the longest and the shortest route.

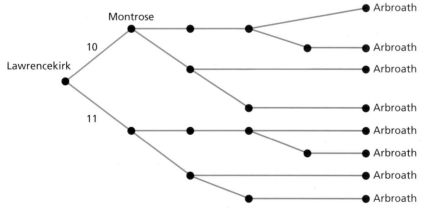

Montrose
Arbroath
10
Arbroath
Lawrencekirk
Arbroath
11
Arbroath
Arbroath
Arbroath
Arbroath
Arbroath

(iii) How many of the routes visit all six towns?
(iv) Which of these routes is the shortest?
(v) Draw a tree diagram to help you find how many routes there are in network B
joining Brechin to Inverkeilor without going through the same town twice.
(vi) Do any of these routes visit all six towns?

5 A road repair team want to check the whole network of roads.
   They wish to start at Lower Largo and
   finish at Anstruther.
   They don't mind passing through a town
   twice but they do mind travelling the same
   stretch of road.

   a **(i)** Describe a route that suits them.
   (ii) How long is the route?
   b Copy and complete this table.

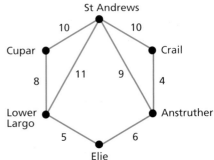

All distances are in miles.

Vertex	Degree	Even/odd
St Andrews	4	even
Cupar	2	even
Lower Largo	3	odd
Elie		
Anstruther		
Crail		

   c Try to explain why your route had to start
   at an odd vertex and end at an odd vertex.

Hint
Think of 'passing through'
places – you need a road in
and also a road out.

6 **a** Find a route covering all 73 miles of the map
   in question **4a.**
   b Is it possible to find such a route for the map
   in question **4b**?
   Give a reason for your answer.
   When such a route is possible in a network,
   we say that the network is **traversable**.

Hint
Use even and odd vertices
to find your starting and
finishing places.

Challenge

All of these networks are traversable.
Copy each network diagram by starting at one vertex, not lifting your pencil and
finishing at another vertex.
You are not allowed to retrace any of the arcs.

a   **b**   **c** 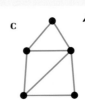 **d**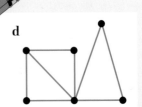

Other uses of networks

This is the plan of a flat.

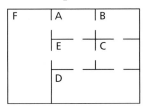

The gaps are connecting doors.

Using a vertex for a room

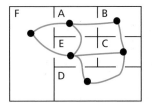

... and an arc for a connection,

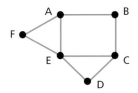

we can draw a simplified network of the situation.

Can the rooms be connected by a single unbroken wire that runs through each doorway only once?

EXERCISE 7

1 a Copy the network above.
   b Label each vertex odd or even.
   c Can you find a suitable route?

Reminder

If there are odd vertices you must use them to start and finish. But what if there are more than two odd vertices?

2 a Make a network for each of these flats.
   b Use the network to help you find a wiring route. (One of the problems is impossible.)

(i)   **(ii)**

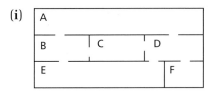   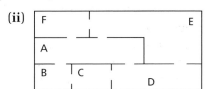

(iii)

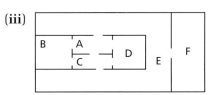

3 a Draw room systems for these networks.
   b Show how they may be wired by a single wire passing through each doorway once and only once.

(i)   **(ii)**

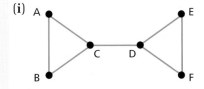   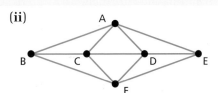

Activity networks

In this kind of network the vertices represent the start and finish of a step in a job.
The arc represents the step.
Each arc is labelled with the step description and the time it takes to do the step.

Example 1

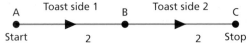

This simple network describes how to make a piece of toast under the grill.
Note that it takes 2 + 2 = 4 minutes to make the toast.

Example 2

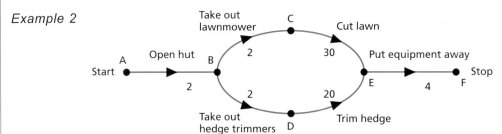

With more than one person it is possible that two steps happen at the same time.
This network shows two people doing the garden.
Note that the longest path is ABCEF: a total of 2 + 2 + 30 + 4 = 38 minutes.
So from start to finish, doing the garden will take 38 minutes.
This longest path is often called the **critical path**.

EXERCISE 8

1 This simple network shows the time in minutes it takes to plant a row of potatoes.

   a How many **(i)** vertices   **(ii)** arcs does the network have?
   b How long does it take to **(i)** dig a drill   **(ii)** cover the drill?
   c How long does it take to complete the job?

2 This network describes cooking a meal of meat and two vegetables. All times are in
   minutes. There are three rings on the cooker. This lets all the items cook at the same
   time if you wish.

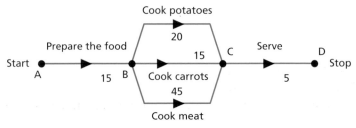

   a How many **(i)** vertices   **(ii)** arcs does the network have?

b How long does it take to **(i)** prepare the food   **(ii)** serve the food?
c **(i)** What is the length of the longest path?
  (ii) How long then does it take to do the job?

3 To lay a pipe workmen need to dig a trench, lay the pipe sections, join the sections and fill it in. The men joining the sections must wait for the first two lengths to be laid. This network describes the activity. Times are in hours.

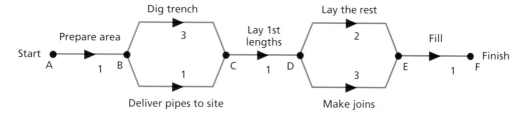

a What is the length of the longest path?
b How long will the job take?

4 In this activity network describing a decorating job, each vertex stands for the *start* of a step. The arc leaving a vertex is labelled with the time required to complete the step. Times are in hours. (Note that it takes 0 hours to start.)

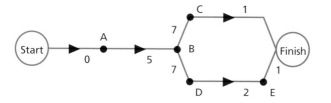

A: Paint woodwork
B: Hang wallpaper
C: Put up curtains
D: Lay carpet
E: Set up furniture

a How long does it take to lay the carpet?
b What is done after the carpet is laid?
c Which three tasks have to wait until after the wallpaper has been hung?
d What is the shortest possible time to complete the whole task?

Challenge

A grill pan can hold two slices of bread for toasting.
It takes the grill 3 minutes to toast one side.
What is the quickest that three pieces of bread can be toasted on both sides?

Flowcharts

This is an example of a flowchart.
This one helps you decide when a number is even and when it is odd.

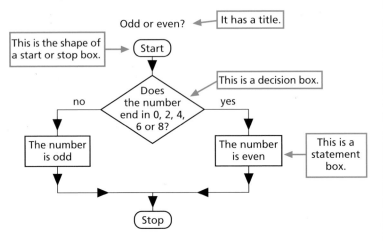

Follow the arrows, read the questions and act on the statements.

EXERCISE 9

1 Use each flowchart to answer the questions.

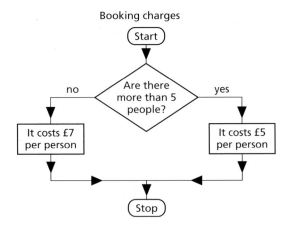

a What is the charge for:
  (i) 1 person
  (ii) 20 people
  (iii) 5 people?

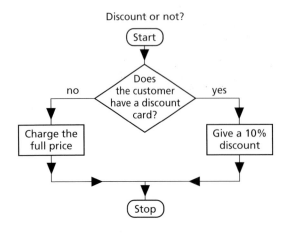

b What does a customer pay for:
  (i) a £20 item with no discount card
  (ii) a £50 item with a discount card?

c Calculate P when:

   (i) $a = 5$

   (ii) $a = 2$

   (iii) $a = 3$.

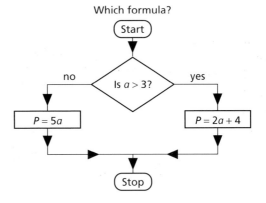

Which formula?

2   Sales commission

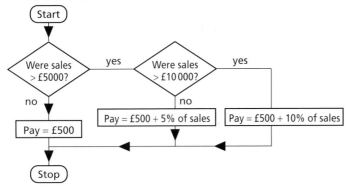

Calculate the salary for a saleswoman whose sales were:

a   £8000

b   £250

c   £12 000

d   £10 000.

3   The charge for sailing lessons depends on various things.

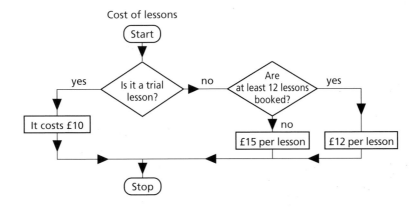

Cost of lessons

What is the charge for:

a   1 trial lesson

b   8 lessons

c   14 lessons?

4 A variety of flowchart called a decision tree diagram is often used when sorting or classifying objects:

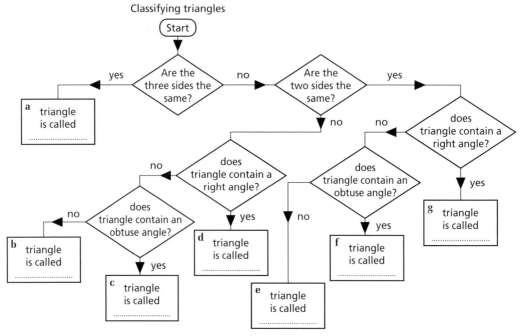

Classifying triangles

Use the terms: equilateral, right-angled isosceles, obtuse isosceles, acute isosceles, acute-angled scalene, obtuse-angled scalene, right-angled scalene to complete the terminal boxes.

5

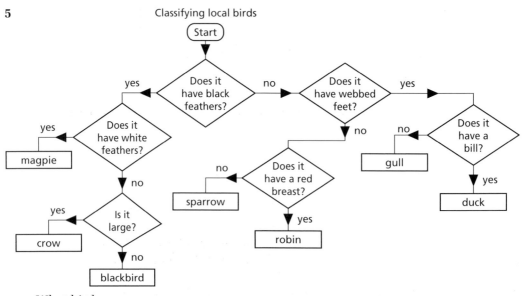

Classifying local birds

a What bird
   (i) has black feathers and white feathers?
   (ii) is not black, has webbed feet and no bill?
   (iii) has black but no white feathers and is not large?
b Describe the robin.

CHAPTER 20 REVIEW

1 A new bakery opens. Takings for the first three days are shown on this spreadsheet.

	A	B	C	D	E
1		Bread	Cakes	Rolls	Daily total
2	Day 1	£78.53	£38.50	£56.40	£173.43
3	Day 2	£123.72	£105.70	£79.76	
4	Day 3	£156.90	£206.80	£67.89	
5	3-day total				
6				Grand total	

  a What is the amount in cell C3?
  b What information does column D give?
  c What format is being used in cells B2 to D4?
  d The formula in cell E2 is = B2 + C2 + D2. What formula should go into cell E3?
  e B5 holds the formula = SUM(B2..B4). What similar formula should go into
     (i) cell C5   **(ii)** D5?
  f Find a suitable formula for cell E6.

2 A salesperson clocks up the following mileages during three weeks of work.

	Mon	Tue	Wed	Thu	Fri	Sat
Week 1	220	105	0	316	112	47
Week 2	0	0	430	455	212	147
Week 3	53	27	39	514	612	23

Design a spreadsheet to:
- display the data
- calculate the weekly average mileage for each of the three weeks, working to 1 decimal place.

3

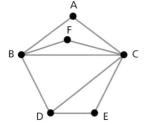

  a For this network diagram, make a table showing:
    (i) the degree of each vertex and
    (ii) whether it is odd or even.

  b Describe how this network can be copied without lifting your pencil and without retracing any of the arcs.
  c **(i)** Draw a tree diagram to find how many routes connect A to E without passing through the same node twice.
    (ii) Do any of the routes pass through all six nodes?

4

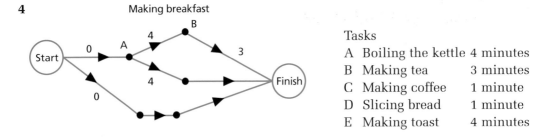

Making breakfast

Tasks

A	Boiling the kettle	4 minutes
B	Making tea	3 minutes
C	Making coffee	1 minute
D	Slicing bread	1 minute
E	Making toast	4 minutes

The dots represent the start of the task.

The numbers next to the arrows give the length of time the task takes.

a Copy and complete this activity network.

b Use it to find the shortest time 'Making breakfast' can take.

5　Charges for Felihome Luxury Cattery

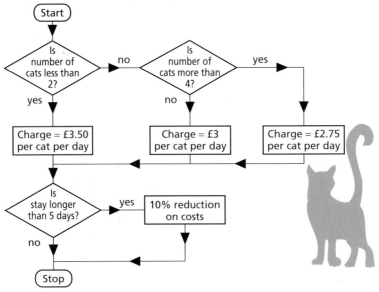

Calculate the charge for:

a　1 cat for 1 day

b　1 cat for 7 days

c　3 cats for 2 days

d　5 cats for a fortnight.

21 Scale Drawings

STARTING POINTS

1 Estimate, then measure the size of these angles.

a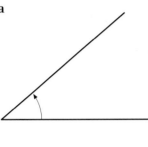

b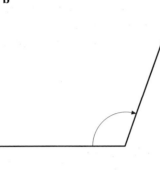

c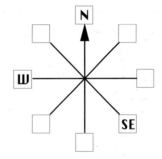

2 Draw angles of: **a** 50° **b** 120° **c** 245°.

3 Copy this compass rose and fill in the missing directions.

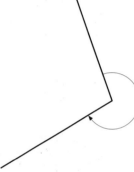

4 a Copy and complete:
  (i) 1 kilometre = ... metres
  (ii) 1 metre = ... centimetres
  (iii) 1 centimetre = ... millimetres

  b Use your answers to part **a** to help you complete these:
  (i) 7 kilometres = ... metres
  (ii) 5.6 metres = ... centimetres
  (iii) 17 centimetres = ... millimetres

  c Copy and complete:
  (i) 3 000 000 millimetres = ... centimetres
  (ii) 300 000 centimetres = ... metres
  (iii) 3000 metres = ... kilometres

5 Write down the abbreviation for:
  a kilometre   **b** metre   **c** centimetre   **d** millimetre.

Scales

Maps and plans are drawn to represent something in real life.
The sizes have to be scaled down to make the plan easy to use.

The **scale** tells you how to turn a length on the map into a length in real life. For example, a scale of **1 cm represents 10 m** means that 1 cm on the map stands for 10 m in real life.

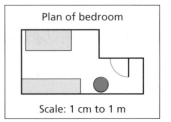

Plan of bedroom

Scale: 1 cm to 1 m

Example 1
Scale: 1 cm represents 100 m.
What real-life distance would 5 cm on the map represent?

       Map   Actual distance

       1 cm ⟶ 100 m

Multiply to scale up.   5 cm ⟶ $5 \times 100 = 500$ m

Example 2
Scale: 1 cm represents 10 km.
What distance would be drawn on the map to represent a real distance of 95 km?

       Map   Actual distance

       1 cm ⟶ 10 km

Divide to scale down. $95 \div 10 = 9.5$ cm ⟵ 95 km

EXERCISE 1

1 Copy and complete:
a scale of **1 cm represents 5 km** means that 1 cm on the map stands for …

2   Scale: 1 cm represents 100 m.

What real-life distance would each of these lengths on a map represent?
a 4 cm   **b** 7 cm   **c** 12 cm   **d** 9.6 cm

3   Scale: 1 cm represents 10 m.

What lengths would be drawn on a map to represent these real-life distances?
a 30 m   **b** 70 m   **c** 120 m   **d** 65 m

4   Scale: 1 cm represents 50 m.

What real-life distance does each length represent?
a 2 cm   **b** 9 cm   **c** 10 cm   **d** 4.5 cm

5   Scale: 1 cm represents 2 km.

What lengths would be drawn to represent these real-life distances?
a 6 km   **b** 20 km   **c** 7 km   **d** 13 km

6 Copy and complete each table.

a

| | ×5 → |
| | ← ÷5 |

Distance on map	Actual distance
1 cm	5 m
2 cm	
	45 m
8.2 cm	

b

| | ×20 → |
| | ← ÷20 |

Distance on map	Actual distance
1 cm	20 km
3 cm	
5.5 cm	
	180 km

7 These lines represent distances on a map.
(**i**) Measure the lengths of the lines in centimetres.
(**ii**) Work out the actual distances that these lines represent.

a —————————————

b ————————————————————

c ——————————

d ————————————————————————

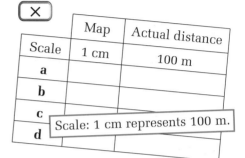

	Map	Actual distance
Scale	1 cm	100 m
a		
b		
c		
d		

Scale: 1 cm represents 100 m.

8 a On this map, work out the distances between:
(**i**) the summits of Skelfhill and Hoghill
(**ii**) Skelfhill and Deerpike
(**iii**) Deerpike and Hoghill
(**iv**) the church and the bridge.

Scale: 1 cm represents 5 km.

b *Estimate* the length of Burndale Water from the southern edge of the map to the northern edge.

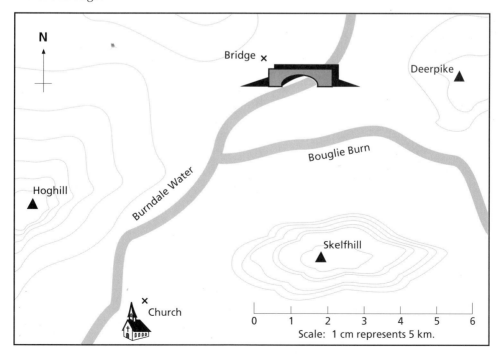

Scale: 1 cm represents 5 km.

9 This is a plan of a bedroom.

   a What does 1 cm on the plan represent?

   b Measure the lengths asked for and work out the actual sizes.

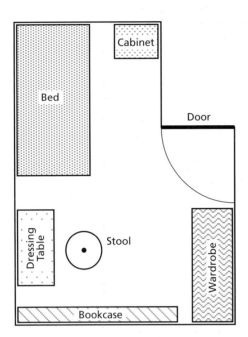

Scale: 2 cm represents 1 m.

	Distance on plan	Actual distance
Scale	1 cm	... m
Width of door		
Length of bed		
Breadth of bed		
Longer diagonal of room		
Diameter of stool		

Scaled rulers

To avoid lots of calculations, a scaled ruler is often provided on a map or plan.
The ruler shows the real-life sizes of the places on the map.

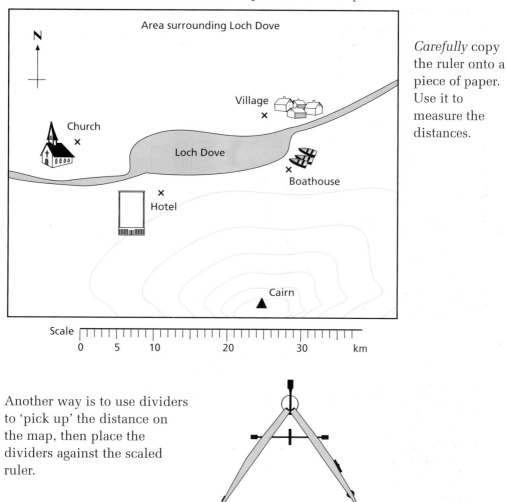

Carefully copy the ruler onto a piece of paper. Use it to measure the distances.

Another way is to use dividers to 'pick up' the distance on the map, then place the dividers against the scaled ruler.

EXERCISE 2

1 Use the map of the area surrounding Loch Dove for this question.
   a Check that the distance from the church to the hotel is 13 km.
   b Measure the distances from:
      (i)   the cairn to the boathouse
      (ii) the church to the village
      (iii) one end of the loch to the other.
   c How far is the hotel from the village?

2 Copy (carefully) the scaled ruler on this plan onto card or use dividers.
Find the actual size of:

a the width of the window

b the length of the fireplace

c the length and the breadth of the room at its widest part

d the length of the table

e the width of the doorway.

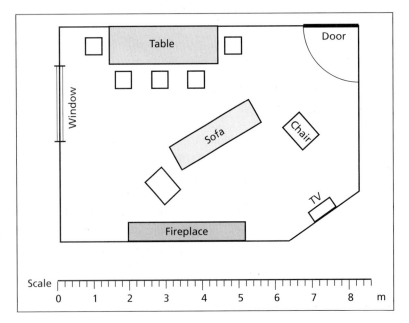

3

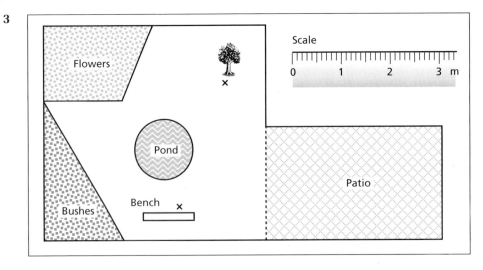

Use the scaled ruler to find:

a the distance between the tree and the bench

b the diameter of the pond

c the area of the patio.

Scale as a fraction

On some maps, the scale is given as a fraction.

Scale: $\frac{1}{10\,000}$ or 1 : 10 000.

The above scale indicates that the actual sizes are ten thousand times those on the map. One on the map represents 10 000 on the ground.

For example,
1 cm represents 10 000 cm
1 m represents 10 000 m
1 inch represents 10 000 inches.

For this exercise it is assumed that a centimetre ruler is being used.

Example On the map, the distance between P and Q is 5 cm.

Scale: $\frac{1}{10\,000}$

Scale $\frac{1}{10\,000}$ means
1 cm represents 10 000 cm
so 5 cm represents 50 000 cm
or 5 cm represents 500 m.

The actual distance from
P to Q is 500 m.

EXERCISE 3

1 Copy and complete:

   a Scale: $\frac{1}{5000}$ means 1 cm represents ... cm
                   so 1 cm represents ... m.

   b Scale: $\frac{1}{1000}$ means 1 cm represents ... cm
                   so 1 cm represents ... m.

2 An old map showed the scale as $\frac{1}{63\,360}$.
   Investigate why this scale is so different from a modern scale.
   Can you work out what this scale means?

3 A map has a scale of 1 : 2 000 000.
   On the map two towns are 3 cm apart.
   How far apart are the towns in real life?

4 A balloonist used a map with a scale of 1 : 10 000.
   He measured two hills as being 4 cm apart.
   How far apart are the hills in real life?

5 This map shows Bridgekey's town centre.

   a How many metres are represented by a centimetre on the map?

   b Calculate the real distance between the following pairs of points:

      (i) leisure centre and town hall   **(ii)** church and school

      (iii) supermarket and cinema   **(iv)** school and leisure centre.

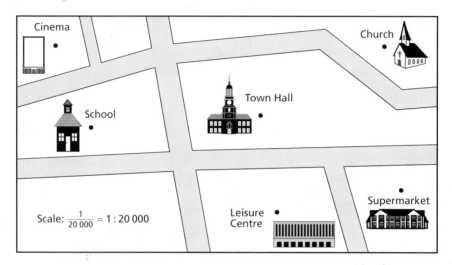

Scale: $\frac{1}{20\,000}$ = 1 : 20 000

Using compass directions to describe positions

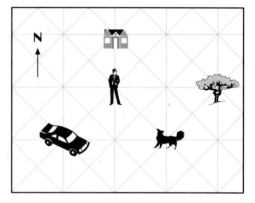

The house is **north** of the man.
The dog is **south-west** of the tree.
The car is **west** of the dog.

EXERCISE 4

1 The diagram shows the position of five oil-rigs. Write down the missing words in the following statements.

   a ... is south of Alpha.

   b Hero is ... of Swallow.

   c North-west of Alpha is the ... oil-rig.

   d ... is south-west of Bruce.

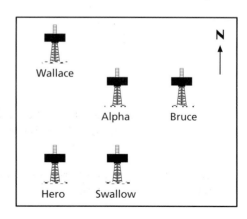

2 Describe the journey from Roberton to Stowe, giving
   (i) the direction and
   (ii) the distance to be travelled in each leg of the journey.

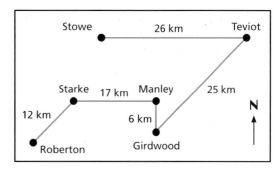

3-figure bearings

James faces north.
He turns clockwise through some angle.
The direction in which he now faces can be described by stating the angle.
The angle is given as a 3-digit number.
When there are only 2 digits a zero is put in front, e.g. 40° becomes 040°.
This angle is then known as a **3-figure bearing**.

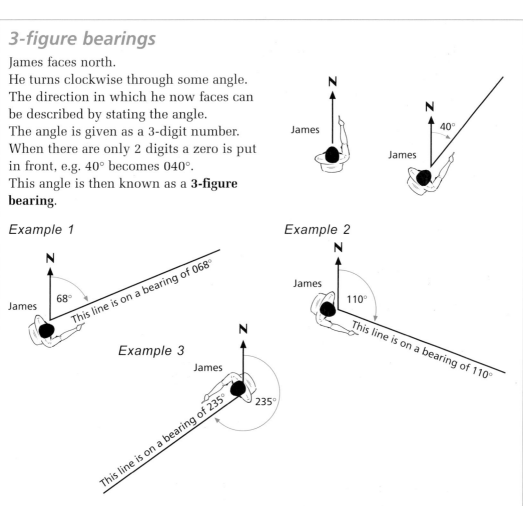

EXERCISE 5

1 North has a 3-figure bearing of 000°. (Since the angle turned clockwise from North is 0°.). Write down the 3-figure bearing of:
   a east   **b** south   **c** west   **d** south-east.

2 Which of the main compass points has a 3-figure bearing of:
   a 045°   **b** 315°   **c** 225°?

3 The diagram shows the position of five ships in relation to the lighthouse, A.

   a Use an angle measurer to check that the bearing of ship P from the lighthouse A is 105°.

   b Estimate, then measure the bearing, from A, of each of the other ships.

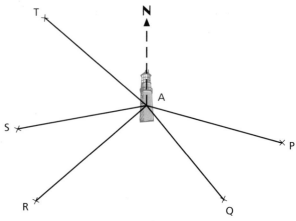

4

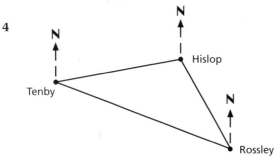

The map shows the position of three towns, Tenby, Hislop and Rossley. Estimate, then measure the bearing of:

   a Hislop from Tenby

   b Rossley from Tenby

   c Rossley from Hislop

   d Hislop from Rossley.

5 Estimate, then measure the bearing of:

   a the wreck from the tree

   b the cave from the port

   c the tree from the cave.

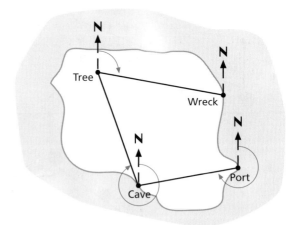

6 Follow these instructions to draw a line to represent a bearing of 150°.

   a Mark a point, P, on a plain piece of paper.

   b Draw a line to represent north from point P.

   c Measure an angle of 150° from north in a clockwise direction.

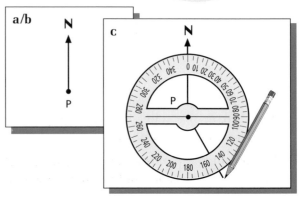

d Draw in the line which has a
bearing of 150° from P.

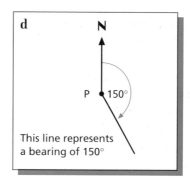

This line represents
a bearing of 150°

7 On separate diagrams, draw lines to represent bearings of:
   a 080°   **b** 130°   **c** 255°   **d** 310°.

8 On a plain piece of paper, mark a point X near the centre of the page.
   a From point X, draw a line to represent north.
   b Draw lines from X to represent these bearings:
     (i) 030°   **(ii)** 240°   **(iii)** 125°   **(iv)** 290°   **(v)** 355°.

Measuring bearings and distances

EXERCISE 6

1 A lighthouse, R, has a radar screen to monitor
the ships around it.
The radar screen shows the position of six ships.
   a Check that ship A is 30 km from the
     lighthouse, on a bearing of 080°.
   b Write down the distance and bearing
     of each ship from R.

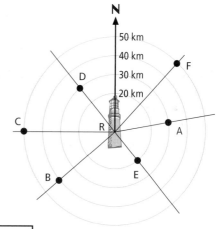

2

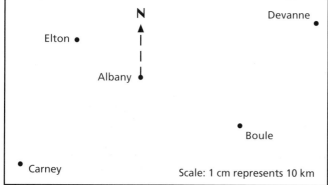

The map shows the position of five towns. The scale of the map is 1 cm to 10 km.
Work out the distance and bearing of each town from Albany.

3 This scale drawing shows an orienteering course.
Instructions for each leg of the course are stated by giving:
a the distance to be run and
b the direction as a 3-figure bearing.

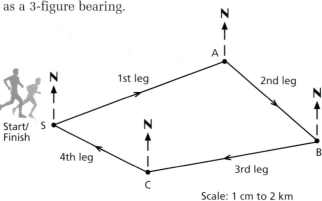

Scale: 1 cm to 2 km

Complete the instructions for the course.

1st leg	10 km	070°
2nd leg	...	...
3rd leg	...	...
4th leg	...	...

Drawing maps and plans

Lauren Pringle is a landscape gardener.
Before arranging a garden she likes to draw up a plan.
The garden of this cottage is a 20 m by 14 m rectangle.

Step 1   Make a rough sketch showing all angles and sizes.

Step 2   Decide on a scale,
e.g. 1 cm represents 2 m.

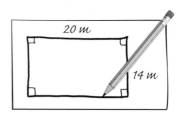

Step 3   Scale all the sizes:

	Actual	On map
Scale	2 m	1 cm
Breadth	20 m	10 cm
Length	14 m	7 cm

Step 4   Make an accurate drawing of a 10 cm by 7 cm rectangle.
(You will need a sharp pencil, ruler and set square.)

EXERCISE 7

1 a (i) Make an accurate full sized drawing of a square of side 5 cm.
   (ii) Measure the length of the diagonal of the square.
  b (i) Make an accurate full sized drawing of a rectangle measuring 6 cm by 4 cm.
   (ii) Measure the length of the diagonal of the rectangle.

2 This sketch shows the lengths of two sides of a triangular field.
The third side, by the river, is to be fenced.
  a Make an accurate scale drawing of the field.
   (Use 1 cm to 2 m.)
  b Measure the side of the field that runs along the riverbank.
  c What is the actual length of fence needed?

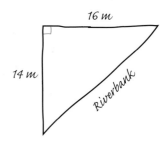

3

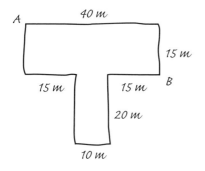

This is a sketch of a building site. The angles are all right angles.
  a Make an accurate scale drawing of the site.
  b Work out how far it is from A to B.

4 Kevin is going to buy new furniture for his bedroom.
The sketch shows the size and shape of his bedroom.
All the angles are right angles.
  a Make an accurate scale drawing of the bedroom.
   (Use a scale of 1 cm to 0.5 m.)
  b On your diagram, draw where Kevin could place a bed that measures 2 m by 1.5 m.

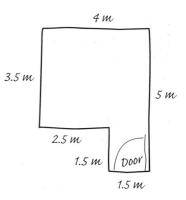

5

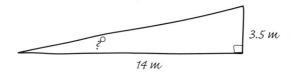

The sketch shows the plan for ramp to be built from a road up to a garage.
The planning authorities will not pass the plans if the angle the ramp makes with the ground is more than 10°.
Make a scale drawing of the ramp and decide if the plans will be passed.

Angles of elevation and depression

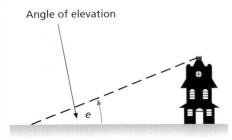

Angle of elevation

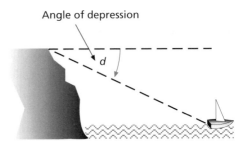

Angle of depression

The **angle of elevation** is measured from the horizontal up to the line of sight.

The **angle of depression** is measured from the horizontal down to the line of sight.

Example

From a point 50 m from the base of a tower block, the angle of elevation to the top of the tower is 25°.

a Make a scale drawing. (Use a scale of 1 cm to 5 m.)

b Work out the height of the tower.

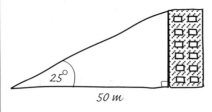

÷ 5 →	
Actual (m)	Drawing (cm)
5	1
50	10

Step 1 Sketch the situation.

Step 2 Scale down all sizes.

Step 3 Draw an accurate right-angled triangle to represent the situation.
Scale: 1 cm represents 5 m.

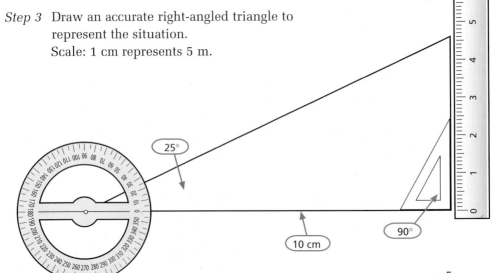

Step 5 Scale up. 4.6 cm $\xrightarrow{\times 5}$ 23 m.
The tower is 23 m high.

Step 4 Measure the height. It is 4.6 cm.

EXERCISE 8

1 From a point 70 m from the foot of a chimney, the angle of
elevation to the top is 50°.
Find the height of the chimney.
Use a scale of 1 cm to 10 m.

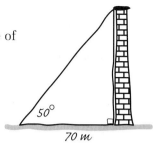

50°

70 m

2

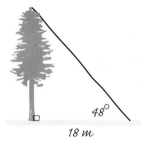

48°

18 m

Find the height of the tree.
Use a scale of 1 cm to 2 m.

3 From the top of a 100 m high
cliff the angle of depression
to a boat is 40°.
Find out how far the boat is
from the foot of the cliff.

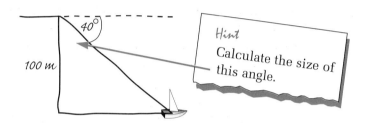

40°

100 m

Hint
Calculate the size of
this angle.

A **theodolite** is used to measure the angle of elevation. Find out about theodolites.

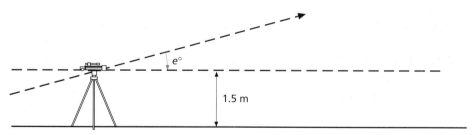

e°

1.5 m

The theodolite measures from a position above the ground.
In questions **4** and **5** the theodolite is 1.5 m above the ground.
Make your scale drawings as you did before, then add 1.5 m to your answer to get
the real height of the object.

4 Find the height of the block of flats.
Use a scale of 1 cm to 10 m.
(Remember to add 1.5 m to your
answer.)

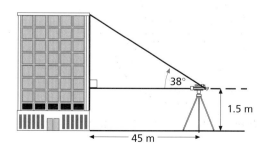

38°

1.5 m

45 m

5 Find the height of the mosque.
Use a scale of 1 cm to 10 m.

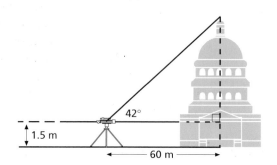

42°

1.5 m

60 m

Using bearings

Example
A hilltop, H, is observed on a bearing of
105° from town A.
The hill is 30 km from A.
Make a scale drawing to show the
position of the town and the hill.
Use a scale of 1 cm to 5 km.

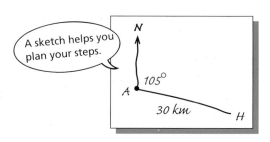

A sketch helps you plan your steps.

N

A

105°

30 km

H

a Mark a point A and draw a north
line.
b From north measure an angle of
105° in a clockwise direction.
c Draw the line longer than you
think you need.
d Scale down the distance:
30 ÷ 5 = 6.
e Measure 6 cm on the line and
mark the point H.

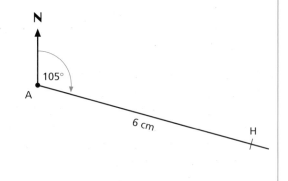

N

A

105°

6 cm

H

EXERCISE 9

1 A ship, S, is on a bearing of 070° from a port, P.
The ship is 10 km from the port.
Make a scale drawing to show the positions of the port
and the ship.
Use a scale of 1 cm to 1 km.

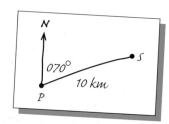

N

070°

10 km

P

S

2

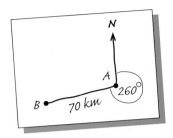

Towns Allandale, A, and Billerwell, B, are 70 km apart.
Billerwell is on a bearing of 260° from Allandale.
Make a scale drawing to show the positions of the two towns.
Use a scale of 1 cm to 10 km.

3 Two lighthouses are positioned 95 km apart.
Lighthouse S is on a bearing of 155° from Lighthouse T.
Make a scale drawing to show the position of the two lighthouses.
Choose a reasonable scale to fit your page.

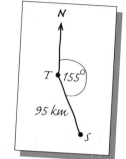

4 From a radar station, R, the positions of five ships are recorded.

Ship	Distance	Bearing from R
Sea Princess, P	70 km	045°
Tatania, T	40 km	110°
Gardenia, G	105 km	200°
Queen Bee, Q	84 km	250°
Cassandra, C	58 km	305°

a (i) Mark a point, R, in the middle of a page.
   (ii) Draw in a north line.
   (iii) Make a scale drawing to show the position of each ship.
      Use a scale of 1 cm to 10 km.
b (i) Measure your drawing to find out which two ships are closest to each other.
   (ii) How far apart are they?

5 Two planes leave an airport, P.
Their cruising heights are the same.
Plane A flies for 80 km on a bearing of 070°.
Plane B flies for 55 km on a bearing of 150°.
Make a scale drawing to find out how far apart the planes are at this point.
Use a scale of 1 cm to 10 km.

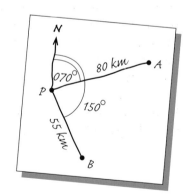

6

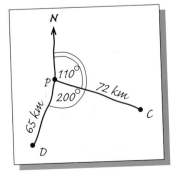

Two yachts leave a port, P.
Yacht C sails on a bearing of 110° for 72 km.
Yacht D sails on a bearing of 200° for 65 km.
a Make a scale drawing of the situation.
b Measure the distance between C and D.
   Work out the real distance between the yachts.

Bearings from two positions

Example

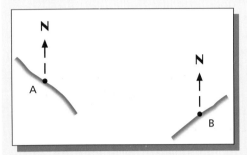

Two coastguard stations, A and B, pick up a distress signal from a ship.
The bearing of the ship from A is 060°.
The bearing of the ship from B is 310°.
Find the position of the ship on the drawing.

Draw an angle of 60° clockwise from A.
Make your line longer than you think you
need.
Draw an angle of 310° clockwise from B.
Make your line long enough to cross over
the first.
Mark the intersection as the position of
the ship.

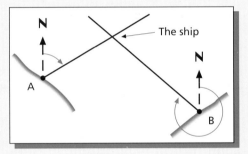

EXERCISE 10

1

  a Trace the position of coastguard stations P and Q onto plain paper.
    (Draw in the north lines too.)
  b A ship is on a bearing of 075° from P. The bearing of the ship from Q is 270°.
    Complete the drawing to find the position of the ship.
  c Is the ship closer to P or Q?

2

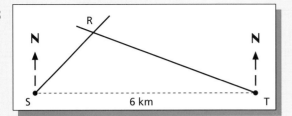

The *Silver Dancer*, S, is 6 km due west of the *Tempest*, T. A third ship, the *Princess Rose*, R, is on a bearing of 045° from the *Silver Dancer* and 290° from the *Tempest*.
Make a scale drawing to show the positions of the three ships.
Use a scale of 1 cm to 1 m.

3 Jake is standing 300 m north of Patrick.
The bearing of the church from Jake
is 105°, and from Patrick it is 070°.
 a Make a scale drawing using a scale
 of 1 cm to 50 m.
 b How far is each man from the
 church?

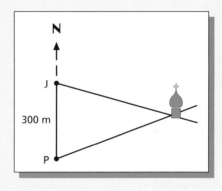

4

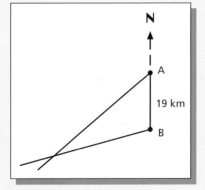

A lifeboat at A picks up an SOS signal
from a yacht in distress.
This yacht is on a bearing of 230° from A.
Another boat, B, is 19 km due south of
the lifeboat.
The yacht is on a bearing of 255° from B.
 a Make a scale drawing to show the
 positions of A, B and the yacht.
 b Use your drawing to work out whether
 the yacht is closer to A or B.

5 A tower is 400 m south-east of a bridge.
The car park is on a bearing of 095° from the bridge, and on a bearing of 010°
from the tower.
 a Make a sketch of the situation.
 b Work out a suitable scale.
 c Make a scale drawing.
 d Use the scale drawing to work out if the tower or the bridge is closer to the car
 park.

CHAPTER 21 REVIEW

1 a Which tree is east of the pear tree?

b Which tree is north of the willow?

c Is the holly east or west of the willow?

d Which tree is north-west of the pear tree?

e Which two trees are south-east of the beech?

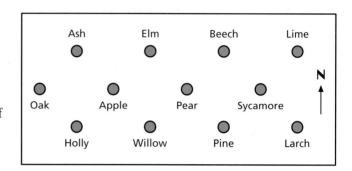

2

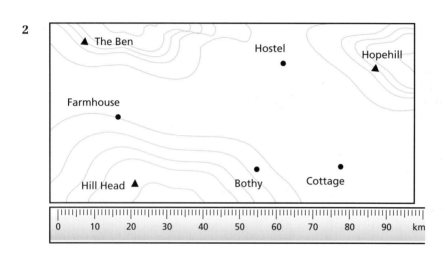

Use the scaled ruler to work out the distance between:

a the farmhouse and the bothy

b Hill Head and The Ben

c the hostel and the cottage

d Hopehill and The Ben.

3

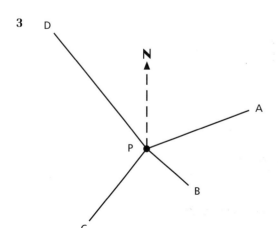

A, B, C and D are four ships. Calculate the bearing and distance of each of ship from the port, P.

Scale: 1 cm to 10 km.

4 Make a scale drawing to find the
height of the building. Use a scale
of 1 cm to 5 m.

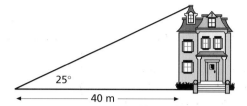

25°

◄——— 40 m ———►

5

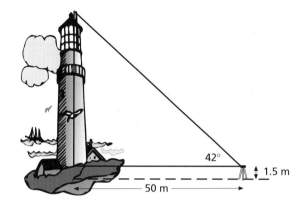

42°

‡ 1.5 m

◄——— 50 m ———►

A surveyor is 50 m from a lighthouse.
The angle of elevation to the top of the lighthouse is 42°.
This has been measured from a height of 1.5 m above the ground.
a Make a scale drawing using the data.
b Find the height of the lighthouse.

6

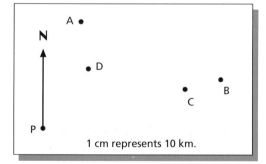

A •

N

• D

•
C

•
B

P •

1 cm represents 10 km.

Four fishing vessels are near Peterhead, P.
a *Gallant Gal* is on a bearing of 038°.
   How far is she from port?
b *Hello Helen* is furthest from port.
   Give her bearing and distance from Peterhead.
c *Indigo Ina* is 30 km away.
   What is her bearing from Peterhead?
d To the nearest degree what is the bearing of C from D?

22 Nets

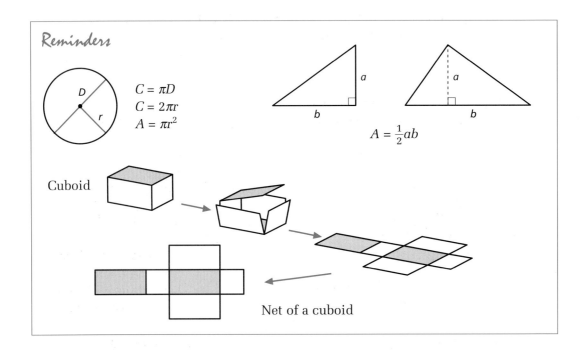

Reminders

$C = \pi D$
$C = 2\pi r$
$A = \pi r^2$

$A = \frac{1}{2}ab$

Cuboid

Net of a cuboid

STARTING POINTS

1 Name each solid.

a   **b**   **c**   **d**   **e**   **f**

2 Which of these is a net of a cube?

A   B   C   D

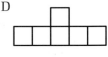

3 Calculate the area of each shape.

a 9 cm, 4 cm   **b** 5 cm, 5 cm   **c** 4 cm, 6 cm   **d** 4 cm, 3 cm, 7 cm

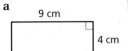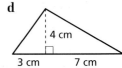

4 a

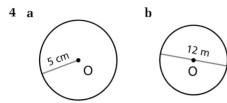

b

Calculate the area of each circle.
(Give your answers to 1 decimal place.)

5 a

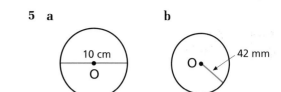

b

Calculate the circumference of
each circle.

Prisms

A prism is a solid with a uniform cross-section.
This means no matter where it is sliced along its length, the cross-section is exactly the same shape.

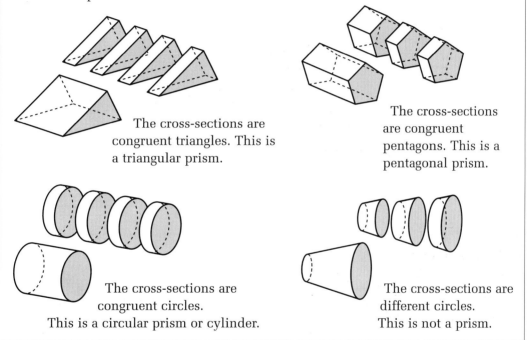

The cross-sections are congruent triangles. This is a triangular prism.

The cross-sections are congruent pentagons. This is a pentagonal prism.

The cross-sections are congruent circles.
This is a circular prism or cylinder.

The cross-sections are different circles.
This is not a prism.

EXERCISE 1

1 a Which of these solids are prisms?

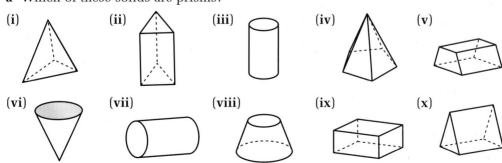

(i) **(ii)** **(iii)** **(iv)** **(v)**

(vi) **(vii)** **(viii)** **(ix)** **(x)**

b Which are triangular prisms?   **c** Which are cylinders?

Challenge

Collect a variety of boxes. Investigate which are prisms.
Take apart some of the boxes. Look at the faces.
What shapes are they? How many faces are there?
Are the boxes for holding solids or liquids?
How convenient is the shape for stacking and packing?
Report your findings.

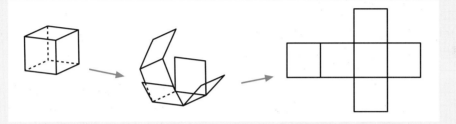

Nets of solids

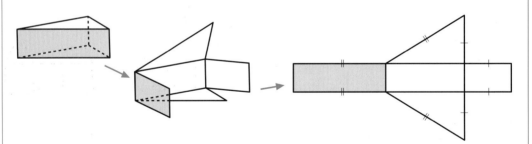

The net of a triangular prism has two congruent triangles and three rectangles for the sides.

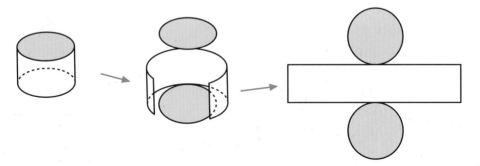

The net of a cylinder has two identical circles and one rectangle for the curved part.

Example 1
Sketch the net of this triangular prism.

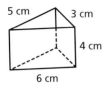

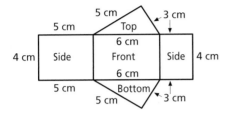

It is important to mark equal edges
which will become the same edge
in the solid.

Example 2
Sketch the net of this cylinder.

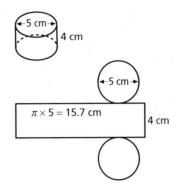

The rectangle fits round the circle,
so its length equals the circumference
of the circle.
Length = $\pi \times$ diameter

EXERCISE 2

1 Which of these is a
net of a triangular
prism?

a 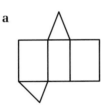 **b**   **c**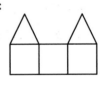

2 One of these is the
net of a cylinder.
Which one?

a 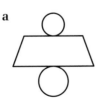 **b** 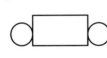 **c**

3

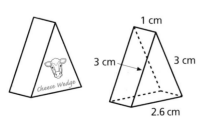

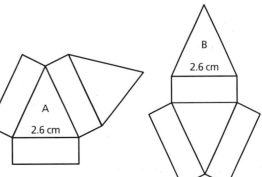

A and B are two nets of the same box.
Make a sketch of each net and mark the length of each edge.

4 Make a sketch of the net of this triangular prism. Mark the length of each edge.

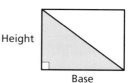

5 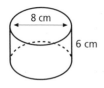 Make a sketch of the net of this cylinder. Mark the length of each edge.

Area of a triangle

Reminder

The area of a right-angled triangle is half the area of the rectangle that surrounds it.

Area of triangle = $\frac{1}{2}$ base × height

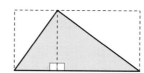
Height
Base

Every triangle can be drawn as two right-angled triangles …

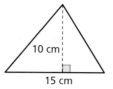

and again the area of the triangle is half the area of the rectangle that surrounds it.

The formula area = $\frac{1}{2}$ base × height holds for all triangles.

Example 1

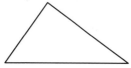
8.1 cm
4 cm
7 cm

$A = \frac{1}{2} b \times h$

$= \frac{1}{2} \times 4 \times 7$

Area of triangle = 14 cm²

Example 2

10 cm
15 cm

$A = \frac{1}{2} b \times h$

$= \frac{1}{2} \times 15 \times 10$

Area of triangle = 75 cm²

EXERCISE 3

1 Calculate the area of each right-angled triangle.

a 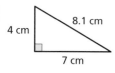 5 cm / 5 cm

b 6 m / 9 m

c 18 cm / 27 cm / 20 cm

2 Calculate the area of each triangle.

a 4 cm / 5 cm

b 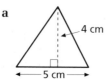 9 cm / 13 cm

c 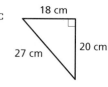 30 cm / 24 cm

3 Calculate the area of each triangle. Be careful, you have been given more information than you need. Look for the base and the height.

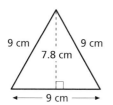

b

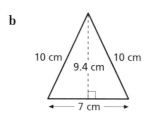

c

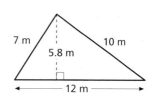

Surface area of a triangular prism

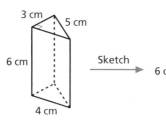

Step 1   Sketch the net.
Step 2   Calculate the area of each part.
Step 3   Add up the parts.

Sketch →

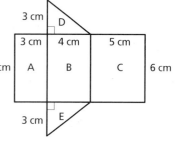

Example

Rectangles: Area of A = $l \times b$ = 6 × 3   = 18 cm²

                Area of B = $l \times b$ = 6 × 4   = 24 cm²

                Area of C = $l \times b$ = 6 × 5   = 30 cm²

Triangles: Area of D = $\frac{1}{2}b \times h = \frac{1}{2} \times 4 \times 3$ =   6 cm²

                Area of E = Area of D   =   6 cm²

Total surface area = 18 + 24 + 30 + 6 + 6   = 84 cm²

EXERCISE 4

1 Calculate the surface area of each prism.

a

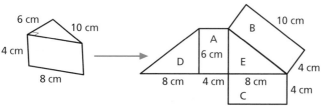

b

2 The diagram shows a floating plastic ramp used for waterskiers. It is in the shape of a right-angled triangular prism.
Calculate the area of plastic needed to make it.

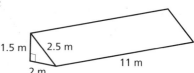

3 Calculate the surface area of each triangular prism.

a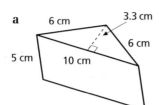

b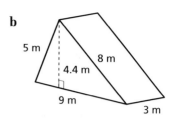

4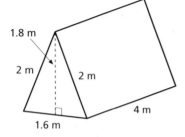

This tent is in the shape of a triangular prism.
Calculate the area of canvas needed to cover the tent.
(Include the floor and the ends.)

5 This is the new design for a chocolate box.
It is a triangular prism, 5 cm deep.
The top is a triangle as shown.
Calculate the area of cardboard needed.

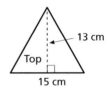

Surface area of a cylinder

The net of a cylinder is made up of two circles and one rectangle.

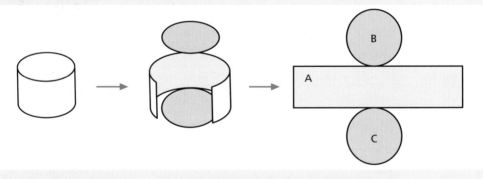

The length of the rectangle A equals the circumference of the circle B
= $\pi \times$ diameter.

Example Calculate the surface area of this cylinder.

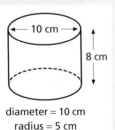

diameter = 10 cm
radius = 5 cm

Length of rectangle A = $\pi \times$ diameter = $\pi \times 10$ = 31.4 cm.

Area of rectangle A	= $l \times b$ = 31.4 × 8	= 251.2 cm^2
Area of circle B	= πr^2 = $\pi \times 5^2$	= 78.5 cm^2
Area of circle C	= Area of circle B	= 78.5 cm^2
Total surface area	= 78.5 + 78.5 + 251.2	= 408.2 cm^2

EXERCISE 5

1 Copy and complete to calculate the surface area of this cylinder:

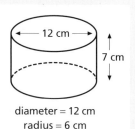

12 cm

7 cm

diameter = 12 cm
radius = 6 cm

Length of rectangle A = $\pi \times$ diameter = $\pi \times 12$ = ... cm.

Area of rectangle A = $l \times b$ = ... $\times 7$ = ... cm^2
Area of circle B = $\pi r^2 = \pi \times 6^2$ = ... cm^2
Area of circle C = Area of circle B = ... cm^2

Total surface area = ... + ... + ... = ... cm^2

2 Calculate the surface area of each cylinder.

a

8 cm 2 cm

b

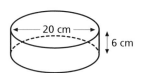

20 cm 6 cm

c

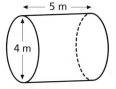

5 m

4 m

3 Calculate the surface area of each coin.

a

£1
diameter 24 mm
thickness 3 mm

b

10p
diameter 26 mm
thickness 2 mm

c

5p
diameter 18 mm
thickness 2 mm

4 These tin cans are all cylindrical.
Calculate the area of tin needed to make each one.

a

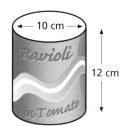

10 cm

12 cm

b

8 cm

11 cm

c

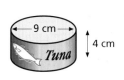

9 cm

4 cm

5 A bale of silage is cylinder-shaped with a diameter of 1.2 m and length 1.2 m.
It has to be covered in polythene wrap to preserve it.
Calculate the area of wrap needed to cover the whole bale.

CHAPTER 22 REVIEW

1

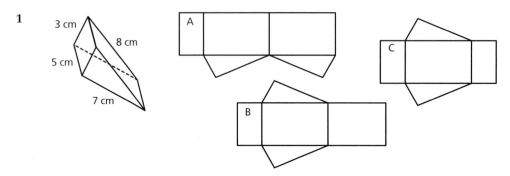

a Which is the net of the prism, A, B or C?

b Sketch it and mark the length on each edge.

2 Calculate the surface area of each triangular prism.

a

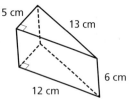

b

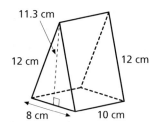

3 Draw the net of this cylinder.

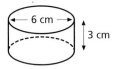

4 A manufacturer makes children's building bricks.
For safety reasons they must be coated with a special paint.
Calculate the area to be painted on each brick.

a

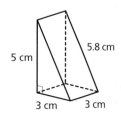

b

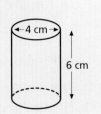

23 Statistical Assignment

STARTING POINTS

1 A garden centre is testing a new variety of pea.
The lengths of the pods are measured after picking.
The stem plot shows the results.

Length of pod	
6	4 8
7	6 8 8
8	4 5 7 7 9
9	0 1 5
10	3

$n = 14$ 6 | 4 represents 64 mm

  a What is
    (i) the longest
    (ii) the shortest length?
  b Which level has the most data?
  c Which length ocurred the most often?

2 Helen drives to her work in the town.
She makes a note of the time it takes over a two-week period.
All the times are in minutes.

43   36   27   34   24   41   30   29   41   38

Make a stem-and-leaf diagram to represent the list.

3 John lists the prices of second-hand disc drives he sees in a magazine:

£49 £52 £34 £67 £58 £47 £53 £46 £76 £63 £36 £42 £50 £44 £52 £65.
  a Put the list in order.
  b Calculate **(i)** the range   **(ii)** the median   **(iii)** the mean price.

Five-figure summary of data

When there are lots of data it is a good idea to summarise it.

The **mean** is a one-number summary, but it would be better if the summary included an idea of how the data are spread out.

To help us in this we use *five* numbers.

First we put the list in order.

This makes it easy to find:

- the highest number
- the lowest number
- the **median** (Q_2), which splits the list into two equal halves
- the median of the lower half, called the **lower quartile** (Q_1)
- the median of the upper half, called the **upper quartile** (Q_3).

Example 1

These are the ages, in years, of 19 children, youngest first:

3, 3, 4, 4, 4, 6, 6, 6, 7, 7, 7, 8, 8, 8, 9, 9, 10, 11, 12.

Imagine this data written evenly spaced on a piece of paper.
The paper is folded into four parts.

3, 3, 4, 4, 4, 6, 6, 6, 7, 7, 7, 8, 8, 8, 9, 9, 10, 11, 12

lower quartile	median	upper quartile
$Q_1 = 4$	$Q_2 = 7$	$Q_3 = 9$

Look at the folds.
The five-figure summary is:

Lowest value	$L = 3$	
Lower quartile	$Q_1 = 4$	
Median	$Q_2 = 7$	
Upper quartile	$Q_3 = 9$	
Highest value	$H = 12$	

Example 2

In another sample there are 18 children with ages:

5, 5, 6, 6, 6, 7, 7, 7, 8, 8, 9, 9, 9, 10, 10, 11, 12, 13.

5, 5, 6, 6, 6, 7, 7, 7, 8, 8, 9, 9, 9, 10, 10, 11, 12, 13

$Q_1 = 6$ Q_2 lies between $Q_3 = 10$
8 and 8.
$Q_2 = 8$

Example 3

In this sample there there are 17 children with ages:

6, 6, 7, 7, 7, 8, 8, 8, 9, 9, 10, 10, 10, 11, 12, 13, 13.

6, 6, 7, 7, 7, 8, 8, 8, 9, 9, 10, 10, 10, 11, 12, 13, 13

Q_1	$Q_2 = 9$	Q_3
lies between		lies between
7 and 7.		10 and 11.
$Q_1 = 7$		$Q_3 = 10.5$

Example 4

In a sample of 16 children the ages are:

6, 6, 7, 7, 7, 8, 8, 8, 9, 10, 10, 10, 11, 12, 13, 13.

6, 6, 7, 7, 7, 8, 8, 8, 9, 10, 10, 10, 11, 12, 13, 13

Q_1	Q_2	Q_3
lies between	lies between	lies between
7 and 7.	8 and 9.	10 and 11.
$Q_1 = 7$	$Q_2 = 8.5$	$Q_3 = 10.5$

In each of the above examples, we are dividing the list into four equal parts.

$19 \div 4 = 4$ remainder 3   All parts have 4 numbers in them and 3 numbers lie on creases.

$18 \div 4 = 4$ remainder 2   All parts have 4 numbers in them and 2 numbers lie on creases.

$17 \div 4 = 4$ remainder 1   All parts have 4 numbers in them and 1 number lies on a crease.

$16 \div 4 = 4$ remainder 0   All parts have 4 numbers in them and 0 numbers lie on creases.

With a list of 37 numbers,

$37 \div 4 = 9$ remainder 1   All parts have 9 numbers in them and 1 number lies on a crease.

EXERCISE 1

1 Copy and complete each sentence.

  a With a list of 51 pieces of data,

   $51 \div 4 = 12$ remainder 3.

   All parts have ... numbers in them and ... numbers lie on a crease.

  b With a list of 26 pieces of data,

   $26 \div 4 = ...$ remainder ... .

   All parts have ... numbers in them and ... numbers lie on a crease.

  c With a list of 9 pieces of data,

   $9 \div 4 = ...$ remainder ... .

   All parts have ... numbers in them and ... number lies on a crease.

2 Make a five-figure summary of each list.

a

4, 5, 5, 5, 6, 6, 6, 7, 9, 9, 9, 9, 10, 10, 12, 13, 13

b

1, 1, 2, 2, 2, 3, 4, 6, 6, 6, 6, 7, 9, 11, 14

3 Make a five-figure summary of the following lists.
  a 2, 3, 3, 4, 4, 5, 5, 5, 6, 6, 7, 7, 8, 8, 9, 9, 9, 10 (18 pieces of data)
  b 2, 3, 3, 4, 4, 5, 5, 5, 6, 6, 7, 7, 8, 8, 9, 9, 9, 10, 10, 11, 12, 12, 12, 13, 14
  (25 pieces of data)

4 The number of babies born in a maternity unit each day is recorded for two weeks:
  6, 2, 9, 1, 9, 13, 6, 7, 1, 4, 8, 8, 11, 5.
  a Write the list of numbers in order, lowest first.
  b Make a five-figure summary of the list.

5 Over one year the number of new cars sold each month at Galaxy Garage are:
  8, 11, 16, 13, 18, 16, 10, 24, 21, 21, 7, 5.
  a Put the list of figures in order.
  b Make a five-figure summary of the sales.

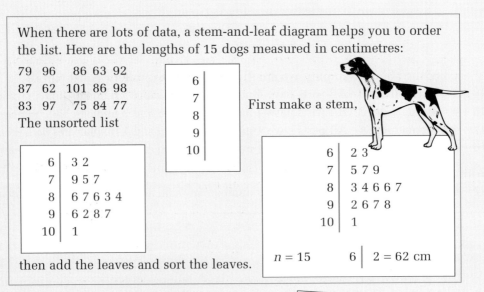

When there are lots of data, a stem-and-leaf diagram helps you to order the list. Here are the lengths of 15 dogs measured in centimetres:

79 96   86 63 92
87 62 101 86 98
83 97   75 84 77
The unsorted list

```
 6 |
 7 |
 8 |
 9 |
10 |
```

First make a stem,

```
 6 | 3 2
 7 | 9 5 7
 8 | 6 7 6 3 4
 9 | 6 2 8 7
10 | 1
```

then add the leaves and sort the leaves.

```
 6 | 2 3
 7 | 5 7 9
 8 | 3 4 6 6 7
 9 | 2 6 7 8
10 | 1
```

$n = 15$ 6 | 2 = 62 cm

6 The cars in a showroom are priced in hundreds
  of pounds, as follows:
  104 143 113 106 108 134 133
  117 107 115 125 122 116 106
  111 120 112 137 105 122 130
  127 141 145 123 101 126 105
  Make a five-figure summary of the figures.

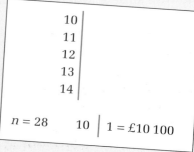

```
10 |
11 |
12 |
13 |
14 |
```

$n = 28$ 10 | 1 = £10 100

Box plots

When we have the five-figure summary we can show the spread effectively using a diagram called a **box plot**.

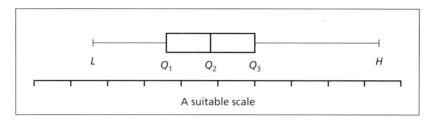

A suitable scale

Example

Lowest score = 16; highest score = 94; Q_1 = 36; Q_2 = 48; Q_3 = 60.

For an exam out of 100:

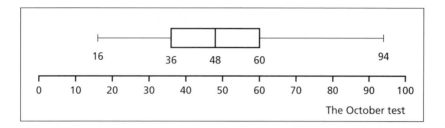

The October test

Note that a quarter of the candidates got between 16 and 36 (the lower whisker), half of the candidates got between 36 and 60 (in the box) and a quarter of the candidates got between 60 and 94 (the upper whisker).

EXERCISE 2

1 A group of students go ten-pin bowling. The box plot gives a summary of the number of strikes they each get in the evening.

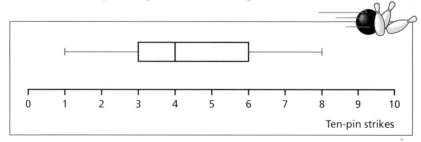

Ten-pin strikes

What is:
a the lowest number of strikes (L)
b the lower quartile (Q_1)
c the median (Q_2)
d the upper quartile (Q_3)
e the highest number of strikes (H)?

2 The points scored by ten rugby teams one weekend have been put in order.
4 6 9 15 22 23 27 35 49 50
a Make a five-figure summary.
b Copy and complete the box plot.

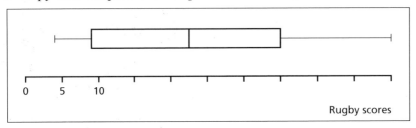

Rugby scores

3 Workers at the Lastlong Exhaust Company note the number of car exhausts they fit each day.
The box plot summarises their data.

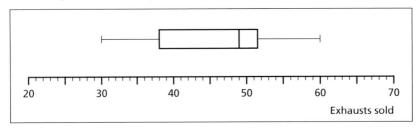

Exhausts sold

Write down:
a (i) the lowest   **(ii)** the greatest number they fit in a day
b the median
c (i) the lower   **(ii)** the upper quartile.

4 The Plaza cinema lists the lengths of its films, in minutes, for one month.
The times are given in order.
88 91 93 93 96 99 103 103 104 106 107 112 126 128 139
a Find the median time.
b Work out the lower quartile.
c Find the upper quartile value.
d Use this scale to draw a box plot.

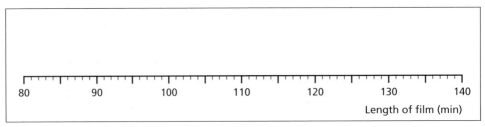

Length of film (min)

5 A group of friends compare the prices they pay for their jeans.
These are the prices, in order, cheapest first.
£18 £22 £26 £30 £32 £35 £39 £45 £50
a Make a five-figure summary.
b Draw a box plot.

The interquartile range

Often it is helpful to measure the spread of data. One way is to calculate the **range**.

Range = Highest value – Lowest value

However, one untypical value can give a false impression.
For example, the marks of a group of students in a test are:
40, 42, 46, 50, 50 and 98.
The range = 98 – 40 = 58
This makes it look as if the whole group is well spread out.
A more useful measure of spread is the **interquartile range**.
This is the difference between the upper and lower quartiles.

Interquartile range = $Q_3 – Q_1$

Nine people share plenty of space...

...but is it crowded or not?

Ignore the extremes and you see...

...it is rather crowded.

Example

40 42 46 50 50 98

Interquartile range = 50 – 42 = 8 marks
This means the middle 50% have a spread of 8 marks.

EXERCISE 3

1 A doctor records the number of patients she sees at her surgery over a seven-day period.
   In order of size the numbers are: 15 18 20 25 26 30 30.
   a What is the **(i)** upper **(ii)** lower quartile?
   b Calculate the interquartile range.

2 This box plot shows the times, in seconds, of a group of students running 100 m.

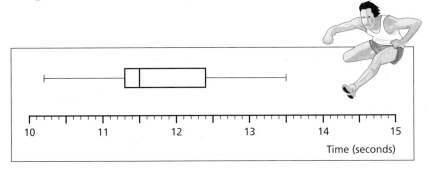

10   11   12   13   14   15
Time (seconds)

   a What is the **(i)** upper **(ii)** lower quartile?
   b Calculate the interquartile range.

3 The heights of a group of girls and a group of boys of a similar age are measured. The means and interquartile ranges are calculated.

	Mean height (cm)	Interquartile range (cm)
Boys	175	5
Girls	168	9

    a Which group is the taller overall?

    b Which group has the greater spread?

4 The results of two exams are shown in the box plots.

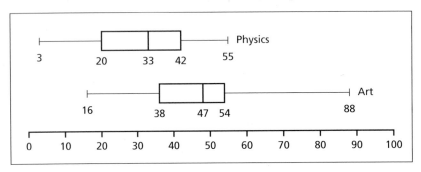

    a Write down the median for each exam.

    b **(i)** Write down the upper and lower quartiles.

        (ii) Calculate the interquartile range for each exam.

    c Which exam has the best results?

    d Comment on the spread of the marks.

When comparing situations, comment using:
- the median as a typical score
- the interquartile range as a measure of how much the scores vary.

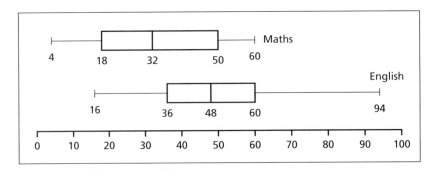

Example

The English marks are typically higher than the maths marks. The median is 16 marks higher.

The maths marks vary more than the English marks. (The maths interquartile range is 32 marks compared with 24 for English.)

5 Compare each of the following pairs of results.

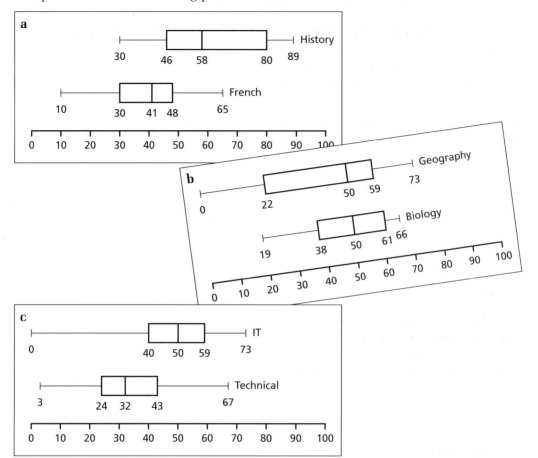

6 The diagram shows the rainfall, in millimetres, at two different sites, Dalebottom and Hillhead, one month.

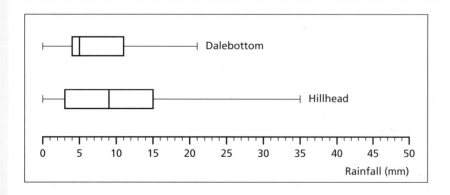

   a Find the median and interquartile range for each site.
   b Compare the rainfall at the two places.

Your statistical assignment

Your statistical assignment is intended to give you a chance to show the statistics you have learned on your course.

It should include:

a collecting data (describe its source)

b making a five-figure summary of the data (show any working)

c drawing a box plot

d calculating the range and interquartile range

e comparing sets of data using box plots

f a short report with a sensible conclusion.

Clarity and attractiveness

For what sort of things is data easy to collect?

Sources:
Newspapers
Ceefax
Internet
Other people
Experiments

Here is an example of a statistical assignment.

A Comparison of the Temperatures of Two Continents

A title.

The task is to compare the temperatures of cities in Europe and the USA on a particular day.

State your aim.

This data is taken from the weather section of a national newspaper on one day in June.

Describe your data and its source.

The European cities chosen are all capital cities.
All the USA cities that are listed in the newspaper are given.

Present your data.

Europe	Temp. °C	Europe	Temp. °C
Amsterdam	14	Lisbon	21
Athens	31	London	16
Belfast	19	Madrid	22
Berlin	17	Paris	19
Brussels	15	Prague	12
Budapest	28	Rome	31
Dublin	15	Vienna	20
Edinburgh	17	Warsaw	26
		16 cities	

USA	Temp. °C
Boston	33
Chicago	28
Dallas	32
Denver	28
Los Angeles	23
Miami	31
New Orleans	31
New York	32
San Francisco	19
Washington	33
10 cities	

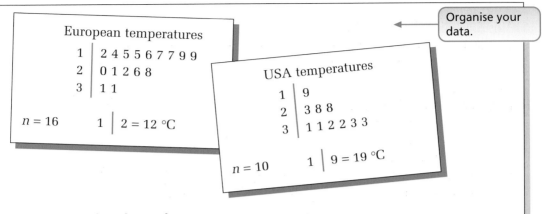

Organise your data.

Temperatures listed in order:

Europe   12   14   15   15   16   17   17   19   19   20   21   22   26   28   31   31

USA   19   23   28   28   31   31   32   32   33   33

The temperature range:

Analyse your data.

Europe   Maximum = 31 °C   Minimum = 12 °C

$\Rightarrow$ Range = 31 − 12 = 19 °C

USA   Maximum = 33 °C   Minimum = 19 °C

$\Rightarrow$ Range = 33 − 19 = 14 °C

Five-figure summaries:

Europe

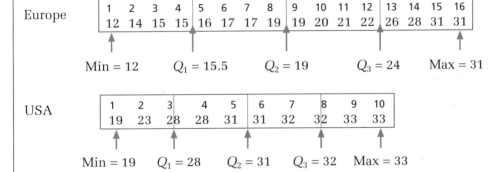

USA

Show your data on box plots.

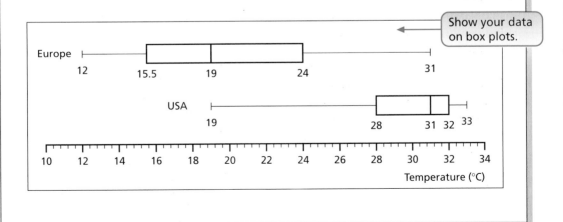

Interquartile range:
Europe $24 - 15.5 = 8.5$ °C
USA $32 - 28 = 4$ °C

The mean temperature:
Europe $323 \div 16 = 20.2$ °C
USA $290 \div 10 = 29$ °C

Further analysis.

Conclusion
On the chosen day it seems that the USA was much warmer than Europe.

Describe your findings.

The median temperatures are 31 °C and 19 °C.
This difference of 12 °C is a large gap.
I checked the mean temperatures and again there is quite a large difference between 29 °C and 20.2 °C.

Most European cities are reasonably warm with two or three quite hot and one or two cold.
Apart from San Francisco and Los Angeles the USA cities are hot.

There is a big difference between the minimum temperatures (12 °C and 19 °C).
However, the maximum temperatures (31 °C and 33 °C) are quite close.

The spread of temperatures for Europe is much greater than the USA.
This is shown by both the ranges, 19 °C for Europe and 14 °C for the USA, and the interquartile ranges of 8.5 °C for Europe and 4 °C for the USA.

It must be noted that I found temperatures for more European cities (16) than the USA (10). This might affect my data, although checking in an atlas shows that the USA cities are well spread out, including ones from the east coast, the west coast and central districts. Also my data is only for one particular day. It would be interesting to repeat this survey over several weeks to see if the USA really does have a much warmer summer than most of Europe.

Mention other questions which may turn up.

24 Revising Unit 4

Calculations in a social context

Reminders

How much are you paid for 8 hours of work at £4.20 per hour?

$8 \times 4.20 = 33.6$

Pay = £33.60

Overtime is paid at time and a half. How much are you paid for 6 hours of overtime when the basic rate is £4.30 per hour?

$6 + \frac{1}{2}$ of $6 = 9$ hours at the basic rate

$9 \times 4.30 = 38.7$

Pay = £38.70

Jeremy borrows £2000. He repays it over 12 months at £181 per month.
a What is his total repayment?
b What is the cost of the loan?

a $181 \times 12 = 2172$
   Total repayment = £2172
b $2172 - 2000 = 172$
   Cost of loan = £172

Anna earns £125 as a basic wage. She is also paid £26 commission and a £50 bonus. She has the following deductions:

tax	£40.20
National Insurance	£12.06
pension plan	£16.08

Calculate: a her gross earnings
            b her net earnings.

a $125 + 26 + 50 = 201$
   Gross earnings = £201
b $201 - 40.20 - 12.06 - 16.08 = 132.66$
   Net earnings = £132.66

EXERCISE 1

1 How much would you earn for:
   a 10 hours of work at £5 per hour
   b 6 hours of work at £4.35
   c 16 hours of work at £5.24 per hour?

2 Overtime is paid at double time.
   How much would you earn for:
   a 8 hours of overtime when the basic rate is £4 per hour
   b 12 hours of overtime when the basic rate is £5.35
   c 1 hour of overtime when the basic rate is £6.24 per hour?

3 Calculate the gross earnings in each case.
   a Basic rate = £4.00 per hour. 35 hours at the basic rate; £50 bonus.
   b Basic rate = £5.20 per hour. 40 hours at the basic rate; 8 hours at double time; £20 commission.
   c Basic rate = £6.40 per hour. 34 hours at the basic rate; 10 hours at time and a half; £35 bonus.
   d Basic rate = £6 per hour. 36 hours at the basic rate; 4 hours at double time; 6 hours at time and a half.

4 Calculate the total deductions in each case.
   a Tax £80; National Insurance £24; pension fund £28.
   b Tax £50; National Insurance £15; pension fund £16; union dues £2.50.
   c Tax £110; National Insurance £33; superannuation £35.40; pension fund £24.30; others £18.30.

5 Margaret Jamieson is a construction engineer. She is paid a basic rate of £4.80 per hour. One week she works 40 hours at the basic rate and does 8 hours at time and a half.
   a Calculate her gross earnings.
   b She has to pay £50 tax and £12.50 for National Insurance.
      (i) Calculate the total deductions.   **(ii)** What is her net pay?

6 Peter Marshall is a salesman. He is paid a basic rate of £3.80 per hour.
   He gets 3% commission on all sales.
   One week he works 35 hours and does £10 000 worth of business.
   a Calculate his gross earnings.
   b He pays £87 tax, £26 for National Insurance and £30 towards his pension fund.
      (i) Calculate the total deductions.   **(ii)** What is his net pay?

7 James McPhee works as a courier. His basic pay is £4.60 per hour. He gets a bonus of £40 if he makes enough deliveries. He works 40 hours at the basic rate, 8 hours at time and a half, and 4 hours at double time. He gets his bonus.
   a Calculate his gross earnings.
   b He has deductions of £63.20 for tax, £18.96 for National Insurance and £22.12 for superannuation. Calculate his net wage.

8 Calculate: **a** 2% of £3000   **b** 3.5% of £8000   **c** 29% of £6000.

9 Calculate the cost of a loan when:
   a £2000 is borrowed and £2540 is repaid   **b** £5000 is borrowed and £6450 is repaid.

10 Calculate the interest after one year when:
   a £4000 is borrowed and the APR is 28%   **b** £6000 is borrowed and the APR is 29%.

11 Jyoti Patel borrows £10 000 to improve his shop. He takes the loan out for 18 months. His monthly repayment is £60 for each £1000 borrowed.
   Calculate:
   a the monthly repayment   **b** the total repayment   **c** the cost of the loan.

12 This loan table shows the monthly repayments on a loan of £1000.
Answer the following questions using the table.

Period of loan in months	Annual interest rate				
	8%	9%	10%	11%	12%
12	£87	£87.50	£88.00	£88.50	£89
18	£59	£59.50	£60.00	£60.50	£61
24 (2 years)	£45	£45.50	£46.00	£46.50	£47
36 (3 years)	£31	£31.50	£32.00	£32.50	£33
48 (4 years)	£24	£24.80	£25.30	£25.80	£26
60 (5 years)	£20	£20.70	£21.25	£21.70	£22

a What is the monthly repayment
on £1000 when it is repaid over:
   (i) 18 months at 10% interest
   (ii) 36 months at 12% interest
   (iii) 5 years at 9% interest?

b Calculate the monthly repayment
on £5000 when it is repaid over:
   (i) 18 months at 10% interest
   (ii) 36 months at 12% interest
   (iii) 5 years at 9% interest.

c Calculate the monthly repayment on:
   (i) £6000 when it is repaid over 24 months at 11% interest
   (ii) £5000 when it is repaid over 48 months at 9% interest
   (iii) £5000 when it is repaid over 3 years at 10% interest.

13 This table gives the repayment terms on loans with and without loan protection.

Amount of loan £	Repayment term									
	5 years		4 years		3 years		2 years		1 year	
	With	Without	With	Without	With	Without	With	Without	With	Without
500	15.35	13.00	17.10	15.00	20.55	18.35	27.65	25.25	49.35	46.10
1000	30.80	26.02	34.25	30.00	41.15	36.75	55.35	50.50	98.77	92.23
3000	92.40	78.10	102.70	89.95	123.45	110.20	166.10	151.50	296.30	276.70
5000	154.10	130.20	171.15	149.95	205.78	183.70	276.80	252.45	493.80	461.20
7000	215.70	182.20	239.60	209.90	288.10	257.15	387.55	353.40	691.35	645.65
10 000	308.16	260.30	342.30	299.85	411.50	367.40	553.65	504.90	987.65	922.40

Using the table, calculate:
a the monthly repayment on a 3 year loan of £7000 with protection
b the monthly repayment on a 4 year loan of £10 000 without protection
c the *total* repayment on a 5 year loan of £3000 with protection.

14 A father and son take out a £10 000 loan to improve their family business.
They wish to repay the loan over 5 years. They want to protect the loan.
   a What is their total repayment?
   b Calculate the cost of the loan.

Logic diagrams

Reminders

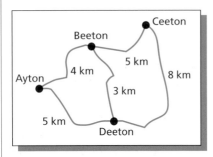

Ceeton
Beeton
5 km
Ayton
4 km
8 km
3 km
5 km
Deeton

The shortest route from Ayton to Ceeton (ABC) is 9 km long.
The longest route from Ayton to Ceeton (ABDC) is 15 km long.
For a journey we normally want the shortest route.

The map can be shown as a **network**, for example:

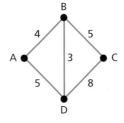

or even

This is a network diagram for preparing and eating a snack. The figures show the times in minutes.

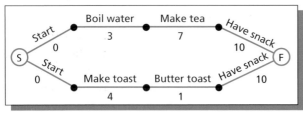

Boil water Make tea
Start   3   7   Have snack
0   10
S   F
Start
0   Make toast Butter toast Have snack
            4   1   10

The shortest path is 15 minutes long. The longest path is 20 minutes long. We need the 20 minutes to complete the task.

EXERCISE 2

1

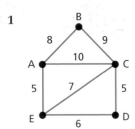

B
8   9
A   10   C
5   7   5
E   6   D

Each vertex on this network is a village. Each arc is a route. Each number is the time in minutes it takes to travel the route by car.

a Which two vertices are connected by a 10 minute route?
b Which of the nodes (vertices) are **(i)** odd   **(ii)** even?
c What is the shortest route from: **(i)** B to D   **(ii)** A to D
   (iii) A to C passing through at least one other village?

2

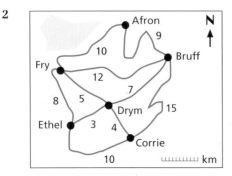

Afron   N
9   ↑
10   Bruff
Fry
12
7
8   5
Drym   15
Ethel 3   4
Corrie
10   ⊔⊔⊔⊔⊔⊔⊔ km

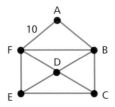

A
10
F   B
D
E   C

a The network represents the map. Copy and complete the network.

b Which are the odd nodes?

c What is the shortest route from Afron to Drym?

d An engineer wants to check each road for pot holes.
Is it possible for him to travel each route only once?

3

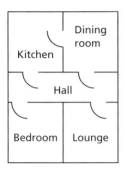

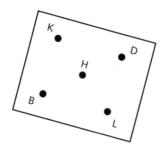

a Copy and complete this network to show how the rooms are connected.

b Each vertex is a room and each arc is a connecting door. Bryan wants to check all the rooms are tidy. Describe an efficient route.

4 Three people work together to clean a car. It takes 2 minutes to get a bucket of water. The wheels take 5 minutes; the body takes 10 minutes; the windows take 7 minutes. Setting up the hose takes 4 minutes. Hosing down the car takes 3 minutes. Here is one possible network to get the job done:

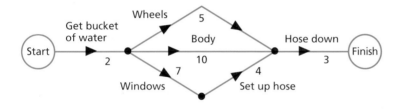

a What is the shortest time from start to finish?

b What is the longest path?

c How long will the job take?

5 It takes 5 hours to dig 100 m of trench.
It takes 6 hours to lay and join 100 m of pipes in the trench.
It takes 4 hours to fill 100 m of trench.
The pipe-layers won't start until the diggers have done 100 m.
The fillers won't start until the pipe-layers have done 100 m.

The network shows the laying of 200 m of pipe.
Each vertex represents the completion of a task.
Each arc is the task being done and its time.

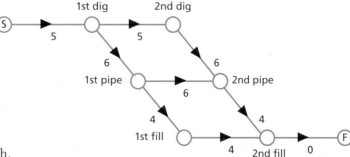

a (i) Find the longest path.

(ii) What is the quickest the job can be done?

b (i) Draw a similar network to show the job to lay 300 m of pipe.

(ii) What is the quickest this job can be done?

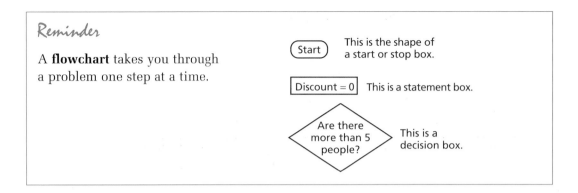
6 This flowchart helps you work out the fines due on overdue books.

Use the flowchart to work out the fine when:

a one book is
   (i) 3 days
   (ii) 6 days
   (iii) 10 days overdue.

b (i) 4 books are
       3 days overdue
   (ii) 3 books are
       12 days overdue.

Working out the fine for overdue library books

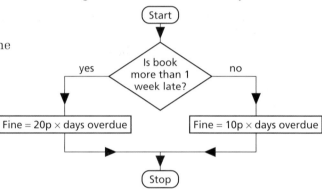

7   Theatre charges (10% discount for parties over 5)

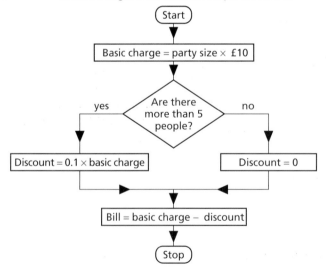

A theatre charges £10 per person. Parties of 6 or more get a 10% discount. This flowchart helps the theatre work out the bills.

Use the chart to work out the bill for a party of:
a 3 people
b 5 people
c 6 people.

8   Working out travelling expenses

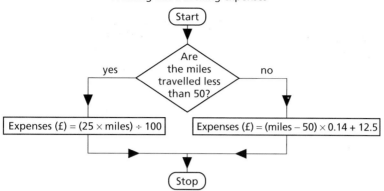

This flowchart helps the employees of Kenneth and Sons work out their expenses when they have to travel on business.

a Use the chart to work out the expenses for a journey of length:
  (i)   42 miles
  (ii) 50 miles
  (iii) 80 miles.

b Examine the statement box in the 'no' branch. Where does the 12.5 come from?

9 The more electricity you use, the bigger the discount.

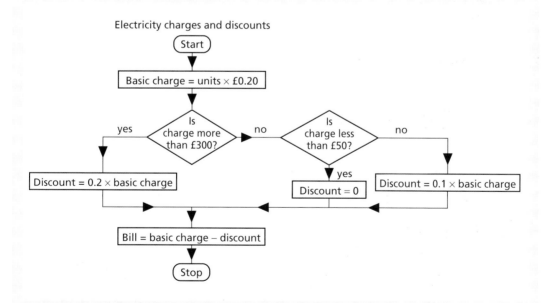

This flowchart helps small businesses calculate their electricity bill.
Calculate the bill for:
  a 2000 units
  b 1400 units
  c 200 units.

This is a **spreadsheet**.
Cell A1 contains a label.
Cell A2 contains a number.
Cell C3 contains the formula:
= A3*B3.
So C3 = 3 × 10 = 30

C3	× ✓	= A3*B3	
	A	**B**	**C**
1	Party size	Basic charge	Total charge
2	2	10	20
3	3	10	30
4	5	9	45

10 A mail order company set up this spreadsheet to calculate the cost of orders.

	A	**B**	**C**	**D**
1	Item	Unit price	Number of units	Charge
2	Calculator	£5.25	35	
3	Rulers	£0.45	100	
4	Pencil	£0.12	144	
5			Total	246.03
6				

a (i) How many calculators were ordered?
　(ii) What is the cost of one calculator?
　(iii) What value should appear in cell D2?
b In cell D2 there is a formula: = B2*C2.
　What formula belongs in cell **(i)** D3　**(ii)** D4　**(iii)** D5?
c (i) Calculate the values which will appear in cells D3 and D4.
　(ii) Check that the value in D5 is correct.

11 This spreadsheet shows the wages bill for one week for a small 3-man firm.

	A	**B**	**C**	**D**
1	Employee	Basic rate	Number of hours	Wage (£)
2	J. Brown	£4.20	35	
3	P. Connolly	£6.20	28	
4	T. Stimp	£4.00	45	
5			Total	£500.60

a (i) For how many hours did J. Brown work?
　(ii) What is his basic rate?
　(iii) What value should appear in cell D2?
b In cell D2 there is a formula: = B2*C2.
　What formula belongs in cell **(i)** D3　**(ii)** D4　**(iii)** D5?
c (i) Calculate the values which will appear in cells D3 and D4.
　(ii) Check that the value in D5 is correct.

12

	A	B	C	D
1	Employee	Basic wage	Overtime	Total wage
2	P. Green	£157.50	£36.80	£194.30
3	D. Side	£230.45	£49.00	
4	G. Force	£184.20	£45.00	
5			Total	

Pamela Green earned a basic wage of £157.50. She earned £36.80 overtime. Her wage was £194.30.

a What formula belongs in cell D2?

b State the formulae which should appear in column D.

c Work out the values which appear in column D.

13 VAT is charged at 17.5%.

The spreadsheet works out the bill for the number of items bought.

Column B gives the cost for one item.

Column C gives the number of items purchased.

	A	B	C	D	E	F
1	Item	Cost for 1	Quantity	Total	VAT	Cost inc VAT
2	Protractor	£0.25	50			
3	Set square	£0.40	80			
4	Eraser	£0.01	120			
					Total	

Work out:

a the formula for each empty cell

b the value which will appear in each cell for the given entries.

14 This spreadsheet gives the names and scores of five students in an exam.

The exam was marked out of 75.

The purpose of the spreadsheet is to convert each score to a percentage score, to find the sum of the scores and to work out the average mark.

Work out the appropriate formula for each cell used.

	A	B	C
1	Name	Score	Percentage
2	A. Bailley	25	
3	B. Craig	32	
4	C. Drummond	65	
5	D. Edwards	48	
6	E. Fleming	30	
7		Total	
8		Average	

Scale drawings

Reminder

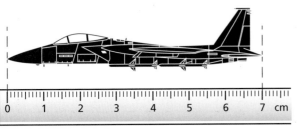

On this model aircraft **1 cm represents 2.5 m**.

We can also say 1 cm represents 250 cm or the scale is 1 to 250.

The model is 7 cm long.

The real plane is 250 × 7 = 1750 cm or 17.50 m long.

Bearings are measured clockwise. North is on a bearing of 000°.

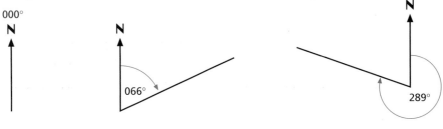

EXERCISE 3

1 On this map of the UK
1 cm represents 160 km.

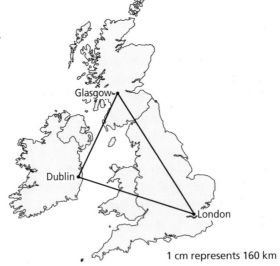

1 cm represents 160 km

a **(i)** Measure the distance from Glasgow to London.
(ii) Multiply by 160 to find the actual distance from Glasgow to London in kilometres.
b Find the actual distance from:
(i) Glasgow to Dublin
(ii) London to Dublin.

2

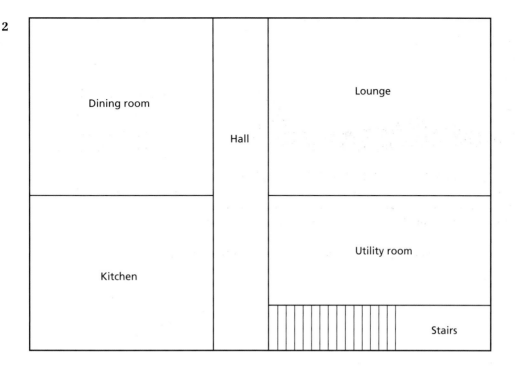

This is a plan of the ground floor of a house.

It is drawn to a scale of 1 to 80.

a **(i)** Measure the width of the hall to the nearest millimetre.

(ii) What is the actual width of the hall?

b What is the actual length of the hall?

c Calculate the actual:

(i) length of the lounge

(ii) breadth of the lounge

(iii) area of the lounge.

d Building regulations state that the stairs should be more than 90 cm wide.
Do these stairs meet with the regulations?

3 The actual length of this guitar is 1 m.

a What is the scale of the drawing?

b Calculate the actual width of the guitar.
The drawing gives a measured width of
1.7 cm.

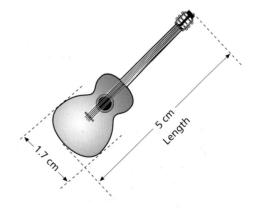

4 Jade wanted to find the height of the steeple.
She made some measurements as shown.
She then made a drawing to a scale of 1 cm to 4.5 m.
  a Measure the line representing the steeple.
  b Calculate the height of the steeple.

Scale: 1 cm to 4.5 m

36°

22.5 m

22.5 ÷ 4.5 = 5

36°

5 cm

5 A surveyor wants to find the width of a river.
He stands opposite a tree on the other bank.
He walks along the bank for 75 m.
He measures the angle to the tree as shown as 19°.
  a Make a scale drawing using a scale of
    1 cm to 10 m.
  b How wide is the actual river?

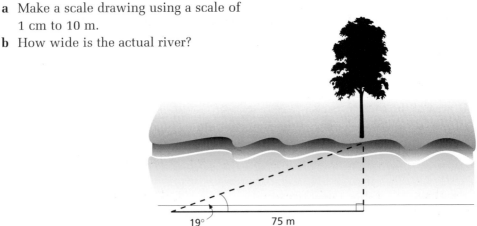

19°   75 m

6 Two yachts left harbour at the same time.
One travelled on a bearing of 050° for 60 km.
The other was on a bearing of 120° for 40 km.
  a Make a scale drawing of the situation.
  b Work out how far apart the yachts are.

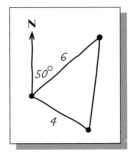

N

50°

6

4

7 A coastguard sees a canoeist in trouble.

From the station his bearing is 050°.

From 1 km due east of the station his bearing is 304°.

  a Using a scale of 1 cm to 100 m, make a drawing of the situation.

  b How far out from the shore is the canoeist?

8

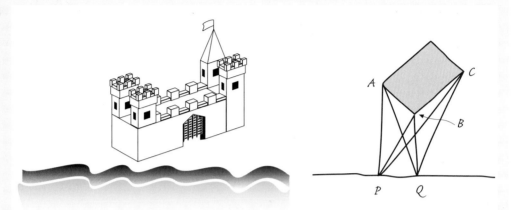

A castle is rectangular and sits on the opposite bank of a river from an observer.
The observer can see three of the corners, A, B and C.
She takes bearings of these three corners from points P and Q which are 100 m apart.
The table shows her results.

	A	B	C
P	008°	035°	050°
Q	347°	000°	038°

  a Make a drawing showing the positions of P and Q using a scale of 1 cm to 10 m.

  b Use the bearings to find the position of **(i)** A   **(ii)** B   **(iii)** C.

  c Construct the rectangle to find the fourth corner.

Nets

Reminder

Some nets of familiar shapes:

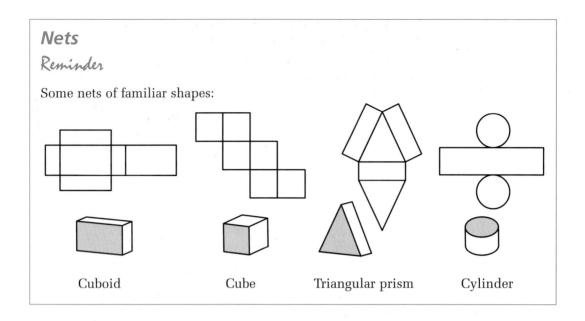

Cuboid   Cube   Triangular prism   Cylinder

EXERCISE 4

1   A manufacturer wants boxes like this for packing cheese.
Which of the following are suitable nets?

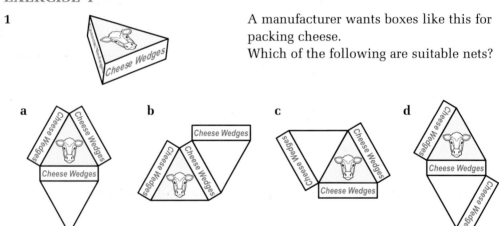

a   **b**   **c**   **d**

2 Dinosaur models come packed in triangular prism boxes as shown.

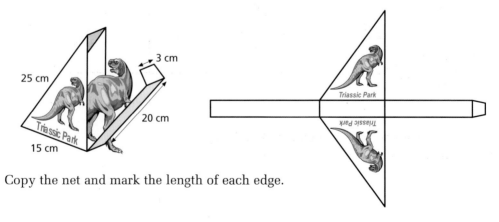

Copy the net and mark the length of each edge.

3
Souvenir golf balls are packed in see-through cylinders.
The cylinder is as deep as it is wide.
Which of the following would
make suitable nets for the
containers?

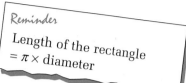
Reminder
Length of the rectangle
= $\pi \times$ diameter

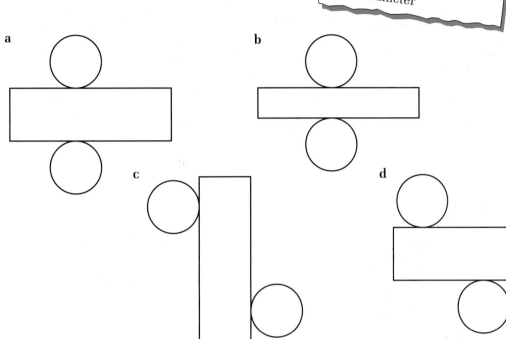

4 A cafeteria sells sandwiches in right-angled triangular prism containers.

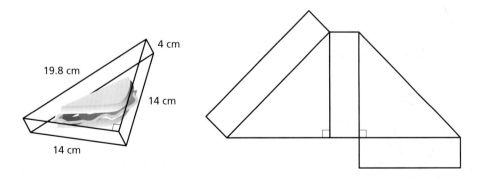

    a Copy the net and mark the length of each edge.
    b Calculate the surface area of the box.

5

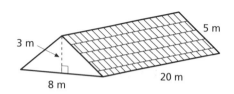

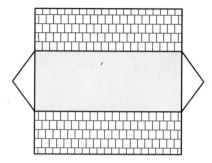

The loft of a house, including its floor, forms a triangular prism.
Heat loss is affected by the total surface area.
Calculate the total surface area of the loft.

6 The tin of cat food has a diameter of 4 cm. Its height is 6 cm.
The cost of making the tins depends on the surface area.
The formula for the length AB is πD.
The formula for the area of a circle is πr^2.
Calculate the surface area of the tin.

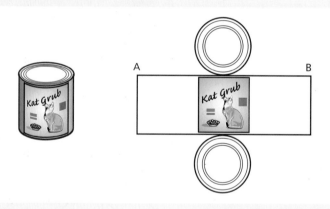

UNIT 1

1 Using Your Calculator in Unit 1

Page 1 Exercise 1

1 **a** 20.74 **b** 155.7 **c** 234.8 **d** 118
2 **a** 247 **b** 539 **c** 162 **d** 3.2
  e 66.5 **f** 54.88 **g** 20.4 **h** 6.22

Page 2 Exercise 2

1 **a** 318.42 **b** 297 **c** 8242 **d** 1404
  e 278.8 **f** 15.16 **g** 647.92
2 **a** 28.2 **b** 261.8 **c** 422 **d** 2835
  e 269 **f** 12.6 **g** 21.6 **h** 1020
  i 30.52 **j** 252.2 **k** 803 **l** 4.488
3 **a** It should end in 9 **b** 459 pence

Page 3 Exercise 3

1 **a** $\frac{1}{2}$ **b** $\frac{2}{3}$ **c** $\frac{3}{5}$ **d** $\frac{2}{3}$
  e 1 **f** $\frac{3}{4}$
2 **a** $\frac{7}{12}$ **b** $\frac{17}{30}$ **c** $\frac{2}{15}$ **d** $\frac{5}{8}$
3 **a** 16 **b** 48 **c** 4 **d** 6

Page 5 Exercise 4

1 **a** 12.39 **b** 0.48 **c** 12.20
  d 176.55 **e** 0.01
2 **a** £11.33 **b** £9.63 **c** £0.90
  d £0.56 **e** £8.50
3 Check while display shows answer,
  e.g. 34 ÷ 3 = 11.33, pressing '× 3' now gives
  34.00 while 11.33 × 3 gives 33.999 999…
4 **a** £8.96 · **b** Check
5 £5.56
6 **a** £24.67 **b** 46.3 cm **c** 5.667 kg
  d £2181.82 **e** £4.09 **f** 0.375 l

Page 6 Exercise 5

1 Akmal 92   Alison 80   Betty 68
  Karen 72   Ashley 58   Faizel 48
  Rizwan 96   Stephen 72   Cari 76
  Danny 28   Jill 40   Lisa 52
  Claire 60   Sarah 100   Derek 54
  May 72   Lee 66   Ricky 44
  Ross 20   Graeme 36
2 Travel £70.83,
  Food £22.83,
  Entertainment £54.75,
  Insurance £5.95
3 **a** £2943.38 **b** £1445.25 **c** £1056.33

2 Basic Calculations

Page 7 Starting Points

1 **a** 31.93 **b** 26.25
2 **a** 86.34 **b** 123.53 **c** 157.51
3

Th	H	T	U	.	t	h	th
		2	3	.	4	7	
			2	.	5	0	4
		1	0	.			
8	3	2	4	.			
		5	5	.	2	5	3
1	0	0	1	.	0	1	
			0	.	2	2	
		8	3	.	2	4	

4 £37.70
5 **a** 430 **b** 4300 **c** 43 000 **d** 43
  e 430 **f** 4300 **g** 2.6 **h** 0.26
  i 0.324 **j** 11.8 **k** 39.84 **l** 4.536
6 £6.50
7 F. Bothwick 10.08, H. Cairns 10.18,
  P. Everett 10.54, A. Duncan 10.79,
  C. Adams 10.8

Page 9 Exercise 1

1 **a** 20 **b** 50 **c** 130 **d** 850
  e 970 **f** 340
2 **a** 100 **b** 300 **c** 2200 **d** 3100
  e 4400 **f** 2000 **g** 100 **h** 300
  i 600
3 **a** 5000 **b** 3000 **c** 53 000
  d 72 000 **e** 21 000 **f** 21 000
  g 3000 **h** 1000 **i** 3000
4 **a** 6 **b** 13 **c** 137 **d** 530
  e 96 **f** 1 **g** 13 **h** 20
  i 200
5 Dens Park 8500, Ibrox Park 15 900,
  Tannadice 12 000, Celtic Park 16 700,
  Hampden Park 23 200, Bayview 1900,
  Starks Park 5400, Pittodrie 13 800
6 Hillview H. S. 150, Blake H. S. 320,
  Norton Academy 270, Linfield H. S. 120,
  Freel College 510, Longside H. S. 70,
  Trest Academy 360, Forthill H. S. 210

Page 10 Exercise 2

1 **a** 3 **b** 7 **c** 1 **d** 0 **e** 2
  f 7 **g** 2 **h** 0 **i** 5 **j** 0

2 a 1 **b** 1 **c** 2 **d** 2 **e** 2
f 5 **g** 1 **h** 3 **i** 0 **j** 1
3 a 6.3 **b** 7.1 **c** 36.1 **d** 5.7
e 31.0 **f** 40.2 **g** 6.2 **h** 7.7
i 6.4
4 a 5.61 **b** 7.03 **c** 258.71 **d** 1.57
e 3.59 **f** 23.44 **g** 0.83 **h** 8.02
i 3.05

Page 11 Exercise 3

1 a £0.42 **b** £1.56 **c** 14 eggs
d 4 trips **e** £20.84
2 a 1.12 m **b** 0.75 m **c** 0.56 m
d 0.45 m **e** 0.37 m **f** 0.32 m
3 a 2.650 kg **b** 1.766 kg **c** 1.325 kg
d 1.060 kg **e** 0.883 kg **f** 0.757 kg

Page 12 Exercise 4

1 Table 1 £10.77, Table 2 £11.66,
Table 3 £9.83, Table 4 £11.70
2 Mon £2.41, Tue £4.29, Wed £2.38, Thu £3.13
3 a £96.96 **b** £66.57

Page 13 Exercise 5

1 a $\frac{1}{4}$ **b** $\frac{1}{2}$ **c** $\frac{3}{4}$ **d** $\frac{3}{25}$ **e** $\frac{1}{10}$
f $\frac{1}{100}$ **g** $\frac{1}{20}$ **h** $\frac{1}{5}$ **i** $\frac{4}{5}$ **j** 1
2 a 0.54 **b** 0.17 **c** 0.33 **d** 0.06
e 0.125 **f** 1.25 **g** 0.175 **h** 0.08
i 2.5 **j** 0.24
3 a 15 **b** 54 **c** 3.5 **d** £3.60
e £6.25 **f** 90 **g** 60 **h** £27.75
i 10.75 **j** 8.88
4 a £20 **b** £28.80 **c** £15.20 **d** £44
5 a Rome £47.55, Corfu £43.50, Paris £28.35,
Athens £68.25, Brussels £39.90
b Rome £269.45, Corfu £246.50,
Paris £160.65, Athens £386.75,
Brussels £226.10
6 a £20.70 **b** £74.58 **c** £7.23 **d** £12.66
e £6.50 **f** £139.20 **g** £34.72 **h** £4.54
7 a £1527.50 **b** £4112.50 **c** £2872.88

Page 15 Exercise 6

1 a 72% **b** 60% **c** 70% **d** 69%
e 75%
2 a 12.5% **b** 12.5% **c** 10% **d** 6.25%
e 7.9%
3 a £12 **b** 10%
4 a 15% **b** 85%
5 a £72 **b** 60%

Page 16 Exercise 7

1 a £6500 **b** 18%
2 a £25 **b** 21%
3 a £13.52 **b** 9%
4 12.6%

Page 17 Exercise 8

1 a **(i)** £3.60 **(ii)** £27 **(iii)** £60
(iv) £33 **(v)** £210 **(vi)** £6.60
b **(i)** £63.60 **(ii)** £477 **(iii)** £1060
(iv) £583 **(v)** £3710 **(vi)** £116.60
2 Northern Star £18, Berwick £21,
Caledonia £24
3 a 7% **b** £54.60 **c** £834.60

Page 18 Exercise 9

1 a £20 **b** £4.50 **c** £62.40
2 £8.40
3 a £18 **b** Peter

Page 19 Exercise 10

1

Number of cream cakes	1	2	3	4	5
Cost	48p	96p	£1.44	£1.92	£2.40

2

Number of drawers	1	2	3	4	5
Number of files	30	60	90	120	150

3 a 10 min **b** 50 min **c** 1 h 30 min
4 a 12 min **b** 1 h 24 min **c** 2 h 36 min
5 a 2.5p **b** £1.75
6 a £2.25 **b** 13.50
7 a 36 miles **b** 180 miles

Page 20 Exercise 11

1 a 0.05 **b** 5
2 a 0.008 **b** 6
3 a 0.002 **b** 14
4 a 0.017 094 017 09 **b** 14

Page 21 Exercise 12

1 £1750
2 30 m
3 35 mm
4 a 48 miles **b** 6 gallons
5 a 18 h **b** 60p
6 a 1050 **b** 2 min 40 s

Page 22 Review

1 a 6 **b** 13 **c** 305
2 b 900, 900, 1000 **c** 1010, 1000, 1000
3 a 3.7 **b** 13.5 **c** 0.8
4 a 1.56 **b** 5.88 **c** 2.43
5 a $\frac{23}{100}$ **b** $\frac{87}{100}$ **c** $\frac{9}{100}$
6 a 0.25 **b** 0.72 **c** 0.19
7 a 32 **b** 24 **c** 12.5
8 a Microwave £10, TV £33, Video £26.80
b Microwave £90, TV £297, Video £241.20
9 English 60%, Maths 75%
10 a £15.60 **b** 12%
11 5%
12 a £23 **b** £483
13 a £160 **b** £80
14 a 20 s **b** 2 min **c** 3 min 40 s
15 a £12 **b** 8 days

3 Basic Geometry

Page 24 Starting Points

1 a 10 cm^2 **b** 17 cm^2 **c** 8 cm^2

2 a cm^2 **b** m^2 **c** m^2 **d** km^2

3 18 cm^2

4 16 cm^2

5 a 45.92 cm^2 **b** 10.56 cm^2

6 A 10 cm^3, B 14 cm^3

7 a cm^3 **b** m^3 **c** cm^3 **d** mm^3

Page 25 Exercise 1

1 32 cm^2

2 310 cm^2

3 48 cm^2

Page 26 Exercise 2

1 a 90 cm^2 **b** 96 cm^2 **c** 36 m^2
d 208 mm^2 **e** 120 cm^2

2 a 34 cm^2 **b** 60 cm^2 **c** 192 cm^2

3 2.03 m^2

4 37.5 m^2

5 190 m^2

Page 28 Exercise 3

1 a 81 m^2 **b** £688.50

2 a 243 cm^2 **b** 27 cm **c** 486 cm^2

3 7500 cm^2

Page 29 Exercise 4

1 72 m^2

2 300 cm^2

3 3.5 m^2

4 64 m^2

5 145 cm^2

6 5.82 m^2

Page 30 Exercise 5

1 125 cm^3

2 1050 cm^3

3 210 m^3

4 27 cm^3

5 9 cm^3

Page 31 Exercise 6

1 a 216 cm^3 **b** 5184 cm^3

2 Zing

3 a 35 m^3 **b** 17.5 tonnes

4 a 7.5 m^3 **b** 7500 litres

Page 32 Exercise 7

1 Own investigation

2 a 30 cm **b** 21 m **c** 120 cm **d** 45 mm

3 a $6 \text{ cm}, 18 \text{ cm}$ **b** $12 \text{ cm}, 36 \text{ cm}$
c $22 \text{ cm}, 66 \text{ cm}$ **d** $50 \text{ cm}, 150 \text{ cm}$

4 a 12 cm
b (i) 8 cm (ii) 10 cm (iii) 6 cm

5 a 2 cm **b** 0.5 cm **c** 0.6 cm

Page 33 Exercise 8

1 a 12.6 cm **b** 5.3 m **c** 34.6 mm
d 19.8 cm

2 a 31.4 cm **b** 56.5 mm **c** 37.7 m
d 5.0 m

3 37.7 cm

4 314.2 m

5 37.7 cm

6 $47.1 \text{ cm} + 62.8 \text{ cm} = 109.9 \text{ cm}$

7 251.3 cm

Page 34 Area of Circles

1 Approximate answers:
a 28 cm^2 **b** 12 cm^2 **c** 8 cm^2 **d** 52 cm^2

2 Own investigation

Page 35 Exercise 9

1 a 113.1 cm^2 **b** 201.1 cm^2 **c** 63.6 cm^2

2 a (i) 5 cm (ii) 78.5 cm^2
b (i) 14.5 cm (ii) 660.5 cm^2
c (i) 5.5 cm (ii) 95.0 cm^2

3 a 128.7 cm^2 **b** 2.0 m^2

4 a 113.1 cm^2 **b** 1017.9 mm^2 **c** 22.9 cm^2
d 78.5 m^2

5 132.7 cm^2

6 $10 \text{ mm}, 314.2 \text{ mm}^2$; $13 \text{ mm}, 530.9 \text{ mm}^2$;
$9 \text{ mm}, 254.5 \text{ mm}^2$; $12 \text{ mm}, 452.4 \text{ mm}^2$;
$11 \text{ mm}, 380.1 \text{ mm}^2$

7 706.5 cm^2

8 153.4 mm^2

9 a 9.6 m^2 **b** 21 m^2 **c** 11.4 m^2

Page 36 Exercise 10

1 66.4 cm^2

2 314.2 cm^2

3 35.3 m^2

4 a 706.9 cm^2 **b** 153.9 cm^2 **c** 553 cm^2

5 97.9 cm^2

6 a 9.82 m^2 **b** 10 m^2 **c** 19.8 m^2

7 a 706.9 cm^2 **b** 960 cm^2 **c** 1666.9 cm^2

Page 37 Review

1 90 m^2

2 27 cm^3

3 60 m^3

4 a 40.8 mm **b** 44.6 cm

5 38.5 cm^2

6 a 104 cm^2 **b** 30 cm^2 **c** 74 cm^2

4 Formulae

Page 38 Starting Points

1 a 12   **b** 3   **c** 3   **d** 40

2 Top row: 5 °C, 13 °C, 17 °C;
bottom row: 5 °C, 10 °C, 18 °C

3 a 9   **b** 14   **c** 10   **d** 5
   e 20

4 Top row: 10, 34; bottom row: 1, 13, 6.4, 2998

Page 39 Exercise 1

1 a £30   **b** £75   **c** £150   **d** £225

2 a 300   **b** 2900   **c** 3320   **d** 1361
   e 6869

3 a £0.80   **b** £0.30   **c** £1.25

4 a 5   **b** 480

Page 40 Exercise 2

1 a 3.50, 5.00, 6.50, 8.00, 9.50, 11.00, 12.50, 14.00
   b No (£11.50)

2 a £60   **b** £66   **c** £80

3 a £117
   b (i) £383   (ii) £497   (iii) £1713

4 a £17   **b** £14

Page 41 Exercise 3

1 a 6   **b** 10   **c** 10   **d** 50
   e 7   **f** 3   **g** 8   **h** 13
   i 20   **j** 10   **k** 2   **l** 0
   m 10   **n** 8   **o** 16   **p** 17
   q 4   **r** 25   **s** 26   **t** 3

2 a 42   **b** 16   **c** 14   **d** 28
   e 3   **f** 28   **g** 105   **h** 22
   i 38   **j** 3   **k** 49   **l** 16
   m 21   **n** 30   **o** 28   **p** 1
   q 1   **r** 72

3 a 19   **b** 20   **c** 38   **d** 14
   e 2   **f** 1   **g** 29   **h** 5
   i 16

Page 42 Exercise 4

1 a 4   **b** 20   **c** 16   **d** 48
   e 64   **f** 128   **g** 2   **h** $\frac{1}{2}$
   i 4   **j** 2   **k** $\frac{1}{2}$ **l** $\frac{1}{4}$

2 a 42   **b** 12   **c** 2   **d** 52
   e 16

3 a 6.3   **b** 28.3   **c** 44.0   **d** 17.4
   e 31.4   **f** 7.1   **g** 11.5   **h** 1

4 a 31.4   **b** 28.3   **c** 78.5   **d** 25.7
   e 34.4

5 a (i) 4   (ii) 1   (iii) 12
   b (i) 13   (ii) 11   (iii) 14

Page 43 Exercise 5

1 a 11   **b** 18   **c** 26   **d** 1   **e** 26
   f 7   **g** 8   **h** 12   **i** 4   **j** 16

2 a 21   **b** 16   **c** 20   **d** 2   **e** 54

3 a (i) 39   (ii) 21   (iii) 120
   b (i) 80   (ii) 52   (iii) 22   (iv) 880

Page 44 Exercise 6

1 a $C = 25T$ **b** $S = 6G$ **c** $t = p + 1$
   d $C = 15t + 5$ **e** $f = 2s + 1$

2 a 7   **b** 11   **c** 15   **d** 21

3 a 12   **b** 17

4 a (i) 28 cm   (ii) 49 cm^2
   b (i) 42 cm   (ii) 108 cm^2
   c (i) 36 cm   (ii) 81 cm^2
   d (i) 12 cm   (ii) 8 cm^2

5 a 300   **b** 480   **c** 180

6 a 40   **b** 9   **c** 50

7 a (i) 11   (ii) 10.5   (iii) 17
   b (i) 7   (ii) 3.5   (iii) 2.5

8 a 16   **b** 28   **c** 36

9 a 52 cm^3 **b** 343 cm^3 **c** 30 cm^3
   d 503 cm^3 **e** 188 cm^3

Page 47 Review

1 15, 30, 65, 67.5

2 a (i) £32   (ii) £140   (iii) £188
   b £760

3 a 10   **b** 35   **c** 17   **d** 6
   e 11   **f** 75

4 a 32 cm   **b** 32 cm   **c** 44 cm

5 a 45 ft   **b** 125 ft   **c** 245 ft

5 Calculations in Context

Page 48 Starting Points

1 £2

2 £12.60

3 a 34p   **b** 42p   **c** 55p

4 $\frac{10}{100}$ $\frac{1}{100}$ $\frac{25}{100}$ $\frac{50}{100}$ $\frac{20}{100}$
   0.1   0.01   0.25   0.5   0.2

5 a £132   **b** £120   **c** £32

6 £24

Page 49 Exercise 1

1 a £1250   **b** £1350

2 a £157.50   **b** £7875

3 a £3   **b** £140

4 a £200   **b** £100

5 a £72   **b** £180

6 a £50   **b** £20

7 a £68   **b** £9.60

8 a £825   **b** £2750

Page 51 Exercise 2

1 a £210   b £230   c £20
2 a £9.99   b £15.01
3 a (i) £175   (ii) £185
   b £10
4 a £320   b £1220
5 a £36   b £70.40

Page 52 Exercise 3

1 a £18   b £20   c £45.60
   d £30.50   e £68
2 a £140   b £48   c £188
3 a £114   b £30.40   c £144.40
4 a £164   b £98.40   c £262.40
5 a £180   b Sandra £174, Thomas £164
   c Bryan

Page 53 Exercise 4

1 a £24   b £27   c £108
   d £121.50   e £136.80
2 a £126
   b (i) £37.80   (ii) £33.60
   c £197.40
3 a £87.50
   b (i) £21   (ii) £14
   c £122.50
4 a (i) £156   (ii) £171   (iii) £235
   b Harry

Page 55 Exercise 5

1 a £212   b £28 000   c £4.60
   d £324   e £19 040   f £4.40
2 a £200   b £5.20   c £208
3 a £327   b £19084   c £367
4 a £26 500   b £19 080
5 a Helen £5.50, Matthew £5.06, Tony £6.60,
      Clark £7.15, Moira £8.80
   b £20

Page 56 Exercise 6

1 a 1600   b 20 000   c 155 220
   d 1550   e 70.5   f 5425
   g 1175   h 930   i 4480
   j 93 750   k 594 612   l 281 250
   m 477 600   n 6112   o 470
2 a 4800   b 238 800
3 1600, 852.5, 2 388 000, 156 000, 36 375
4 a 600 000   b 120 000
5 850Ff, 7650Bf, 750Dm
6 a £62.50   b £1.25   c £297.87
   d £322.58   e £40   f £0.90
   g £937.50   h £274.19   i £19.90
   j £10.21
7 a £130   b £35   c £250
   d £18   e £73
8 a 792 francs   b £105
9 a 85 500 drachmas   b £228

Page 59 Exercise 7

1 a £120   b £240   c £2000
   d £210   e £337.50   f £231
2 a £150   b £225   c £212.50
   d £312.50   e £217.50
3 a (i) £625   (ii) £622.50
   b (i) 1p   (ii) £2.50
4 a 60   b £150
5 £82.50
6 a £149.40   b £12.45
7 £121.44, £94, £171.60, £255
8 a £46.80   b £52   c £88.40
   d £31.20   e £910
9 a £61.50   b £98.40   c £266.50
   d £311.60   e £984
10 £35.20
11 £82
12 a Detached   b Extra damage
13 £44.40
14 a £20.50   b £89   c £8.50
   d £41.60   e £14   f £178
   g £75   h £100
15 £14
16 £50
17 a Area 3   b £192
18 a £25   b £62.50

Page 62 Exercise 8

1 a £180   b £100   c £280
   d £199   e £156
2 a 50%   b £190   c £190
3 a 60%   b £296
4 a 1 year   b £144   c £336
5 £215.20

Page 63 Exercise 9

1 a £260   b £225   c £256
   d £264   e £2020
2 a £54   b £64   c £6
3 a £420   b £500   c £50
4 a £12 600   b £600
5 a £510   b £265   c £1040
6 a £30   b £258   c £8
7 a £270   b £1560   c £1830
8 a £15 600   b £600

Page 65 Review

1 a £120   b 8
2 £52
3 a £210   b £230
4 £48
5 £28 890
6 480 francs
7 a 60 000 pesetas   b 41 500 pesetas
   c £207.50
8 £63

9 £45.54
10 a £48   **b** £356
11 a 40%   **b** £168   **c** £252
12 a £410   **b** £10
13 £557

6 Revising Unit 1

Page 67 Exercise 1

1 a (i) 350   (ii) 400   **b** (i) 870   (ii) 900
  c (i) 970   (ii) 1000   **d** (i) 860   (ii) 900
  e (i) 6750   (ii) 6700   **f** (i) 9820   (ii) 10 000
  g (i) 67 430 (ii) 67 400
2 a 4.80   **b** 60   **c** 49.60
  d 390   **e** 72   **f** 4.55
  g 157.50   **h** 10   **i** 3.50
3 a 70%   **b** 25%   **c** 33%
  d 25%   **e** 92.8%   **f** 50%
4 a 40%, 45%   **b** Chemistry
5 a £1.08   **b** £8.64
6 £42
7 a 8070   **b** 8100
8 a £262.50
  b (i) £1763   (ii) £1760
9 a £1.70   **b** 15p
  c 4 special packs and 2 individual bars
10 a £165   **b** 16 vouchers
11 a £680   **b** £68
  c (i) £76 320   (ii) £710
12 a 77%, 80%   **b** essay 2
  c (i) B1   (ii) A2
13 a £4.20   **b** £29.40
14 a £39.90
  b (i) £78.12   (ii) £80.50
  (iii) A case of 24 bottles is cheaper than 23 individual bottles.
15 a £30
  b (i) £15   (ii) £2.50   (iii) £8.22

Page 70 Exercise 2

1 a 15 cm^2 **b** 28 cm^2 **c** 20.88 cm^2
  d 9 cm^2
2 a 40 cm^2 **b** 33.07 cm^2 **c** 52 cm^2
  d 50.78 cm^2
3 a 140 m^2 **b** 104 cm^2 **c** 43.01 cm^2
4 a (i) 25.13 cm   (ii) 50.27 cm^2
  b (i) 18.85 cm   (ii) 28.27 cm^2
  c (i) 35.19 cm   (ii) 98.52 cm^2
5 a 12 m^2 **b** £240
6 a 2800 cm^2 **b** 3 tins
7 a 60 000 cm^3
  b (i) 3 bags   (ii) £6
8 a 18.85 cm   **b** 56.55 cm   **c** no

9 a 45 m^2 **b** 7.07 m^2 **c** 32.93 m^2
10 a 23 cm by 19 cm
  b (i) 285 cm^2 (ii) 152 cm^2
11 a 8.75 cm^2
  b (i) 56   (ii) 490 cm^2
12 a 6   **b** 4   **c** 24

Page 73 Exercise 3

1 a 25   **b** 25   **c** 7   **d** 0.3
  e 42   **f** 40
2 a £24   **b** 1800°   **c** £18   **d** £26
3 a 21   **b** 19   **c** 17   **d** 27
4 a 80   **b** $S = 4V$
5 a (i) £7   (ii) £11   (iii) £15
  b $C = 2H + 1$
6 a (i) £40   (ii) £55
  b $C = 15H + 25$
7 a $xy + ab$ **b** 22
8 a $S = 0.75C$ **b** £562.50
9 a (i) £4.40   (ii) £14.40   (iii) £15.15
  b £21.90
10 a 1809.56 cm^2 **b** 5 footballs
11 a $P = 2a + 6b + 4c$ **b** 62

Page 76 Exercise 4

1 a £2   **b** £10   **c** £30
2 a £180   **b** £540   **c** £72
3 a (i) £315   (ii) £315
  b One day less to work
4 £45.60
5 £27 621
6 £21.25
7 27 710 francs
8 a £314   **b** £14
9 a £1440   **b** £12 240
10 a (i) £233.75   (ii) £217.50
  b Highland by £16.25
11 a (i) £143.50   (ii) £49.20   (iii) £49.20
  b £241.90
12 a deposit = £480 and £160 per month
  b deposit = £75 and £25 per month
  c deposit = £36 and £12 per month
13 a 4480 francs   **b** 67.2 francs
  c 4412.8 francs
14 a £36.40   **b** £24.90   **c** £102

UNIT 2

7 Using Your Calculator in Unit 2

Page 78 Exercise 1

1 a −1   **b** −14   **c** −20   **d** −2
    e −10   **f** −5   **g** −2   **h** 15
    i −3

2 a 35   **b** 6   **c** 5   **d** 25
    e 42   **f** 2   **g** 2   **h** 12

3 a 5   **b** 13   **c** 117   **d** 37
    e 10   **f** 5.2   **g** 29   **h** 17

Page 79 Exercise 2

1 a 1   **b** 4   **c** 9   **d** 16
    e 25   **f** 36   **g** 49   **h** 64
    i 81   **j** 100

2 a 67.24   **b** 376.36   **c** 56.25
    d 789.61   **e** 99.8001   **f** 282.24
    g 8968.09

3 a 1.7   **b** 2.7   **c** 3.4   **d** 4.8
    e 5.9   **f** 6.1   **g** 9.5   **h** 1.3
    i 2.5   **j** 5.1   **k** 7.3   **l** 8.4
    m 6.4   **n** 2.1

Page 80 Exercise 3

1 a **(i)** 36, 4.5   **(ii)** 206, 25.75
    (iii) 94.5, 9.45   **(iv)** 8.3, 4.61
   b **(i)** 8   **(ii)** 8   **(iii)** 10   **(iv)** 18

2 a Check
   b **(i)** 133, 7   **(ii)** 91, 4.55

8 Graphs, Charts and Tables

Page 81 Starting Points

1 a 4   **b** 3, 7   **c** 4   **d** £2

2 a 7   **b** Wren and hawk   **c** 23

3 A Bogeys, C Birdies, D Eagles

4 a £3   **b** 70 km

Page 82 Exercise 1

1 a Heights of bars: 2 7 9 3 1
   b Heights of bars: 6 4 5 8 4; 8 5 5 4 1;
          9 4 2 6 1

2 Heights of bars: 8 12 11 6 4

3 A steady downward trend

4 a Heights of points: 30 10 20 50 70 90
                      40 20 30 50 70 80
   b Upward trend at weekends

5 a **(i)** Heights of points: 3 5 7 7 8 1 7 6
     (ii) Getting brighter
     (iii) At 2 pm
   b **(i)** Heights of points: 1 4 4 5 1 7 8 10
                         7 6
     (ii) Getting wetter
     (iii) The middle of the second week

Page 85 Exercise 2

1 a 20, 22 and 25 km   **b** 41 km   **c** 10

2 a 11, 13 and 18 seconds
   b 42, 38, 37, 36, 34, 29, 26, 26, 25, 22, 18,
     13, 11, 07, 04
   c 15

3 a **(i)** £10 400   **(ii)** £14 100
   b 10
   c £12 300 and £12 500

4 a 4.8, 4.9, 5.0, 5.1, 5.3, 5.6, 5.8, 5.8, 5.9, 6.1,
     6.2, 6.4, 6.7, 6.8, 7.3, 7.6, 8.1
   b 8
   c 17

5

1	2 6 8 9
2	0 0 4 5 5 8 8
3	0 2 2
4	3 8

Page 87 Exercise 3

1 a **(i)** 131   **(ii)** 82
   b Yes, absences slightly lower

2 a Region A £52, £56; Region B £54
   b **(i)** £87   **(ii)** Region B

3 a

With feed		Without feed
2 2 1	9	1 3 5 5 7
6 5 4	10	0 4 6 6
8 8 4 3	11	2 4 7 9
6 6 5 0 0	12	0 3 3
7 4 0	13	2 7 7
3 2	14	3

   b Yes, the plants grow higher with the feed

Page 88 Exercise 4

1 a Number of houses
     (i) 2 6 4 5 2 0 1 2 0 1
   b **(ii)** 7 6 3 2 0 0 2 1 1 0
     (iii) 1 3 4 6 7 6 3 2 1 2
   c 2
   d 22
   e 5

2 a **(i)** 0   **(ii)** 6
   b Wed
   c Increasing

3 a **(i)** 90   **(ii)** 0
   b **(i)** Dec   **(ii)** Oct
   c She sells more in winter

4 a (i) Jul and Aug, or summer
(ii) Jan or winter
b 800
c Sales increase in summer, decrease in winter

Page 90 Exercise 5

1 a (i) 90° **(ii)** 20° **(iii)** 50°
(iv) 40° **(v)** 160°

2 a 180°, 60°, 70°, 50°
b (i) $\frac{1}{6}$ **(ii)** $\frac{1}{2}$
c (i) 10 **(ii)** 30

3 a (i) $\frac{1}{10}$ **(ii)** $\frac{1}{12}$
b (i) 6 **(ii)** 5 **(iii)** 9
(iv) 40

4 b (i) $\frac{72}{360}$ or $\frac{1}{5}$ **(ii)** $\frac{108}{360}$ or $\frac{3}{10}$
c (i) 20 **(ii)** 30
d 10

Page 92 Exercise 6

1 a 9p
b Increasing
c Yes, because the graph goes down

2 a (i) 8 **(ii)** 4
b (i) Decreasing **(ii)** Increasing

3 a Decreasing, though an increase in 1996
b 1989, 1991 and 1996
c They add up to 100

4 a 4 times
b 30p
c $\frac{3}{10}$
d The gap between the bottom and £1 is not 10p

5 a 2 times
b 2 and 8, 4 times greater

6

Attendance has risen but not by as much as the advert shows.

Page 94 Exercise 7

1 a With feed: 3 4 4 8 8 6 7
Without feed: 9 7 6 5 4 4 5
b Yes

2 a R 18, S 13, L 8, A 13, V 8
b Heights of bars: 18 13 8 13 8
c R 18, S 13, A 13, L 8, V 8

3 a 12 noon–1 pm: C 6, S 10, A 2, O 18;
3 pm–4 pm: C 30, S 10, A 15, O 5

b (i) 36 **(ii)** 60
c (i) 6 **(ii)** 30
d (i) $\frac{6}{36}$ or $\frac{1}{6}$ **(ii)** $\frac{1}{2}$
e Children go home from school between 3 and 4 pm

4 a 3 miles: 1; 4 miles: 2; 5 miles: 3;
6 miles: 3; 7 miles: 4; 8 miles: 5;
9 miles: 6; 10 miles: 6
b Heights of bars: 1 2 3 3 4 5 6 6

Page 97 Exercise 8

1 a

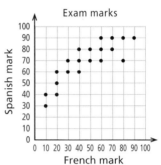

b Positive
c The students with a high mark in French score a high mark in Spanish

2 a

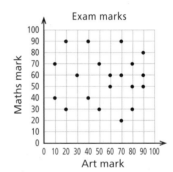

b Examples:
(i) Maths and Science
(ii) PE and English

3 a

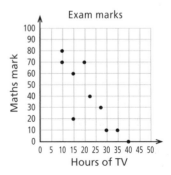

b Negative

Page 98 Exercise 9

1 **a** Positive
 c (i) Approx. 220 km
  (ii) Approx. 10 litres

2 **a** Negative
 c Approx. 180
 d September

3 **a**

 c (i) £18 (ii) 10 hours

4 **a**

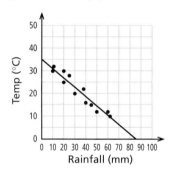

 b Negative correlation
 d (i) 0 mm (ii) 17 °C

Page 100 Review

1 Heights of bars: 9 4 6 5 2
2 Plotted points: (0.5, 5), (1, 8), (1.5, 13),
  (2, 16), (2.5, 21), (3, 25), (3.5, 27), (4, 30)
3 **a** 144°, 72°, 72°, 72°
 b (i) $\frac{1}{5}$ (ii) $\frac{2}{5}$
 c 20
4 **a** 21, 23 and 24 fish
 b 45
 c 281
5 **a** May
 b July
 c Increasing
6 **a** Jan 97
 b Time axis is not uniform
7 **a** 1: 8; 2: 9; 3: 12; 4: 5; R: 6
 b Heights of bars: 8 9 12 5 6
 c (i) Screen 3
  (ii) Screen 4

8 **a**

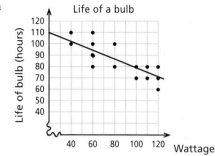

 b Negative **d** 80 hours

9 Time, Distance and Speed

Page 102 Starting Points

1 **a** 10 am **b** 10.30 pm **c** 1.15 am
 d 6.35 pm
2 **a** 11 am **b** 6.30 am **c** 3.30 pm
 d 7.15 pm
3 **a** 13 00 **b** 16 00 **c** 06 20
 d 23 45
4 **a** $2\frac{1}{2}$ hours **b** $3\frac{3}{4}$ hours
5 **a** 10 am **b** 60 miles **c** 11.30 am
 d $2\frac{1}{2}$ hours **e** 1 hour
6 **a** 60 km **b** 15 km **c** 75 km
 d $7\frac{1}{2}$ km

Page 103 Exercise 1

1 **a** 3 hours **b** 3 hours 15 minutes
 c 2 hours 20 minutes **d** 2 hours 45 minutes
 e 3 hours 40 minutes
2 2 hours 50 minutes
3 Channel 1: 2 hours;
 Channel 2: 1 hour 30 minutes;
 Channel 3: 1 hour 45 minutes;
 Channel 4: 2 hours 25 minutes;
 Channel 5: 2 hours 45 minutes
4 Newsagent 8 hours,
 Baker 8 hours 30 minutes,
 Butcher 7 hours,
 Grocer 8 hours 45 minutes,
 Chemist 9 hours 30 minutes
5 **a** 8 hours 45 minutes
 b 15 hours 15 minutes

Page 104 Exercise 2

1 **a** 8 hours 48 minutes
 b 8 hours 46 minutes
 c 8 hours 52 minutes
2 **a** 12 hours 22 minutes
 b 9 hours 25 minutes
 c 7 hours 59 minutes
3 11.55 pm

4 a 12.20 pm **b** 1.21 pm **c** 12.18 pm
5 6.59 pm

Page 105 Exercise 3

1 a 4 km **b** 70 minutes
  c 45 minutes **d** 15 minutes
2 a 30 minutes **b** 1 hour 30 minutes
  c 3 hours **d** 12 km **e** 2 hours
3 a 100 metres **b** 200 metres
  c 500 metres **d** 600 metres
  e 200 metres
4 a 15 minutes **b** 1 hour
  c 30 minutes **d** 15 minutes **e** 40 km
5 a 4 hours 15 minutes **b** 30 minutes
  c 80 km **d** 160 km

Page 106 Exercise 4

1 The middle one
2 a (i) A (ii) B (iii) C
  b 5200 metres **c** 8 minutes
3 a 6 km **b** 12.30 pm
  c 30 minutes
  d Between 11.48 am and 12.30 pm
4 a Cy, Abe, Bert
  b Cy 54 seconds, Abe 62 seconds,
    Bert 72 seconds
  c About 50 metres ahead of Abe and about
    100 metres ahead of Bert

Page 108 Exercise 5

1 a 50 minutes **b** 8.20 am **c** 6 km
2 a Train from Glasgow 33 minutes,
    train from Edinburgh 40 minutes
  b 10.18 am **c** 22 miles **d** 18 miles
3 a 7 pm **b** 7.45 pm **c** 1200 metres
  d 9.00 pm **e** 1000 metres
4 a Mavis 11 am, Norah 11.30 am
  b Perth **c** 1 hour **d** 1 pm
  e Mavis 2.30 pm, Norah 1.30 pm
5 a (i) Arnie's (ii) Tom's
  b 0.7 mile
  c 7 minutes
  d Tom 31 minutes, Arnie 25 minutes

Page 110 Exercise 6

1 a 10 30
  b 200 miles
  c The car overtakes the coach which has
    stopped
  d 30 minutes
  e The coach overtakes the car which has
    stopped
  f The coach
2 a 38 km
  b *Sea Voice* 11 50, *Lady Day* 12 15
  c *Sea Voice*

d *Sea Voice* and *Lady Day* passed each other
e *Lady Day* overtook *Sea Voice*
f (i) *Lady Day* (ii) 30 minutes
  (iii) By about 15 kilometres

Page 111 Exercise 7

1 a 5 km/h **b** 48 km/h **c** 96 km/h
  d 2785 km/h
2 50 miles/h, 160 m/s, 37.1 km/h,
  11.6 miles/h, 571 km/h
3 a 10.1 m/s **b** 17.2 m/s **c** 18.7 m/s
  d 19.1 m/s **e** 2.08 m/s **f** 13.9 m/s
4 1083 miles/h
5 a Alice's **b** By 0.3 km/h

Page 113 Exercise 8

1 a $\frac{1}{6}$ **b** $\frac{1}{3}$ **c** $\frac{1}{2}$ **d** $\frac{2}{3}$
  e $\frac{5}{6}$ **f** $\frac{1}{5}$ **g** $\frac{2}{5}$ **h** $\frac{1}{12}$
  i $\frac{1}{4}$ **j** $\frac{3}{10}$
2 a 200 m/min **b** 32 km/h
3 a 48 km/h **b** 8 m/min
4 24 miles/h, 6 cm/min, 12 m/s, 16 cm/s,
  16.4 km/h
5 a $\frac{2}{3}$ **b** 18 km/h

Page 114 Exercise 9

1 a 36 km **b** 50 miles **c** 270 m
  d 26 km **e** 175 cm **f** 136 m
2 a John **b** 3 km
3 a 16 miles **b** 62.4 miles
  c 133.4 miles

Page 115 Exercise 10

1 a (i) 0.8 hour (ii) 40 miles
  b (i) 120 miles (ii) 90 miles
    (iii) 95 miles
  c (i) 3.1 hours (ii) 155 miles
2 a (i) $\frac{1}{4}$ (ii) $\frac{1}{6}$
  b Monday 2.25 km, Tuesday 1.5 km,
    Wednesday 1.8 km, Thursday 0.75 km,
    Friday 0 km

Page 116 Exercise 11

1 a 3 hours **b** 4 hours **c** 12 hours
  d 6 hours **e** 12 seconds **f** 28 hours
2 a 4 hours **b** 7 hours **c** 3 hours
3 a (i) 3 hours (ii) 6 hours
    (iii) 5 hours (iv) 11 hours
  b (i) 380 miles (ii) No

Page 117 Exercise 12

1 a 2 hours 6 minutes
  b 3 hours 30 minutes
  c 7 hours 36 minutes
  d 2 hours 15 minutes

e   3 hours 9 minutes
f   8 hours 27 minutes
2 a Neil's   **b** 18 minutes
3 9 hours 30 minutes
4 3 hours 15 minutes
5 a Mr Dun   **b** 3 minutes

Page 118 Review

1 29 hours 30 minutes
2 a 2.15 pm
  b 2 hours 15 minutes
  c 2 hours 15 minutes
  d The tortoise, 30 minutes
  e 2.45 pm   **f** 30 minutes
3 a 1800 metres   **b** 7.30 am
  c 30 minutes   **d** At about 8.40 am
  e About 750 metres
4 120 metres
5 5 hours
6 4 hours
7 1.6 million miles per day

10 The Theorem of Pythagoras

Page 119 Starting Points

1 25, 49, 9, 64, 144, 400, 6.25, 11.56
2 a 16 cm^2 **b** 100 cm^2 **c** 36 cm^2
  d 1.69 cm^2
3 a 2 cm, 4 cm^2 **b** 1.5 cm, 2.25 cm^2
  c 2.5 cm, 6.25 cm^2
4 a 64   **b** 81   **c** 900   **d** 121   **e** 6.76
5 a 1   **b** 4   **c** 5   **d** 3   **e** 6
  f 1.5
6 a 8   **b** 12   **c** 7   **d** 40   **e** 1.2
7 a 4   **b** 6   **c** 7

Page 120 Exercise 1

1 a 81   **b** 169   **c** 42.25   **d** 0.25
  e 625
2 a 25   **b** 130   **c** 25   **d** 36
3 a 0.36   **b** 0.09   **c** 6.25   **d** 1.44
  e 576
4 a 2.41   **b** 6.25   **c** 12.82   **d** 2.56
5 49
6 a 64   **b** 576 cm^2
7 a 10   **b** 17   **c** 0.6   **d** 0.7
  e 0.05
8 a 5   **b** 25   **c** 1   **d** 3
9 a 13   **b** 25   **c** 29   **d** 40
10 a 15 cm   **b** 19 cm   **c** 13 cm
  d 100 cm
11 Width of machine is 48 cm so yes there is room
12 80 metres

Page 123 Exercise 2

1 a $x^2 = 9 + 16$, $x^2 = 25$, $x = \sqrt{25}$, $x = 5$
  b $x^2 = 81 + 144$, $x^2 = 225$, $x = \sqrt{225}$, $x = 15$
  c $x^2 = 64 + 225$, $x^2 = 289$, $x = \sqrt{289}$, $x = 17$
  d $x^2 = 12^2 + 16^2$, $x^2 = 144 + 256$, $x^2 = 400$, $x = 20$
2 a 25 cm   **b** 26 cm   **c** 29 cm   **d** 34 cm
  e 41 cm   **f** 3.7 cm   **g** 4 cm   **h** 4.5 cm
  i 5.2 cm   **j** 6.1 cm
3 73 cm
4 a The square on the hypotenuse is equal to the sum of the squares on the other two sides
  b 10.1 metres

Page 124 Exercise 3

1 a 6.71 cm   **b** 5.39 cm   **c** 10.82 cm
  d 10.63 cm   **e** 9.43 cm   **f** 13.89 cm
  g 6.81 cm   **h** 3.29 cm   **i** 4.38 cm
  j 11.79 cm
2 3.61 m
3 6.40 m
4 253.03 m

Page 125 Exercise 4

1 a $x^2 = 121$, $x = \sqrt{121}$, $x = 11$
  b $x^2 = 5^2 - 4.8^2$, $x^2 = 1.96$, $x = \sqrt{1.96}$, $x = 1.4$
  c $x^2 = 15^2 - 12^2$, $x^2 = 81$, $x = \sqrt{81}$, $x = 9$
  d $x^2 = 5.3^2 - 4.5^2$, $x^2 = 7.84$, $x = \sqrt{7.84}$, $x = 2.8$
2 a 30 cm   **b** 24 cm   **c** 12 cm
  d 7 cm
3 a 44.72 cm   **b** 6.24 cm   **c** 5.77 cm
  d 6.71 cm

Page 126 Exercise 5

1 a 24 m   **b** 25 m
2 165 cm
3 16 cm
4 6.24 m
5 a 3.95 m   **b** 3.6 m
6 67.41 km

Page 127 Exercise 6

1 a 25 cm   **b** 15 cm   **c** 8.5 cm
  d 1.6 cm   **e** 6 cm   **f** 8.06 cm
  g 4.42 cm   **h** 4.50 cm   **i** 8 cm
  j 3.95 cm
2 5.66 m
3 1 m
4 21.33 m
5 3.48 m

Page 128 Exercise 7

1 241 m
2 10.61 km
3 **a** 72 cm **b** 65 cm
4 4.84 m

Page 129 Review

1 **a** 17 cm **b** 2.8 cm
2 **a** 15.06 cm **b** 5.50 cm
3 14.42 km
4 22.91 m

11 Integers

Page 130 Starting Points

1 B(4, 5), C(1, 2), D(3, 1)
3 **a** Singapore **b** Moscow **c** 28 °C
   d 15 °C **e** 17 °C
4 11 °C

Page 131 Exercise 1

1 **a** −2 °C **b** −5 °C **c** −1 °C
   d −3 °C **e** 6 °C
2 −5 °C, −3 °C, −2 °C, −1 °C, 6 °C
3 **a** 5 °C, 4 °C, 2 °C, 1 °C, 0 °C, −2 °C, −3 °C,
       −3 °C, −9 °C
   b 4 degrees **c** 2 degrees
   d (i) 2 degrees (ii) 6 degrees
       (iii) 13 degrees (iv) 10 degrees
   e 13 degrees
4 **a** 6 am **b** 3 °C
   c (i) Fell 2 degrees (ii) Rose 1 degree
       (iii) Fell 3 degrees (iv) Remained at 2 °C
       (v) Rose 2 degrees (vi) Rose 7 degrees
   d 8

Page 133 Exercise 2

1 **b** T(3, 1), U(−2, 4), V(−5, −1), W(2, −3)
2 A(5, 2), B(7, 6), C(0, 5), D(−4, 4), E(−8, 5),
   F(−7, 0), G(−6, −2), H(−3, −7), I(0, −3), J(5, −6),
   K(2, −8)
4 P(2, 3), Q(−3, 2), R(−2, −3), S(3, −2)
5 A(−7, 2), B(−6, 4), C(−5, 2), D(−6, −4);
   E(−4, 4), F(−4, 7), G(2, 7), H(2, 4);
   I(4, 4), J(6, −2), K(4, −7), L(2, −2)

Page 134 Exercise 3

1 **b** (−1, 2), (−4, 5), (−7, 2), (−7, −3), (−4, −6),
       (−1, −3), (−1, 2)
   c (2, 5), (2, 10), (−1, 13), (−4, 10),
       (−4, 5), (−1, 2), (2, 5)
2 **a** Dumfries (−2, −4), Campbeltown (−6, −2),
       Ayr (−4, −2), Glasgow (−3, 0),
       Edinburgh (0, 0), Stirling (−2, 1),
       Perth (−1, 2), Aberdeen (2, 5),

Inverness (−3, 6), Ullapool (−5, 9),
Wick (0, 10)
   b Dumfries (−1, −6), Campbeltown (−5, −4),
       Ayr (−3, −4), Glasgow (−2, −2),
       Edinburgh (1, −2), Stirling (−1, −1),
       Perth (0, 0), Aberdeen (3, 2),
       Inverness (−2, 4), Ullapool (−4, 7),
       Wick (1, 8)
3 **b** C(4, −7), D(−5, −7) **c** $(-\frac{1}{2}, -2\frac{1}{2})$
4 **c** M(−1, 0) **d** No

Page 136 Exercise 4

1 **a** 1 °C **b** 0 °C **c** −1 °C
   d −2 °C **e** −4 °C **f** −6 °C
2 **a** −2 °C **b** −3 °C **c** −5 °C
   d −7 °C **e** −9 °C **f** −11°C
3 **a** −2 °C **b** 0 °C **c** 1 °C
   d 3 °C **e** 4 °C **f** 7 °C
4 **a** 2 **b** 2 **c** 11
   d 3 **e** 7
5 **a** 2000 m **b** 2000 m **c** 2900 m
   d (i) 5000 m (ii) 4000 m (iii) 200 m
       (iv) 1500 m (v) 400 m
   e (i) −3 °C (ii) −8 °C (iii) 0 °C
6 **a** 6 **b** 4
   c (i) £6000 profit (ii) Broke even
       (iii) £4000 loss
   d Profit, £28 000

Page 138 Exercise 5

1 **a** 9 **b** 1 **c** 2 **d** 2
   e −4 **f** −5 **g** 0 **h** 7
   i −1
2 **a** 5 **b** 2 **c** 0 **d** −1
   e −1 **f** −3 **g** −3 **h** −5
   i −8 **j** −9
3 **a** 2 **b** −7 **c** −3 **d** −4
   e −2 **f** 2 **g** −3 **h** 0
   i −3 **j** −5
4 **a** 24 **b** AD 24
   c (i) AD 5 (ii) 26 BC (iii) AD 44
5 **a** (i) 3 (ii) −11
   b (3, −11)
   c (i) (1, 3) (ii) (−7, 1) (iii) (0, −9)
6 0 °C

Page 139 Exercise 6

1 **a** 1 + (−2) **b** 6 + (−2) **c** 8 + (−1)
   d 5 + (−7) **e** 4 + (−5) **f** 0 + (−2)
2 **a** −1 **b** −4 **c** −3 **d** −3
   e −1 **f** −10 **g** −6 **h** 5
   i −2 **j** −2 **k** −3 **l** −12
   m −7 **n** −8

Page 140 Exercise 7

1 a 8   b 9   c 12   d 9
   e 4   f 2   g 4   h 7
   i 7   j 1   k −1   l 0

2 a −4   b −1   c −7   d 8
   e 11   f −7   g −4   h −7
   i 7   j −5   k −12   l −10
   m −10   n −3

3 a 9   b 6   c 10   d 5
   e 10   f 1   g 4   h 2
   i 1   j −1   k −4   l −1
   m −4   n 12   o 0

4 a 7 degrees
   b −2 − (−5) = −2 + 5 = 3 degrees

5 a 1530 m   b 399 m
   c 1415 m   d 13 m

Page 141 Exercise 8

1 a −6   b −20   c −6   d 0
   e −3   f −16   g −10   h 0
   i 18   j −12   k −7   l −100

2 a −2   b −2   c 0   d −1
   e −3   f −3   g −1   h −2
   i −2   j −3   k −10   l −7
   m −6

3 a −3   b −5   c −4   d −5
   e −2   f −4   g −17   h −27
   i −4   j 0   k −1

4 a −6 °C   b −1 °C

5 a A(−4, 4), B(2, 4), C(2, −2), D(−4, −2)
   b A(−8, 8), B(4,8), C(4, −4), D(−8, −4)
   d A(−2, 2), B(1, 2), C(1, −1), D(−2, −1)

Page 143 Exercise 9

1 a 4   b 20   c 14   d 5
   e −24   f −54   g 40   h −35
   i 120   j −12   k −63   l −100
   m 88   n −28   o −39

2 a 3   b 3   c 5   d 11
   e 1   f −2   g −3   h 4
   i 21   j −6

3 a 5   b 2   c 5   d 16
   e −12   f −5   g 7   h 13
   i −24   j 6   k 5   l −18
   m −32   n 7

4 a 15   b −15   c 15   d −6
   e 0   f −40   g 18   h −1
   i 40   j −18   k 35   l −60

5 a −8   b 1   c −27   d 16

Page 143 Exercise 10

1 −1   2 5   3 −7   4 −4
5 −7   6 −20   7 −5   8 −6
9 −14   10 −8   11 −20   12 9

13 −9   14 −5   15 −21   16 −2
17 −15   18 2   19 −6   20 −1
21 −18   22 −7   23 −13   24 −4
25 1   26 6   27 24   28 2
29 6   30 5   31 1000   32 −1
33 −42   34 60   35 −32   36 1

Page 144 Review

1 Station (−5, 1), Bridge (−3, 5), Shop (−3, −1),
   Hotel (−2, −3), Cairn (0, 4), Bothy (2, −4),
   Farm (3, 2), Camp (4, −2)

2 a They lie in a straight line
   b $y = -6$ c $x = -8$

3 a −5 °C   b 3 °C

4 a 90 m
   b (i) 55 m   (ii) 120 m

5 AD 25

6 −2 °C

7 a −6   b 2   c −18   d −13
   e −1   f 2   g −21   h −5
   i −21   j −8   k −8   l −7
   m −9   n −6   o −5

12 Statistics

Page 145 Starting Points

1 a 6: 1; 7: 3; 8: 5; 9: 1   b 8   c 10
2 a 175, 178, 178, 179, 180, 182, 184
   b (i) 184   (ii) 175
3 a 12 °C   b 18 °C

Page 146 Exercise 1

1 2 kg
2 a 12 kg   b 4 kg
3 a 32 cm   b 4   c 8 cm
4 a 15   b 3
5 a 71   b 5
6 a 50 km
   b (i) Sat   (ii) 8

Page 147 Exercise 2

1 a 2.4   b Yes, by 1.6
2 a 68, 65   b Kanti 3
3 a 200, 210   b Sarah
4 a 2nd   b 87.6 kg, 88.2 kg
   c 0.6 kg

Page 148 Exercise 3

1 a 7
   b (i) 7, 29   (ii) Moorside College
2 22
3 a (i) 480 yards   (ii) 120 yards
   b 360
4 210

5 a 2, 6, 1, 3, 5, 2, 3, 4
  b (i) 6   **(ii)** 1
  c 5
6 a 6, 8   **b** B

Page 149 Exercise 4

1 0.17 m
2 a (i) 6 s   **(ii)** 60.5 s
  b (i) 2 s   **(ii)** The second
3 a (i) 8, 7.5   **(ii)** 13, 3
  b Kosy Kitchens: lower mean and more
    consistent
4 a Classic Chains: 8.3, 0.6;
    Super Strength: 8.5; 5.9
  b Classic Chains: similar means but more
    reliable
5 A Debbie, B Trevor, C Sarah, D Mike

Page 150 Exercise 5

1 a 3   **b** 5
2 a B   **b** No
3 a S: 6; M: 9; L: 7   **b** M
4 a 3: 9; 4: 7; 5: 2   **b** 3
5 a 8   **b** 28: 2; 30: 4; 32: 4; 34: 2; 36: 1
  c 30 and 32   **d** In the middle, average

Page 151 Exercise 6

1 a 1: 4; 2: 10; 4: 6   **b** 2   **c** 2.4
  d Mode
2 a 0, 1   **b** No, both scored a total of 12
3 a 5.6   **b** 5.8   **c** Mean
4 Rockton-on-Sea; 8 hours is most common
  and range is only 3 so at least 5 hours of sun
  each day

Page 152 Exercise 7

1 a 4   **b** 20   **c** 4   **d** 12
2 a 30, 50, 100, 125, 200   **b** 100
3 a 1, 2, 2, 3, 3   **b** 2
4 a 15   **b** 66   **c** 16   **d** 51.5
  e 257
5 a 19, 21, 25, 28   **b** 23
6 a 10, 20, 24, 30, 50, 80   **b** 27
7 a 53   **b** 61

Page 153 Exercise 8

1 a 9.4   **b** 9.6   **c** Median
2 a 9.6   **b** 9.4   **c** Median
3 a 10   **b** 5   **c** 6
  d Mode   **e** Median
4 a Each occurs once
  b (i) £1.25   **(ii)** £0.57
  c Two dear calls make mean high

Page 154 Exercise 9

1 a 1, 2, 3, 4, total 10; 3, 8, 15, 24, total 50
  b 5   **c** 6

2 a 10, 2, 4, total 16; 60, 16, 36, total 112
  b 7   **c** 6   **d** Mean
3 a 6, 8, 6, 4, 2, 4, total 30;
    6, 16, 18, 16, 10, 24, total 90
  b 3   **c** 2   **d** Mean
4 a 10, 2, 6, 2, total 20;
    10, 10, 60, 40, total £120
  b £6   **c** £1
  d Mode   **e** £19
5 a 5, 2, 2, 1, total 10;
    50, 30, 40, 80, total £200
  b £20 000   **c** £10 000
  d £70 000   **e** Mode

Page 157 Exercise 10

2 a (i) 1, 2, 3, 4, 5, 6   **(ii)** 2, 4, 6
  (iii) $\frac{3}{6}$ or $\frac{1}{2}$
  b (i) 1, 2   **(ii)** $\frac{2}{6}$ or $\frac{1}{3}$
  c (i) $\frac{1}{6}$ **(ii)** $\frac{1}{6}$ **(iii)** $\frac{4}{6}$ or $\frac{2}{3}$
3 a (i) 26   **(ii)** $\frac{1}{2}$
  b (i) 13   **(ii)** $\frac{13}{52}$ or $\frac{1}{4}$
  c (i) 4   **(ii)** $\frac{4}{52}$ or $\frac{1}{13}$
  d $\frac{1}{52}$
4 a (i) 12   **(ii)** 6   **(iii)** $\frac{1}{2}$
  b (i) 3   **(ii)** $\frac{3}{12}$ or $\frac{1}{4}$
  c 0.08
5 a $\frac{4}{16}$ or $\frac{1}{4}$ **b** $\frac{1}{16}$ **c** $\frac{11}{16}$
6 a 60
  b (i) $\frac{8}{60}$ or $\frac{2}{15}$ **(ii)** $\frac{24}{60}$ or $\frac{2}{5}$
7 a 100
  b (i) 0.12   **(ii)** 0.25   **(iii)** 0.18
  (iv) 0.28
8 a 276
  b (i) 0.18   **(ii)** 0.17   **(iii)** 0.08
  (iv) 0.23

Page 159 Review

1 30
2 6
3 a £587.50   **b** £470
4 a 140 m   **b** 1000 m
5 a 50 s   **b** 7 s
6 a 6   **b** 2   **c** 0
  d Mean, most of these students go to the
    cinema
7 a (i) 5   **(ii)** 2   **(iii)** $\frac{2}{5}$
  b $\frac{1}{5}$
8 a (i) 80   **(ii)** 16   **(iii)** $\frac{16}{80}$ or $\frac{1}{5}$
  b $\frac{8}{80}$ or $\frac{1}{10}$

13 Revising Unit 2

Page 161 Exercise 1

1 B(4, 1), C(−2, 4), D(−5, 3), E(−3, −2), F(−4, −5), G(2, −4), H(4, −2), I(2, 0), J(0, −2)

3 a 3 °C   **b** 0 °C   **c** −2 °C   **d** −4° C
   e −7 °C

4 a 5 °C   **b** 3 °C   **c** 1 °C   **d** −3 °C
   e −6 °C

5 a Aberdeen fell 2 degrees, Edinburgh fell 6 degrees, Glasgow fell 6 degrees, London fell 5 degrees, Torquay fell 5 degrees
   b Aberdeen rose 8 degrees, Edinburgh rose 3 degrees, Glasgow rose 4 degrees, London rose 11 degrees, Torquay rose 10 degrees

6 a 1   **b** 6   **c** 4   **d** 1
   e 4   **f** −1   **g** −6   **h** −5
   i −8   **j** −11   **k** 0   **l** 0

7 a −8   **b** −5   **c** −7   **d** −5
   e −3   **f** −1   **g** 0   **h** −3
   i 5   **j** 2   **k** 12   **l** 8

8 a −12   **b** −14   **c** −8   **d** −3
   e −10   **f** −16   **g** −2   **h** −42
   i −100   **j** −12   **k** −9   **l** 0

9 a Rectangle   **b** (0, −2)

10 a/b Black Rock (−5, 5), School (−2, 5), Town Hall (−4, 2), Harbour (1, 2), Library (4, −1), Airport (−4, −2), Leisure Centre (0, −3)
   c (i) (−5, 0)   **(ii)** (−5, −4)   **(iii)** (−3, 3)
   (iv) (−1, −5)

11 2753 years (in the year AD 2000)

12 a −6   **b** A = 2, B = −4, C = −2

13 a A loss
   b (i) £200 profit   **(ii)** £400 loss
   c (i) −£200   **(ii)** £0
   d £300

14 a Mick −8, Monty −5   **b** Monty by 3
   c 4
   d (i) 12   **(ii)** 9
   e No. After 9 throws Mae's score is −2, so Mae's best possible score is 3 which is less than Molly's score.

15 a Train 3   **b** −1, i.e. 1 minute early
   c 1 minute early

16 a 9   **b** 2   **c** 4   **d** −12
   e 2   **f** −2   **g** −4   **h** 1
   i 12   **j** 40   **k** 4   **l** 1

17 a −24   **b** −60   **c** 60

Page 164 Exercise 2

1 a 350 km   **b** 5 hours   **c** 5.5 hours
   d 45 minutes   **e** 2.15 pm   **f** 200 km
   g 4.30 pm

2 a Fleetfoot
   b At the Double overtook Fleetfoot, 20 seconds
   c At the Double
   d At the Double, 34 seconds; Fleetfoot, 36 seconds

3 a Monday 8 hours, Tuesday 7 hours 50 minutes, Wednesday 6 hours 45 minutes, Thursday 8 hours 17 minutes, Friday 7 hours 25 minutes
   b 38 hours 17 minutes

4 a 120 km   **b** 8 hours
   c 90 km/h   **d** 9.43 m/s

5 a 1200 m   **b** 84 minutes
   c Ali overtook Tariq; after 10 minutes
   d Tariq; after 54 minutes
   e 34 minutes
   f Tariq coming down passed Ali on his way up

6 a 57 minutes   **b** 98 km/h
   c More; the 90 km are covered in less than 1 hour

7 a 3 hours 15 minutes   **b** 57.6 mph
   c 220 miles

Page 167 Exercise 3

1 a 15 cm   **b** 26 cm   **c** 31.3 cm
2 a 20 cm   **b** 21 cm   **c** 20 cm
3 a 11.4 cm   **b** 17.3 cm   **c** 9.7 cm
4 a 11.7 cm   **b** 8.1 cm   **c** 4.2 cm
   d 7.1 cm
5 9.7 m
6 No, the tree is 7.5 m tall and it is 8 m from the house
7 84 m
8 No, it only reaches 4.7 m up the wall
9 a 10.3 cm   **b** AC = 8 cm, BD = 14.9 cm
10 a (ii) 6.3 units   **b** 4.5 units
11 17.2 km
12 a (ii) 3.6 m   **b** 3.3 m

·A·N·S·W·E·R·S·

Page 170 Exercise 4

1

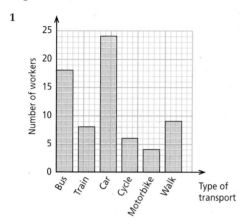

2

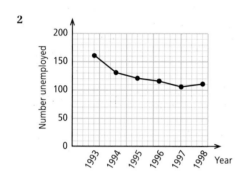

3 a 12 km, 17 km, 23 km, 24 km
  b 291 km   **c** £87.30

4 a (i) $\frac{1}{4}$ (ii) 180
  b (i) $\frac{1}{3}$ (ii) 240   **c** 220

5 a

Letter	Frequency
G	1
H	2
J	1
K	3
L	6
M	5
N	2
P	2

b

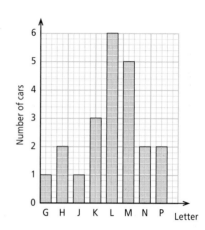

6 Week 1: 580 miles, Week 2: 820 miles,
    Week 3: 960 miles, Week 4: 1380 miles
  b The mileage increased every day from
    Monday to Thursday
  c The mileage increased every week

7 a Lott
  b Dott 9000, Pott 1000, Knott 4500,
    Watt 6000, Lott 15 500

8 a 06 00, 4 °C
  b (i) 8.5 °C   (ii) 22.5 °C   (iii) 20 °C
  c (i) 10 00 and 12 00
    (ii) 20 00 and 22 00
  d About 8 hours 40 minutes
  e 11 hours

9 a/c

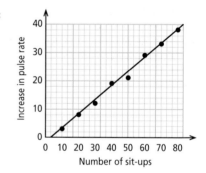

  b The pulse rate increases as the number of
    sit-ups increases
  d 25 or 26

10 a/c

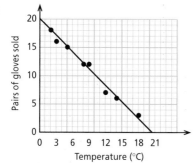

Pairs of gloves sold

Temperature (°C)

b The number of pairs of gloves sold decreases as the temperature increases

d About 10

11 a It falls from February to August and rises from August to December

b Down

c (i) 600 tonnes

(ii) End of June to end of August of year 3

d 4200 tonnes

e Year 1, 22 400 tonnes;
year 2, 15 600 tonnes;
year 3, 9600 tonnes

12 a 2 minutes 23 seconds

b 3 minutes 11 seconds

c 3 minutes 9 seconds

13 a Unleaded, 500 000 litres;
leaded, 2 500 000 litres

b Unleaded, 2 800 000 litres;
leaded, 300 000 litres

c 1997, 3 100 000 litres

d Unleaded increases each year and leaded decreases each year

Page 175 Exercise 5

1 a 80   **b** 76.5   **c** 86

2 a 5

b (i) 19.7   (ii) 20   (iii) 18

c 44

3 a (i) £160   (ii) £145   (iii) £145

(iv) £266

b 9

c £360 is £200 above the mean, £94 is £66 below the mean

4 a 38.7   **b** 38   **c** 38 hours

5 a $\frac{1}{3}$ **b** $\frac{1}{2}$ **c** $\frac{1}{3}$

6 a (i) 25.8   (ii) 27.9

b (i) 32   (ii) No mode

c (i) 25.5   (ii) 26.5

d (i) 18   (ii) 26

e The mean age of the brides is about 2 years less than the mean age of the grooms

f The range of ages of the brides is considerably less than that of the grooms

7 a −1 °C   **b** −1 °C   **c** −2 °C

d 5 degrees

8 a (i) $\frac{1}{5}$ (ii) $\frac{1}{4}$ (iii) $\frac{1}{4}$ (iv) $\frac{1}{3}$

b (i)

c (ii) and (iii)

UNIT 3

14 Basic Algebra

Page 177 Starting Points

1 a 8   b 10   c 12
2 a 15   b 7   c 0   d 13
3 a $5x$ b $3m$ c $3a + 4b$
4 a true   b false   c true   d true
  e false   f true
5 a 2, 4   b 5, 7, 5, 7, 35   c a, b, ab
6 a 1.41   b 2.24   c 4.12   d 28
  e 5.70

Page 178 Exercise 1

1 a 4   b 20   c 14   d 5
  e 1   f 8   g 16   h 11
  i 6   j 2   k 56   l 4
2 a 14   b 11   c 10   d 18
  e 15   f 27   g 36   h 7
  i 9   j 108   k 1   l 52
3 a 11   b 25   c 1   d 60
  e 10   f 10   g 4   h 10
  i 2   j 25   k 6   l 7
4 a 20   b 21   c 10   d 0
  e 5   f 1   g 4   h 29
  i 0   j 2   k 2   l 3
5 c greatest, a and d least
6 a 7   b 11   c 7   d 5
7 a 51.5   b 8   c 17.1   d 75.2

Page 180 Exercise 2

1 a (i) 26 cm   (ii) 30 cm^2
  b 2520 cm^3 c 8 cm^3 d 40.84 cm
  e 153.94 cm^2 f 36 cm^2
2 a 373   b 16   c 6   d 22
  e 18   f 60   g 43   h 8
3 a 31   b 13   c 6
4 a 175 km   b 50 km/h   c 5 hours
  d 105 miles
5 a 13 cm   b 29 cm   c 37 cm

Page 181 Exercise 3

1 a 15 cm^2 b 9 cm^2
2 a 50%   b 75%   c $33\frac{1}{3}$% or 33.3%
3 a 18.85   b 150.80   c 50.27
4 a 17.55 m/s   b 24.82 m/s

Page 183 Exercise 4

1 a $2a$ b $3x$ c $4l$
  d $3b$ e x f $2l$
  g $4y$ h $5t$ i $4k$
  j $4b + 2c$ k $2x$ l $2x + 6y$
  m $2q - 2p$ n $7h - 4n$ o g
  p $2x^2$

2 a m^2 b $3n$ c a^2
  d p^2 e $5k$ f $7b$
  g $5x$ h $6b$ i $4r^2$
  j $6x$ k $6b$ l $12r$
  m $5p^2$ n ab o $5pq$
  p $3fg$ q $4k^2$ r $14rt$
3 a $3y$ b $2y^2$ c $2a^2$
  d $3y$ e $21q^2$ f $12p^2$
  g $5a$ h $15xy$ i $4m$
  j $11a$ k $40x^2y$ l $6m$
4 a $3x^2$ b $3x^2$ c $7x^2$
  d $3x + y$ e $a + 3$ f $2x + 7$
  g $5 + 2c$ h $6 + 4c$ i $3a^2 - 3$
  j $8y^2$ k $2k^2 + l^2$
5 a (i) $3x$ (ii) 21
  b (i) $2x + y$ (ii) 18
  c (i) $x + 2y$ (ii) 15
  d (i) $4y$ (ii) 16
  e (i) $3x + 3y$ (ii) 33
  f (i) $x + 3y$ (ii) 19
  g (i) $4x + y$ (ii) 32
  h (i) $4x + 2y$ (ii) 36
  i (i) $x + 3y$ (ii) 19
  j (i) $7y$ (ii) 28
  k (i) $5x + 2y$ (ii) 43
  l (i) $6y - x$ (ii) 17
  m (i) $5x + y$ (ii) 39
  n (i) $7x + 2y$ (ii) 57
  o (i) $x^2 + 2y^2$ (ii) 81
  p (i) $6x^2 + 5y^2$ (ii) 374

Page 184 Exercise 5

1 a (i) $3 \times 4 + 3 \times 6$ (ii) 30
  b (i) $2 \times 5 + 2 \times 1$ (ii) 12
  c (i) $6 \times 8 - 6 \times 3$ (ii) 30
  d (i) $5 \times 6 - 5 \times 4$ (ii) 10
2 a $3y + 6$ b $2x - 6$ c $3a + 9$
  d $2y - 2$ e $7x + 21$ f $5t - 10$
  g $2y + 10$ h $9m - 9$ i $3y + 6$
  j $8k + 40$ k $3b + 21$ l $2b - 14$
  m $5d - 15$ n $6g + 6$ o $8l + 16$
  p $6x - 6$
3 a $2 + 2x$ b $6 - 3y$ c $21 + 7t$
  d $24 - 3u$ e $45 + 5v$ f $4 - 2y$
  g $5x - 5y$ h $8x + 8y$ i $7a - 7b$
  j $8m + 8n$ k $14 - 2m$ l $4y - 8$
  m $100 + 10k$ n $12a - 12b$ o $70 - 7c$
  p $70 - 5a$
4 a (i) $6(x + 4)$ (ii) $6x + 24$

b (i) $3(y-2)$ (ii) $3y-6$
c (i) $8(m+3)$ (ii) $8m+24$
d (i) $2(n-1)$ (ii) $2n-2$
e (i) $4(12-m)$ (ii) $48-4m$
f (i) $6(10-x)$ (ii) $60-6x$

5 a $6x+2$ **b** $21y-7$ **c** $6b+2$
   d $21b-14$ **e** $18d+12$ **f** $6x-9$
   g $14m-7$ **h** $18k-3$ **i** $3a+6b$
   j $14a-21b$ **k** $24x-16y$ **l** $21l+35m$

6 a $2a^2-3a$ **b** x^2-2x **c** m^2+mn
   d $3b^2+bc$ **e** y^2-xy **f** $5x^2-xy$
   g $2n+5n^2$ **h** $2x^2-6x$ **i** $10y+5y^2$
   j $6xy-10x^2$ **k** $10r^2+15rs$ **l** $5x^2+6xy$

Page 185 Exercise 6

1 a $2x+5$ **b** $2y+8$ **c** $110-10m$
   d $5k+13$ **e** $1+3x$ **f** $26-3y$
   g $6p+9$ **h** $4+5r$ **i** $16-5f$
   j $7c+4$ **k** $19+9x$ **l** $7+3p$
   m $5x+3$ **n** $6y-12$ **o** $2+4m$
   p $8k-6$ **q** $18+4x$ **r** $5+2y$
   s 6 **t** $15x+21$ **u** $3p+14$

2 a $10x+4$ **b** $12y+12$ **c** $14+26m$
   d $4k-2$ **e** $4+9x$ **f** $20+19y$
   g $c-15$ **h** $10+16x$ **i** $11p+4$
   j $9x+3y$ **k** $4y+3z$ **l** $12n+26m$
   m $12k+5p$ **n** $4w+35x$ **o** $21x+33y$
   p $16c-18d$ **q** $20q+18p$ **r** $8p+r$

3 a $5x+1$ **b** $8y$ **c** $7z+3$
   d $12+3p$ **e** $7+t$ **f** $18m+14$
   g $14k+2$ **h** $14+x$ **i** $23s+4t$

4 a $4x+6$ **b** $6x+8$ **c** $12x+1$
   d $21x+13$

Page 187 Exercise 7

1 a 1, 2, 4, 8   **b** 1, 2, 3, 6, 9, 18
   c 1, 2, 3, 4, 6, 9, 12, 18, 36   **d** 1, 5
   e 1, 2, 4, 5, 10, 20   **f** 1, 5, 25
   g 1, 2, 3, 5, 6, 10, 15, 30

2 a 1, 2   **b** 1, 2, 3, 6, 9, 18   **c** 1, 2, 4
   d 1, 2, 4, 8   **e** 1

3 a 3   **b** 4   **c** 18   **d** 1   **e** 1

4 a $1, x, y, xy$ **b** $1, a, b, ab$
   c $1, 2, a, 2a$ **d** $1, 2, 3, 6, a, 2a, 3a, 6a$
   e $1, 2, a, 2a, b, 2b, ab, 2ab$
   f $1, 2, 4, 8, p, 2p, 4p, 8p, q, 2q, 4q, 8q, pq,$
     $2pq, 4pq, 8pq$
   g $1, 5, x, 5x, x^2, 5x^2$
   h $1, 2, 3, 6, a, 2a, 3a, 6a, a^2, 2a^2, 3a^2, 6a^2$

5 a $1, x$ **b** $1, 2, q, 2q$ **c** $1, 3, b, 3b$
   d $1, m$ **e** $1, 2, g, 2g$

6 a $3x$ **b** $4b$ **c** $6p$ **d** $3k$
   e $6a$

Page 188 Exercise 8

1 a $3(3x+2)$ **b** $4(x+2)$ **c** $7(2x-3)$
   d $5(2x+3)$ **e** $6(4x+3)$ **f** $8(7x+2)$
   g $2(7-5x)$ **h** $3(7+11x)$ **i** $5(6x+7)$
   j $4(9x+11)$ **k** $12(1-2x)$ **l** $8(2+5x)$
   m $x(2+y)$ **n** $2x(2+9y)$ **o** $2x(1-x)$

2 a $2(2x-1)$ **b** $3(2y+1)$ **c** $3(x-1)$
   d $5(m+1)$ **e** $6(x-3)$ **f** $4(y+2)$
   g $3(3x-2)$ **h** $2(m+5)$ **i** $7(x-2)$
   j $4(2y+3)$ **k** $5(3x-1)$ **l** $6(3m+2)$
   m $12(3x-1)$ **n** $2(4y+3)$ **o** $4(x-1)$
   p $5(2m+5)$ **q** $2(3m+4)$ **r** $5(2t-3)$
   s $2(ab+1)$ **t** $3(2-ab)$ **u** $2(4pq+1)$

3 a $a(b+2)$ **b** $d(1-c)$ **c** $7x(2y-1)$
   d $3k(2+3h)$ **e** $q(p+4)$ **f** $6d(1-2c)$
   g $4k(2j-1)$ **h** $6g(y+4)$ **i** $a(5-b)$
   j $b(2a+1)$ **k** $k(3l-2)$ **l** $n(5m-7)$
   m $e(9+7f)$ **n** $2q(2p-1)$ **o** $2a(b+2)$
   p $4r(2s-3)$ **q** $4h(2g+7)$ **r** $6s(7t-2)$

4 a $a(a-3)$ **b** $y(y+4)$ **c** $m(6-m)$
   d $n(2-n)$ **e** $t(3t+2)$ **f** $c(4-c)$
   g $2x(x+2)$ **h** $y(5x+y)$ **i** $b(2a+3b)$
   j $2p(2p-1)$ **k** $3q(2+q)$ **l** $5(m^2+3n^2)$
   m $5n(n-3)$ **n** $6x(3x-2)$ **o** $4y(4+5y)$

Page 189 Exercise 9

1 a $y=12$ **b** $x=1$ **c** $x=2$
   d $y=2$ **e** $x=3$ **f** $t=10$
   g $m=4$ **h** $r=5$ **i** $x=3$
   j $x=1$ **k** $n=2$ **l** $r=6$

2 a $c=4$ **b** $k=0$ **c** $m=0$
   d $k=0$ **e** $d=0$ **f** $x=4$
   g $n=4$ **h** $l=3$ **i** $l=5$
   j $q=5$ **k** $w=5$ **l** $x=10$

3 a $x=2$ **b** $y=0$ **c** $m=5$
   d $t=4$ **e** $n=2$ **f** $c=7$
   g $y=0$ **h** $x=2$

Page 190 Exercise 10

1 a $x=4$ **b** $x=4$ **c** $x=2$
   d $x=14$ **e** $x=2$ **f** $x=2$
   g $x=1$ **h** $m=7$

2 a $y=5$ **b** $x=2$ **c** $m=3$
   d $x=3$ **e** $k=1$ **f** $y=3$
   g $w=3$ **h** $t=3$ **i** $c=3$
   j $u=5$ **k** $y=6$ **l** $n=12$
   m $a=4$ **n** $e=3$ **o** $x=1$

3 a (i) $4x-1=x+8$ (ii) $x=3$ (iii) 11 m
   b (i) $4x-1=x+2$ (ii) $x=1$ (iii) 3 m
   c (i) $3x-4=x+2$ (ii) $x=3$ (iii) 5 m
   d (i) $2x-3=6x-15$ (ii) $x=3$ (iii) 3 m
   e (i) $2x-1=14-x$ (ii) $x=5$ (iii) 9 m

Page 192 Exercise 11

1 a $p \leq 8$ **b** $e \leq 6$ **c** $m > 4$ **d** $p < 5$
  e $p \leq 10000$ **f** $e < 36$

2 a $<$ **b** $>$ **c** $>$ **d** $<$
  e $>$ **f** $<$ **g** $>$ **h** $<$
  i $>$ **j** $<$ **k** $>$ **l** $>$
  m $<$ **n** $>$ **o** $>$ **p** $<$

3 a 4, 5, 6   **b** 1   **c** 1, 2, 3
  d 5, 6   **e** 4, 5, 6   **f** 3, 4, 5, 6
  g 1   **h** 4, 5, 6   **i** 5, 6
  j 1, 2   **k** 1, 2, 3   **l** 4, 5, 6

4 a true   **b** false   **c** false
  d true   **e** true   **f** false
  g true   **h** false

5 a $<$ **b** $>$ **c** $>$ **d** $>$
  e $<$ **f** $>$ **g** $<$ **h** $>$

6 a 0, 1, 2   **b** 4   **c** 0, 1
  d 3, 4   **e** 3, 4   **f** 3, 4
  g 0, 1   **h** 2, 3, 4   **i** 0, 1, 2

Page 193 Exercise 12

1 a 2, 3, 4, …   **b** 0, 1, 2
  c 0, 1, 2, … , 8   **d** 8, 9, 10, …
  e 0, 1, 2, 3, 4   **f** 1, 2, 3, …
  g 3, 4, 5, …   **h** 3, 4, 5, …
  i 0   **j** 3, 4, 5, …
  k 0, 1, 2   **l** 0, 1, 2, … , 10

2 a $m > 3$ **b** $x < 6$ **c** $y \leq 2$
  d $k \geq 0$ **e** $k > 14$ **f** $h < 2$
  g $f \leq 11$ **h** $y \geq 3$ **i** $x < 11$
  j $y \geq 7$ **k** $t > 3$ **l** $y \leq 2$

3 a 0, 1, 2, 3   **b** 6, 7, 8, …
  c 0, 1, 2, 3   **d** 9, 10, 11, …
  e 5, 6, 7, …   **f** 0, 1, 2, 3, 4
  g 4, 5, 6, …   **h** 0, 1, 2, 3, 4
  i 0, 1, 2, 3, 4, 5

Page 194 Review

1 a 19   **b** 9

2 a 10 °C   **b** 7.5 °C   **c** 6.25 °C

3 a $7b - 6$ **b** $6a + 8b$ **c** x^2
  d r^3 **e** $2t^2$ **f** $24m + 3$

4 a $5m + 30$ **b** $28 + 4x$ **c** $6n - 15m$
  d $a^2 + a$ **e** $2xy - x^2$ **f** $12 - 18k$

5 a $2x + 4$ **b** $14 + 11y$ **c** $5x - 2$

6 a $3(2m + 1)$ **b** $3b(a - 3)$
  c $4x^2(4 - 3a)$ **d** $m(m - 1)$

7 a $x = 5$ **b** $y = 3$ **c** $m = 7$
  d $k = 3$

8 a $8n - 3 = 5n + 3$ **b** $n = 2$ **c** $13m$

9 a $m < 6$ **b** $m < 3$ **c** $x < 8$

15 Graphical Relationships

Page 195 Starting Points

1 a 2   **b** 4   **c** (3, 4)

2

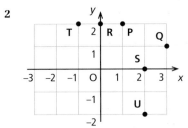

3 8, 11, 14

4 a No   **b** (0, 2), (1, 3), (2, 4) or (3, 5)

Page 196 Exercise 1

1 a (i) B, D   (ii) B, F   (iii) A
  (iv) A, E (and O)
  b (i) $y = 4$ (ii) $x = 3$

2 a C, D, K   **b** E, G
  c C, I and O   **d** E, F, J
  e A, B and O   **f** D, F, L
  g D, G (and O)   **h** L
  i K

3 a $x = 4$ and $y = 1$ **b** to the right
  c $x = 2$ **d** $y = 2$ **e** $x = 2$

4 a (i) (1, 0), (1, 1), (1, 2), etc.
  (ii) (0, 3), (1, 3), (2, 3), etc.
  (iii) (0, 1), (1, 1), (2, 1), etc.
  b (1, 3)   **c** $x = 1$ and $y = 1$
  d $x = 1$ and $y = -2$
  e (ii) and (iv)

5 a $x = 1$ **b** $x = 3$ **c** $y = 4$
  d $y = 2$ **e** $x = -3$ **f** $y = -2$

6 a $x = 2$ **b** $y = 1$ **c** $x = 5$
  d $x = 4$ **e** $x = -1$ **f** $y = -6$

7 a above   **b** left   **c** above
  d right

8 a (i) $x = 1$, $x = 4$, $y = 1$, $y = 5$
  (ii) $x = 1$, $x = 6$, $y = 3$, $y = 5$
  (iii) $x = 1$, $x = 5$, $y = 1$, $y = 2$

  b (i)

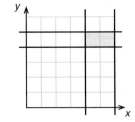

(ii)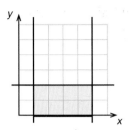

(iii)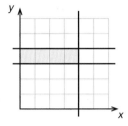

(iv)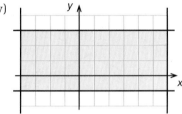

(v)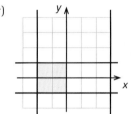

(vi)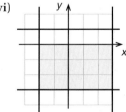

Page 199 Exercise 2

1 a 9, 12

b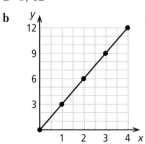

c $y = 3x$

2 a 18, 27, 36

b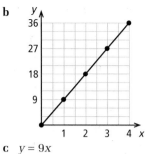

c $y = 9x$

3 a 10, 15, 20

b

c $y = 5x$

4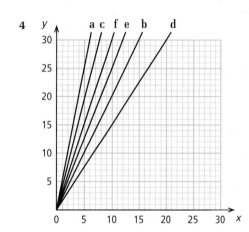

5 a **(i)** 5 **(ii)** 2 **(iii)** 6 **(iv)** a
b **(i)** $y = 10x$ **(ii)** $y = 5x$ **(iii)** $y = 3x$
(iv) $y = 2x$ **(v)** $y = x$ **(vi)** $y = \frac{1}{2}x$

6 a $y = -3x$ **b** $y = -2x$ **c** $y = -\frac{1}{2}x$

7 a 12, 8, 4, 0, −4, −8, −12
b 15, 10, 5, 0, −5, −10, −15
c 4.5, 3, 1.5, 0, −1.5, −3, −4.5
d 7.5, 5, 2.5, 0, −2.5, −5, −7.5

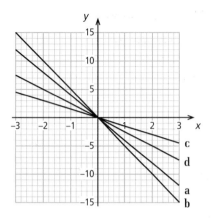

4 a 10, 8, 6, 4, 2

b

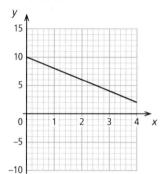

Page 202 Exercise 3

1 a 14   **b** 6   **c** −1   **d** 3   **e** 13

2 a −5, −3, −1, 1, 3, 5, 7, 9

   b 1, 2, 3, 4, 5, 6, 7, 8

   c −8, −7, −6, −5, −4, −3, −2, −1

   d −13, −11, −9, −7, −5, −3, −1, 1

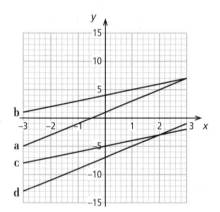

5 a–d

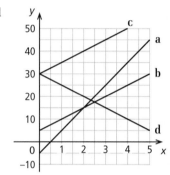

6 a −1   **b** −3   **c** −5   **d** 6   **e** −1

7 a −1, 0, 1, 2, 3, 4, 5

   b −7, −5, −3, −1, 1, 3, 5

   c −6, −5, −4, −3, −2, −1, 0

   d −5, −3, −1, 1, 3, 5, 7

3 a 12, 11, 10, 9, 8

   b 3, 1, −1, −3, −5

   c 5, 4, 3, 2, 1

   d 3, 5, 7, 9, 11

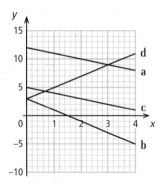

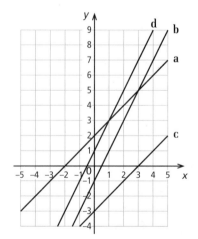

8 a (i) $y = 5$ **(ii)** $y = 7$ **(iii)** $y = 2$

     (iv) $y = 10$ **(v)** $y = b$

   b (i) 4   **(ii)** 2   **(iii)** 5

     (iv) 1   **(v)** 3

Page 204 Exercise 4

1 a 1, 4, 7, 10, 13   **b** 0, 3, 6, 9, 12
   c $y = 3x + 1$

2 a $y = 2x + 1$ **b** $y = x + 3$
   c $y = 4x + 2$ **d** $y = 3x + 2$
   e $y = 2x + 4$

3 a $y = 2x - 2$ **b** $y = x - 2$
   c $y = 4x - 12$ **d** $y = 3x - 3$

4 a 42, 44, 46, 48, 50   **b** $y = 2x + 22$

5 a y ; 3, 4, 5, 6, 7   **b** $y = x + 2$

Page 207 Review

1 a $x = 2$ **b** $x = 5$ **c** $y = 2$

2 a $x = 2$ **b** $y = 3$

3 a $-3, -2, -1, 0, 1, 2, 3$
   b $0, -1, -2, -3$
   c $-9, -6, -3, 0, 3, 6, 9$
   d $-3, -1, 1, 3, 5, 7, 9$

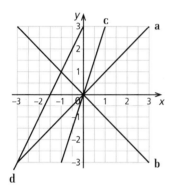

4

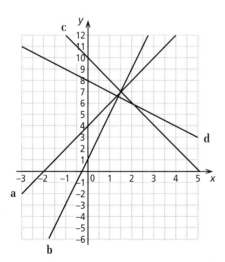

16 Basic Trigonometry

Page 208 Starting Points

1 a   **b**

   c   **d**

2 a (i) 43.7   (ii) 43.72
   b (i) 5.7   (ii) 5.68
   c (i) 0.4   (ii) 0.36
   d (i) 28.0   (ii) 27.98

3 a 63.6   **b** 40.5

4 a $T = \dfrac{D}{S}$ **b** $D = S \times T$ **c** $S = \dfrac{D}{T}$

Page 209 Exercise 1

1 a   **b**

   c 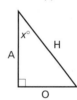   **d**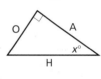

   e

2 a (i)   (ii)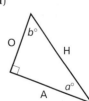

   b (i) 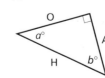   (ii)

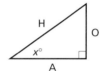

Page 212 Exercise 2

1 **a** 0.4   **b** 0.375   **c** 0.632
   d 0.462 and 2.167
2 **a** 0.364   **b** 2.356   **c** 0.748
   d 4.829   **e** 0.112
3 **a** 30.0°   **b** 51.3°   **c** 41.9°   **d** 45°

Page 212 Exercise 3

1 **a** $\tan x° = \frac{4}{5} = 4 \div 5$, $\tan x° = 0.8$, $x° = 38.7°$
   b $\tan x° = \frac{2}{6} = 2 \div 6$, $\tan x° = 0.3333$,
     $x° = 18.4$
   c 36.7°   **d** 53.3°   **e** 69.2°
   f 50.0°   **g** 40.9°   **h** 33.7°
2 59.0°
3 10.0°

Page 214 Exercise 4

1 **a** 0.810   **b** 0.673   **c** 0.729   **d** 0.75
2 **a** 0.707   **b** 0   **c** 0.998   **d** 1
   e 0.724   **f** 0.984   **g** 0.368
3 **a** 61.2°   **b** 7.9°   **c** 30°   **d** 23.6°
4 **a** 0.5, 30°   **b** 0.810, 54.0°
   c 0.741, 47.8°   **d** 0.465, 27.7°
5 34.5°
6 53.1°
7 10.6°
8 **a** 57.1°   **b** 32.9°
9 angle W = 4.7°, angle G = 85.3°

Page 216 Exercise 5

1 **a** 0.75   **b** 0.558   **c** 0.709   **d** 0.364
2 **a** 0.707   **b** 1   **c** 0   **d** 0.978
   e 0.651   **f** 0.831   **g** 0.103
3 **a** 0°   **b** 90°   **c** 60°   **d** 71.3°
4 **a** 0.857, 31.0°   **b** 0.75, 41.4°
   c 0.831, 33.8°   **d** 0.735, 42.7°
5 69.9°
6 **a** 75.1°   **b** 14.9°
7 60°, 30°

Page 218 Exercise 6

1 **a** 20.6°   **b** 48.6°   **c** 52.3°   **d** 40.2°
   e 43.8°   **f** 46.2°   **g** 41.8°   **h** 39.7°

Page 219 Exercise 7

1 **a** 5.1 cm   **b** 13.0 cm   **c** 8.7 m
   d 1.2 cm   **e** 20.0 cm
2 35.0 m
3 383.9 m

Page 220 Exercise 8

1 **a** 5.7 cm   **b** 13.0 cm   **c** 13.9 mm
   d 4.0 cm   **e** 7.3 km
2 1.8 m
3 48.8 m

Page 221 Exercise 9

1 **a** 6.6 cm   **b** 3.5 cm   **c** 33.5 cm
   d 27.4 km   **e** 34.8 cm
2 4.5 km

Page 222 Exercise 10

1 **a** 2.1 cm   **b** 11.0 cm   **c** 19.7 cm
   d 6.0 cm   **e** 7.0 cm   **f** 2.6 cm
   g 3.5 cm   **h** 2.7 cm   **i** 62.8 cm
   j 14.5 cm
2 2.1 m
3 36.3 m
4 9.3 m
5 4.6 m

Page 223 Exercise 11

1 **a** 24.9 m   **b** 39.9 m
2 **a** 12.3 m   **b** 7.5 m
3 **a** 1.4 m   **b** 1.8 m
4 **a** 1.6 m   **b** 3.1 m
5 30°
6 26.6°
7 11.4 m
8 728.9 m

Page 225 Review

1 **a** 41.1°   **b** 53.1°   **c** 50.5°
2 **a** 16.4 cm   **b** 5.3 cm   **c** 3.3 m
3 31.8 m
4 48.6°

17 Standard Form

Page 226 Starting Points

1 **a** **(i)** $10 \times 10 \times 10 \times 10 \times 10 \times 10 = 1\,000\,000$
     (ii) $10 \times 10 \times 10 \times 10 \times 10 = 100\,000$
     (iii) $10 \times 10 \times 10 \times 10 = 10\,000$
     (iv) $10 \times 10 \times 10 = 1000$
     (v) $10 \times 10 = 100$
   b **(i)** 6 zeros   **(ii)** 5 zeros   **(iii)** 4 zeros
     (iv) 3 zeros   **(v)** 2 zeros
   c **(i)** $10^1 = 10$ **(ii)** $10^0 = 1$
3 **a** 186   **b** 186 m   **c** 186 kg

Page 227 Exercise 1

1 **a** 12×100 **b** $275 \times 1\,000\,000$
   c 34×1000 **d** 3×100
   e $974 \times 10\,000$ **f** 8×10
2 **a** 2300   **b** 456 000
   c 4 000 000   **d** 780
   e 310   **f** 6750
3 **a** 1 200 000 000   **b** 1 016 000 000
   c 5 202 000 000 000
   d 23 936 400 000
4 48 000 000 years

5 a 314   **b** 6290   **c** 84 100
   d 7 210 000   **e** 1 450 000 000
   f 97.9

6 a $9.42 \times 10\,000$ **b** $8.41 \times 100\,000$
   c 2.14×100 **d** $6.16 \times 100\,000\,000$
   e 9.2×10

Page 228 Exercise 2

1 a 4 560 000   **b** 8 410   **c** 29.6
   d 4.11   **e** 546 000   **f** 719
   g 88.2   **h** 6.17   **i** 89 000
   j 2 300

2 a 3.21×10^2 **b** 4.726×10^3
   c 5.21×10^1 **d** 5.12×10^0
   e 4.96×10^1 **f** 5.964×10^2
   g 3.96×10^5 **h** 4.56×10^7
   i 1.3×10^4 **j** 1.7×10^1
   k 2×10^0 **l** 4.25×10^2
   m 1.4×10^7 **n** 8×10^5
   o 2.5×10^8 **p** 6.1×10^5
   q 2.01×10^8 **r** 5.622×10^6

3 a 496 000   **b** 890 000
   c 723 000 000   **d** 550 000 000
   e 74 418 000   **f** 518 750 000

4 8.949×10^9

Page 228 Exercise 3

1 a **(i)** 0.14   **(ii)** 0.014   **(iii)** 0.0014
   (iv) 0.000 14   **(v)** 0.000 014
   (vi) 0.000 001 4   The number of decimal places in the answer = the number of decimal places in the question
   b **(i)** 0.1   **(ii)** 0.01   **(iii)** 0.001
   (iv) 0.0001   **(v)** 0.000 01
   c **(i)** 6.2×0.01 **(ii)** 8.57×0.1
   (iii) $4.56 \times 0.000\,01$ **(iv)** $9.1 \times 0.000\,01$
   (v) $2.38 \times 0.000\,000\,000\,1$
   (vi) 3.5×0.01 **(vii)** 2.1×0.01
   (viii) $4 \times 0.000\,1$ **(ix)** $7.8 \times 0.000\,01$
   (x) $9.16 \times 0.000\,000\,1$
   d **(i)** 6.2×10^{-2} **(ii)** 8.57×10^{-1}
   (iii) 4.56×10^{-5} **(iv)** 9.1×10^{-5}
   (v) 2.38×10^{-4}

2 a 0.721   **b** 0.003 85
   c 0.000 061 1   **d** 0.000 000 127
   e 0.0889   **f** 0.749
   g 0.0004   **h** 0.000 005

3 a 10^{-2} **b** 3.4×10^{-3}
   c 5.41×10^{-6} **d** 9.3×10^{-5}
   e 4.6×10^{-2} **f** 9×10^{-1}

4 a 0.051 25   **b** 0.000 047 0 8
   c 0.000 000 442 74   **d** 0.004 898 4

e 0.000 000 000 609   **f** 0.000 000 577 7
g 0.000 000 000 669 6

Page 230 Exercise 4

1 a 0.000 046   **b** 42 000
   c 29 000 000   **d** 65 100
   e 2 017 000 000   **f** 0.000 115
   g 0.000 000 32   **h** 713 000 000
   i 76 100 000

2 a 2.472×10^6 **b** 3.032×10^9
   c 6.45×10^{10} **d** 2.874×10^5
   e 1.884×10^{-2} **f** 1.132×10^{-7}
   g 5.771×10^{-8} **h** 3.164×10^{-5}

3 a 1.7×10^4 **b** 2.13×10^6
   c 1.73×10^3 **d** 2.48×10^5
   e 1.13×10^{-3} **f** 2.25×10^{-7}
   g 4.42×10^3 **h** 4.83×10^7

4 a 2.95×10^2 **b** 3.8×10^1
   c 7.05×10^2 **d** 6.47×10^{-1}
   e 1.82×10^1 **f** 3.87×10^2
   g 7.3×10^1 **h** 7×10^{-1}

5 a 1.579×10^5 **b** 8.881×10^{12}
   c -3.564×10^9 **d** 1.425×10^7

Page 232 Exercise 5

1 a 3.154×10^7 **b** 1.262×10^8
   c 1.667×10^{-2} **d** 1.14×10^{-4}

2 a 4.65×10^3 **b** 1.277×10^4
   c 7.776×10^8 **d** 2.811×10^9

3 a 2.7×10^{-23} **b** 1.686×10^{-24}
   c 1.64×10^{-24} **d** 4.926×10^{25}

Page 233 Exercise 6

1 a 2.262×10^7 **b** 2.306×10^{10}

2 a 9.6×10^{12} **b** 4.967×10^2

3 2.22

4 6.724×10^{11}

Page 234 Review

1 a 10^4 **b** 10^6 **c** 10^{-4}
   d 10^{-7} **e** 10^1 **f** 10^0

2 a 3.245×10^3 **b** 3.41×10^1
   c 3.4×10^7 **d** 7.3×10^{-3}
   e 4.56×10^0

3 a 31 400   **b** 624   **c** 4.15
   d 95 600 000   **e** 0.000 802
   f 0.007   **g** 0.000 000 611

4 a 2 400 000 000 000
   b 0.000 000 000 000 05

5 a 3180   **b** 80 900
   c 0.000 745   **d** 0.000 007 9

6 a 4.715×10^5　　**b** 1.99×10^4
c 1.368×10^{-4}　　**d** 3.889×10^{-7}
e 2.7946×10^4　　**f** 7.5×10^{-5}
7 a 8.72×10^6　　**b** 2.592×10^{15}
c 2.254×10^2　　**d** 4×10^9

18 Revising Unit 3

Page 235 Exercise 1

1 a 20　　**b** 9　　**c** 252　　**d** 85
2 a 576 cm^2　　**b** 1357.2 cm^3
3 a 14　　**b** 102
4 a $5a + 4b$　　**b** $4x^2$
c $2x - 2y$　　**d** $2c + 5d$
5 a $3(x + 4)$　　**b** $x(1 - 6x)$
c $5(2y + 1)$　　**d** $x(2y - 3)$
6 a $x = 7$　　**b** $x = 7$　　**c** $x = 4$

7 a

x	0	1	2	3	4	5
y	3	5	7	9	11	13

b

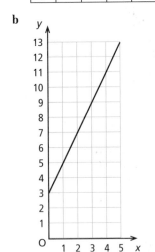

8 a $x < 4$　　**b** $x > 17$　　**c** $x \le 4$　　**d** $x \ge 8$
9 $x = 9$
10 a **(i)** $3x$　　**(ii)** $3(x + 4)$　　**(iii)** $x(x + 4)$
b $2x^2 + 20x + 24$
11 a Yes, max weight = 782 kg　　**b** 350 kg
12 a $x \ge 3$　　**b** 3, 4, 5, 6, 7, 8, 9
13 $x < 6$
14 13 h 4 min
15 a **(i)** 1, 2, 3, 4, 5, ...
(ii) 1, 4, 9, 16, 25, ...
(iii) 2, 4, 6, 8, 10, ...
(iv) 13, 14, 15, 16, 17, ...
(v) 29, 28, 27, 26, 25, ...
b 16

Page 238 Exercise 2

1 a (i)

x	-3	-2	-1	0	1	2	3
y	2	2	2	2	2	2	2

(ii)

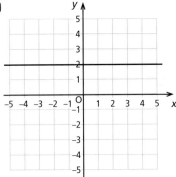

b (i)

x	-3	-2	-1	0	1	2	3
y	-3	-2	-1	0	1	2	3

(ii)

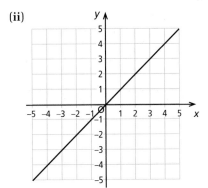

c (i)

x	-3	-2	-1	0	1	2	3
y	-6	-4	-2	0	2	4	6

(ii)

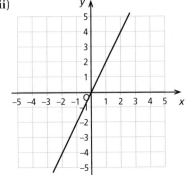

d (i)

x	−3	−2	−1	0	1	2	3
y	−5	−3	−1	1	3	5	7

(ii)

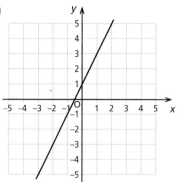

e (i)

x	−3	−2	−1	0	1	2	3
y	4	3	2	1	0	−1	−2

(ii)

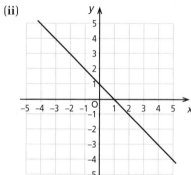

f (i)

x	−3	−2	−1	0	1	2	3
y	9	7	5	3	1	−1	−3

(ii)

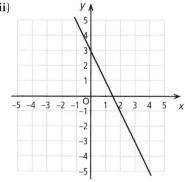

2 a

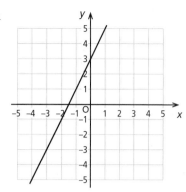

b below

3 a/b

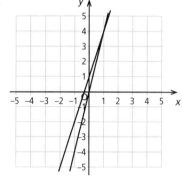

c (1, 4)

4 a

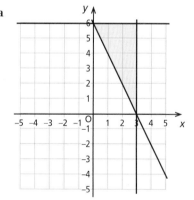

b 9 cm²

5 a

Number of slides (x)	0	2	4	6	8	10
Cost (y)		2	3	4	5	6	7

b

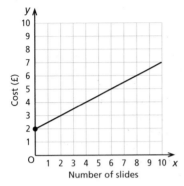

6 a

Number of tickets (x)	1	2	3	4	5	6
Charge (y)		5	8	11	14	17	20

b

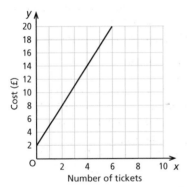

7 a

Number of hours (x)	0	1	2	3	4	5
Litres of fuel left (y)	10	8	6	4	2	0

b

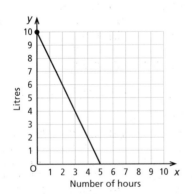

Page 239 Exercise 3

1 a 52.1°   **b** 53.1°   **c** 30°
2 a 3.7 cm   **b** 4.7 cm   **c** 29.7 cm
3 62.2°
4 No, the angle is 4.1°
5 2.4 km
6 a 4 m   **b** 4 m   **c** 54 m
7 a 1.6 km   **b** 1.1 km   **c** 2.7 km

Page 241 Exercise 4

1 a 3.14×10^3 **b** 6.28×10^0
  c 4.56×10^{-2} **d** 2.134×10^6
  e 7×10^0 **f** 4×10^{-1}
  g 5.2×10^{12} **h** 6.4×10^{10}
  i 4.4444×10^{11} **j** 9.3×10^{-6}
  k 6×10^{-12}
2 a (i) 3.9×10^{-2} **(ii)** 0.039
  b (i) 6.3×10^5 **(ii)** 630 000
  c (i) 8.47×10^3 **(ii)** 8470
  d (i) 1.309×10^4 **(ii)** 13 090
3 a 1.333×10^6 **b** 1.819×10^4
  c 1.250×10^5 **d** 9.25×10^{-8}
  e 1.56×10^{-2} **f** 2.957×10^{-4}
  g 6.4×10^{-6} **h** 8×10^1
4 7.3×10^4
5 3.154×10^9
6 a 2 300 000   **b** 2.3×10^6
  c 2.875×10^5
7 0.13×10^7
8 a (i) 0.025   **(ii)** 2.5×10^{-3}
  b (i) 0.004   **(ii)** 4×10^{-3}
  c (i) 0.0002   **(ii)** 2×10^{-4}
  d (i) 0.0005   **(ii)** 5×10^{-4}
9 1.667×10^8 seconds
10 a (i) 3.5×10^6 **(ii)** 7.5×10^5
  b £(3.875×10^7)
11 a 1.83×10^8 **b** 1.227×10^8
  c $\frac{409}{610}$ (0.6705)

UNIT 4

19 Calculations in a Social Context

Page 243 Starting Points

1 **a** commission **b** piecework **c** bonus
  d overtime
2 £127.50
3 £16 000
4 £235
5 £189
6 £30
7 **a** 0.02 **b** 0.13 **c** 0.022
  d 0.0195
8 **a** £50 **b** £210
9 **a** £36 **b** £636 **c** £53

Page 245 Exercise 1

1 **a** 12 **b** 15 **c** 7.5
  d 10.5 **e** 27 **f** 36
2 **a** £30 **b** £45 **c** £75
  d £22.50 **e** £67.50 **f** £90
3 £54
4 **a** £170 **b** £30 **c** £200
5 **a** £107.80 **b** £142.45
6 **a** £163.10 **b** £27.96 **c** £46.60
  d £237.66
7 **a** £173.25 **b** £31.50 **c** £31.50
  d £236.25 **e** £257.25
8 £216

Page 246 Exercise 2

1 £5390
2 £25 200
3 £1526
4 **a** £154 **b** £7392
5 £6450
6 **a** £13 624 **b** £1048
7 £6031.50
8 £9418

Page 247 Exercise 3

1 £627
2 £1436
3 **a** £9024 **b** £10 427
4 £38.74
5 £355
6 £1540
7 £9365
8 **a** £226.31 **b** £410 **c** £1229.22
  d £189.20 **e** £1428
9 **a** £364.98 **b** £839.48

Page 249 Exercise 4

1 £56.17
2 £578.72
3 £2.07
4 **a** £152.05 **b** £35.69 **c** £724.14
5 £24.60

Page 250 Exercise 5

1 **a** £126.82 **b** £941.34
  c £15 610.15 **d** £16 273.20
2 **a** Gross wage = £364.63,
    total deductions = £59.25,
    net wage = £305.38
  b Gross wage = £937.66,
    total deductions = £137.80,
    net wage = £799.86
  c Gross wage = £1889,
    total deductions = £532.90,
    net wage = £1356.10
3 **a** Gross wage = £1968,
    total deductions = £500, net wage = £1468
  b Gross wage = £2214,
    total deductions = £610, net wage = £1604
  c Gross wage = £420,
    total deductions = £123, net wage = £297

Page 252 Exercise 6

1 £243.85
2 7, 7, 8, 8, 7, 4, 3.5 hours; basic pay £199.50;
  6 hours at time and a half = £51.30;
  3.5 hours at double time = £39.90;
  gross pay = £290.70;
  total deductions = £54.89; net pay = £235.81
3 £182, £41.60, £223.60, £37.93, £185.67

Page 253 Exercise 7

1 **a** (i) £25 (ii) £1025
  b (i) £15.41 (ii) £685.41
  c (i) £63 (ii) £3563
  d (i) £51.45 (ii) £2501.45
  e (i) £15.60 (ii) £815.60
2 **a** (i) 1.3% (ii) £20.80
  b (i) 23.2% (ii) £696
  c 15.5%
  d (i) £89.50 (ii) £92.80
  e Albion Gold
  f £60.324, £2478.324, £54.52, £2208.85

Page 255 Exercise 8

1 **a** (i) £88 (ii) £1056 (iii) £56
  b (i) £31 (ii) £1116 (iii) £116
  c (i) £302.50 (ii) £5445 (iii) £445
  d (i) £41.40 (ii) £2484 (iii) £484
  e (i) £91 (ii) £4368 (iii) £868
2 **a** £120 **b** £5760 **c** £760
3 **a** £143 **b** £8580 **c** £2080

Page 256 Exercise 9

1 a £196.72   b £180.95 c £15.77
  d 20.1%
  e (i) £116.24   (ii) £102.59
  f (i) £2573.52   (ii) £2322.96

2 a £92.40   b £257.15   c £663.60

3 a £342.30   b £16 430.40
  c £6430.40

4 a £154.10   b £9246   c £4246

5 a (i) £110.20   (ii) 123.45
  b £13.25   c £477

6 1 year without protection = £11 068.80;
  2 years with protection = £13 287.60; cheaper
  to pay back in 1 year without protection

Page 258 Review

1 £9058
2 £247.25
3 £244.80
4 Gross wage = £625.12; deductions = £93.46;
  net wage = £531.66
5 a £44   b £2044
6 a £96.60   b £3477.60   c £477.60
7 a £84.40   b £1172.40

20 Logic Diagrams

Page 259 Starting Points

1 a (i) Depth (mm)   (ii) 457
   (iii) E52   (iv) £114.00
  b B45, C38, D27   c £156

2 £6.19

3 a 4.5   b £167   c 25 km   d £3

4 a 14 miles   b 17 miles   c 4 miles
  d 49 miles

Page 261 Exercise 1

1 a (i) D2   (ii) B3   (iii) A2
   (iv) D3   (v) D4   (vi) F2
   (vii) E2   (viii) B5
  b C3   c C
  d 1   e C3 is highlighted

2 a (i) D5   (ii) D6   (iii) E5
  b (i) B3   (ii) B4   (iii) C3
  c (i) D7   (ii) D8   (iii) E7
  d (i) A3   (ii) A4   (iii) B3

3 b (i) 160 cm   (ii) Ian   (iii) Amer
   (iv) Amer

4 a C1   b C2   c A3   d D5

5 a 9.9   b 7.8

Page 263 Exercise 2

1 a (i) 20 appears   (ii) 38 changes to 46
  b nothing   c 37

2 a 67

b (i) = B3 + C3 + D3 + E3 + F3
  (ii) = B4 + C4 + D4 + E4 + F4
c = G2 + G3 + G4
  or = B5 + C5 + D5 + E5 + F5

3 a (i) = SUM(C2..C4)   (ii) = SUM(E2..E4)
  b (i) = SUM(B3..F3)   (ii) = SUM(B4..F4)

Page 266 Exercise 3

1 a (i) = SUM(C2..C4)
   (ii) = SUM(D2..D4)
   (iii) = SUM(E2..E4)
   (iv) = SUM(F2..F4)
  b (i) 540   (ii) 300
   (iii) 520   (iv) 280

2 a (i) = B2 – C2   (ii) = B3 – C3
   (iii) = B4 – C4
  b (i) 109.45   (ii) 171.56
   (iii) 145.09

3 a (i) = C1*C2   (ii) = D1*D2
  b (i) 11 250   (ii) 12 250

4 a 280/40
  b (i) = B3/C3   (ii) = B4/C4
  c (i) 8.8   (ii) 10.5

5 a (i) = B2*C2   (ii) = B3*C3
   (iii) = B4*C4   (iv) = SUM(D2..D4)
   (v) = D5*0.175   (vi) = D5 + D6
  b (i) £85.31   (ii) £146.88
   (iii) £342.63

6 a = B2*B3
  b (i) 3.68   (ii) 3.7   (iii) 4

7 a (i) = B2/2   (ii) = C2/2   (iii) D2/2
  b (i) = PI( )*B2   (ii) = PI( )*C2
   (iii) = PI( )*D2
  c precision 2
  d (i) PI( )*C3*C3   (ii) = PI( )*D3*D3

Page 269 Exercise 4

1 a (i) = A2 + 1   (ii) = A3 + 1
   (iii) 3, 4
  b (i) = B2*2   (ii) = B3*2
   (iii) 4, 8
  c (i) = C2 – 1   (ii) = C3 – 1
   (iii) 98, 97
  d (i) = D2/2   (ii) = D3/2
   (iii) 256, 128
  e (i) = 2*E2 – 1   (ii) = 2*E3 – 1
   (iii) 5, 9

2 a = A1 + 2   b = B1*3
  c (i) = C1/2   (ii) = D1*2 + 1
  d 6, 8, 10, 12, 14, 16   e 32, 16, 8, 4, 2, 1

Page 270 Exercise 5

1 a = B2 + C2   b = B6 + C6
  c (i) = AVERAGE(C2..C6)
   (ii) = AVERAGE(D2..D6)

d **(i)** Yvonne, Siobhan, Michael, Peter
(ii) John

2 a = A2/B2   **b** = A5/B5
   c precision 2   **d** = AVERAGE(C2..C6)
   e 285 km and 110 km

3 a £4.60   **b** £44.30   **c** £131.25

Page 271 Exercise 6

1 a

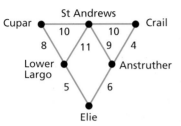

b (i)

(ii)

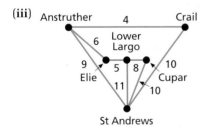

(iii)

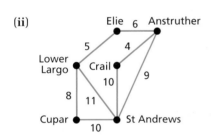

   c 15 miles
   d Crail: 2; Anstruther: 3; Elie: 2;
       Lower Largo: 3; Cupar: 2

2 a (i) 6   **(ii)** 6   **(iii)** 4
   b (i) 6   **(ii)** 6   **(iii)** 2
   c (i) 7   **(ii)** 7   **(iii)** 4

3 a (i)

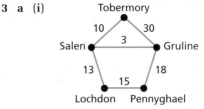

(ii)

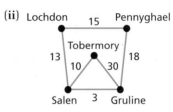

   b (i) Tobermory: 2; Salen: 3; Gruline: 3;
       Lochdon: 2; Pennyghael: 2
   c 31 miles

4 a A

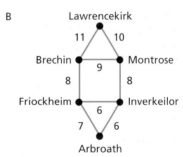

   b (ii) longest 46 miles; shortest 22 miles
      (iii) longest 54 miles; shortest 21 miles
   c (i) longest 41 miles; shortest 24 miles
      (ii) 2
      (iv) 39 miles via Montrose, Brechin,
        Friockheim, Inverkeilor
      (vi) No

5 a (i) Lower Largo, Cupar, St Andrews,
       Crail, Anstruther, Elie, Lower Largo,
       St Andrews, Anstruther
      (ii) 63 miles
   b Elie, 2, even; Anstruther, 3, odd;
      Crail, 2, even
   c 'Passing through' uses an even number of
      arcs so travelling once on all arcs requires
      a start or a stop at an odd degree vertex

6 a Kenmore, Aberfeldy, Tummel Bridge, Pitlochry, Ballinluig, Birnam, Milton, Aberfeldy, Ballinluig

b There are 4 odd vertices so no such route is possible (such a route requires at most 2 odd vertices)

Page 275 Exercise 7

1 c A, F, E, D, C, B, A, E, C

2 b (i) F, D, A, B, C, D, E, B
(ii) E, F, A, B, C, D, E, A, D
(iii) F, E, A, B, C, D, A, C, E

3 b (i) C, A, B, C, D, E, F, D
(ii) B, A, C, B, F, C, D, A, E, D, F, E

Page 276 Exercise 8

1 a (i) 4   (ii) 3
b (i) 5 min   (ii) 3 min
c 10 min

2 a (i) 4   (ii) 5
b (i) 15 min   (ii) 5 min
c (i) 65 min   (ii) 65 min

3 a 9 hours   **b** 9 hours

4 a 2 hours   **b** Set up furniture
c Curtains, carpet and furniture
d 15 hours

Page 277 Challenge

9 min

Page 278 Exercise 9

1 a (i) £7   (ii) £100   (iii) £35
b (i) £20   (ii) £45
c (i) 14   (ii) 10   (iii) 15

2 a £900   **b** £500
c £1700   **d** £1000

3 a £10   **b** £120   **c** £168

4 a equilateral
b acute-angled scalene
c obtuse-angled scalene
d right-angled scalene
e acute isosceles
f obtuse isosceles
g right-angled isosceles

5 a (i) magpie   (ii) gull
(iii) blackbird
b not black, not webbed feet, red breast

Page 281 Review

1 a £105.70
b Takings for rolls on days 1–3
c Currency   **d** = B3 + C3 + D3
e (i) = SUM(C2..C4)   (ii) = SUM(D2..D4)
f = SUM(E2..E4) or = SUM(B5..D5)

3 a Degree: 2 (even), 2 (even), 4 (even), 5 (odd), 3 (odd) and 2 (even)

b Start at one of the odd vertices and finish at the other odd vertex
c (i) 10   (ii) Yes, 2

4 b 7 minutes

5 a £3.50   **b** £22.05   **c** £18
d £173.25

21 Scale Drawings

Page 283 Starting Points

1 a 40°   **b** 110°   **c** 260°

2 Check angles measure 50°, 120° and 245°

3 N, NE, E, SE, S, SW, W, NW

4 a (i) 1000   (ii) 100   (iii) 10
b (i) 7000   (ii) 560   (iii) 170
c (i) 300 000   (ii) 3000   (iii) 3

5 a km   **b** m   **c** cm   **d** mm

Page 284 Exercise 1

1 5 km in real life

2 a 400 m   **b** 700 m   **c** 1200 m
d 960 m

3 a 3 cm   **b** 7 cm   **c** 12 cm
d 6.5 cm

4 a 100 m   **b** 450 m   **c** 500 m
d 225 m

5 a 3 cm   **b** 10 cm   **c** 3.5 cm
d 6.5 cm

6 a 10 m, 9 cm, 41 m
b 60 km, 110 km, 9 cm

7 a 4 cm, 400 m   **b** 6.3 cm, 630 m
c 2.5 cm, 250 m   **d** 8 cm, 800 m

8 a (i) 40 km   (ii) 30 km   (iii) 60 km
(iv) 36 km
b 60 to 65 km

9 a 0.5 m
b 2 cm, 1 m; 4 cm, 2 m; 2 cm, 1 m; 10 cm, 5 m; 1 cm, 0.5 m

Page 287 Exercise 2

1 a Student's check
b (i) 17.5 km   (ii) 25 km   (iii) 21 km
c 17 km

2 a 2 m   **b** 3.2 m   **c** 8 m by 5.6 m
d 2.9 m   **e** 1.5 m

3 a 2.6 m   **b** 1.2 m   **c** 7.6 m^2

Page 289 Exercise 3

1 a 5000 cm, 50 m   **b** 1000 cm, 10 m

2 1 inch represents 1 mile

3 60 km

4 400 m

5 a 200 m
b (i) 520 m   (ii) 1660 m   (iii) 2040 m
(iv) 1120 m

Page 290 Exercise 4

1 **a** Swallow   **b** West   **c** Wallace
   d Swallow
2   12 km NE, 17 km E, 6 km S, 25 km NE,
   26 km W

Page 291 Exercise 5

1 **a** 090°   **b** 180°   **c** 270°   **d** 135°
2 **a** NE   **b** NW   **c** SW
3 **b** Q 140°, R 230°, S 260°, T 310°
4 **a** 080°   **b** 110°   **c** 150°   **d** 330°
5 **a** 100°   **b** 260°   **c** 340°
6   Check bearing on diagram is 150°

7 **a**   **b**

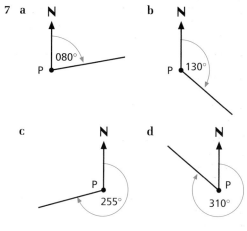

c   **d**

8

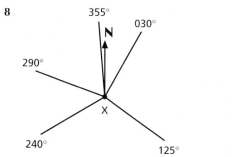

Page 293 Exercise 6

1 **a** Student's check
   b B 40 km 230°, C 50 km 270°,
      D 30 km 320°, E 20km 140°, F 50 k, 043°
2   B 30 km 117°, C 40 km 237°, D 50 km 075°,
   E 20 km 300°
3   6.6 km 130°, 9.4 km 260°, 6 km 300°

Page 295 Exercise 7

1 **a** (**i**) Own drawing   (**ii**) 7.1 cm
   b (**i**) Own drawing   (**ii**) 7.2 cm
2 **a** Own drawing   **b** 10.6 cm   **c** 21.2 m
3 **a** Own drawing   **b** 42.7 m
4   Own drawing
5   No, angle is 14°

Page 297 Exercise 8

1   83.4 m
2   20 m
3   119 m
4   36.7 m
5   55.5 m

Page 298 Exercise 9

1   Own drawing
2   Own drawing
3   Own drawing
4 **a** Own drawing
   b *Sea Princess* and *Titania* 64.3 km
5   88.9 km
6 **a** Own drawing   **b** 97 km

Page 300 Exercise 10

1 **a/b** Own drawing   **c** P
2   Own drawing
3 **a** Own drawing
   b Jake 491 m, Patrick 505 m
4 **a** Own drawing   **b** Ship B
5 **a–c** Own drawing   **d** Tower

Page 302 Review

1 **a** sycamore   **b** elm   **c** west
   d elm   **e** sycamore and larch
2 **a** 41 km   **b** 40 km   **c** 31 km
   d 80 km
3   A 30 km 070°, B 15 km 130°, C 25 km 220°,
   D 40 km 320°
4   18.7 m
5 **a** Own drawing   **b** 46.5 m
6 **a** 20 km   **b** 075° 50 km   **c** 020°
   d 102°

22 Nets

Page 304 Starting Points

1 **a** cuboid   **b** cube   **c** cylinder
   d sphere   **e** triangular prism
   f triangular pyramid
2   A, B
3 **a** 36 cm²   **b** 25 cm²   **c** 12 cm²
   d 20 cm²
4 **a** 78.5 cm²   **b** 113.1 cm²
5 **a** 31.4 cm   **b** 263.9 mm

Page 305 Exercise 1

1 **a** (**ii**), (**iii**), (**v**), (**vii**), (**ix**), (**x**)   **b** (**ii**), (**x**)
   c (**iii**), (**vii**)

Page 307 Exercise 2

1 **a** and **b**
2 **c**

3 A

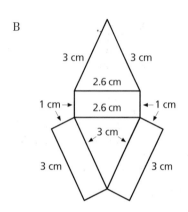

B

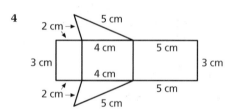

4

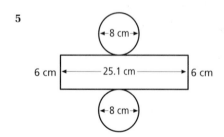

5

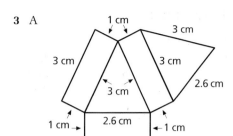

Page 308 Exercise 3

1 **a** 12.5 cm^2 **b** 27 m^2 **c** 180 cm^2

2 **a** 10 cm^2 **b** 58.5 cm^2 **c** 360 cm^2

3 **a** 35.1 cm^2 **b** 32.9 cm^2 **c** 34.8 m^2

Page 309 Exercise 4

1 **a** 144 cm^2 **b** 96.8 m^2

2 69 m^2

3 **a** 143 cm^2 **b** 105.6 m^2

4 25.28 m^2

5 420 cm^2

Page 311 Exercise 5

1 37.7, 37.7 × 7 = 263.9 cm^2,
113.1 cm^2, 113.1 cm^2,
263.9 + 113.1 + 113.1 = 490.1 cm^2

2 **a** 150.8 cm^2 **b** 1005.3 cm^2 **c** 88.0 m^2

3 **a** 1131 mm^2 **b** 1225 mm^2 **c** 622 mm^2

4 **a** 534.1 cm^2 **b** 377 cm^2 **c** 240.3 cm^2

5 6.79 m^2

Page 312 Review

1 **a** B

b

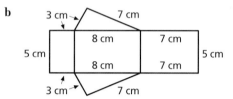

2 **a** 240 cm^2 **b** 666.4 cm^2

3

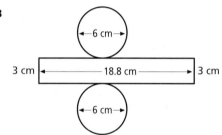

4 **a** 56.4 cm^2 **b** 100.5 cm^2

23 Statistical Assignment

Page 313 Starting Points

1 **a** (i) 103 mm   (ii) 64 mm

   b 8

   c 78 and 87

2

2	4 7 9
3	0 4 6 8
4	1 1 3

$n = 10$ 2 | 4 represents 24 minutes

3 **a** 34, 36, 42, 44, 46, 47, 49, 50, 52, 52, 53, 58, 63, 65, 67, 76

   b (i) 42

     (ii) 51

     (iii) 52.125

Page 315 Exercise 1

1 a 12, 3   b 6, 2, 6, 2   c 2, 1, 2, 1
2 a 4, 5.5, 9, 10, 13   b 1, 2, 6, 7, 14
3 a 2, 4, 6, 8, 10   b 2, 5, 8, 10.5, 14
4 a 1, 1, 2, 4, 5, 6, 6, 7, 8, 8, 9, 9, 11, 13
   b 1, 4, 6.5, 9, 13
5 a 5, 7, 8, 10, 11, 13, 16, 16, 18, 21, 21,24
   b 5, 9, 14.5, 19.5, 24
6 101, 107.5, 118.5, 128.5, 145

Page 317 Exercise 2

1 a 1   b 3   c 4   d 6   e 8
2 a 4, 9, 22.5, 35, 50
3 a (i) 30   (ii) 60
   b 49
   c (i) 38   (ii) 51
4 a 103   b 93   c 112
   d

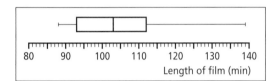

5 a 18, 24, 32, 42, 50
   b

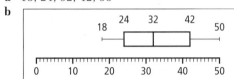

Page 319 Exercise 3

1 a (i) 30   (ii) 18
   b 12
2 a (i) 12.4   (ii) 11.3
   b 1.1
3 a Boys   b Girls
4 a 33, 47
   b (i) 42, 20, 54, 38   (ii) 22, 16
   c Art
   d The art results vary less
5 a History median is higher and results vary
        more
   b Medians are equal but the geography
        results vary more
   c IT median is higher but the interquartile
        range is the same
6 a 5, 7, 9, 12
   b Hillhead has more rain.
        Hillhead median = 9,
        Dalehead median = 5.
        The rainfall at Hillhead varies more. Its
        interquartile range is 12 compared to 7 at
        Dalehead.

24 Revising Unit 4

Page 325 Exercise 1

1 a £50   b £26.10   c £83.84
2 a £64   b £128.40   c £12.48
3 a £190   b £311.20   c £348.60
   d £318
4 a £132   b £83.50   c £221
5 a £249.60
   b (i) £62.50   (ii) £187.10
6 a £433
   b (i) £143   (ii) £290
7 a £316   b £211.72
8 a £60   b £280   c £1740
9 a £540   b £1450
10 a £1120   b £1740
11 a £600   b £10 800   c £800
12 a (i) £60   (ii) £33   (iii) £20.70
   b (i) £300   (ii) £165   (iii) £103.50
   c (i) £279   (ii) £124   (iii) £160
13 a £288.10   b £299.85   c £5544
14 a £18 489.60   b £8489.60

Page 328 Exercise 2

1 a A and C
   b (i) A, E   (ii) B, C, D
   c (i) BCD 14 min   (ii) AED 11 min
      (iii) AEC 12 min
2 a

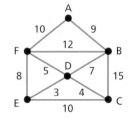

   b C and E   c AFD
   d

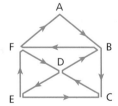

3 a

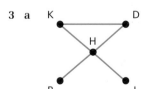

   b BHKDHL
4 a 10 min   b 16 min   c 16 min

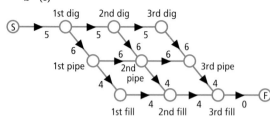

5 a (ii) 21 h
b (i)

(ii) 27 h
6 a (i) 30p   (ii) 60p   (iii) 200p
  b (i) 120p   (ii) 720p
7 a £30   **b** £50   **c** £54
8 a (i) £10.50   (ii) £12.50   (iii) £16.70
9 a £320   **b** £252   **c** £40
10 a (i) 35   (ii) £5.25   (iii) 183.75
  b (i) = B3*C3   (ii) = B4*C4
    (iii) = SUM(D2..D4)
  c (i) 45, 17.28   (ii) check
11 a (i) 35   (ii) £4.20   (iii) £147
  b (i) = B3*C3   (ii) = B4*C4
    (iii) = SUM(D2..D4)
  c (i) £173.60, £180
12 a = B2 + C2
  b = B3 + C3, = B4 + C4, = SUM(D2..D4)
  c £279.45, £229.20, £702.95
13 a D2, "= B2*C2"; D3, "= B3*C3";
    D4, "= B4*C4"; E2, "= 0.175*D2";
    E3, "= 0.175*D3"; E4, "= 0.175*D4";
    F2, "= D2 + E2"; F3, "= D3 + E3";
    F4, "= D4 + E4"; F5, "= SUM(F2..F4)"
14 C2, "= B2/75*100"; C6, "= B6/75*100";
  C7, "= SUM(C2..C6)";
  C8, "AVERAGE(C2..C6)"

Page 334 Exercise 3

1 a (i) 3.8 cm   (ii) 608 km
  b (i) 400 km   (ii) 528 km
2 a (i) 15 mm   (ii) 1.2 m
  b 7.04 m
  c (i) 4.88 m   (ii) 3.76 m
    (iii) 18.35 m^2 (2 d.p.)
  d Yes, 96 cm
3 a 1 cm represents 20 cm   **b** 34 cm
4 a 3.6 cm   **b** 16.2 m
5 a Own drawing   **b** 25.8 m
6 a Own drawing   **b** 59.7 m
7 a Own drawing   **b** 374 m
8 a–c Own drawing

Page 338 Exercise 4

1 a and d

2

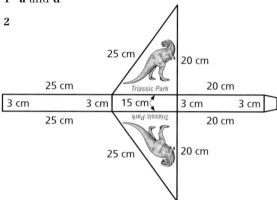

3 a and c
4 a

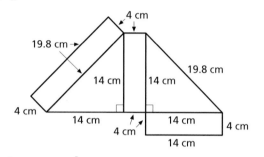

  b 387.2 cm^2
5 384 m^2
6 100.5 cm^2